AF765735

Public–Private Partnerships and the Law

For Lancelot and Enguerrand

Public–Private Partnerships and the Law

Regulation, Institutions and Community

Yseult Marique

University of Essex, UK

Edward Elgar

Cheltenham, UK • Northampton, MA, USA

© Yseult Marique 2014

All rights reserved. No part of this publication may be reproduced, stored in a retrieval system or transmitted in any form or by any means, electronic, mechanical or photocopying, recording, or otherwise without the prior permission of the publisher.

Published by
Edward Elgar Publishing Limited
The Lypiatts
15 Lansdown Road
Cheltenham
Glos GL50 2JA
UK

Edward Elgar Publishing, Inc.
William Pratt House
9 Dewey Court
Northampton
Massachusetts 01060
USA

A catalogue record for this book
is available from the British Library

Library of Congress Control Number: 2014937774

This book is available electronically in the ElgarOnline.com Law Subject Collection, E-ISBN 978 1 78100 455 5

MIX
Paper from responsible sources
FSC® C013056

ISBN 978 1 78100 454 8

Typeset by Columns Design XML Ltd, Reading
Printed and bound in Great Britain by T.J. International Ltd, Padstow

Contents

Foreword

Public–private partnerships (PPPs) have become popular with governments and the European Union as a way of providing public infrastructure and public services. There are a number of reasons. One is the sense that the private sector will do a better (and less bureaucratic) job. Another is that the private sector is used to paying attention to cost and that the provision of private finance will reduce the need for the taxpayer to pay the cost in a period when public sector budgets need to be kept in check. These instrumental aims of PPPs do not give the full picture of the legal and social mechanism that has been created. Many lawyers would treat a PPP like any other contract made with a public body – a set of terms to regulate the provision of services by the private sector and the money provided by both to a design made by the public body. But PPPs are not just any other contract. They are contracts built to last. A twenty-five- or thirty-year PPP between a contractor and a public body will last longer that a typical marriage or even the typical relationship between a customer and her bank. That length, over a generation, has profound consequences which the concept of 'contract' does not capture.

It is the merit of this work by Yseult Marique that she takes the distinctiveness of PPPs as her starting point. For her, a PPP is a set of relationships, not just a set of terms (or duties) agreed by the parties. As in any long-term relationship, a PPP is not just a set of reciprocal obligations, but a way of life. The relationship between the contractor who builds and runs a school and the local education authority will be one of constant interaction. The relationship will not work well if either side insists on its contractual rights and duties; there needs to be flexibility. Most of all, as Marique points out, there needs to be a commitment to make the PPP project (for instance a PFI school) work. The PPP sets a relational context within which the parties need to view their contractual responsibilities. That perspective of the project brings into the understanding of the contractual relationship the beneficiaries of the public service – in the case of the school, the pupils, parents and teachers whose place of learning it is. The PPP contract thus requires a sense of 'community', a sense of belonging together. Passengers on a train all have contracts with the train operator, but their short moment of sharing that common relationship does not create a real community. Within the school PPP, it is the constant need to interact in order to fulfil the project of delivering a place of learning which creates a community. Over many years, parents, pupils and teachers will place (typically non-legal) requirements on the contractors and on the local authority, and the commitment of the latter to the project makes them keen to satisfy those legitimate needs.

This regular and long-term interdependence requires a sense of community to make it work. The sense of community also brings with it values which are distinct from the classical one-off contract – the single train journey which will not be repeated. If parties have a common project and need to belong to a community of interest to achieve it, then the idea of each contracting party as a rational maximiser of their own self-interest is inadequate. Alongside the need to ensure that their own interests are satisfied through the project, Marique carefully points out that they have to adopt an 'ethic of care' for the interests of the other contracting party and of the third party beneficiaries of the public service. Such an ethic is not pure benevolence. It is rather a recognition that, in a relationship of interdependence, one's personal fulfilment is bound up with the fulfilment of other people. A proactive ethic of caring for the interests of the others ensures the project succeeds and that one can satisfy the goals that you have for yourself. Ultimately, commitment to the project, rather than playing by the rules determines the culture of the PPP.

John Bell
University of Cambridge, 16 December 2013

Acknowledgements

The subject of this book is public–private partnerships (PPPs) and more generally relationships between public and private actors and their impact on third parties. PPPs attract passionate debates on their ability to secure public goods with private finance for long durations. While their political, social or economic stakes are abundantly discussed, there is often silence over their legal makeup, even if technical discrete issues such as public procurement have received more sustained attention. This statement prompted my curiosity and led me to embark on the doctoral research at the basis of this monograph. It mainly seeks to highlight that, although the state and (financial) industry may be the most prominent drivers of PPPs, other groups and individuals in a range of capacities – from taxpayers to service users, from patients to commuters and pupils – need to be accounted for and involved in the decision making of public actors and the implementation of the common good. In that sense, this monograph seeks to engage with researchers who also take an interest in contemporary public contracting and public resources allocation.

This research benefited from much advice from a range of English academics. In particular, I was privileged to carry out my doctoral research under the supervision of Professor John Bell at the University of Cambridge. Professor Bell paid unfailing consideration to this research from day one and became a trusted mentor whose generous attention and moral strength have uniquely contributed to my personal and professional development. Thanks to his mastery of time, patient listening and engaged questioning, I owe to him the distinct belief that extending oneself is endlessly rewarding.

My thanks also go to my academic colleagues for contributing ideas and discussing drafts of this monograph. I am especially indebted to Professor David Feldman and Professor Anne Davies, who acted as my examiners, for their careful discussion of the thesis and their helpful and encouraging suggestions. Furthermore, Professor Davies kindly agreed to comment on parts of this monograph and I am grateful for her time and remarks, which help sharpen some of my key ideas. Professor Tony Prosser also provided positive criticisms which helped to simplify Chapter 5. Colleagues from the School of Law at the University of Essex

– Dr Audrey Guinchard, Professor Ellie Palmer, Professor Maurice Sunkin and Professor Christopher Willet – also provided encouragement and/or a fresh look at some of the chapters presented here, as did colleagues outside Essex, especially Nikiforos Meletiadis and Dr Sophie Turenne. I have also benefited greatly from discussions, formal and informal, with different audiences. Most prominent are the debts I owe to the discussions emerging from the CRASSH Business and Society Research Group, the Comparative Law Discussion Group at the Cambridge Faculty of Law and the Public Law Section Stream at the Society of Legal Scholars, in Bristol in 2012.

As far as possible I endeavoured to integrate my colleagues' comments and they have greatly helped to limit mistakes and misunderstandings. Remaining shortcomings would require me to take the work further with different methods. This undoubtedly applies to the further elaboration of ethic of care and a more sociological approach to community. However it is hoped that, in its present form, the research will still be useful for fostering discussions with colleagues in the United Kingdom and abroad.

Finally, my thanks go to my family and especially my brothers, Enguerrand and Lancelot. Welcoming me back time and again, my brothers offer me constant enlightening confidence rooted in deep affection.

I have been deeply privileged to meet such stimulating and patient colleagues and friends, whose care immensely enriches my research and my character. So, thank you.

Abbreviations

4Ps	Public Private Partnership Programme
AC	Audit Commission
BEC	Business and Enterprise Committee (House of Commons)
BMA	British Medical Association
BMJ	British Medical Journal
BsF	Building Schools for the Future
CBI	Confederation of British Industry
CCT	Compulsory Competitive Tendering
CHP	Community Health Partnership
CIC	Construction Industry Council
CLG	Communities and Local Government
CSR	Comprehensive Spending Review
DCSF	Department for Children, Schools and Families
Defra	Department for Environment, Food and Rural Affairs
DfE	Department for Education
DH	Department of Health
FRAB	Financial Reporting Advisory Board
FOI 2000	Freedom of Information Act 2000
GLA 1999	Greater London Authority Act 1999
HC	House of Commons
HL	House of Lords
HRA 1998	Human Rights Act 1998
HSCA 2012	Health and Social Care Act 2012
IUK	Infrastructure UK
LA	London Assembly
LIFT	Local Improvement Finance Trust
LIFTCo	Local Improvement Finance Trust Company

LU (PPP)	London Underground (Public–Private Partnerships)
MEAT	Most Economically Advantageous Tender
MP	Member of Parliament
MPA	Major Projects Authority
NAO	National Audit Office
NATS	National Air Traffic Services
NEDO	National Economic Development Office
NHS	National Health Service
NHSA	National Health Service Act
OGC	Office of Government Commerce
ODPM	Office of the Deputy Prime Minister
OTF	Operational Taskforce (HM Treasury)
PAC	Public Accounts Committee (House of Commons)
PASC	Public Administration Select Committee (House of Commons)
PCR 2006	Public Contracts Regulations 2006
PCT	Primary Care Trust
PF2	Private Finance 2
PFI	Private Finance Initiative
PfS	Partnership for Schools
PPN	Public Procurement Note
PPP	Public–Private Partnership
PRG	Project Review Group
PRIME	Private Sector Resource Initiative for the Management of the Estate
PSBP	Priority School Building Programme
PSBR	Public Sector Borrowing Requirement
PSED	Public Sector Equality Duties
PS(SV) Act 2012	Public Services (Social Value) Act 2012
PUK	Partnerships UK
SCEA	Select Committee on Economic Affairs (House of Lords)
SLHT	South London Healthcare Trust
SoPC3	Standardisation of PFI Contracts (SoPC) Version 3

SoPC4	Standardisation of PFI Contracts (SoPC) Version 4
SoS	Secretary of State
SPV	Special Purpose Vehicle
STEPS	Strategic Transfer of the Estate to the Private Sector
SHA	Strategic Health Authority
TC	Treasury Committee (House of Commons)
TfL	Transport for London
TTPF	Treasury Taskforce Private Finance
TUPE	Transfer of Undertaking (Protection of Employment) Regulations
VfM	Value for Money
WIDP	Waste Infrastructure Delivery Programme
WGA	Whole of Government Accounts

OFFICIAL DOCUMENTS REFERRED TO IN ABBREVIATED FORM

Classic directive	Directive 2004/18/EC of the European Parliament and of the Council of 31 March 2004 on the coordination of procedures for the award of public works contracts, public supply contracts and public service contracts [2004] OJ L134/114
PF2 (draft)	Treasury, *Standardisation of PF2 Contracts (draft),* 2012
Remedies directive	Directive 2007/66/EC of the European Parliament and of the Council of 11 December 2007 amending Council Directives 89/665/EEC and 92/13/EEC with regard to improving the effectiveness of review procedures concerning the award of public contracts [2007] OJ L335/31
Treasury and IUK, 2013	Treasury and IUK, *Infrastructure Procurement Routemap: A Guide to Improving Delivery Capability*, 2013

Treasury, 2012	Treasury, *A New Approach to Public Private Partnerships*, 2012
Treasury, 2010	Treasury and IUK, *Strategy for National Infrastructure*, 2010
Treasury, *Joint Ventures*, 2010	Treasury, *Joint Ventures: A Guidance Note for Public Sector Bodies Forming Joint Ventures with the Private Sector*, 2010
Treasury, 2008	Treasury, *Infrastructure Procurement: Delivering Long-Term Value*, 2008
Treasury, 2007	Treasury, *Project Governance: A Guidance Note for Public Sector Project*, Draft, 2007
Treasury, 2006	Treasury, *PFI: Strengthening Long-Term Partnerships*, 2006
Treasury, 2003	Treasury, *PFI: Meeting the Investment Challenge*, 2003
Treasury, 2000	Treasury, *Public Private Partnerships: The Government Approach*, 2000
Treasury, 1997	Treasury Taskforce Private Finance, *Partnerships for Prosperity – The Private Finance Initiative*, 1997
Treasury, 1995	Treasury, *Private Opportunity, Public Benefit – Progressing the Private Finance Initiative*, 1995
Treasury, 1993	Treasury, *The Private Finance Initiative – Breaking New Ground – Towards a New Partnership between the Public and the Private Sectors*, 1993
TSA Report	Office of the TSA, *Securing Sustainable NHS Services: the Trust Special Administrator's Report on South London Healthcare NHS Trust and the NHS in South East London* (3 vol 2013)
Utilities directive	Directive 2004/17/EC of the European Parliament and of the Council of 31 March 2004 coordinating the procurement procedures of entities operating in the water, energy, transport and postal services sectors [2004] OJ L134/1

PRINCIPLES APPLIED TO THE ABBREVIATION OF OFFICIAL DOCUMENTS

Audit Commission and NAO reports are abbreviated with the most significant word(s) of their title and date (e.g. NAO, *Department of Social Security: The PRIME Project: The Transfer of the Department of Social Security Estate to the Private Sector*, 1999 = NAO, *PRIME*, 1999. This is distinguished from NAO, *Transfer of Property to the Private Sector under the Expansion of the PRIME Contract*, 2005 = NAO, *PRIME Expansion*, 2005).

WORKS REFERRED TO IN ABBREVIATED FORM

Arrowsmith and Craven	S Arrowsmith and R Craven, 'Competitive Dialogue in the United Kingdom' in S Arrowsmith and S Treumer (eds) *Competitive Dialogue in EU Procurement* (CUP 2012) 181–271
Arrowsmith and Kunzlik	S Arrowsmith and P Kunzlik (eds), *Social and Environmental Policies in EC Procurement Law* (CUP 2009)
Arrowsmith	S Arrowsmith, *The Law of Public and Utilities Procurement* (Sweet and Maxwell 2005)
Cane	P Cane, *Administrative Law* (5th edn, OUP 2011)
Collins	H Collins, *Regulating Contracts* (OUP 1999)
Cotterrell	R Cotterrell, *Law, Culture and Society – Legal Ideas in the Mirror of Social Theory* (Ashgate 2006)
Craig	P Craig, *Administrative Law* (7th edn, Sweet and Maxwell 2012)
Davies	A Davies, *The Public Law of Government Contracts* (OUP 2008)
Engster	D Engster, *The Heart of Justice – Care Ethics and Political Theory* (OUP 2007)
Harlow and Rawlings	C Harlow and R Rawlings, *Law and Administration* (3rd edn, Law in Context, CUP 2009)

Hodge and Greve	G Hodge, C Greve and A Boardman (eds), *International Handbook on Public–Private Partnerships* (Edward Elgar 2010)
Prosser	T Prosser, *The Regulatory Enterprise – Government, Regulation, and Legitimacy* (OUP 2010)
Tronto	J Tronto, *Moral Boundaries – A Political Argument for an Ethic of Care* (Routledge 1993)
Vincent-Jones	P Vincent-Jones, *The New Public Contracting – Regulation, Responsiveness, Relationality* (OUP 2006)

NOTES

Except where otherwise stated, all references in the footnotes are to page numbers; websites were last accessed on 15 August 2013 and I have endeavoured to update the documentation up to June 2013.

Table of cases

Table of statutes

EUROPEAN UNION

Directives

INTERNATIONAL INSTRUMENTS

Table of statutory instruments

Introduction

'Public–Private Partnerships bring public and private sectors together in long-term partnership for mutual benefit'.[1] So wrote the British Treasury about public–private partnerships (PPPs) in 2000. Since then, they have become an emblematic form of contractual relationship providing public infrastructures and services at both international and domestic levels. The question arises, therefore, of the role that the law plays in ensuring that PPPs deliver these infrastructures and services for the public good.

This monograph provides a narrative for the dynamics involved in coordinating competing public, private and individual interests in PPPs. Three problems of coordination have to be tackled. Firstly, the fragmented features of PPPs and their public and private partners; secondly, the multiple tensions between PPPs, their public and private partners and third parties, such as taxpayers or users; and thirdly, the constant changes in definitions and techniques used in these schemes. In addressing these issues, public authorities use their discretion. Institutions, law and communities shape this use of their discretion by public authorities. Pragmatism may explain the concrete implementation of these interplays between institutions, law and communities in PPPs. However, my narrative suggests a more principled, yet more demanding, analysis of how discretion coordinates public, private and individual interests in PPPs: the law does not account fully for discretion; it needs to be supplemented by an ethical framework, namely an ethic of care.

PPPs, PUBLIC SPENDING AND FINANCIAL CRISES

Tight pressures on public budgets inform the background against which PPPs have been developed. Officially born following the financial crisis triggered by the September 1992 'Black Wednesday', English Private Finance Initiatives (PFIs) were rebranded as PPPs in 1997. They do not have a statutory definition. Since their launch, however, two main requirements have been ascribed to them; namely that:

---

[1] Treasury, 2000, 10.

1. the private sector must genuinely assume risk;
2. value for money must be demonstrated for any expenditure by the public sector.[2]

In 2000, PPPs were broken down into three different kinds: firstly, private ownership in otherwise state-owned businesses; secondly, PFIs; and thirdly, government services sold to wider private markets.[3] Since then, various definitions have appeared in Treasury documentation. For instance, in 2007, the notions of structured arrangement, value for money (*VfM*) and control were highlighted;[4] while in 2008, PPPs were associated with joint working, collaboration and risk sharing.[5] PFIs often link assets and services. However, the official definitions emphasise either the services purchased[6] or the construction of assets and the provision of 'associated services of a specified quality'.[7] PPPs/PFIs are thus associated with features such as *VfM*, risk allocation, joint working, control, the long term, assets and specific outcomes. The weights attached to these elements vary. This monograph starts from the following working definition, underlining the main recurring features of PPPs/PFIs. PPPs/PFIs are understood as:

> a long-term cooperation between public and private partners to deliver a public infrastructure or service, according to principles of risk allocation between the parties and value for money (*VfM*).

Under the multiple forms mentioned above, the Labour government (1997–2010) experimented with PPPs/PFIs and developed them into a policy to finance public projects in nearly all policy fields, ranging from defence to social housing, from prisons to highways and from schools to hospitals. By 2010, approximately 600 PPPs/PFIs had been set up. They financed school refurbishments, hospitals, the London Underground and a major waste treatment project in Manchester, to name just a few of the projects where PPPs/PFIs have been critical. By March 2010, the net book value of PFI assets was officially £30.9 bn and the associated liability for capital repayments was £28.1 bn. The 2010 value of future obligations was estimated at £131.5 bn, including service charges and

---

[2] Treasury, 1993, 7.
[3] Treasury, 2000, 10.
[4] Treasury, 2007, glossary, 61.
[5] Treasury, 2008, 18.
[6] Ibid 18.
[7] Treasury, 2007, glossary, 61.

some life cycle replacement costs.[8] By comparison, the overall assets of the British government were £1,207.5 bn in 2010 and its overall gross liabilities were £2,480 bn. PFI assets thus represent 2.55% of these overall assets and 1.12% of these overall liabilities.

When the coalition government came into power (2010), it announced spending cuts worth £30 bn,[9] almost equal to the value of the PFI assets. A period of hesitation followed: PFI programmes such as Building Schools for the Future (BsF) were cancelled; few new PFIs were signed; and reviews were carried out. However, by December 2012, PFIs had been relaunched in the form of *Private Finance 2* (PF2).[10] Negotiations for new projects progressed, for instance for the building of a new state-of-the-art hospital in Birmingham and the delivery and maintenance of rolling stock for the Thameslink project. The Buckinghamshire Waste PFI reached financial close. The Treasury announced that PF2 would represent a market of £1 bn per year. PPPs were coming back. Under the new modalities of PF2, *VfM* remains the key objective that public authorities pursue; yet risks are allocated differently between public and private partners. Therefore, further developments in PPPs would gain from building on lessons learned from past mistakes in delivering public infrastructures and services.

Developing and implementing PPPs/PFIs requires the involvement of many actors, from financial institutions and insurance companies to facilities management firms, as well as from directors deciding on submitting a bid to the architects designing the project. Among all the relationships involved in PPPs/PFIs, this monograph focuses on three. The first is the relationship linking public and private partners together. The second is the relationship linking public entities with individuals, especially users. The third is the relationship linking PPPs/PFIs with individuals. This monograph suggests a narrative for mapping the interplays, potential weaknesses and available corrective devices between these three relationships.

PPPs, LAW AND PUBLIC CONTRACTS

English legal literature does not examine PPPs/PFIs comprehensively but often analyses the specific techniques used in them in a separate manner.

---

8 Treasury, *Whole of Government Accounts – Year Ended 31 March 2010* (1601 HC 2011), para 3-69.

9 Treasury, *Comprehensive Spending Review* (2010 Cm 7942), para 1.11.

10 Treasury, 2012.

Economic law scholarship investigates the contractual and financial mechanisms guiding the private finance[11] or the building construction[12] side of PPPs/PFIs. Public law scholarship analyses issues such as *ultra vires,*[13] accountability,[14] public procurement,[15] local finance[16] or human rights.[17] A couple of handbooks systematise the technical issues arising from both contract and public law.[18] However, different contributors write on specialised issues without articulating the different sides of PPPs/PFIs as a whole. This results in a patchwork of issues being treated for idiosyncratic purposes. However, PPPs/PFIs are forms of economic power that the government uses to implement its policies. As such, a more comprehensive framework is needed.

Recent scholarship on public contracts contributes to developing such an overarching framework for government action. Davies and Vincent-Jones both seek to channel the discretion that public authorities enjoy in

---

[11] G Vinter and G Pierce, *Practical Project Finance* (3rd edn, Sweet and Maxwell 2005); N Morrison, 'Project Finance in the United Kingdom' (1996) IBFL 25.

[12] E.g.: S Brookes, 'A Critical Evaluation of the Success of Project Partnering' (2008) 24 Const LJ 314; R Honey and J Mort, 'Partnering Contracts for UK Building Projects: Practical Considerations' (2004) 20 Const LJ 361; S Roe and J Jenkins, 'Partnering and PPP', Sixth KCCLA Annual Lecture, 27 November 2003, www.kccla.org.uk/pdfs/PARTNERING_PPP_%20WAY_FORWARD.pdf; J Hughes-D'Aeth, 'Sub-contract Issues on PFI Projects' (2002) 18 Const LJ 449; B Colledge, 'Obligations in Good Faith of Partnering in UK Construction Contracts' (2000) ICLR 175.

[13] A Davies, 'Ultra Vires Problems in Government Contracts' (2006) 122 LQR 98.

[14] M Freedland, 'Public Law and Private Finance – Placing the Private Finance Initiative in a Public Frame' [1998] PL 288.

[15] E.g.: A Brown, 'The Impact of the New Procurement Directive on Large Public Infrastructure Projects: Competitive Dialogue or Better the Devil You Know' [2004] PPLR 160; P Braun, 'Selection of Bidders and Contract Award Criteria: The Compatibility of Practice in PFI Procurement with European Law' [2001] PPLR 1; P Badcoe, 'Public Private Partnerships in Local Government: The Legal, Financial and Policy Framework' [1999] PPLR 279.

[16] S Bailey and C Crawford, *Cross on Principles of Local Government Law* (Sweet and Maxwell 2004) 622–3; W Birtles and A Forges, *Butterworths Local Government Finance* (Butterworths 2000) 273.

[17] M Edwards, 'Case Comment' (2002) JPEL 304.

[18] S Cirell, J Bennett and R Hann, *The PFI and Major Strategic Procurement in Local Government* (Thomson Sweet and Maxwell 1997–); S Arrowsmith (ed), *Public Private Partnerships and PFI* (Sweet and Maxwell 1999–); J Fox and N Tott, *The PFI Handbook* (Jordan 1999); G Lindrup and E Godfrey (eds), *Butterworths PFI Manual* (Butterworths 1998–).

these public contracts. Davies focuses on the modalities for developing 'a public law of government contracts to control, facilitate and render accountable the government's activities'.[19] She mostly argues in favour of formal, in the sense of statutory, solutions to address uncertainties arising from public contracts, such as the scope of powers granted to public authorities or their power to change the law during the contracts to reflect changes in the public interest. Formal legal solutions to these specific issues arising in public contracts would ensure a greater accountability of public authorities and help to strengthen the confidence of citizens and private contractors in public action and decisions.[20] Vincent-Jones considers that public law has failed to develop such an appropriate framework for calling public authorities to account. Suggesting a renewed social contract, he is mostly concerned with the legitimacy and efficiency of public decisions and government contracts, which regulate the behaviour of individuals and social and economic actors.[21] He advocates hybrid regulation to limit discretion, combining formal law and legal procedures with informal institutional processes.[22] This should ensure that decisions related to the organisation of public services are rationally and democratically taken. Furthermore, this hybrid regulation should help citizens to enjoy the full benefits of contracts.[23]

This monograph engages with this scholarship on public contracts. It focuses on PPPs/PFIs, however, and does not suggest a theory for government contracts based on a discussion of the accountability, efficiency or legitimacy of PPPs/PFIs. Davies' and Vincent-Jones' emphases on, respectively, formalisation and hybridity, are used as a starting point for an investigation into how the commitments and interests involved in PPPs/PFIs are structured. The narrative presented here accepts that both approaches may be traced in PPPs/PFIs, that PPPs/PFIs are hybrids and that there is an ongoing process of formalisation. However, my narrative nuances these two trends with a more systemic approach to these schemes. The methods used for developing such a narrative are detailed in the next section.

---

[19] A Davies, *The Public Law of Government Contracts* (OUP 2008) 331.

[20] E.g.: Ibid Chapter 6.

[21] P Vincent-Jones, *The New Public Contracting: Regulation, Responsiveness, Relationality* (OUP 2006).

[22] Ibid 308 and nearly in the same wording, 333.

[23] Ibid 359–60.

RESEARCH APPROACH: A NARRATIVE FOR PPPs

Facing the dearth of case law and statutory provisions expressly related to PPPs/PFIs, this monograph seeks to develop a narrative for these PPPs/PFIs. One of the research's central themes is that PPPs/PFIs are not fully encapsulated in legal norms or institutional mechanisms. In order to understand a PPP/PFI, we need to look at its 'cultural side', i.e. the informal way in which the public and private relationships are organised and operate in PPPs/PFIs. PPPs/PFIs such as the London Underground PPPs (LU PPPs) have consisted of different sets of contractual documents running to hundreds of pages with many appendices. In this case, these documents organised the relationships between London Underground Ltd, a public body, and Tube Lines, one of the two private contractors, on the one hand, and between London Underground Ltd and Metronet, the other private contractor, on the other hand. These relationships were the outcome of financial and political negotiations between the London authorities, the central government and market actors during the procurement process. The differences in the performance and termination of the contracts with Tube Lines and Metronet cannot be explained solely with the help of the contractual documents which were to a large extent similar. Other political, technical, social or managerial factors need to be considered. For this reason, understanding PPPs/PFIs needs to build on a narrative that encapsulates their cultural dimensions and these non-legal factors.

Against a backdrop of sparse and diverging legal techniques whose scope may be rather inappropriate, narratives focus on key issues underlying the diverging techniques and the overarching solution to be privileged. In cases of conflicts between techniques or loopholes, narratives direct attention to the general aim that the system promotes. Narratives then allow one to find techniques which best match this general aim. Narratives thus foster creativity within the constraints of relating the means to the end. They provide explanations fitting the whole story line. Narratives may also draw attention to who is telling them and how.

My narrative accounts for the specificity of PPPs/PFIs in the ways in which discretion articulates tensions between the competing public, private and individual interests involved in them. To construct this narrative, three strands of resources have been brought together in a framework detailed in Chapter 1. Here, the basic tenets are briefly presented.

The starting point for this research lies in the statement that most of the research carried out on PPPs/PFIs belongs to public management literature.[24] The emerging questions there relate to assessing PPP/PFI success,[25] to their generalisation as a way of governing[26] or to their hybrid nature between public and private sectors.[27] Across these questions emerges the idea that PPPs/PFIs are a specific mix of government tools[28] such as money, authority or information. My narrative builds on this concept in order to understand PPPs/PFIs as a bundle of various techniques, legal and non-legal, which need coordination in order for them to deliver the common good.

The second resource for developing my narrative is the officially available material, namely the wealth of guidelines, codes of practice, standardised documentation, recommendations etc., along with the scarce available legal solutions. As PPPs/PFIs can prove to be highly technical arrangements, a series of case studies have been especially chosen to illustrate the basic features of PPPs/PFIs in England. These cases bring to mind practical questions as they supervene in their context and reveal the factors influencing how solutions are developed. The following case studies inform my narrative: accommodation PFIs (PRIME[29] and STEPS[30]), the London Underground PPPs (LU PPPs), school refurbishment programmes (BsF[31] and then PSBP[32]), waste PFIs, the NHS LIFT programme[33] and hospital PFIs. These case studies are spread over different policy areas where PFIs have been widely used (real estate operations, transportation, education, waste and healthcare). They have

---

24 E.g.: G Hodge, C Greve and A Boardman (eds) *International Handbook on Public–Private Partnerships* (Edward Elgar 2010); G Hodge and C Greve (eds), *The Challenge of Public–Private Partnerships – Learning from International Experience* (Edward Elgar 2005).

25 C Greve and C Hodge, 'Introduction – Public–Private Partnerships in Turbulent Times' in C Greve and C Hodge (eds), *Rethinking Public–Private Partnerships: Strategies for Turbulent Times* (Routledge 2013) 1.

26 L Salamon, *The Tools of Government – A Guide to the New Governance* (OUP 2002).

27 C Skelcher, 'Public–Private Partnerships and Hybridity' in E Ferlie and others (eds), *The Oxford Handbook of Public Management* (OUP 2007) 348.

28 C Hood and H Margetts, *The Tools of Government in the Digital Age* (Palgrave 2007) 5–11.

29 Private Sector Resource Initiative for the Management of the Estate.

30 Strategic Transfer of the Estate to the Private Sector.

31 Building Schools for the Future.

32 Priority School Building Programme.

33 Local Improvement Finance Trust.

been developed at different moments from the end of the 1990s to current fine tuning. This illustrates possible evolutions across PPPs/PFIs and a variety of issues in both their elaboration and implementation. All these cases have attracted sustained attention from the National Audit Office (NAO), which provides detailed analysis of these PPPs/PFIs.

The final contributing resource to my narrative is anchored in public law concerns and the functions that PPPs/PFIs perform: they constitute ways for the government to spend taxpayers' money and to implement its policies on transportation, education, healthcare etc. Developing a narrative for PPPs/PFIs seeks to give an account of the connections between the techniques, means and aims involved in governmental action and public discretion. Therefore, my narrative adheres to the idea that law, politics and morality are connected and that the values involved in these connections and choices need to be acknowledged.[34] It suggests that the defining values for the discretion used in PPPs/PFIs are concerns for autonomy, solidarity and trust. Chapter 1 returns to defining these values, which run across this monograph.

NARRATIVE IN A NUTSHELL

Building on the resources drawn from public management, case studies and values in public law, my narrative suggests that PPPs/PFIs are located within a 'regulatory space', i.e. a framework composed of the main elements structuring the context in which PPPs/PFIs are embedded. These elements include the legal and non-legal techniques that public and private sectors rely on to develop PPPs/PFIs. From this starting point, the hypothesis is that, within the regulatory space, commitments and interests related to PPPs/PFIs are structured by three features: institutions, law and community. As these structures are under tension, discretion is required to balance concerns for autonomy, solidarity and trust when public authorities decide on commitments and interests. My narrative then seeks to assess the specific role of the law in this process, its limits and its interplay with the community. In this sense, my narrative departs from Davies' and Vincent-Jones' approaches. Firstly, it departs from Davies' focus on legal formalism as it does not assume that human behaviour has to be regulated through formal norms to reach a certain level of stability. Regular non-legal practices may also create stability. It also underlines

[34] P Craig, 'Theory, "Pure Theory" and Values in Public Law' [2005] PL 440; N MacCormick, *Institutions of Law – An Essay in Legal Theory* (OUP 2008) 176–80.

that formalism may be seen as a spectrum and not only conceived of in its ultimate form of statutory enactment. Secondly, my narrative departs from Vincent-Jones' hybridity in displacing hybridity from characterising the regulatory and legal *system* to depicting PPP/PFI *arrangements* themselves. It also suggests that the main contrast within hybridity lies in institutions versus community and not state versus market. My narrative underlines that the state is not necessarily a single entity and that the market is a form of community of interests.

Overall, this monograph accounts for one specific tool of state intervention in economic life: PPPs/PFIs. It suggests that formalisation and hybridity are both needed to explain PPPs/PFIs but are not sufficient: formal certainty and maximising calculation do not fully explain how discretion is used in terms of coordinating public, private and individual interests in PPPs/PFIs. It therefore highlights the structures which shape how discretion is used in PPPs/PFIs and how these different structures both narrow down and widen discretion in attempting to articulate concerns for autonomy, solidarity and trust in daily decisions. Explaining the tensions between these constraints on discretion leads me to suggest a narrative where the law is supplemented with an ethic of care; namely, an ethical framework seeking to chart the discretion that a person in a position of trust enjoys when meeting the needs of those individuals for whose well-being they are responsible.

ARGUMENT AND OUTLINE OF CHAPTERS

In order to articulate a narrative for PPPs/PFIs, this monograph is divided into five chapters, each contributing to highlighting how public and private commitments and interests are organised in these schemes.

Chapter 1 explains the frames of reference, providing a general overview of the recurring concepts used throughout this monograph, including regulatory space, techniques and narratives. As PPPs/PFIs are hybrids in how they structure public and private commitments and interests, they may develop according to different models, namely market-analogue, state-analogue and community-analogue. This monograph tests these models on English PPPs/PFIs to highlight their distinctiveness.

Relying on these concepts, Chapter 2 details English PPPs/PFIs in terms of both their legal context and in their practical development. It underlines how the regulatory space is shaped in England and then discusses how PPPs/PFIs have been linked to changes in public administration. Case studies are also brought in here to illustrate the key features of PPPs/PFIs and their main practical issues. This chapter concludes by suggesting the hypothesis that discretion is shaped by institutions, law and community but that, in turn, discretion needs to balance concerns for autonomy, solidarity and trust.

This hypothesis is then tested in the following two chapters. Chapter 3 details how public and private commitments are structured between PPP/PFI partners and how market logics present in PPP/PFI contracts have evolved away from competition towards formalisation and cooperation. Chapter 4 explores how these commitments and interests are structured with regard to outsiders, mainly the PPP/PFI machinery and individual users. The lack of coordination between market-analogue and state-analogue models results in fragmentation of and intermediation in the protection of individual interests. The interplay between the techniques and narratives on which the public and private partners rely in the PPP regulatory space is highlighted in both chapters. While Chapter 3 underlines that narratives extend the reach of legal techniques, Chapter 4 suggests that narratives developed to address deficiencies in legal techniques fail to strengthen the coordination of public, private and individual interests in PPPs/PFIs. These market-analogue and state-analogue models do not provide for a direct coordination of public, private and individual interests. At most, *VfM* conveys an economic logic across the two models: it focuses on individuals in their capacity as abstract taxpayers but remains silent on individuals as concrete PPP/PFI users or third parties and on their needs for public infrastructures and services.

Building on the preceding statement, Chapter 5 returns to the hypothesis suggested in Chapter 2 and highlights the ways in which PPP/PFI users and third parties are understood in their collective dimension. A community-analogue model would indeed outline the mutual support and tensions between institutions, law and communities in coordinating collective interests, beyond the public, private and individual interests in PPPs/PFIs. It would highlight the limits of the law in this coordination and suggest a more encompassing way to articulate the tensions between PPP/PFI commitments and interests, which rest on ethical considerations of care emphasising the needs of PPP users and other third parties.

Analysing how institutions, law and communities coordinate the interests involved in PPPs/PFIs leads to the suggestion that market-analogue and state-analogue models overly focus on *VfM,* leaving out any other standard of assessing how public discretion is used. Therefore, the Conclusions highlight how an ethic of care may be developed to assess this use of public discretion in PPPs/PFIs in a more comprehensive way. Such development would have three main aspects: community, flexibility and trust. Communities are needed to provide a stable framework supporting this integration of competing public, private, collective and individual interests. Flexibility is needed to give space for the balancing of public, private, collective and individual interests over time in the public decision-making process related to PPPs/PFIs. A balance between flexibility and stability needs to be developed. To that end, trust appears to play a constitutive part in how discretion is used to tackle these tensions between the various interests involved in PPPs/PFIs. Suggesting a narrative of care to account for PPP/PFI dynamics highlights this crucial role of trust and the need to foster its multiple forms within PPPs/PFIs or, more generally, within public–private relationships providing public infrastructures and services.

1. PPPs in regulation

INTRODUCTION

Public–private partnerships/Private Finance Initiatives (PPPs/PFIs) bring together public and private actors, state and market logics to provide public infrastructures and services to individual users who rely on them for their economic and social lives, as well as their physical integrity. PPPs/PFIs represent investments in expensive public projects: for instance, the Greater Manchester Waste PFI amounted to £3.8bn[1] and the London Underground PPPs (LU PPPs) to £17bn.[2] These investments have to be compared with the £720bn that the British government expected to have as overall total public expenditure for 2013–14.[3] Of course, the Greater Manchester Waste PFI and the LU were exceptionally large PFIs and the figures mentioned here related to their whole expected duration, namely thirty years. Yet such large investments in PFIs involve high financial risks. LU PPPs were transferred back into public ownership after Metronet failed in 2007 and Tube Lines negotiated its exit out of the PPP in 2010. Seven NHS PFI hospitals were struggling financially in 2012. The Department of Health wiped off the £65m debt of the South London Health Trust, a large part of which was due to its PFI. These cases illustrate the effects of relying on PPPs/PFIs to develop critical public projects such as hospitals, schools, highways, waste treatment plants or prisons. The developing, maintaining and terminating of PPPs/PFIs involves coordinating public, private and individual interests over time. This monograph analyses the factors shaping how public discretion is used to coordinate these interests and how far the law contributes to this coordination.

PPPs/PFIs are embedded in a sphere of public discretion as they are developed through a succession of choices from a general policy level to their day-to-day implementation. So, for instance, the Treasury decides at

[1] http://news.bbc.co.uk/nol/ukfs_news/hi/newsid_7990000/newsid_7991200/7991263.stm.

[2] Harlow and Rawlings, 2009, 425.

[3] Treasury, *Budget 2013*, 2013, 6.

policy level that PPPs/PFIs should be considered as part of the economic planning policy underlying the development of a modern infrastructure in the country. It then depends on the Department of Health to decide that 100 new hospitals will be operated thanks to PPPs/PFIs by 2025, or on the Department for Education to refurbish schools through PPPs/PFIs. In turn, the local NHS trust may decide to reorganise its hospitals with a PPP/PFI or the local council may decide to modernise its housing estate or its schools through PPPs/PFIs. These public authorities need to choose between the different procurement procedures (open, restricted or competitive dialogue procedures), selecting the one which will best allow them to realise their PPPs/PFIs.[4] They then need to award the contract to a private contractor, choosing, for instance, between Veolia and Sita UK in a waste PFI or between Siemens and Bombardier in a PPP used to provide and maintain railway carriages. Finally, discretion pervades the performance of these PPPs/PFIs: the public authority has to decide constantly how and when to best handle changing circumstances, failing private partners, monitoring compliance and performance, prospects of termination etc.

These choices entail varying scopes of discretion. Choosing a contracting partner and setting other candidates aside has impact on the contracting party which differs from negotiating the modalities of the relationships. This in turn differs from forcing the contracting party to behave according to the agreed terms. Discretion is not only contextualised according to the specific phase of the PPP/PFI process. The factual or legal presence of alternatives (such as other serious candidates) or constraints (such as EU requirements to proceed with a new public procurement in cases of additional works or new legal technical standards targets), gives rise to more or less interdependence between the public and private partners. Discretion has to constantly balance various constraints and interests. From here on, there flow formal and informal commitments and expectations between PPP/PFI partners and towards users and third parties. This process is at the core of this monograph.

This chapter presents the key elements necessary to analyse the techniques and dynamics in PPPs/PFIs and to address the tensions that public authorities face when they use their discretion in relation to PPPs/PFIs. For this purpose, this chapter suggests locating PPPs/PFIs within a 'regulatory space', tracing limits around them, thanks to their specific focus on given public projects. It then explores how the

[4] Treasury, 2008, 35.

relationships between the public authorities, the contractors and individuals within the regulatory space may be coordinated: such coordination may rely on legal and non-legal techniques and on narratives and communities. This leads this chapter to suggest three models of coordination: a market-analogue model, a state-analogue model and a community-analogue model. Each of these emphasises institutions, law and communities differently. As an interface between these, PPPs/PFIs reflect these three models of coordination in their regulatory space.

TENSIONS IN PPPs

Discretion in PPPs/PFIs is structured in a distinctive manner because of three key tensions that characterise them: a tension between their public and private dimensions, a tension between flexibility and stability, and a tension between efficient resource allocation and fair distribution of benefits. The first tension finds its source in the hybrid nature of PPPs/PFIs, bringing together public and private actors in the provision of a given infrastructure or service. The second tension relates to the long-term relationships that PPPs/PFIs set-up and which require adjustments as circumstances change. Finally, the last tension refers to the polycentric issues in PPPs/PFIs: PPPs/PFIs affect multiple categories of individuals whose interests public authorities need to take into account when entering and managing these schemes. This section develops each of these tensions.

PPPs as Hybrids

As PPPs/PFIs seek to deliver a public good (public infrastructure or service) with a determining contribution from private corporations, their first defining feature is their hybrid nature. PPPs/PFIs bring together public and private actors. They rely on contracts and corporate bodies to organise the delivery of public infrastructure and services. They are used by public authorities for the common good and by private contractors to generate profits. PPPs/PFIs cannot therefore be categorised neatly as legal or non-legal, public or private, contract or institution. They straddle all of these pairings. This hybridity triggers specific issues in relation to the use of public authorities' discretion. Indeed, it makes it more difficult to gain a comprehensive understanding of who decides what, through which decision-making process, for what end and with which legal and financial means. It is then tempting to see PPPs/PFIs as a tool of government,[5] a sort of composite of different resources available to public authorities by virtue of being public authorities and upon which they can draw to carry out their policies.[6]

Such an analysis would be supported by the conceptual origins often attributed to PPPs/PFIs: namely organisational theory, (neo) institutional theory and mainly *New Public Management*.[7] This *New Public Management* literature especially presents PPPs/PFIs as hybrids. In this context, hybridity is 'associated with an indistinct boundary between public and private interests as a result of the close engagement of business and not-for-profits in the governmental process'.[8] This indistinctiveness may need to be nuanced. Indeed, the three parties identified as central for this analysis – public authorities, corporations and individuals – are essentially different from each other: in nature, needs, functions and aims. Public authorities primarily represent the common good or public interest; private contractors are entitled to pursue their economic interests; users and other third parties may also protect or promote their individual interests. This monograph seeks to identify how these public, private and individual interests are articulated in PPPs/PFIs. It suggests that these interests may at times overlap but only at times. The aim is thus to identify when and how this happens.

Therefore the hybridity of PPPs/PFIs needs to be taken seriously. It fragments the decision-making process and brings complexity into the understanding of the relationships, and thus the respective commitments and expectations, among PPPs/PFIs and their users. Problems of coordination arise from this hybridity. Hybridity may make identifying the body of rules applicable to PPPs/PFIs and their relationships complex. However, the hybridity of PPPs/PFIs may also be positive: as PPPs/PFIs bring public and private actors into cooperation, they may also facilitate the

---

[5] L Salamon, 'The New Governance and the Tools of Public Action: An Introduction' (2001) 28 Fordham Urb LJ 1611.

[6] Adapted definition from C Hood and H Margetts, *The Tools of Government in the Digital Age* (Palgrave 2007) 5.

[7] For a critical perspective on the link between PPPs and the *New Public Management*, see C Greve and G Hodge, 'A Transformative Perspective on Public–Private Partnerships' in T Christensen and P Laegreid (eds), *The Ashgate Research Companion to New Public Management* (Ashgate 2010) 265. For a survey of the paradigms used in social sciences to understand PPPs, see T Bovaird, 'A Brief Intellectual History of the Public–Private Partnership Movement' in Hodge and Greve, 2010, 43.

[8] C Skelcher, 'Public–Private Partnerships and Hybridity' in E Ferlie and others (eds), *The Oxford Handbook of Public Management* (OUP 2007) 347, 348.

coordination of their respective interests in the long term. This may need the development of adequate accountability and regulatory techniques or standards to assess this coordination. In this respect, this monograph asserts that the law needs to be supplemented by an ethical framework. This is strengthened by the second tension in PPPs/PFIs, arising from their long duration.

Long-term Relationships and Changing Circumstances

The second source of tensions in PPPs/PFIs originates in the long duration of the relationship to which public and private partners commit themselves: PPPs/PFIs are usually signed for minimum periods of twenty to thirty years. Therefore changes are 'inevitable', 'whether because of new policy initiatives or from changing local needs'.[9] Legislative changes may have direct or indirect influences on PPPs/PFIs, for instance when statutory or regulatory standards (e.g. in health or safety) are strengthened or if specific transparency requirements for PPPs/PFIs are brought into the statutes dealing with freedom of information. The evolution of the political or financial context may also cause changes, as the 2008 financial crisis and the 2010 change of government in the UK evidence. Furthermore, various elements need adaptation during the course of PPPs/PFIs, from changing locks and electrical sockets, to changing the use of rooms or adding a new building.[10] The assessing, pricing and implementing of these changes is costly and time-consuming. Planning these changes and their legal consequences structures how parties may use their discretion to adapt their relationships accordingly.

Given the above, long-term contracts have to find solutions for changing circumstances. Contract law offers more or less appropriate exit solutions depending on the seriousness of the changing circumstances, the disturbance of the contractual balance or the rationality and caution with which parties were supposed to be endowed at the time of the contractual agreement. However, relational contract theory highlights that parties tend to maintain their relationships by adapting agreed commitments to changing circumstances. A balance is struck between preserving expectations (parties need to get what they hoped for when signing the

---

[9] NAO, *Changes*, 2008, 9.

[10] For illustrations, Ibid App 2.

contracts) and adapting them to supervening events. Parties develop solidarity and share risks.[11]

In PPPs/PFIs, however, public authorities are not fully free to derogate to the contractual commitments they agreed with the contractor. For instance, changes in the contract may require a new public procurement procedure. Public authorities are also subject to external control over the good use of public money, constraining how contractual rights may be waived for the sake of preserving a relationship or continuing a public service.

PPPs/PFIs also challenge contract law when the changing circumstances are related to a change in the conception of public interests: public authorities have the duty to continually serve the public good, which may change over time, especially over such long periods of twenty or thirty years as those involved in PPPs/PFIS. For instance, PPPs/PFIs in the underground transportation have to be adapted as new policies promoting the mobility of disabled people in public transportation are developed. PFI hospitals also have to adjust to changing policies promoting the delivery of care to patients in their own homes. As this risk is inherent to the contract, one may suggest that the contractor is aware of it. However, making the contractor bear it would have adverse effects on the price paid for the service provided. For these reasons, private law does not adequately solve issues arising from changes in the context in which PPPs/PFIs operate. Any model of regulation relying on private law and contract needs to be adapted to take into account this feature of PPPs/PFIs.

Public authorities acting as contracting parties in PPPs/PFIs represent third parties. However, third parties also need to be distinguished in terms of the specific interests they have in PPPs/PFIs.

Polycentricity and Differentiation of Interests

The third tension in PPPs/PFIs relates to the polycentric issues that PPPs/PFIs are meant to address. PPPs/PFIs often entail sensitive projects, such as hospitals, prisons and schools. Projects may be carried out through closing down or merging existing facilities, therefore making it more difficult for patients to access hospitals or specific services, for instance. PPPs/PFIs thus involve a decision-making process regarding how best to allocate scarce resources between competing needs, as well

---

[11] I Macneil, 'Economic Analysis of Contractual Relations: Its Shortfalls and the Need for a Rich Classificatory Apparatus' (1981) 75 Nw ULRev 1018, 1046–48.

as an implementation process to achieve the goals set. Therefore public authorities are faced with polycentric issues, namely a subset of intricate questions, which affect not only the parties to the issue but other groups in a manner that cannot be foreseen easily. This is not least because the affected parties need to be redefined for each question.[12] Polycentric issues cannot be solved with straightforward decisions. The best way to factor these consequences into a decision and its implementation is uncertain. Due to the long chain of decisions involved in PPPs/PFIs, they offer an opportunity for a wide range of individuals to voice their interests and expectations in relation to the infrastructure or service provided by them. However, they also bring highly differentiated categories of users and individuals into competition, and their needs and interests may be challenging to balance.

An illustration taken from an NHS PFI hospital clarifies these difficulties. In 2007, the Department of Health approved a PFI contract for the Peterborough and Stamford Hospitals NHS Trust in order to bring its operations into one single location. The Trust entered a period of financial difficulties in 2010. The reasons identified for this situation were twofold. Firstly, its modern facilities attracted far more patients than anticipated; secondly, spending cuts in the wake of the English financial crisis meant that its commissioning body did not increase the payments made to the hospital accordingly. Therefore, the PFI hospital was delivering services without adequate payment. This led the PFI hospital to seek alternative income sources from its natural commissioning body and to seek to attract patients from a neighbouring catchment area. In doing so, however, the PFI hospital was depriving another hospital of its own patients and income streams. The overall result was then a global threat to the local health economy and a need to consider whether the services provided should be reconfigured.[13] A set of decisions involving a PFI in need of meeting its financial obligations thus had direct implications for immediate patients, neighbouring patients, prospective patients and taxpayers. This case illustrates the interplay between a range of decisions taken by the PFI hospital and the difficulty of appreciating the short- and long-term effects of a set of decisions or their geographic impact.[14]

---

[12] L Fuller, 'The Forms and Limits of Adjudication' (1978–79) 92 Harv LRev 353, 395.

[13] NAO, *Peterborough and Stamford Hospitals NHS Foundation Trust*, 2012.

[14] See Chapter 5, pp 235–42.

This monograph focuses on third parties understood mostly as individuals, in terms of their relationships to a PPP/PFI.[15] Individuals may be users, intended beneficiaries or third parties who justifiably rely on the performance of the contract. Their legal or material situation changes thanks to or because of PPPs/PFIs. In the case of patients, their position is altered because they get healthcare services delivered elsewhere, maybe more quickly but further away. LU commuters are affected in terms of safety, costs or service provision. London ratepayers also see their financial situation affected if the LU needs additional investments not covered by tickets and governmental grants. In short, third parties are affected either positively or negatively. They need to adapt their expectations in light of the modalities in which a service is delivered. Three main categories of individuals are relevant to this research: taxpayers, users and especially wronged, dissatisfied or aggrieved parties.

These three categories of individuals have the impacts of PPPs/PFIs on their interests or expectations in common. Taxpayers seek value for money (*VfM*)[16] for the services delivered through PPPs/PFIs. Users expect a service to be designed and implemented so that their specific needs are met. Aggrieved parties have developed a given picture of their entitlement and of what they will build their expectations on, as a patient, parent, prisoner or neighbour. The consequences that these third parties are likely to bear need to be assessed. Possible involvement needs to be contemplated in terms of its modalities and timing. Possible changes need to be planned. Given the series of decisions involved in PPPs/PFIs, these changes may have various repercussions for third parties and these affected parties may need ongoing redefinition. However, PPPs/PFIs may not meet all the expectations and interests of third parties, thus forcing them to adapt their life plan according to new modalities.

PPPs/PFIs involve all three categories of individuals and have to seek ways to coordinate their interests, as well as the possible changes they may undergo alongside the interests that the PPP/PFI partners pursue. This monograph analyses the legal and non-legal techniques used in PPPs/PFIs to tackle this question. It maps out if and how PPPs/PFIs, in bringing together public and private actors, develop concepts or techniques which acknowledge third parties' interests in their service delivery. It starts from the assumption that public authorities exercise discretion in addressing the problems of polycentricity, unpredictability

---

15 Staff constitute an important category of third party but are not considered.

16 See Chapter 3, pp 119–23 and Chapter 4, pp 160–68.

in changing circumstances and the importance of differentiating third parties. A conventional legal contract will thus not provide a full account of PPPs/PFIs. Therefore, the rest of this chapter suggests key tools for charting how these issues are tackled within PPPs/PFIs. First, the regulatory space is explained. Then the techniques and narratives developed regarding PPPs/PFIs are detailed, before turning to the three models of regulation available for coordinating interests within them.

BACKGROUND: REGULATORY SPACE AND RELATIONAL DISTANCE

In order to be able to suggest a framework to analyse PPPs/PFIs, one first difficulty needs to be addressed. PPPs/PFIs are highly flexible concepts in need of further delineation: their nature and purpose are imprecise. PPPs/PFIs are hybrids relying on a variety of legal and non-legal techniques, on contracts and organisations and on public and private actors. Similarly, PPPs/PFIs seek to address a range of financial, social or regulatory issues: for instance, the long-lasting lack of investment in public infrastructures such as the LU, the EU and environmental pressure to divert from landfill or the need for more room in prisons. They are used to provide a public service and fulfil a regulatory aim, in the sense of an 'activity valued by a community'.[17] Therefore, this section takes a different approach to identifying PPPs/PFIs and, more especially, to identifying the discretion that public authorities use in them. The highly fragmented and elusive picture that emerges from PPPs/PFIs can indeed be structured within the 'regulatory space' that is created by public authorities' use of discretion in relation to PPPs/PFIs. This regulatory space results from public authorities developing policy guidelines related to the development of PPPs/PFIs, models of documents to organise the contractual commitments between PPP/PFI partners or design other facilitative techniques supporting the funding and the procurement of PPPs/PFIs. Once this notion of regulatory space is elucidated, the organisation of relationships within that space may be analysed thanks to the concept of 'relational distance', which captures the extent to which public and private partners are aware of each other's interests and may decide to act upon this awareness in their own decision-making process.

[17] P Selznick, 'Focusing Organizational Research on Regulation' in R Noll (ed), *Regulatory Policy and the Social Sciences* (Berkeley 1985) 363, quoted in A Ogus, *Regulation: Legal Form and Economic Theory* (Hart 2004) 1.

Regulatory space and relational distance highlight legal and non-legal content in the relationships between the actors involved in PPPs/PFIs.

External Boundaries: Discretion and Regulatory Space

PPPs/PFIs are embedded in a sphere of discretion, especially of public authorities' discretion. Discretion has been seen as a danger, as the 'antithesis of law'.[18] One way to prevent abuse of discretion has been the deployment of techniques leading to the fragmentation of discretion. Regulation theories attempt to understand this fragmentation and to draw an institutional design harnessing the dispersed resources of discretion.[19] Hancher and Moran use the notion of 'regulatory space' as an analytical tool, defined 'by the range of regulatory issues subject to public decision'.[20] According to these authors, the concept of 'regulatory space' underlines:

> [the] defining [...] character of the social relations between the occupants of that space. The notion of a 'regulatory space' focuses attention not only on who the actors involved in regulation are, but on structural factors which facilitate the emergence and development of networks and which contribute to the institutionalization of linkages.[21]

These linkages are the ways in which the actors interact. They may be articulated in different ways: 'formal, binding legal rules, standard operating procedures, or indeed in the form of mere conventions'.[22] The role of institutions and structures (legal culture and organisational forms) in shaping a space and delimiting the possibilities within it is thus underlined.[23] In this description, the regulatory space seems to be neatly defined and its boundaries delineated. Such a pictorial representation leads to connecting the regulatory space to Dworkin's metaphor of

---

18 T Prosser, 'Towards a Critical Public Law' (1982) 9 JLS 1, 6.

19 C Scott, 'Analysing Regulatory Space: Fragmented Resources and Institutional Design' [2001] PL 329, 331.

20 L Hancher and M Moran, 'Organizing Regulatory Space' in L Hancher and M Moran (eds), *Capitalism, Culture and Economic Regulation* (Clarendon Press 1989) 271, 277.

21 Ibid 292.

22 Ibid 291.

23 Scott (n 19 above) 334.

discretion as 'the hole in the doughnut'.[24] This expression emphasises that discretion may be seen as an open space shaped and structured by rules.[25]

In the case of PPPs/PFIs, however, the boundaries do not match any specific rule or even a closely knitted together collection of rules. The boundaries are set through the discretion available to the public and private actors when faced with issues arising from PPP/PFI projects (in conception or implementation) or the issues they seek to address. Talking about a PPP/PFI regulatory space is useful because it helps to detach a range of practice, norms and choices especially connected to PPPs/PFIs, as distinct from other sectional activities. PPPs/PFIs are developed as a policy for investing in public infrastructures and services, regardless of the specific service (healthcare, highways, defence) provided. Then, the PPPs/PFIs are adapted to incorporate the specificities of particular policy fields to implement concrete projects such as hospitals, bridges, training soldiers to pilot military aircrafts etc. It is also necessary to integrate 'external' regulatory aims, such as health, safety and consumer protection when developing PPPs/PFIs. Furthermore, PPPs/PFIs need to be implemented at a local level, with local actors. Finally, PPPs/PFIs need to be distinguished from the range of other activities in which local government or central departments are involved. In this sense, the regulatory space is a useful concept as it focuses on the discretion exercised by a range of players in their peculiar involvements within PPPs/PFIs. It helps us to look at the various players in the specific light of PPPs/PFIs and the constraints bearing on PPPs/PFIs from the outside.

The regulatory space uses the institutional framework to explain how relationships are designed between public and private partners and in relation to third parties. It allows for distinguishing between the law and the cultural and administrative contexts within which PPP/PFI relationships are embedded. Chapter 2 will proceed to do so by detailing the techniques available in the PPP/PFI regulatory space in England and their evolution.

Once the external boundaries of PPPs/PFIs are set, a space is open for shaping how public and private discretion, commitments and interests are coordinated. Figure 1.1 depicts the key elements structuring the space. The notion of relational distance, explained in the following section, sets out a possible way to organise the relationships, commitments and

---

[24] R Dworkin, *Taking Rights Seriously* (Duckworth 1977) 31. The metaphor is commonly used, e.g. Harlow and Rawlings, 2009, 203 or R Baldwin and K Hawkins, 'Discretionary Justice: Davis Reconsidered' [1984] PL 570, 573.

[25] Harlow and Rawlings, 2009, 203.

interests involved in PPPs/PFIs internally. Then the key notions of techniques, narratives and communities are explained. This will lead us to suggest that the regulatory space can be organised through three different models (market-analogue, state-analogue and community-analogue).

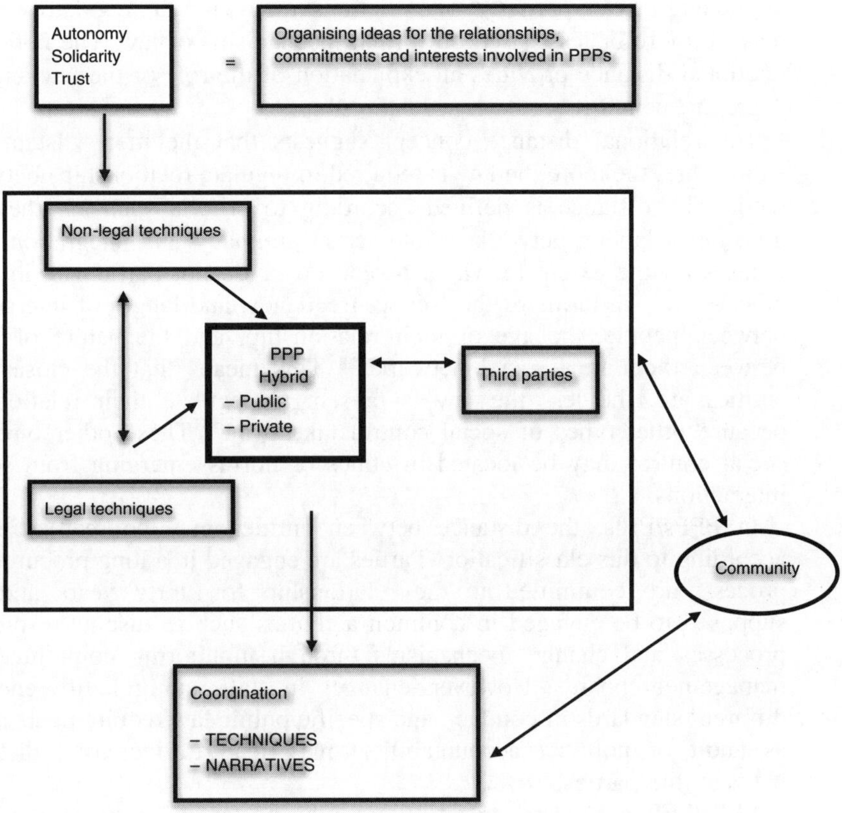

Note: *PPP regulatory space involves a series of relationships between public and private actors and third parties. These relationships are connected within that space according to ideas of autonomy, solidarity and trust, leading to non-legal mechanisms of coordination to support the relationships between public and private actors and between PPPs/PFIs and the community of users.*

Source: Author.

Figure 1.1 PPP regulatory space

Internal Organisation and Relational Distance

Organising relationships between PPP/PFI actors within this regulatory space rests on more or less sophisticated mechanisms: from social bonds in general, to refinement of the relationship content in contractual or organisational terms. The specificity of the assets used to develop PPPs/PFIs may inform the design used for the relationships between the public and private parties.[26] The relationships within the regulatory space may be more or less based on formal mechanisms or law. The notion of relational distance provides an explanation of the role of the law and the degree to which it regulates a relationship.

The relational distance concept suggests that the more distant two entities are, the more the law is required to regulate relationships between them. The distance is defined according to criteria such as 'the [...] division of labour, network of interaction, intimacy, and integration'.[27] It focuses on the extent to which people do or do not participate in each other's lives, in terms of the 'scope, frequency, and length of interaction between people, the age of their relationship, and the nature of links between them in a social network'.[28] This means that the closer two entities are, the less the law is present to regulate their relationship because other types of social control take over.[29] These other types of social control may be located in ethics or norms emerging from social interactions.

In PPPs/PFIs, the distance between entities may be seen as short according to this classification. Parties are engaged in a long procurement process, are committed to the relationship for thirty years and are supposed to be engaged in common activities such as dispute resolution processes and change mechanisms through monitoring committees or management boards. However, changes in staff, cultural differences,[30] different standards of conduct, and specific public law requirements (such as audit or political accountability) may lead to increased distance between the parties.

PPPs/PFIs are characterised by an enduring tension between the need to bring the public and private partners closer to each other and the need

---

[26] O Williamson, 'Transaction-Cost Economics: The Governance of Contractual Relations' (1979) 22 JLE 233.

[27] D Black, *The Behavior of Law* (Academic Press 1976) 37.

[28] Ibid 41.

[29] Ibid 41.

[30] Treasury Guidance prepared by PUK, *A Guidance Note for Public Sector Bodies Forming Joint Venture Companies with the Private Secto*r, 2001, 10.

to maintain an appropriate distance. Narrowing down the distance reduces the energy dissipated in finding solutions. If the parties share a common goal regarding PPPs/PFIs and their associated issues (e.g. addressing education needs in deprived areas, providing affordable housing to disadvantaged communities), decisions are smoother and more straightforward. However, PPPs/PFIs relate to social issues and involve public money. Public goals cannot be subsumed into the private partner's pursuit of profit. Therefore, distance needs to be maintained. This ongoing tension surfaces repeatedly in the analysis of PPPs/PFIs, both in the relationships between public and private partners and in their relationships with external bodies and third parties. The legal system offers various tools to organise the logics at play in the regulatory space, in the form of either contracts or the rule of law.[31] Reliance on solutions provided by the legal system may be a determining factor in ensuring that contractors enter PPPs/PFIs.[32] Similar considerations may be held for the acceptance of PPPs/PFIs by third parties. However, little law has been formally and explicitly developed in support of PPPs/PFIs, while extensive administrative and other structures have developed complex ways of interacting.

This monograph investigates the internal organisation of PPP regulatory space in England, namely how public, private and individual actors and interests are coordinated at one point in time and over time. Key to this organisation are techniques of coordination and dynamics developed on the basis of narratives. The following two sections explain, in turn, the techniques and narratives shaping PPPs/PFIs and organising the relational distance between the public and private actors.

TECHNIQUES OF COORDINATION

The previous two sections have underlined common features across PPPs/PFIs in terms of their hybridity, the polycentric issues they face and the regulatory space and relational distance shaping the relationships involved in PPPs/PFIs. No single technique is used to coordinate the mutual commitments and interests of PPP/PFI partners in the regulatory space but a package of them, in which the law is more or less present. This section looks at the legal and non-legal techniques that are available in the regulatory space.

---

[31] T Allan, 'Rule of Law' in P Cane and J Conaghan (eds), *The New Oxford Companion to Law* (OUP 2008) 1037.

[32] Davies, 2008, 108.

This section starts with three key techniques coordinating public and private actors: competition, cooperation and authority. It then details how the law can be used in the regulatory space. The law on its own does not give a full picture of how the space is structured, however. This statement is strengthened by the need for techniques ensuring a balance between stability and flexibility[33] and thus the provision of a possible accommodation over time between public and private commitments and interests. Soft law and reflexive processes are techniques which offer such a balance.

Competition, Cooperation and Authority

Among the techniques available in the regulatory space, competition, cooperation and authority bring together public and private discretion in the development and implementation of PPPs/PFIs. They are encapsulated in the specific contractual documents organising PPPs/PFIs and in the logic underpinning successful examples of them. Chapter 3 shows that PPPs/PFIs rely on these techniques in different forms, from competition to competitive dialogue in public procurement and from contracts to partnering agreements. The contract epitomises the meeting of competing interests. However, the contract is also understood as a framework for organising accountability and control of the private partner.[34] Given the complexity and long duration of PPPs/PFIs, cooperation is especially emphasised in them. Cooperation and competition, however, reach beyond the contractual relationships between the public and private partners. They are part of how the regulatory space is structured in general and they shape the dynamics within PPP/PFI projects.

Cooperation is linked to authority and competition. They can be seen in opposition or in harmony depending on the individual or systemic perspective.[35] Two corporations competing for the same bid are actually cooperating to develop what the system elects as the best solution (or the

---

[33] J Black, '"Which Arrow"?: Rule Type and Regulatory Policy' [1995] PL 94, 104–6.

[34] A Davies, *Accountability – A Public Law Analysis of Government by Contract* (OUP 2001) 80.

[35] For cooperation as an outcome of competition or an alternative to competition and hierarchy: S Deakin and F Wilkinson, 'Contracts, Co-operation and Trust: The Role of the Institutional Framework' in D Campbell and P Vincent-Jones (eds), *Contract and Economic Organisation* (Dartmouth 1996) 95, 96.

VfM solution).[36] This differs from the cooperation between two firms putting their energies, staff and know-how together to design the most suitable solution for a bid or to deliver the service contractually agreed in the PPP/PFI. Then, cooperation in the form of partnering – a non-legally binding technique – appears.

Cooperation and competition bring market benefits (e.g. resource allocations) and problems (e.g. monopolies). The law is supposed to police competition problems without disturbing competition benefits. The law may have to find an even more subtle balance regarding cooperation than for competition. The law alone may not compel entities to cooperate if they do not wish to do so. Fostering cooperation between entities may be needed. Often, however, the law takes competition and opposition of interests based on self-interests as a likely starting point for explaining entities', especially private parties', attitudes. Hence the difficulty of shifting the legal starting points towards cooperation and mutual interests in a project without falling into the trap of monopoly.

Authority and control may be needed to monitor how cooperation and competition are effectively implemented. Formalisation of the relationships between PPP parties may then be needed. How to pursue this balance between control, competition and cooperation lies at the centre of Chapter 3, where the contractual relationships between the public and the private entities are detailed.

The Law: More than a Set of Techniques

In discussing relational distance, the interplay between law and non-law has been underlined. Although PPPs/PFIs are prominently organised around non-legal techniques such as competition, cooperation and authority, this does not mean that the law is absent from PPPs/PFIs. As Yeung and Morgan highlight, the law is very often implied by these techniques.[37] One task of this research is to take a reverse position towards the relationship between the non-legal and legal techniques. It will therefore make the law and its functions within PPPs/PFIs explicit before assessing the extent to which the law gives a structure to public discretion. While the law does not provide a full account of the use of discretion, it offers a useful starting point which can be complemented by both non-legal techniques and narratives. Here, the possible functions of the law in PPPs/PFIs are briefly surveyed.

---

36 See Chapter 3, pp 119–23.

37 B Morgan and K Yeung, *An Introduction to Law and Regulation* (CUP 2007) 91–2.

The first function of the law is to set techniques shaping social behaviour. It 'forms part of the infrastructure that links the state to the market, to the community and the individuals'.[38] The legal norms – in the sense of formalised, externally generated norms – are likely to have multiple functions in establishing, maintaining or reducing the distance between the parties to PPPs. This monograph looks at the place of the law in PPPs/PFIs in six different ways:

1. the statutory provisions as sources of power (Chapter 2) – in this, the law shapes the regulatory space;
2. the legal principles and rules developed in procurement and contract (Chapter 3) – in this, the law provides for the tools to exercise public discretion;
3. the legal requirements regarding the accountability and regulation involved in PPPs/PFIs (Chapter 4) – in this, the law limits the use of public discretion;
4. the entitlements that the law confers on individuals to protect their interests (Chapter 4);
5. the connections between the law and the coordination of public, private and collective interests (Chapter 5) – in this, the law may suggest the purpose for which discretion is used and may organise frameworks for discussions between disagreeing parties;
6. the limits of the law and the need to develop an ethical framework to supplement them (Chapter 5).

The first two points are rather thick and sharp regarding the issues they expressly tackle. However, they are more concerned with authorising and allowing than with imposing definitive solutions. Their articulation is not well settled yet but there is little doubt that they are at the core of PPPs. The third and fourth points refer to binding mechanisms but the law is limited to extreme cases. The last two points invite us to discuss how the law and PPPs balance and prioritise interests over time, as well as the need for an alternative to the law in doing so.

In addition to this first function of providing techniques, the law fulfils a specific function that non-legal techniques such as competition, cooperation and authority lack; the law also encompasses a (set of) narrative(s), as we will discuss shortly. It interacts with morality as it

---

[38] Ibid 5.

provides a framework for economic and social transactions.[39] It 'institutionaliz[es] and giv[es] expression to certain values that democracy presupposes'.[40] These values are not only imposed by the state. They may also mirror the 'shared or agreed morality of the community of players'.[41] This monograph highlights these narratives and relates them to key techniques which structure the regulatory space in which PPP/PFI relationships are developed.

Soft Law and Reflexive Processes

PPPs/PFIs are embedded in a paradoxical context of experimentation[42] and routinisation.[43] PPPs/PFIs indeed seek to break new ground for complex issues. However, PPPs/PFIs are developed in a context of ongoing formalisation. Coordination of the experiments is highlighted by two techniques: soft law and reflexive processes.

Firstly, formal law does not feature prominently within the PPP regulatory space. However, a wide array of procedures and techniques breathes life into policy guidelines and technical notes through a combination of different techniques. These documents are used as a yardstick for funding projects. They shape partners' behaviour to a significant extent – albeit in a way which is difficult to ascertain clearly. Soft law supports the legal techniques and fills gaps in legal solutions. Soft law is located between repeated and incentivised practice and authorisation from the law. In the process from law to practice and vice-versa, soft law plays the role of balancing the need for predictability and flexibility. For instance, soft law provides for standardised contractual documents which allow for customising solutions according to the specificities of the PPP/PFI projects. The competitive dialogue is organised in England by the Public Contracts Regulations 2006 (PCR 2006)[44] and has been detailed in successive guidelines issued by the Treasury.[45] The formalisation of commitments and relationships refers to a spectrum between assigned but loose forms (process, document or body) and binding mechanisms –

---

39 Ibid 6.
40 Ibid 6.
41 Ibid 6.
42 Harlow and Rawlings, 2009, 414.
43 In general regarding the use of discretion: Baldwin and Hawkins (n 24 above) 574.
44 PCR 2006, SI 2006/5, reg 18.
45 See Chapter 3, pp 106–16.

factually or in law. Chapters 3[46] and 5[47] provide illustrations for this formalisation in PPP/PFI-related matters. They also, however, highlight that formalisation often goes along with informal developments.

Secondly, PPPs/PFIs seem, at first sight, to be organised in such a way that they should achieve specific outcomes as agreed in the contracts.[48] However, PPPs/PFIs also incorporate techniques helping to adapt the contracts or solve issues. They look more like a process of accommodation, related to agreed starting points between the public and private parties. Beyond individual projects, the ways in which the policy related to PPPs/PFIs is developing seem to incorporate lessons from previous mistakes. PPPs/PFIs evolve through a learning process and they rely on reflexive processes to this end. Present throughout this monograph, this learning process is mainly detailed in Chapters 4[49] and 5.[50]

Soft law and reflexive processes help us to sketch expectations and commitments regarding PPPs/PFIs, at least to some superficial levels, before engraving them further in either contractual documents or legal techniques. The need to provide stability and flexibility explains these accommodating techniques. The soft law techniques and reflexive processes participate in the hybrid nature of PPPs/PFIs as much as the contractual and institutional factors and public and private interests involved. However, describing these components of PPPs/PFIs will not lead further than stating their fragmented character, while specific choices among the mixes might not be accounted for. Looking for a frame of reference to interpret PPPs/PFIs leads us to turn to the narratives PPPs/PFIs convey and where they find justifications for their specific designs and dynamics.

DYNAMICS: NARRATIVES AND COMMUNITY, FROM TRUST TO CARE

The regulatory space is not static. As the outcome of tensions between public and private parties, between short- and long-term concerns, and between scarce resources and users' needs, PPPs/PFIs structure the commitments between public and private entities in a sophisticated way. Public authorities need to balance these tensions in the long succession of

---

[46] passim.
[47] pp 222–32 and pp 235–42.
[48] E.g: *Standardisation of PFI Contracts Version 4 (SoPC4)*, para 3.2.
[49] pp 160–68.
[50] pp 213–22 and pp 235–42.

decisions required between the designing of a PPP/PFI policy and the daily performance of a given PPP/PFI. Changes of focus in both policies and projects may arise as the social, political or financial circumstances may require. Techniques may be useful as a starting point but, although necessary, they are not sufficient to convert a past or present practice into the belief and expectation of continuance in the future. This section seeks to provide a framework of supplementing dynamics.

This section suggests that the dynamics over time in the regulatory space can be coordinated through narratives and communities providing ways to coordinate past commitments, present interests and future expectations. This highlights that autonomy, solidarity and trust have multiple meanings in PPPs/PFIs. As trust is intimately connected to control and power, to formality and distrust, and to the use of discretion, it is critical in PPPs/PFIs. Taken together, narratives, communities and trust will all point away from public management and towards ethics to coordinate public, private and individual interests. Here it is suggested that an ethic of care could offer a standard for assessing how these interests are coordinated in the PPP regulatory space.

Communities and Narratives: Consistency and Shared Meanings

Communities and narratives are closely associated. 'Communities' or 'community' have various meanings. These communities rely on shared interests and goals, shared ideals or beliefs.[51] They refer to a collectivity and are used as a substitute for public bodies.[52] For Macneil, 'community' features communal duties (and not rights), reciprocity (and not equality) and a sense of belonging. Community is thus not the same as the 'society' but an intermediary grouping needed to ensure the smooth working of society.[53] Black uses 'interpretative community' in the distinctive sense of a given set of actors coming together to interpret rules and give them meaning, developing a shared meaning for these rules.[54] Even though communities are differently understood, they provide shared meanings for action among their members so that they may direct their behaviour according to these meanings. They do so in developing narratives providing consistency and connection across the differences of their individual members. Narratives are in this sense processes used for

---

[51] Cotterrell, 2006, 68–9.

[52] E.g.: M Feintuck, *'The Public Interest' in Regulation* (OUP 2004) 38.

[53] I Macneil, 'Bureaucracy, Liberalism and Community-American Style' (1984–85) 79 Nw ULRev 900, 944.

[54] J Black, *Rules and Regulators* (Clarendon Press 1997) 30.

identifying issues and suggesting solutions related to PPPs/PFIs, making sense of the conflicting values or goals related to the various relationships involved in PPPs/PFIs, their public and private partners and third parties. Communities thus have a coordinating effect, as do techniques.

Applied to PPPs/PFIs, community provides a framework for articulating the competing values and interests the involved entities pursue. PPPs/PFIs provide the means to negotiate and articulate ad hoc solutions in a highly complex (legal and regulatory) environment. It is possible that PPPs/PFIs may develop their own narrative, on the basis of the community PPP/PFI actors would form, giving a shared meaning and logic to the project. In this sense, PPPs/PFIs will be definitively distinct from the parts which compose them. However, PPPs/PFI may involve different kinds of communities with different logics, for instance local (public and private) actors on the one hand, and national (public and private) actors on the other hand.

Therefore, a full identification or exact overlap between one interpretative community and one PPP/PFI with its actors is only a theoretical possibility. PPPs/PFIs may not often develop into a distinct source of a consistent narrative for the project or service delivered. This monograph highlights that legal techniques need the support of narratives shared among actors involved in PPPs/PFIs in order to coordinate public, private and individual interests over time. Yet narratives and communities may co-exist without neatly equating with each other. Communities and narratives may partially contribute to connecting commitments or interests inside PPPs/PFIs which would otherwise be far looser. However, they may also be fragmented or under tension and contribute to uncertainty. Chapter 5 examines how communities contribute to PPPs/PFIs and their interplays with institutions and the law. PPPs/PFIs have to coordinate multiple communities. One way to do so is to suggest narratives fostering trust as part of shaping an idea of PPPs/PFIs as a shared project between a public authority, a contractor and individual users. Trust here supplements legal techniques by establishing connections between PPP actors.

Autonomy, Solidarity and Trust

In their regulatory space, PPPs/PFIs are complex arrangements committing large amounts of money for the long term while undergoing changes in circumstances. Public and private partners need to coordinate their commitments and interests. Techniques are available but not necessarily decisive. Parties do not share the same material goals or do not expect benefits of the same nature from PPPs/PFIs. Normally, the public party pursues a public good and the private party a profit. Adopting shared narratives and belonging to common communities may then foster the development of shared modalities for a PPP/PFI through which both partners achieve their individual goals. This process would require that each PPP/PFI partner moves beyond its own long-term interest in a calculative and maximising way. The partners would express solidarity towards the common project, relying on the assumption (rationally backed up) that the contracting party will behave in a similar way. Each partner would believe that the other will direct its choices in such a way that the PPP/PFI project is fostered. Such belief highlights the importance of trust in structuring partners' attitudes towards self-interest and common interest.

This requires us to distinguish between the different meanings of 'autonomy', 'solidarity' and 'trust'. These three notions are expressed in different ways depending on time, space or circumstances. They vary across the relationships and commitments involved in PPPs/PFIs. 'Autonomy' is used in this monograph to indicate the relationship of one entity towards itself or considered in its own right. It refers to the individual level in PPPs/PFIs. 'Solidarity' refers to the collective dimension present in PPPs/PFIs. It mostly expresses how two entities relate to each other and to the common project. 'Trust' is also multifaceted. It is linked to discretion and the risks discretion entails: 'trust involves giving discretion to another to affect one's interests. This move is inherently subject to the risk that the other will abuse the power of discretion'.[55] Trust helps us to deal with the complexity and uncertainty involved in appraising circumstances or relationships. Three aspects of trust need to be explored: firstly, the different levels of trust; secondly, its sources; thirdly, its effects and importance in PPPs/PFIs.

Firstly, trust exists at three levels: personal, interpersonal and systemic. Personal trust is based on a calculation of one's own self-interest. In this case it does not add much to an explanation based on economic rationality. Interpersonal trust exists where the parties share values, history, cultural or family links. In this case, law or contract may co-exist with trust. Trust may also be supported by institutions or processes where trust is rooted in stable institutions;[56] it then becomes systemic.

---

[55] R Hardin, 'The Street-level Epistemology of Trust' (1993) Politics and Society 507 quoted in P Pettit, 'The Cunning of Trust' in P Pettit, *Rules, Reasons, and Norms* (Clarendon Press 2002) 349.

[56] Deakin and Wilkinson (n 35 above) 111–12.

Secondly, the sources of trust are open to speculation. Trust is not declared.[57] Trust needs to be rationally developed but it also requires shared values or frames of reference. 'Trust relationships find a favourable soil in social contexts with the same kind of structure, i.e. are characterised by the relative persistence of the relationship, by reciprocal dependencies, and a certain quality of the unforeseen.'[58] Trust among the participants in markets is enhanced by repetitive and deliberative patterns of social interactions. Contracts may also perform an important trust-building function[59] as they help create a context in which behaviour based on trust is generated. Mechanisms such as quality standards or good faith may also build expectations of trust.[60] Finally, 'institutional forms are an important mechanism for the reproduction of trust'.[61] The interactions between different elements of the context, such as contract law, policy agreements, quality standards or other tacit assumptions related to the ethical behaviour of participants, support trust and cooperation between the partners in a project.[62]

Finally, if it is correct that '[t]rust is only involved when the trusting expectation makes a difference to a decision',[63] then trust is likely to be often involved in PPPs/PFIs. Indeed, trust has three main effects. It guides the selection of the other contracting party as it helps overcome the vulnerability of the first mover because it reduces the complexity of available information.[64] It reduces the need to guard against disappointment by specifying the precise content of the reciprocal undertakings in detail and then monitoring performance closely. Moreover, trust is the antidote to transaction costs.[65]

All these consequences of trust are welcome in PPPs/PFIs, which are complex contractual arrangements involving unpredictable risks, even if the parties attempt to list them as precisely as possible. Negotiating PPPs/PFIs is a time-consuming and costly process. This process may, however, enable the parties to develop a shared project and a shared

---

57 Harlow and Rawlings, 2009, 407.

58 N Luhmann, 'Trust' in *Trust and Power* (John Wiley & Sons 1979) 37.

59 Ibid 23.

60 Ibid 23.

61 S Deakin and J Michie, 'The Theory and Practice of Contracting' in S Deakin and J Michie (eds), *Contracts, Co-operation, and Competition – Studies in Economics, Management, and the Law* (OUP 1997) 20, 23.

62 Ibid 23.

63 Luhmann (n 58 above) 24.

64 Collins, 1999, 100.

65 Ibid 101.

understanding of what the PPP/PFI is expected to deliver: for each of them and in its own right. The trust relationship develops through the personal contacts required to communicate about the identification of risks. These personal contacts may feed trust between the public and private partners. However, systemic trust may be required as well. Here, the links between cooperation at a day-to-day level and cooperation as a general principle for the relationship appear. Trust can be related to the use of discretion, as Chapter 3 explores in relation to contracts, as well as to control over discretion, a matter that Chapter 4 details in relation to accountability and trust. Trust is also related to the purpose that public authorities seek to achieve when coordinating the interests involved in PPPs/PFIs. In this respect, Chapter 5 highlights the role that communities play in fostering trust.

Overall, trust is connected to formalisation, which fosters trust but also expresses distrust. Formalisation does not exhaust all issues, and formalisation of part of the relationship does not prevent another part of the relationship from developing informally. Yet, trust is needed to encourage private parties to commit large resources to the mere tendering process.[66] Trust is continually needed throughout the lifetime of PPPs/PFIs to maintain the relationship. This focus on the importance of the relationship alongside the individual positions of the parties in a PPP/PFI leads us to consider how an ethic of care may be present within PPP/PFI commitments and expectations.

An Ethic of Care

Looking at the techniques organising PPP/PFI commitments and interests in the regulatory space does not lead us to a full understanding of their dynamics. Indeed, we need to know the direction that coordination is aiming at. In short, why would a specific tension between short- and long-term concerns or between resources and needs be resolved in the favour of one over the other, or in giving priority to one over the other? Answering this question with 'discretion' or 'pragmatism' is only partly helpful. Therefore, in order to suggest a more sophisticated approach to the question, insights drawn from an ethic of care are suggested. This may not answer the question in a comprehensive way and it may be highly disputable. However, it may allow for further unpacking of how

---

[66] For the issue of bid costs in the competitive dialogue, see OGC/HM Treasury, *Guidance on Competitive Dialogue*, 2008, para 4.5.

discretion is used to coordinate public, private and individual interests in PPPs/PPPs according to common values within the legal system.

An ethic of care is both a practice and a value[67] which is defined by its attention to meeting the needs of particular individuals for whom somebody has responsibility.[68] It also stresses the importance of developing relationships with these particular individuals which will enable them to progress. It rejects abstract reasoning and universal values to evaluate how decisions are made to achieve these needs in favour of reasoning based on the specific circumstances of each case. An ethic of care suggests a moral framework where decisions are not taken on the grounds of selfish interests. What matters is the well-being of the particular individuals involved in the relationship, as well as 'the well-being of the relationship itself'.[69] Instead of valuing the autonomy and independence of individuals, an ethic of care focuses on the interdependence between people and the differences between them.

These considerations echo the importance that maintaining relationships has in PPPs/PFIs and the position of public authorities entrusted with the provision of welfare to individual users. Besides autonomy, common values of solidarity and trust[70] seem to form recurring patterns across the relationships involved in PPPs/PFIs. These abstract values need to find a translation within each relationship. Autonomy may be translated into carrying out economic maximisation or expressing concern for the self-development of other parties affected by PPPs/PFIs. Solidarity may be connected to the regulatory aims that PPPs/PFIs seek to meet in providing public infrastructures or services. These regulatory objectives are thus activities of public value for a community, here conceived at public authority level. Trust refers to the way in which discretion may fulfil these concerns for autonomy or solidarity in practice. Here an ethic of care may supplement the law when legal techniques are limited in their development, implementation and enforceability. Such an ethic then helps us to revisit autonomy, solidarity and trust in order to bring cohesion across the interplays between institutions,

---

[67] V Held, 'The Ethics of Care' in D Copp (ed) *The Oxford Handbook of Ethical Theory* (OUP 2006) 537.

[68] Ibid 538.

[69] Ibid 540.

[70] Comp D Oliver, *Common Values and the Public/Private Divide* (Butterworths 1999) 60 ff and the five common values: autonomy, dignity, respect, status and security. She treats the first three together.

law and communities. Chapter 5 illustrates how ethic of care may be applied in such a way in the case of PPPs/PFIs.[71]

This monograph looks at how the common values of autonomy, solidarity and trust are translated in PPPs/PFIs and how the (non-) legal techniques concretise these three values in the different configurations of PPP/PFI relationships, namely between public and private partners and between PPPs/PFIs and users. It is suggested that recurring issues of connection between public authorities, contractors and individuals are addressed through developing narratives. The following task is then to specify how techniques and narratives relate to each other. Three models are suggested to this end in the following section.

THREE MODELS OF REGULATION

The discussion so far has suggested that discretion in PPPs/PFIs is wide, although a range of techniques and narratives shapes its use. Patterns can be identified across these techniques and narratives according to the following three models of regulation: a market-analogue model, a state-analogue model and a community-analogue model.[72] Each of these models contrasts the different roles of the law and the community in the relationships between autonomy, solidarity and trust. These models are briefly covered here – the rest of the monograph tests further how far they account for how discretion is used in PPPs/PFIs.

The Market-Analogue Model: Focus on Contract and Responsiveness

The interests involved in PPPs/PFIs may first be coordinated according to a market-analogue model, where the set-up of PPPs/PFIs works according to the logic of the market. Most of the legal literature highlights contracts and competition as the core of PPPs/PFIs. Legal scholarship picks up different elements of PPPs/PFIs in order to distinguish them: partnering or partnership arrangements,[73] presumption of 'a strong competitive element',[74] 'long-term contractual arrangements involving joint-working between the public and private sectors'[75] etc. In short, 'public–

---

[71] pp 244–57.
[72] For an alternative version: Prosser, 2010, Ch 1.
[73] Vincent-Jones, 2006, 175; Harlow and Rawlings, 2009, 413.
[74] Vincent-Jones, 2006, 175.
[75] Davies, 2008, 10.

private partnerships epitomize the idea of contractual governance'.[76] Contracts are indeed one of the ways in which formalisation has been creeping into English administration over the last twenty years.[77] This contractualisation calls for a consideration of what the legal regime should be. Vincent-Jones has developed an answer that relies on private law and private law-related mechanisms as a starting point.

Vincent-Jones suggests a tailored framework for government contracts in which PFIs/PPPs play a large role. He suggests a *New Social Contract*, building on Macneil's relational contract theory. This theory highlights the discrepancy between how contracts work in theory and in practice. According to Macneil, in long-term contracts parties seek to preserve their ongoing relationship. They balance competing needs for stable expectations with necessary adaptations to changing circumstances. In so doing, parties develop specific behaviours and norms outside the legal framework.[78] This theory has been influential in management, mostly through Williamson's contractual governance.[79] However, it relies strongly on economic exchange. It does not detail how to account for the political sphere and its structure, a side Macneil only described from a utopian perspective.[80] Relational theory provides a starting point for Chapter 3, which deals with the relationships between public and private partners in PPPs/PFIs.

Vincent-Jones extends relational theory from the contractual relationship to the overall structure of the state. He underlines the need for responsiveness in government contracts. Responsiveness cumulates the requirements of legitimacy and efficacy. Issues linked to contractualisation need to be resolved through 'responsive institutional and organisational design',[81] more than with (public) law. Mechanisms need to be built into the system so that it responds to citizens' expressed wishes. To this end, democratic experimentalism could be helpful: it both seeks to involve individuals in decision making and relies on experts to provide basic skills to these individuals for understanding the issues at stake.

---

[76] Harlow and Rawlings, 2009, 413 (footnote omitted). Similarly in Davies, 2008, 8: 'PFI policies represent the height of (the) contractualization process'.

[77] On formalisation in general, see C Harlow and R Rawlings, *Law and Administration* (2nd edn, Butterworths 1997) 210. For an illustration, see NAO, *The Privatisation of Qinetiq*, 2007.

[78] I Macneil, 'The Many Futures of Contracts' (1974) 47 SCalLRev 691.

[79] Williamson (n 26 above) 233.

[80] Macneil (n 53 above) 944–8.

[81] Vincent-Jones, 2006, 32 and 296 ff.

Public participation and deliberation should be integrated into contractualisation.[82] This cannot be done only by way of law, as administrative practices in various public, private or other organisations also need to be changed accordingly. So, techniques other than law might be more appropriate.[83] As a result, the *New Social Contract*, Vincent-Jones suggests, is hybrid in many respects: in terms of the law (public and private), in terms of law and regulation, and in terms of substantive and procedural answers.[84]

Relational theory focuses on economic rationality in order to understand and develop social bonds. It sees norms emerging from economic or social interactions. However, in PPPs/PFIs, public authorities also actively develop norms and institutions.

The State-Analogue Model: Focus on Public Law and Accountability

A second model for coordinating the interests involved in PPPs/PFIs can be the state-analogue model, which emphasises the structuring role of institutions (used here as a shorthand for public bodies) in PPPs/PFIs. It highlights that the techniques facilitating the development of PPPs/PFIs mimics a state-like activity. This model may be surprising as English[85] PPPs/PFIs are mostly understood as a contractual arrangement. However, institutions are an important fact to understand PPPs/PFIs for two reasons. Firstly, scholarship draws attention to the institutions involved in supporting PPPs/PFIs. Secondly, the legal literature seeks to institutionalise the concept of PPPs/PFIs, or at least to give them a more comprehensive statutory regime either on their own or within a distinct category of public contracts.

Amidst the general emphasis on the contractual aspects of PPPs/PFIs, Freedland draws attention to the institutional framework developed to support them. He differentiates 'government contracting'[86] from 'government by contracts'.[87] In the former case, contracts with commercial

---

82 Ibid 345.

83 Ibid 345.

84 Ibid 333.

85 For a different approach at EU level: European Commission, *Green Paper on Public–Private Partnerships and Community Law on Public Contracts and Concessions*, COM(2004) 327, para 20.

86 M Freedland, 'Government by Contract Re-Examined – Some Functional Issues' in P Craig and R Rawlings (eds), *Law and Administration in Europe* (OUP 2003) 123, 125.

87 Ibid 125.

providers are used for one-off transactions without further supporting mechanisms. In the latter case, institutional frameworks are set up and operated in order to make something similar to market contracts possible. Different kinds of arrangements may be distinguished in 'government by contracts' and placed on a spectrum from 'market-analogue' to 'state-analogue'.[88] Government by contracts falls more often into the latter category: 'they are long-term relational contracts or arrangements which may possibly be formed in a market environment, but which in any event subsist and function in a context which is not a market environment in any ordinary sense'.[89] However, these highly complex mechanisms fail to provide the necessary environment for the arrangements to come anywhere close to the 'market contract stereotype', i.e. the discrete transaction.[90] PPPs/PFIs require the development of sophisticated institutions and processes (such as Infrastructure UK (IUK), Partnerships UK (PUK), Local Partnerships or the Gateway Process). This interlocking of contractual relationships, public bodies and financial streams is epitomised in the Building Schools for the Future programme (BsF).[91]

PPPs/PFIs stand out as triggering efforts by the legal doctrine to develop a specific regime for government contracts more than any other contractual mechanisms.[92] This matches previous scholarship recommending that contractual powers and money to carry out policies (dominium) should be subject to the same principles and constraints as the use of statutory powers (imperium).[93] Freedland[94] and Davies especially advocate a public law framework for government contracts on the basis of PFIs and their criticisms. Assuming that, overall, private contract law is applicable,[95] Davies advocates the development of an autonomous public law each time a particular public issue is not appropriately dealt with under private (contract) law.[96] Such a case exists, for instance, in the

---

[88] Ibid 126: Freedland uses the term 'market-analogue' but not 'state-analogue'. This seems however an appropriate label for his description.

[89] Ibid 126.

[90] Ibid 126.

[91] E.g.: NAO, *BsF*, 2009, fig 6.

[92] S Boyron, 'The Public–Private Divide and the Law of Government Contracts' in M Ruffert (ed), *The Public–Private Law Divide* (BIICL 2009) 221, 223.

[93] T Daintith, 'Regulation by Contract: The New Prerogative' (1979) 32 CLP 41.

[94] M Freedland, 'Public Law and Private Finance: Placing the Private Finance Initiative in a Public Frame' [1998] PL 288.

[95] Davies, 2008, 71.

[96] Ibid 72.

definition of the power to enter into contracts or in the case of control over power delegation.[97] In these cases, a solution should be formalised and mainly set in a statute.[98] In her argument in favour of statutory solutions, Davies relies on how trust was restored through the Local Government (Contracts) Act 1997, developed to regulate PPPs/PFIs and the uncertainties of their financing.[99] The development of an appropriate public law framework would offer the stability and security public and private parties need for their undertakings, as well as that needed by citizens. Indeed, government contracts should exist in a 'framework of constitutional values, such as respect for the Rule of Law and for the principles of democracy'.[100] Therefore, principles of public law such as accountability should be developed to control the use of public discretion in PPPs/PFIs.

The Community-Analogue Model: Focus on Third Parties and Ethics

Regarding the relationships and commitments between public and private partners, emphasis may be put on the contract or the institutions around the contract. The market-analogue and state-analogue models may be extended from an analysis of the public and private commitments to include third parties. Vincent-Jones does so through proceduralisation.[101] Davies extends the protection offered by public law to situations where individuals are in direct contact with contractors.[102] Here a third model, focusing especially on third parties, is put forward. So far, it has not been explicitly articulated in the legal literature related to PPPs/PFIs. It tentatively builds on the idea of community as an intermediary level of relationships between contracts and state. For instance, BsF was a programme delivering school refurbishment financed by PFIs. However it was not only a contract signed between a local authority and a private contractor or a programme financed by the Department for Children, Schools and Families. BsF can also be approached as a community of actors involving the schools to be refurbished. This community of actors would include the heads of school and the parents, local education

---

97 Ibid 88 and 257.

98 By contrast, Vincent-Jones, 2006, 98 opts for hybrid solutions.

99 Davies, 2008, 108, 325 and 329.

100 A Davies, 'English Law's Treatment of Government Contracts' in M Freedland and JB Auby (eds), *The Public Law/Private Law Divide – Une entente assez cordiale?* (Hart 2006) 114.

101 Vincent-Jones, 2006, 312–15.

102 Davies, 2008, 257.

partnerships (a joint venture created to support long-term partnering between the PPP partners), the various sub-contractors involved in the refurbishment and maintenance of the school buildings, and finally other users of the schools (such as sport societies using the sport facilities of the schools).[103]

This community-analogue model seeks to apprehend the relationships between an individual and a group or between individuals within a group. Along the lines of developmental individualism, individuals are seen as seeking self-development and fulfilment,[104] and the group is only a means to that end. Individuals are seen as socially embedded selves, developing their capabilities thanks to relationships, not just relating to others on the basis of economic exchange or subject to authority. Groups of various kinds become important through the variety of social, economic or human relationships they provide for individuals. For instance, BsF sought to improve the educational environment in schools located in deprived areas in order to improve life opportunities available to their pupils.

A question then arises of how to maintain the balance between individuals and these various groups. This group dynamic may indeed challenge a public/private divide as the groups straddle it. PPPs/PFIs, because of their hybridity, are one of these straddling groups. They may thus participate in breaking down the public/private divide in different ways. They may blur public–private boundaries, bringing public values into private spheres or vice-versa. They may also bridge a collective level where public interests are defined in terms of more particularised and individualised interests involved in the realisation of a specific PPP/PFI. They may also foster collective values, such as trust, and set in motion the elements needed to develop such values further. This monograph, especially Chapter 5, suggests that these collective values may be organised according to an ethic of care, articulating the public, private and individual interests involved in PPPs/PFIs.

---

[103] NAO, *BsF,* 2009.

[104] P Cane, 'Public Law and Private Law: A Study of the Analysis and Use of a Legal Concept' in J Eekelaar and J Bell (eds), *Oxford Essays in Jurisprudence – 3rd Series* (Clarendon Press 1987) 57, 58.

PPPs: INTERFACES BETWEEN INSTITUTIONS, LAW AND COMMUNITIES

This chapter has suggested a framework for making sense of the tensions and interests involved in PPPs/PFIs. Locating PPPs/PFIs in a regulatory space is a first step to delineating their actors and the legal (such as public procurement or contracts) and non-legal (such as competition) techniques used to structure public discretion and breathe life into PPPs/PFIs. The overarching aim in this regulatory space is to secure a common good, to deliver regulatory aims valued by the collectivity. Three main models organise the techniques coordinating public, private and individual interests within the regulatory space: market-analogue, state-analogue and community-analogue. They carry with them a distinctive interpretation of the techniques on which they rely to explain how the ongoing relationships are sustained and directed towards the common good. These three models and their underlying dynamics can be summed up as follows:

- 'Market-analogue' emphasises autonomy in the sense of the self-interest, freedom and equality of PPP/PFI actors. Competition between self-interests defines the common good. Matching the narrative of responsiveness, public institutions have their discretion controlled through hybrid regulatory techniques. Law is limited to framing the market or to norms emerging from economic exchanges. Trust is used to overcome risks connected to opportunism and bounded rationality.
- 'State-analogue' emphasises public authority and institutions as identifying the common good. Private autonomy needs to be protected against public discretion, thus following a public law narrative. In this model, the law offers a way to facilitate and control discretion, as well as to call it to account. It also brings stability, strengthening systemic trust.
- 'Community-analogue' emphasises cooperation and autonomy in the sense of personal self-fulfilment through belonging to a group. The model relies on webs of interpersonal relationships of trust fostered through shared ideals, meanings and identity. Questions arise regarding how the notion of 'shared' is developed, maintained and challenged. The law is required to keep a distance between public and private interests.

These models provide a toolbox for understanding the different patterns created by the interplays between the institutions, law and communities involved in PPPs/PFIs and how these patterns shape the discretion used in such schemes. The remainder of this monograph illustrates these models by applying them to English PPPs/PFIs. Chapter 2 therefore details the PPP regulatory space in England and the techniques that have been used to coordinate public and private interests in English PPPs/PFIs. While Chapter 2 devotes specific attention to institutions, law and communities in this process, it also highlights that these institutions, law and communities do not canvass discretion: discretion is needed to coordinate them and new spheres of discretion are thus created. This will thus help us refine our understanding of how discretion is shaped.

2. English PPPs: Institutions, techniques and changes

INTRODUCTION

Chapter 1 developed a framework for analysing public–private partnerships/Private Finance Initiatives (PPPs/PFIs) within their regulatory space. It suggested possible models for structuring the public discretion used in PPPs/PFIs and concluded that, PPPs/PFIs may result from different articulations of (non-) legal techniques and narratives within the regulatory space. Since PPPs/PFIs are hybrids of public and private partners, they rely on both public institutions and market mechanisms to varying extents. Depending on their specific set-up, PPPs/PFIs may thus follow a 'state-analogue' or a 'market-analogue' model. This chapter maps out the institutions and techniques which shape PPPs/PFIs in the English regulatory space.

Focusing on English PPPs/PFIs,[1] we can highlight how PPPs/PFIs oscillate between state-analogue and market-analogue models. PPPs/PFIs emerged as a means of tackling a backlog of investments in public infrastructure with private finance. This happens despite financial pressures, changes in central-local relationships, the strengthening of audit as a control technique, government policy changes related to PPPs/PFIs and formalisation of PPPs/PFIs. These factors have led to experimentation and an incremental evolution in the organisation of PPPs/PFIs and the cooperation between public and private actors. Overall, PPPs/PFIs have become a sophisticated laboratory for constant balancing between market and state logics and between private and public interests.

In order to map out these swings between market-analogue and state-analogue models in English PPPs/PFIs, this chapter proceeds as follows. Building on the notion of the regulatory space, this chapter first identifies the public institutions in charge of PPPs/PFIs and the general

---

[1] Devolved entities (Northern Ireland, Scotland and Wales) have developed different approaches to PPP policies and projects, as capital spending on public infrastructure is a devolved matter (Treasury 2012, 15).

scope of their discretion to develop relationships with private actors to provide public infrastructures and services. The next step focuses on the changes that PPPs/PFIs were intended to bring in public administration through the introduction of market logic into the provision of public infrastructure. This led to highly refined supporting institutions, the development of statutory provisions framing PPPs/PFIs and the emergence of a community building on the expertise resulting from the experiments carried out with PPPs/PFIs. The interplay between market-analogue and state-analogue logics is then illustrated by three cases showing the concrete implementation of English PPPs/PFIs (accommodation PFIs, London Underground (LU) and Local Improvement Finance Trust (LIFT)). Thus, this chapter showcases the specific roles that institutions, market and law play in organising PPPs.

Having outlined the practicalities and distinctiveness of English PPPs/PFIs, this chapter puts forward a hypothesis for the role that discretion plays in the arrangements of PPPs, namely that discretion is shaped by institutions, law and community but that, in turn, discretion needs to balance concerns for autonomy, solidarity and trust.

INSTITUTIONAL ACTORS:[2] AUTONOMY AND CONTROL

When PPPs/PFIs were introduced in 1992, cooperation between government and industry was not new. Various forms of such cooperation have shaped English regulatory space into a mixed economy. Once the mixed features of PPP regulatory space have been explained, the external boundaries that the law sets for PPPs may be drawn. More especially, the legal techniques shaping the discretion of public bodies call for attention. Two kinds of public bodies play a significant role in PPPs: central institutions such as the Treasury on the one hand, and local government on the other hand. The law organises different spheres of autonomy for them, especially in recognising different degrees of discretion for them. However, both central and local government have to spend taxpayers' money with respect to the value for money (*VfM*) test. This test reflects how market logics and efficiency concerns in spending public money are integrated in public decisions. Legal and non-legal techniques thus shape the public–private relationships and the control over public discretion.

---

[2] Only the public actors are dealt with.

This section first outlines English regulatory space. It then looks at the autonomy enjoyed by central and local government and at the control that audit bodies exercise over this autonomy.

English Regulatory Space before PPPs/PFIs

The English regulatory space structures the relationships involved in PPPs/PFIs; that is, those between the public authorities, the private contractors, their financiers and the individual users of the infrastructures and services provided by PPPs/PFIs. Indeed, PPPs/PFIs evolved from a context in which corporatism was a way to organise state-industry relationships, mostly regarding the strategy of planning for the needs and possibilities of both sides.[3] 'Public/private partnership' was also used to label public and private interactions by way of corporatism in the English constitutional machinery.[4] These relationships between government and the industry need to be understood with regard to their historical background. They mostly took shape from the early nineteenth century on, before moving to successive phases of municipal socialism up to the Second World War. Nationalisation appeared after the Second World War, culminating in an attempt at economic planning in the 1970s. This was followed by the privatisation and deregulation of the 1980s and eventually re-regulation and even bank nationalisation after 2008. This section details how – across this wide spectrum of modalities used by the state to give an overall direction to the economy – non-legal techniques recurred across three main themes. The first was a search for a balance between private autonomy and public control over private actors. The second theme was cooperation as a privileged technique of coordination. And the third was the disputed role of institutions in which public and private actors could meet.

The first feature of the English regulatory space relates to the constantly reworked balance between autonomy and control: the autonomy of private interests to organise themselves and state control over the contribution of these private interests to the general well-being. Starting with the English *laissez faire* emblematic of the nineteenth century, there was a presumption that companies' autonomy should be free from external state interference. While inspectorates appeared in the mid-1850s, they were under-resourced to carry out their inspections and

[3] C Turpin, *Government Contracts* (Penguin 1972) Ch 10.

[4] P Birkinshaw, I Harden and N Lewis, *Government by Moonlight – The Hybrid Parts of the State* (Unwin Hyman 1990) 27.

therefore had to rely on the cooperation of the inspected industries.[5] The English system had turned away from these inspectorates by the 1870s to privilege central government as the organising entity for relationships with industry.[6] In parallel, local government took over an increasing number of missions performed to the benefit of the collectivity (such as waste, health, education),[7] either on their own or through joint ventures with economic actors.

While the central government would progressively take over these local missions, the crucial shift in the relationships between the state and the industry came with the nationalisation of the British economy after the Second World War.[8] A period of economic decline had then started. Attempts to find the proper techniques to rebalance the economy would be repeated in the following years. Boards of nationalised enterprises were, for instance, located at arm's length from the government but the government reserved the right to determine general economic objectives and financial constraints. For instance, the National Coal Board was in theory autonomous for its day-to-day management. However, ministers kept the power to set its policy and to exercise a general economic control. Ministers had the power to appoint and dismiss the board members and to issue general directions to the board. In practice, ministers intervened extensively by using informal channels and contacts to direct the board's policy.[9] Wider attempts to articulate autonomy and control across the economy in the form of economic planning equally came to nothing. The National Enterprise Board was set up in 1974 to act as a source of investment capital for industry. It would normally take a share of equity capital yet was supposed to operate at arm's length from the government.[10] However, it soon triggered issues of parliamentary

---

[5] M Moran, *The British Regulatory State – High Modernism and Hyper-Innovation* (OUP 2003) 46.

[6] Ibid 64.

[7] M Loughlin, *Local Government in the Modern State* (Sweet & Maxwell 1986) 6.

[8] Bank of England, cable and wireless, civil aviation, coal, electricity, road and rail transport, gas, iron and steel (K Morgan, *Britain since 1945* (OUP 2001) 33).

[9] T Prosser, *Nationalised Industries and Public Control – Legal, Constitutional and Political Issues* (Blackwell 1986) 22–5.

[10] Department of Industry, *The Regeneration of British Industry* (1974 Cmnd 5710).

accountability and especially control over the accounts.[11] This failure to devise a satisfying system of public ownership in the economy explains the resulting privatisation in the 1980s.[12] Privatisation then echoed the American programme of state reduction, and the concept of 'regulation' appeared in England:[13] public ownership in the economy was set aside and other economic and social means of controlling private actors' behaviour were developed.

The second feature of the English regulatory space is the extent to which cooperation between the government and industry has been prominent throughout this process with only limited reliance on the law and no constitutional definition of the role of the market in society. We have already mentioned that the Victorian inspectorates sought cooperation from the professions they controlled. This pattern would remain in inspections well into the twentieth century.[14] Cooperation extends beyond particular relationships of enforcement between public authorities and private actors. Informal relationships between the government and nationalised enterprises mushroomed early on after the Second World War, but the government and industries were unwilling to listen to each other by the 1970s.[15] The 1980s privatisations and the resulting overall reduction of public ownership in the economy would decrease the economic power of the state to rely on cooperation. However, legal techniques or constitutional constraints were again lacking or were minimal in this privatisation process. The government could not carry out a privatisation policy on its own in many cases. It had to either rely on persuading the legal owner to cooperate or adjust each specific statutory framework as required.[16] Therefore, public authorities relied on cooperation in their interactions with private actors and legal techniques were only marginally used.

As cooperation between government and industry was privileged, fora where such a cooperation could be fostered, were useful. This third feature of the regulatory space highlights, however, the disputed role of

---

[11] Prosser (n 9 above) 47–52.

[12] Prosser (n 9 above) 135.

[13] T Daintith, 'A Regulatory Space Agency?' (1989) 9 OJLS 534, 535.

[14] K Hawkins, *Law as Last Resort – Prosecution Decision-Making in a Regulatory Agency* (OUP 2002) 16–22.

[15] Prosser (n 9 above) 41.

[16] M Sah and T Daintith, 'Privatisation and the Economic Neutrality of the Constitution' [1993] PL 465.

such institutions and their changing location in the regulatory space. At first, clubs fostered a context in which informal and formal cooperation emerged.[17] They later lost this social function and were replaced by more formalised institutions in the regulatory space. Following up on previous experiments, such as the Economic Advisory Council (1930s) and the Economic Planning Board (1940s), the National Economic Development Council became a forum for ministers, industrialists, and trade unions to debate economic strategy and develop economic planning.[18] It met for the first time in 1962. Its work was supported by NEDO (National Economic Development Office), entrusted with research on economic issues. NEDO's role was heavily contested and the Treasury sought to instrumentalise it in order to direct discussions on economic planning in the direction that it desired.[19] However, the NEDO resisted and attempted to establish its independence from the Treasury,[20] leading the latter to hamper its work. The National Economic Development Council went on meeting until it was wound up in 1992. This shows the need for a meeting place where economic policy is discussed. The Treasury's role in facilitating economic planning – including infrastructure planning – remains a key feature of the English regulatory space and PPPs/PFIs. Bridges between government and industry are needed and PPPs/PFIs may perform this function, as this chapter details.[21]

In light of the above, public authorities have constantly searched to find a balance between autonomy and control in the regulatory space. They relied on cooperation above legal techniques and intermediary bodies bridging public and private actors. English PPPs/PFIs were developed within such a regulatory space, at a time when market logics were given priority over corporatism. Their launch was supposed to break even further away from this approach of state intervention in the economy and to offer alternative means for the private sector to invest in the public sector. As hybrids between public and private, PPPs/PFIs may

---

17 A Sampson, *Anatomy of Britain Today* (Hodder and Stoughton 1965) 54–63.

18 A Ringe and N Rollings, 'Responding to Relative Decline: the Creation of the National Economic Development Council' (2000) 2 Economic History Review 331, 342.

19 Ibid 344.

20 Ibid 347.

21 For an analysis of the contemporary institutions involved in economic planning, NAO, *Planning for Economic Infrastructure* (595 HC 2012–13).

be seen as an indirect move towards privatisation.[22] At the outset, PPPs/PFIs were presented as additional[23] to public investment, however. They would not jeopardise public ownership; only widen the scope of the public projects financed thanks to private finance. Indeed, PPPs have been used for projects where no other funding was available (e.g. LU, National Air Traffic Services (NATS)[24]).

In England, the relationships between public and private actors within the regulatory space are not framed in terms of direct legal or constitutional constraints. However, PPPs/PFIs have been developed in a legal context where an unsuccessful mixed economy, failed planning, and contested privatisation defined the relationships between state and market. Specific ways to articulate social and economic interests have been developed in this context, leading to 'a highly mixed public service economy'.[25] This monograph investigates how public authorities use their discretion in the coordination of these public and private interests when they implement PPPs/PFIs where these competing public and private interests are articulated. The Treasury plays a leading role in this articulation.

The Executive: The Treasury and Spending Powers

PPPs/PFIs develop a long-term cooperation between public and private actors which primarily invest in public infrastructures and ultimately deliver public services to the benefit of their users. PPPs/PFIs are intrinsically a spending mechanism and, thus, interesting to the Treasury for at least three reasons. Firstly, in PPPs/PFIs the Treasury may find leverage to develop the public infrastructure necessary for economic and social transactions. Secondly, the Treasury may want to use PPPs/PFIs as a means of carrying out its policies, such as the promotion of economic growth. In this respect, the Treasury can use PPPs/PFIs as a way to channel public money into the economy, starting with the construction and financial industries. Thirdly, the Treasury may have to commit public

---

22 That PPPs might be 'a disguised form of privatisation' is often written (Harlow and Rawlings, 2009, 420). The Treasury (2003, 3) spelled out the distinction between PFI and privatisation in terms of who determines the service provided and how.

23 This was the main option in Treasury, 1993, 25.

24 NAO, *NATS*, 2002, 11.

25 N Boeger and T Prosser, 'United Kingdom' in M Krajewski and others (eds), *The Changing Legal Framework for Services of General Interest in Europe* (TMC Asser 2009) 357, 381.

funds to the development of these projects. It may appreciate the fact that PPPs/PFIs do not compel it to take up the full investment into its budget at the start of the project: PPPs/PFIs allow public spending to be spread over the lifetime of the project, often twenty to thirty years, as periodic payments are made to the private contractors.[26] It is thus hardly surprising that the English Treasury plays a crucial role in promoting PPP/PFI policies. This section briefly describes the extent of central government's discretion, including the Treasury's, in terms of its action in the regulatory space.

Firstly, the Treasury is '*the* central department of government'.[27] It has actively given a policy impulse to PPPs/PFIs in issuing policy guidelines at regular intervals[28] and promoting PPPs/PFIs through specific entities such as the Office of Government Commerce (OGC), Partnerships UK (PUK) and Infrastructure UK (IUK).[29] Despite this distinctive role played by the Treasury in PPPs/PFIs, it has not assumed undivided leadership of PPPs/PFIs. The allocation of roles among the Treasury, departments and the Cabinet Office has required specific procedures to coordinate PPP/PFI projects.[30] We return to this in the following section.

Secondly, the Treasury structures processes for spending public money and controlling its spending: it does not spend money on policies as such, except occasionally,[31] but departments do. The Treasury is often the main author of the rules and principles binding its own actions and defines the scope of its own autonomy.[32] It exercises its control over departmental spending in various ways, one of which is the appointment of accounting officers responsible for financial management in the departments.[33]

---

[26] For the difficulties of accounting for PPPs/PFIs, see D Heald and G Georgiou, 'The Substance of Accounting for Public–Private Partnerships' (2011) 27 Financial Accountability & Management 217.

[27] A Page and T Daintith, *The Executive in the Constitution: Structure, Autonomy and Internal Control* (OUP 1999) 109 (original emphasis).

[28] Treasury, 2012; Treasury, 2010; Treasury, 2008; Treasury, 2006; Treasury, 2003; Treasury, 2000; Treasury, 1997; Treasury, 1995; Treasury, 1993.

[29] See below this chapter, pp 70–73.

[30] E.g.: HM Treasury and Cabinet Office, *Major Project Approval and Assurance Guidance,* 2011. For a general account of the day-to-day relationships between the Treasury and other departments, see R Rhodes, *Everyday Life in British Government* (OUP 2011) 210–13.

[31] E.g.: the Waste Manchester PFI.

[32] E.g.: HM Treasury, *Managing Public Money,* 2007.

[33] J McEldowney, 'Public Expenditure and the Control of Public Finance' in J Jowell and D Oliver (eds) *The Changing Constitution* (OUP 2011) 334, 349.

Moreover, the Treasury enjoys increased oversight of the funding of major PPPs, notably through the approval and assurance process.[34]

Finally, the Treasury channels public money towards PPPs/PFIs at policy level. Indeed, it widely influences negotiations over the money available in spending reviews. A spending review maps the main orientations required to develop general policies. For instance, the 2010 spending review aimed to reform the public service radically while achieving substantial cuts in government expenditure.[35] In this regard, the spending review presented a mixed picture. On the one hand, PFIs were scaled down with the revision of incentives for PFIs[36] and the withdrawing of PFI projects in waste.[37] On the other hand, funding was confirmed for projects involving PFIs such as highway maintenance[38] and Crossrail.[39] Overall commitment to PPPs/PFIs was also maintained, although the modalities available for them would require longer to be developed.

Between this high level of general policy-making and the concrete development of PPPs/PFIs, implementing measures are taken. In this respect, the English Executive enjoys two main tools for intervening in the regulatory space: statutory powers and common law powers (or inherent powers) to contract.[40] If statutory powers exist, then the government is not free to choose between the statute and the inherent powers; it has to follow the former.[41] The modalities are to a large extent enshrined in conventions and not in statutory/constitutional provisions.[42]

The exercise of these inherent powers by the Executive, and especially by the Treasury, opens up a wide scope for them to exercise their discretion. As a rule, the validity of a decision cannot be challenged under common law as no legal constraints can be identified in such a way that the contractual process could be invalidated by a court.[43] This does

---

[34] HM Treasury and Cabinet Office, *Major Project Approval and Assurance Guidance,* 2011.

[35] Treasury, *Spending Review* (2010 Cm 7942) 8; T Prosser, '"An Opportunity to Take a More Fundamental Look at the Role of Government in Society": the Spending Review as Regulation' [2011] PL 596.

[36] Treasury, *Spending Review* (2010 Cm 7942) 18.

[37] Ibid 64. See below this chapter, p 69.

[38] Ibid 46.

[39] Ibid 45.

[40] C Turpin and A Tomkins, *British Government and the Constitution* (6th edn, CUP 2007) 464 ff.

[41] Ibid 469.

[42] Davies, 2008, 86–92.

[43] T Daintith, 'Regulation by Contract: the New Prerogative' (1979) 32 CLP 41, 52–3.

not mean, however, that no control at all will operate over the exercise of such inherent powers. For instance, both the Committee of Public Accounts (PAC) in the House of Commons and the National Audit Office (NAO) exercise control over the Treasury's decisions. This can be in terms of either their regularity and propriety or their *VfM*. We return to these techniques for constraining public discretion shortly but first we need to assess how far local government enjoys similar discretion to central government and thus its autonomy within the English regulatory space.

Local Government: Limited Autonomy

In England, local authorities and central government can be seen as two different layers with few legal and formal linkages, except for the statutes granting powers to local authorities. There is no legal concept – such as that of the 'state' – that helps to bring them or their justifying supervisory powers into a unified organisation interacting through formal and legal mechanisms. There is a formal autonomy within the legal spheres traced by this dual organisation but nowhere is this autonomy legally protected. In practice, however, cooperation between central and local government is required.[44] Since the Second World War, the relationships between local and central government have oscillated between more or less local autonomy, expressed in terms of the legal powers granted to the local government and of the financial means that local governments enjoy for fulfilling their powers. The changes in local autonomy are examined here from the three perspectives: power, finances and organisation. Three periods are relevant: 1990s–2000, 2000–10 and after 2010. The mere extension of legal power does not automatically lead to increased autonomy if finances and organisation are tightly constrained. While legal powers have been incrementally extended, finances and organisation have not followed suit, which has undermined local autonomy in general and for PPPs/PFIs in particular.

A first expression of the local-central relationship lies in the granting of powers to local government. Local governments are corporate bodies which only have the powers they have been granted by statute.[45] They have, however, always been allowed to use those 'implied powers' necessary to pursue their goals. By the same token, they are entitled to

---

[44] H Wade and C Forsyth, *Administrative Law* (10th edn, OUP 2009) 94.

[45] P Badcoe, 'Public Private Partnerships in Local Government: the Legal, Financial and Policy Framework' [1999] PPLR 279, 298.

set up local authority companies[46] or joint venture companies.[47] Local government used these powers extensively up to the Second World War. Following a period of systematic reduction of local powers,[48] the trend was inversed first in 2000 with the granting of general well-being powers to the local authorities[49] and then with the further granting of a general power of competence to local government, as an expression of the Big Society Agenda in 2011.[50] The Localism Act 2011 grants local authorities the 'power to do anything that individuals generally may do'.[51] However, the activities falling within this provision have not been clarified, leaving a parliamentary select committee sceptical about the impact of the reform.[52] Furthermore, the extent to which this reform increases the autonomy and effective discretion of local authorities depends on the means available for local government to exercise their general power of competence in practice.[53]

A second expression of the relationship between central and local government is found in the autonomy local government has in organising the ways in which it delivers services. Here, the three key moments have been the introduction of market actors into the delivery of public services with 'compulsory competitive tendering' (CCT), CCT's replacement with 'best value', and the current shift towards alternative service provisions. From the 1980s onwards, local authorities had to carry out CCT before awarding a contract inhouse.[54] This CCT brought competition from the private sector into local organisations. Efficiency was to follow. However, it triggered hostility between local government and corporations. Hence, the need developed to promote more partnering and cooperation. By 1999, best value had replaced CCT; best value is a process requiring constant improvement in the delivery of public services but without formally requiring competition to demonstrate improvement.[55] In the case of good performance under best value, broader autonomy was

---

46 J Bennett and S Cirell, *Charging and Trading in Local Government* (Sweet & Maxwell 2005) Ch 8.

47 Ibid Ch 9.

48 Reforms from 1972 and 1982.

49 Local Government Act 2000, s 2.

50 It also limits the Local Government Act 2000, s 2 to Wales (see Localism Act 2011, Sch 1).

51 Localism Act 2011, s 1.

52 CLGC, *Localism* (547 HC 2010–12), para 102.

53 Ibid Ch 3.

54 Local Government Planning and Land Act 1980; Local Government Act 1988.

55 Local Government Act 1999, s 3.

granted to local government. In this context, PPPs were used as a way to achieve this constant improvement at local level and as a way for central government to provide funding to local government within the best value framework. They also fit the partnering motto, needed as a consequence of the adversarial atmosphere following the CCT experience. However, best value was also constraining local authorities because of the numerous performance indicators that the Audit Commission was monitoring.[56] With the coalition government's coming into power, the situation has changed again in two ways. The first change is a relaxation of control over local government, as the Audit Commission's assessments related to local performance have been abolished.[57] Best value as such remains in force but the new guidance focuses on the abolition of local services rather than on their performance.[58] The second change relates to the *Open Public Service – White Paper*, in which central government remains concerned with the organisation of local government and indicates how local services should be delivered, namely thanks to providers from the market or non-profit organisations.[59]

Besides the powers and organisational constraints imposed on local government, a third way to assess local autonomy relates to the financial means of exercising their powers. In practice, local government needs funding to fulfil its statutory duties. In this respect, the result of the last fifty years of reform is that '[t]he larger proportion of local government revenue is either directly provided by central government from national taxation revenues, or is controlled and distributed by central government'.[60] Local government has developed strategies to retain some financial room for manoeuvre and to bypass accounting constraints. It has used financial creativity such as swaps or complicated guarantee schemes to leverage more capital. However, these mechanisms have been challenged in a series of judicial decisions: as the local government had acted *ultra vires*, the contracts were void.[61] If the immediate effect of

---

56 P Badcoe, 'An Overview of the United Kingdom Government's Policy for the Provision and Procurement of Local Authority Services' [2001] PPLR 63, 71–2 (footnote omitted).

57 E.g.: the comprehensive area assessment (CLG Committee, *Audit and Inspection of Local Authorities* (763 HC 2010–12) para 73).

58 CLG, *Best Value Statutory Guidance*, 2011.

59 HM Government, *Open Public Services – White Paper* (2011 Cm 8145) 9.

60 Badcoe (n 56 above) 64.

61 E.g.: *Crédit Suisse v Waltham Forest LBC* [1997] QB 362; *Crédit Suisse v Allerdale BC* [1997] QB 306; *Hazell v Hammersmith LBC* [1992] 2 AC 1.

these decisions was to prevent local authorities from losing huge amounts of money due to mis-investments, the indirect effect was to shatter bankers' confidence in the commitments that local authorities might undertake. There was a risk that banks would refuse to enter such contracts or make them more expensive. Upon coming to power, New Labour passed the Local Government (Contracts) Act 1997 to address such concerns: PFIs could be entered into without fear of the contract being declared void. The Act indeed sets out a certification procedure which, once followed, protects the contractor from claims that the contract might have been signed *ultra vires*.

PFIs have developed into local projects over which central government exercises the most rigorous scrutiny.[62] They have been also a place where financial incentives have been used in various forms, such as granting PFI credits or relaxing financial constraints, either on a general basis[63] or for PPPs/PFIs used in specific sectors such as waste[64] or social housing.[65] However, these strengthened financial resources were altered when PFI credits were abolished in 2010. Furthermore, the Localism Act 2011 links economic activities in a local government more closely with its business rates, which may lead to financial uncertainty for local government.[66] Limits in terms of trading and charging remain and now local residents have been given a right to challenge excessive increases in local taxes.[67] Therefore PPPs will continue to attract financial creativity from local councils eager to use their new general power of competence. The specific forms of these PPPs remain, however, unchartered so far. Local government may need to find creative expressions which meet private contractors' need for confidence in the use of local discretion. Techniques of control over this use may also shape how public discretion is relied on to develop PPPs.

---

62 Treasury, 2008, para 5.9. Compare with the opposite announcement of relaxation of control over local authorities in Treasury, 1995, 8.

63 Under the prudential capital finance system, introduced from 1 April 2004 in the Local Government Act 2003, no specific regulations apply to PFIs.

64 AC, *Responding to the Waste Challenge*, 2008, 18–20.

65 4Ps and Care Services Improvement Partnership, *Shared Equity: Using the Private Finance Initiative to Boost Extra Care Housing*, 2008, 4.

66 NAO, *Financial Sustainability of Local Authorities*, 2013.

67 Localism Act 2011, ss 3, 4 and 72.

Control: Audit and Value for Money (*VfM*)

Even though local and central government enjoy the freedom to choose if and how PPPs are delivered to different extents, both are required to exercise their discretion alongside *VfM*. *VfM* is predominantly a non-legal technique which reflects market logics to some degree. *VfM* is key to the control that audit bodies, especially the NAO, exercises over public discretion. This control has been highly refined with regard to PPPs/PFIs.

VfM in the use of taxpayers' money is a defining feature of PPPs, along with risk allocation between parties. It has also become the guiding principle of public action. Developed from techniques devised to audit performance in private firms, *VfM* encompasses three dimensions: the economy, efficiency and effectiveness of a decision. Public decisions need to ensure that costs are minimised (economy). There must be a relationship between the resources spent and the outcome of the goods or services purchased with the resources (efficiency). Finally, there must be a relationship between the intended and actual results of the public spending (effectiveness). Courts use *VfM* to assess decisions only in extreme cases.[68] It is indeed a fluid concept, open to interpretation, especially regarding the extent to which wider policy considerations and qualitative assessment need to be taken into account to assess the *VfM* of a public decision.[69]

However, the NAO reports to the PAC on the *VfM* of public policies and projects in a highly sophisticated way, especially in relation to PPPs/PFIs. Parliamentary control of public spending is often criticised for its lack of follow-up mechanisms to ensure that the Executive actually complies with and implements PAC recommendations.[70] However, the situation in PPPs/PFIs is markedly different. While these follow-up mechanisms do not exist formally in PPPs/PFIs either, the recurring analyses of PPP/PFI projects and their transversal issues time and again, across more than 80 reports, come close to a result akin to such a systematic follow-up mechanism. The NAO has investigated specific PPP/PFI projects on the grounds that they were major projects (e.g.

---

68 *R v Secretary of State for Foreign Affairs, ex p World Development Movement* [1995] 1 All ER 611.

69 E.g.: Treasury, *Regularity, Propriety and Value for Money*, 2004, 17 defines *VfM* as follows: 'Value for money is not about achieving the lowest initial price: it is defined as the optimum combination of whole life costs and quality'.

70 A Brazier and V Ram, *The Fiscal Maze – Parliament, Government and Public Money* (Hansard Society 2006) 36 ff.

NATS, LU) or in crisis (e.g. the Passport Agency, Bicester Accommodation Centre). They have also been investigated on the occasion of a major event such as refinancing (e.g. NATS) and as part of specific policy areas (defence, prison, transportation). Especially relevant in terms of follow-up mechanisms are the reports investigating projects a few times over their lifetimes (e.g. NATS, the Channel Tunnel Rail Link, LU) or reports highlighting issues cutting across previous NAO reports, such as effective contract management.[71] These strategies regarding *VfM* reports expose shortcomings and lessons for future PPPs, therefore mapping the ways available for public authorities to next use their discretion in PPPs. They encourage public authorities to follow the NAO's recommendations and PAC's reports, despite their lack of binding force.

The NAO mainly focuses on central departments' spending of taxpayers' money. However, it has also reported on projects such as LIFT, *Building Schools for the Future* programme (BsF) or waste PFIs implemented at the local level, as the PFI credits are granted at the central level. Furthermore, the process of abolishing the Audit Commission resulted in a transfer of some of its powers to the NAO, especially to investigate *VfM* at the local level and in the NHS.[72] Pursuant to this power extension, the NAO started to work on local government and PFIs in NHS trusts.[73]

VfM plays a structuring role in PPPs/PFIs and brings the efficient use of taxpayers' money to the core of the use and control of discretion, a topic to which Chapters 3 and 4 return.

Summary

English PPPs are used in a regulatory space marked by the commingling of state and market after waves of mixed economy and privatisation. This section focused on the legal and non-legal techniques underlying public authorities' discretion within this regulatory space. Legal techniques grant public authorities powers. Legal and non-legal techniques are used to control how these powers are exercised.

In England, the law shapes the external boundaries of the PPP regulatory space in recognising more or less extended autonomy for public authorities. A wide autonomy can be found in English central

---

71 NAO, *Lessons from PFI and Other Projects*, 2011.

72 DCLG, *Local Audit Bill* (2012 Cm 8393), draft local audit bill, s 94.

73 E.g.: NAO, *Peterborough and Stamford Hospitals NHS Foundation Trust,* 2012.

government. English local governments enjoy a less extended autonomy, especially due to the constraints on their organisation and finances. However, the law sought to extend this autonomy in specific cases related to PPPs/PFIs in 1997 and then again in more general terms in 2011. These interventions were justified by the wish to increase the confidence of private actors (corporations, non-profit organisations or individuals) when dealing with local authorities.

Moving from the external boundaries to the internal organisation of the PPP regulatory space, we see that England has developed an approach based on non-legal techniques to control how public authorities exercise their discretion to coordinate their relationships with private contractors in the PPP regulatory space. *VfM* is predominantly a non-legal technique used to control how public authorities spend taxpayers' money when developing PPPs/PFIs. *VfM* developed from market logics of auditing brought into the decision-making process related to the delivery of infrastructures and services through PPPs/PFIs. The NAO and the PAC fleshed out *VfM* extensively and controlled it in PPPs more extensively than in other policies. This could enhance the confidence in efficient spending of the large amounts of taxpayers' money in PPPs/PFIs. The law contributes to this control to a limited extent. Firstly, the *VfM* control carried out by the NAO is provided for in a statutory provision; secondly, the control exercised by PAC over governmental spending takes place within a public law framework of accountability. However, the law is mostly facilitative. The modalities are extensively developed through non-legal techniques that need to be worked out to structure public authorities' discretion and autonomy

The following chapters discuss the extent to which the law is able to account for PPPs/PFIs. The following sections focus on the changes in the regulatory space that PPPs/PFIs occupy showing how concerns for solidarity and trust have become embedded in public discretion.

PRAGMATISM: DEVELOPING SUPPORTING INSTITUTIONS

In their earlier days, PPPs (in their PFI form) were described as the 'largest cultural change for decades in the way the public sector operates in the United Kingdom'.[74] However, the policies and projects

[74] P Braun, 'The Practical Application of EC Public Procurement Law to the UK's Private Finance Initiative' (2003) 9 ELJ 575.

implementing PPPs/PFIs have evolved following lessons learned from failed projects, political changes and financial circumstances. This section maps out how PPPs/PFIs have brought change to English public administration and institutions.

At the outset, PFIs were linked to the 'new' role of the state as an enabler[75] rather than provider of services, in line with the *New Public Management*.[76] The backlog of underinvestment in public infrastructure was one of the main drivers of this policy, along with the modernisation of public services in general. In tackling infrastructure underinvestment within tight budgetary constraints, '[t]he means by which this is achieved is less important than the end result':[77] public money would kick-start projects, attracting private investors. Control over the use of public money would follow. However, this new role for the state, away from direct public ownership in the economy, does not lead to public institutions disappearing. PPPs/PFIs illustrate this neatly.

The change was symbolic at first: breaking with endemic underinvestment and strained public finance. Public authorities were to benefit from learning how economic actors take decisions and carry out their business. However, too much discretion and wide choices led to uncertainty for public and private entities alike, long negotiations and high costs. Not many PPPs/PFIs were developed. Concerns for solidarity and trust led to the development of institutions organising the relationships between public authorities and market actors, securing the provision of public infrastructure for the benefit of users and giving confidence that the PPPs/PFIs had been appropriately designed and their contracts well drafted. PPPs/PFIs then gradually evolved along three main trends: institutionalisation, formalisation and standardisation.

Looking at each of these three trends in turn, this section highlights that, beyond the constant tweaking of modalities and readjustments to fit changing political and economic circumstances, institutions are called to take up an increasing role in shaping the proper context for economic growth, giving confidence to private investment in public infrastructure and modernising public services.

---

75 Treasury, 1993, 6.

76 P Falconer and K McLaughlin, 'Public–private Partnerships and the "New Labour" Government in Britain' in S Osborne (ed), *Public–Private Partnerships – Theory and Practice in International Perspective* (Routledge 2000) 120.

77 Treasury, 1997, para 1.02.

Beyond Symbolism: Bringing Private Finance into Public Projects

Norman Lamont, then Chancellor of the Exchequer, announced the *Private Finance Initiative* (PFI) as a new policy in his 1992 Autumn Statement.[78] A few months later, PFIs were detailed with the belief that '[it] will soon be recognised to be a radical and far-reaching change in capital investment in public services'.[79] This 'radical change' would lie in a win-win logic. No definition of PFI was provided, even if three types of projects were identified: financially free-standing projects, joint ventures between public and private sectors, and services sold to the public sector.[80] The only two requirements set by the new approach were that:

1. the private sector must genuinely assume risk;
2. value for money must be demonstrated for any expenditure by the public sector.[81]

To mostly financial and economic issues, a mainly financial and economic solution had been suggested. By 1992–93, the state was deemed to have failed in securing adequate direct investment in public infrastructures. Therefore, PFIs would seek to remedy this failure through market techniques, as far removed as possible from state control over the development of infrastructure projects. These techniques have, however, been fine-tuned over the following twenty years, seeking to rely on private autonomy and innovation, while ensuring that the state keeps control of the services, risks and benefits associated with PPPs/PFIs.

The background: state failure

In the background explanation of the development of PPPs/PFIs in 1992, three factors point towards the systematic failure of the state to provide adequate public infrastructures through public money. The first factor is the budgetary constraints drawn from the public deficit. The second is comprised of the overall economic interactions between private finance and public expenditure. The third involves specific troubles with the public procurement of infrastructure.

---

78 HC Deb 12 November 1992, vol 213, cols 993–1016.

79 Treasury, 1993, Foreword. Similarly, PFIs were said to represent a 'profound change to the culture of government procurement' in Treasury, 1995, Foreword.

80 Treasury, 1993, 10–11.

81 Ibid 7.

The first factor pushing for a change in infrastructure investment was the public deficit, which had been endemic in England and led to privatisation as the ultimate rescue mechanism. Fiscal discipline was necessary, internally as well as externally, notably to take part in the European Monetary System and later to comply with the Maastricht criteria. Due to a financial crash known as 'Black Wednesday' in 1992, the UK had to withdraw from the European Monetary System. However, the UK kept an eye on its balance sheet thereafter. Budgetary constraints, linked to the Public Sector Borrowing Requirement (PSBR), indeed remained applicable as participation in the Euro lingered until 2003.[82] Even thereafter, ambiguity towards the Euro remained. This explains why the PSBR has been invoked for so long to justify choices of financial policy and limits to the budgetary implications of investing in public infrastructure. Indeed, any (major programme of) public investment requires funding expenses and saddles the state with debts, affecting the PSBR. If the debt could be borne by the private sector (at least in its accounting), the PSBR would not suffer.[83]

The second factor pushing for a change in investment in public infrastructure was related to the means available for tackling this endemic public deficit. From 1981, official publications reported on the use of private finance in public spending in general terms and particularly in the nationalised sectors. Especially, the so-called 'Ryrie Rules' were developed. These set criteria under which private finance might be introduced in nationalised industries. These criteria were, firstly, a condition of fair competition with private sector borrowers and, secondly, that privately financed projects would bring improved efficiency and profit.[84] However, the Ryrie Rules received a different application from the one they were intended to have. They were used not to allow more private finance into the public sector but to limit it.[85] Equally, they were extended outside the nationalised industries. Therefore they became seen as hindering private

---

82 P Sinclair, 'The Treasury and Economic Policy' in A Seldon (ed), *Blair's Britain 1997–2007* (CUP 2007) 190 ff.

83 H Randall, 'The Private Finance Initiative' in H Randall (ed), *Local Government Contracts and Procurement* (Butterworth LexisNexis 2002) 279.

84 Appendix A of *Private Finance in Public Expenditure*, prepared by the Treasury for the Civil Engineering Economic Development Committee in 1988.

85 G Clark and A Root, 'Infrastructure Shortfall in the United Kingdom: The Private Finance Initiative and Government Policy' (1999) 18 Political Geography 341, 347–50.

finance in public spending:[86] they did not give any incentives to public bodies to search for private funding when possible.[87] They were progressively set aside at the end of the 1980s.[88] Around that time, various documents on 'Private Finance' were circulated.[89] The September 1992 'Black Wednesday' crash triggered major reductions in government spending. John Major reacted by publishing a 'Strategy for Growth', which encouraged private sector involvement in large infrastructure projects.[90] Thus, by November 1992, a vehicle such as PFI could be presented as a major breakpoint for infrastructure investment as it coincided with the official suppression of the Ryrie Rules:[91] private money could be invested more freely in public infrastructure.

This general move towards private money being welcome in public infrastructure was accompanied by more specific considerations. Public expenditure through public procurement was indeed challenged for its inefficiency, as various infrastructures across England had hugely overrun budgets and deadlines.[92] The construction industry had, however, been identified as an important economic sector, especially at a difficult time of economic trouble.[93] Structural issues in the construction industry had been linked to litigation and blackmail since the end of the Second World War.[94] The bickering between the parties involved in any construction

---

[86] G Allen, *The Private Finance Initiative (PFI)* (research paper 03/79 HC 2003) 12–13. Harlow and Rawlings, 2009, 418.

[87] Treasury, 1995, 6.

[88] Treasury, 1993, 7.

[89] E.g.: *Private Finance in Public Expenditure*, prepared by the Treasury for the Civil Engineering Economic Development Committee in 1988, or *Public Money and Private Finance*, Guidance for the Department of the Environment in 1990.

[90] R Morledge and others, *Building Procurement* (Blackwell 2006) 214.

[91] 'The Government has now made clear that it wants deals, not rules' (Treasury, 1993, 7).

[92] E.g.: The Jubilee Line extension in the LU was delivered two years late and cost £1.4bn more than the original estimates (Treasury, 2000, 18).

[93] The link between PPPs/PFIs and the construction industry in both policy terms and technical terms continued later: e.g. 'Public private partnerships (PPPs) are […] providing a major boost to the construction industry' (Treasury, 2000, Foreword, 4). For the technical implications, see NAO reports such as: *Improving Public Services through Better Construction*, 2005; *PFI: Construction Performance*, 2003; *Modernising Construction*, 2001.

[94] NEDO, *The Public Client and the Construction Industries*, 1975 and *Faster Building for Industry*, 1983.

project had to be addressed: 'partnership' and 'partnering' were introduced and promoted, notably with the Latham[95] and Egan[96] reports. These themes would also be promoted in relation to PFIs.

By 1992, global and structural economic conditions and reflections articulating the roles of market and state in the provision of infrastructure were in the air. The time was ripe to experiment with 'cultural change'[97] in the ways in which infrastructure would be delivered: PFI was launched. Market mechanisms would bring private finance to public projects. This represents a 'radical change' because it departs 'from the assumption that most infrastructure and many public services are inherently public and have to be financed and managed by the public sector'.[98] From then on, the state would only need to remove the barriers which prevented the market from investing in infrastructure.[99] The market would then remedy state failures.

PFIs as a market-analogue model?

Against this backdrop of PFIs as a breakpoint, novelty may be looked at from two perspectives. Firstly, were PFIs a novel technique in 1992–93? Secondly, how was the novelty the Treasury introduced in 1992–93 related to market techniques?

In 1992, the PFI technique as such was not novel. PFIs had been used in the UK before 1992 for specific projects such as the Queen Elizabeth II Bridge.[100] They were partly based on techniques used in leasing[101] and partly on techniques used for international projects,[102] especially the 'DBFO model'[103] (i.e. design, build, finance and operate). The main idea was to bundle in one project the procurement of both assets and future services related to the assets (maintenance, repair, operations).[104] The contractor, the private entity bidding for the contract, would be responsible for both the construction of the asset and the provision of the related services. The contractor would then be remunerated over the whole life

---

95 Sir Latham, *Constructing the Team*, 1994.
96 Sir Egan, *Rethinking Construction*, 1998.
97 Braun (n 74 above) 575.
98 Randall (n 83 above) 281.
99 Treasury, 1993, Foreword, 3 and 7.
100 N Morrison, 'Project Finance in the United Kingdom' (1996) IBFL 25.
101 Treasury, 1993, 11.
102 Morrison (n 100 above) 25.
103 Badcoe (n 45 above) 285.
104 Ibid 280 and 287.

of the project.[105] Savings were expected, as the design of the project would take into account the quality of the asset to minimise future repairs over the course of its life. Similarly, the design would integrate ideas about how to generate third-party revenues from the assets.[106] In its purest form, this would lead to financially free-standing projects where the assets and services remunerated the contractor through the revenues produced.

While not fully new in 1992, PFIs represented a change in impetus by generalising different techniques to deliver public projects. That generalisation put forward two advantages of PFIs: one regarding the financial streams and one regarding the expertise and innovation carried by contractors.

Regarding investment, PFIs hinged upon the idea that corporations would be attracted by new markets and would bring the necessary funds, so that public investments in infrastructures such as bridges and highways could be limited. As such, PFIs are no exception to other provisions (procurement, transfer of undertaking (TUPE), accounting[107]). However, the way PFIs designed the relationships between the assets on which the infrastructure was built and the services provided with that infrastructure could result in the debts not being borne by the public. They also removed the need to comply with public procurement regulations – at least each time the private sector funded the project. When the investment was genuinely[108] borne by a private corporation, the off-balance sheet treatment and the non-application of public procurement rules would actually not have been real exceptions to either the accounting or the procuring system. The guidelines issued by the Treasury mostly contained references to case studies[109] and their concerns were practical. They were interested in how to spread the cost of asset acquisition over an extended period of time rather than paying all at once, and helping to provide more space for other investments each year, for instance,[110] or in

105 K Hartley, 'Problems of Using Partnering and Similar Private Sector Practice in the Public Sector Environment' in S Arrowsmith and M Trybus (eds), *Public Procurement* (Kluwer 2003) 187, 191.

106 Badcoe (n 45 above) 280.

107 A Arden and others (eds), *Local Government Constitutional and Administrative Law* (Sweet & Maxwell 2008) 1127.

108 In the sense that the asset would have been the property of the private entity and that the users would have paid for the service delivered without any state intervention in the costs.

109 Treasury, 1993.

110 Treasury, 1995, 22.

how to avoid too restrictive procurement regulations in favour of the negotiated procedure.[111] However, it was clear from the beginning that the PFI needed some kind of (mild) structuring and a commission was set up for that prospect.[112]

Regarding the creativity or innovation side, the question was to find out where better ways of doing things could be used to gain in efficiency. The techniques used in the private sector would be transplanted into the public sphere in terms of managing, planning, organising, technologies, flexibility etc. However, simultaneously, the concern arose that creativity could be used to sacrifice staff conditions or service quality, in the accountancy system or in the use (or the non-use) of public procurement. In these last two cases, the creativity would lie in the fact that a not genuinely fully privately financed project would be treated 'as if' it were one.[113] Globally, PFIs aimed to separate an asset (a building, an infrastructure) from the service that asset helped to produce. Such separation was indeed helpful for setting PFIs off the balance sheet or using the negotiated procedure in public procurement, creating a more flexible instrument for devising the contractual relationships between the public and private partners.

This background highlights how much PFIs are on the boundary between two different conceptions of how the state and the market are articulated in providing public services and infrastructures. It informs us about some of the key techniques with which PFIs will be closely associated at any given point of their development. However, in the years following those discussed above, PFIs did not meet with huge enthusiasm from the private sector and only few projects made progress.[114] Notably, financially free-standing projects were not developed on any large scale. These would have been the most likely place for market actors to take over the role of the public sector, once barriers to such action had been removed.[115] The tide turned for PFIs when New Labour came to power (1997): PFIs gained new impetus under the title 'PPPs'.[116]

---

111 Ibid 41.

112 Treasury, 1993, 9 and 24 announced a Private Finance Working Group, set up as the Private Finance Panel (Treasury 1995, 7).

113 For an illustration: S Norris, 'Application of EC Public Procurement Rules to Special Purpose Corporate Vehicles Formed Jointly by the Public and the Private Sectors' [1999] PPLR 146.

114 Treasury Committee, *The Private Finance Initiative* (146 HC 1995–96) v.

115 Treasury, 1993, Foreword, 3 and 7.

116 From the beginning, 'PFI' was connected with 'partnership' (see Treasury, 1993).

From PPPs to PF2: Interdependence between State and Market

New Labour endorsed PPP policy formally in their electoral manifesto.[117] The backlog of underinvestment in public infrastructure was one of the main drivers of this policy, as well as the modernisation of public services in general. Fiscal constraints such as the PSBR remained present, narrowing down the possibilities then as now. In 2010, the coalition government also reaffirmed its commitment to PPPs upon coming to power,[118] despite the pressure to cut public spending and the abolition of high-profile PPP programmes such as BsF.[119] This enduring presence of PPPs across changing governments arises from their necessity and yet flexibility: public–private cooperation is required to tackle infrastructure investments. The actual modalities for this cooperation have, however, varied across a wide range of techniques (e.g. joint ventures, contracts or shareholding). While different policies focus on different techniques, they never fully rule out other techniques. The *Private Finance 2* (PF2) developed by the government in 2012 is but one of the latest avatars of this continuous interdependence between state and market.

The flexibility of PPPs/PFIs is best illuminated with the ever-changing definition the Treasury gives to them. Indeed, up to and including *Partnerships for Prosperity* in 1997,[120] no definition was provided for PPPs at all. Only three types of constructions were mentioned; namely, financially free-standing projects, joint ventures between public and private actors and services sold to the public sector.[121] In 2000, *The Government Approach* brought in a distinction between PPPs and PFIs. PFIs are a specific kind of PPP which also encompasses the privatisation of state-owned businesses and the selling of government services into wider markets.[122] Therefore the boundaries between public and private involvement could be expressed in terms of assets, ownership and services that either of them provide to the other. The interplays have never been set once and for all, evidence for which comes from the

---

[117] Also a 1994 document authored by G Brown, J Prescott and R Cook, *Financing Infrastructure Investment: Promoting a Partnership between Public and Private Finance*, Labour Finance & Industry Group, 1994, referred to in Treasury, 2000, Foreword.

[118] Treasury, *Public Private Partnerships – Technical Update*, 2010, 1.

[119] See Chapter 5, pp 217–20.

[120] Treasury, 1997, 2.

[121] Treasury, 1993, 10–11.

[122] Treasury, 2000, 10.

constant attempts to revisit the ways in which public and private relationships are structured.

Two of these attempts are worth mentioning here. Firstly, in 2008 the Treasury issued a policy document, discussing alternatives to conventional procurement to unlock private finance options such as concessions, strategic infrastructure partnerships, integrators, alliancing and joint ventures.[123] These ideas were, however, set aside when the financial crisis pushed the government to seek temporary measures for investing in infrastructure. Secondly, the Lords' select committee on economic affairs drew out a mixed assessment of PPPs' achievements in 2009, recommending the transfer of more risks and services to private actors.[124]

Following these attempts, the coalition government sought to redirect PPPs when it came into power in 2010. In 2012, the newly devised policy, known as the PF2, showed again the flexibility of PPPs.[125] PF2 is part of a new approach to economic planning and strategies for developing infrastructure in England. Building on a paper issued by the Treasury shortly before the end of the Labour government,[126] the coalition government set up a National Infrastructure Plan in order to assess infrastructure needs and prioritise investments. This set up a pipeline of infrastructure projects, therefore giving them the visibility to attract private investments while seeking to ensure the confidence of private investors.[127] Infrastructure UK (IUK) – an entity inside the Treasury to which we return in the following section – is in charge of drafting and updating the plan. The first Plan mentioned a pending reform of PPPs,[128] the 2012 update builds on PF2,[129] as one way to deliver public infrastructure.

Indeed, after a period of uncertainty when the 2010 spending review abolished important financial incentives to use PPPs/PFIs – PFI credits[130] – and after extensive consultations by the Treasury, the dearth of funding for investing in public infrastructure was recognised and the coalition

---

[123] Treasury, 2008, Ch 2.

[124] SCEA, *Private Finance Projects and Off-Balance Sheet Debt* (63 HL 2009–10) recommendations 186–7.

[125] Treasury, 2012.

[126] Treasury and IUK, *Strategy for National Infrastructure*, 2010.

[127] Treasury and IUK, *National Infrastructure Plan*, 2011, 6.

[128] Ibid 8.

[129] Treasury and IUK, *National Infrastructure Plan – Update*, 2012, 33.

[130] Treasury, *Public Private Partnerships – Technical Update*, 2010, 3. Although the PFI credits were sometimes renamed and not abolished (Treasury, *Infrastructure Plan*, 2011, para 3.147).

government adapted PF2 as a new version of PPPs. The overarching ideas extend the two main features of PPPs, namely emphasising appropriate risk allocation and improving the *VfM* of PPPs. Risk allocation, however, implies that more risks will be borne by the public sector so that private investors will be attracted.[131] Public authorities will have a minimum shareholding in PF2 – which should allow them to share in potential gains in the transactions but also to retain risks and therefore reduce the costs of the transactions.[132] *VfM* will be improved as the arrangements for services will be made more flexible, notably in terms of changes. Efficiency and risk allocation again emphasise the market logic in PF2, while state logic remains as IUK pilots the PF2 policy and projects.

Overall, risk allocation and *VfM* are two recurring features across the various versions of PPPs/PFIs. These experiments are evidence that public actors need to encourage private actors' willingness and confidence to invest in public infrastructures. If this pattern of mutual interdependence between state and market in public infrastructure seems accepted at policy level, the concrete consequences in terms of PPP/PFI projects are still in the making. Despite these constant changes, PPPs/PFIs have developed into a policy distinct from other public policies thanks to their supporting institutional framework. Here again, however, changes have been incremental as circumstances have required them.

Institutionalisation and the Treasury

From the launch of PFIs, a specific body has been devoted to supporting them. However, its role has changed over time from very much hands-off[133] to active advising, supporting and even investing financially in PFIs. A Treasury Taskforce was set up after the Bates Review, in 1997, to speed up the flow of projects. The idea was to gather all PFI activities in that body. However, following various reorganisations, the policy and project sides of PPPs/PFIs have been located in different bodies. At one point, the Treasury piloted the policy side and PUK and OGC the project side. Other entities such as Local Partnerships and departmental units were also involved in PPPs/PFIs. This section first surveys the bodies set up under the New Labour government before explaining how the

---

131 Treasury, 2012, Ch 6.

132 Ibid Ch 2.

133 Treasury, 1993, 9 and 24 announced a Private Finance Working Group, set up as the Private Finance Panel (Treasury 1995, 7).

coalition government adjusted the institutional landscape around the Treasury afterwards.

Created in 2000,[134] Partnerships UK (PUK) succeeded to the Treasury Taskforce. It was 'a public private partnership with a public interest mission to make the public sector a more effective client in public private partnership and PFI transactions'.[135] PUK was incorporated as a private sector company, with 51 per cent of its shares owned by private sector institutions and the remaining 49 per cent held by the Treasury and Scottish ministers. Acting as a bridge between public and private entities, PUK did not define or enforce PPP policy. It ensured that the public sector had the necessary expertise to enter into PPPs. To that end, PUK advised public sector entities, set up procurement joint ventures related to specific programmes (such as LIFT and BsF) and entered into development agreements with public entities to jointly procure PPP/PFI projects.[136]

Also created in 2000, the Office of Government Commerce (OGC) was an independent office of the Treasury, established to help the government deliver the best from its spending.[137] It was set up following the Gershon Review,[138] which advocated more centralisation of purchasing power across departments. In general, the OGC fulfilled two roles: guiding departments in their purchasing and developing good practice in government purchasing. The OGC was especially relevant for PPPs/PFIs as it developed the Gateway Process.[139] The OGC not only developed and managed the concept but also issued various sets of guidance, such as its *Achieving Excellence in Construction Procurement Guide* and *OGC Best Practice – Gateway to success*.

Created in 1996, the Public Private Partnership Programme (4Ps) was the main source of advice on PPPs for local government. It was financed by local authorities and run by a board appointed by the Local Government Association.[140] It was transformed in 2009 into Local Partnerships,[141] a joint venture between the Local Government Association and

---

134 Government Resources and Accounting Act 2000, s 16.

135 Treasury, 2003, 61.

136 Treasury, 2003, 64.

137 Davies, 2008, 5ff; C Strassarino and C Mollers, 'Transforming Government Procurement: A Report by HM Treasury' [2007] PPLR 147, 148.

138 P Gershon, *Review of Civil Procurement in Central Government*, 1999.

139 See below this chapter, pp 73–5.

140 Davies, 2008, 9–10.

141 http://www.localpartnerships.org.uk/.

PUK, and now the Treasury. The new structure carries on 4Ps' missions, notably the Gateway Process for local PPPs/PFIs.

In various departments, such as defence, the Department for Environment, Food and Rural Affairs (Defra), health and transport, PFI Units have been set up to support the work carried out in PFI procurement teams, during either the preparation of the contracts or their performance.[142] These departmental units acquire specific commercial skills from their involvement in PFI processes across the department. The idea is to build on this specific acquired expertise for other procurement activities.[143] However, coordination inside the Treasury or across departments requires specific guidelines[144] and taskforces.[145] This process of coordination may stumble on the constant internal changes needed to adapt to specific issues.

This map around the Treasury has been reshuffled with the 2008 financial crisis and the coming to power of the coalition government. The separation between PPP programmes and PPP projects has been redrawn and the involvement of the Treasury has been altered in two opposing directions. The first direction was to depart from previous arrangements in which the Treasury was preeminent. In line with this, the OGC was re-located in the Efficiency and Reform Group within the Cabinet Office in 2010.[146] This group is in charge of developing a strategy to increase efficiency across central government and to improve the reforms related to the provision of public services. It coordinates the actions of different departments, including those of the Treasury. It also has a unit in charge of reviewing major projects, including PPPs/PFIs: the Major Projects Authority (MPA).[147] However, the MPA has fewer financial and human

142 NAO and HM Treasury, *From Private Finance Units to Commercial Champions – Managing Complex Capital Investment Programmes Utilising Private Finance*, 2010.

143 Treasury, 2008, 51.

144 PRG, *Process and Code of Practice*, Revised PRG Code V3.0 2009.

145 For instance, the Operational Taskforce, an advising entity issuing guidance, was acting on behalf of the Treasury but was located in PUK and it further followed suit as part of IUK (Treasury, *Public Private Partnerships – Technical Update*, 2010, 7).

146 However, reporting to the Efficiency and Reform Board, chaired jointly by the Cabinet Office (its minister) and the Treasury (its chief secretary): NAO, *The Efficiency and Reform Group*, 2013, 11.

147 NAO, *The Efficiency and Reform Group's Role in Improving Public Sector Value for Money*, 2011.

resources than the OGC had, which leads it to be more selective in the projects it follows.[148]

The second direction is steered towards closer control by the Treasury over its PPP/PFI unit, more especially, Infrastructure UK (IUK), which had been set up in 2009 as an advisory entity within the Treasury.[149] IUK's primary role was to 'stimulate increased private sector investment in infrastructure' and ensure cooperation between the public and private sectors.[150] It built on the PPP/PFI experience[151] and absorbed PUK's missions and staff. In the course of the following years, IUK developed into a central player in the planning of UK infrastructure investment. Now its missions extend beyond PPPs/PFIs to the drafting, monitoring and updating of the National Infrastructure Plan, as the previous section explained. Therefore, missions which were carried out at arm's length from the Treasury by PUK are now exercised in the Treasury's centre.

These developments have led to the Treasury losing its grip on the functions performed by OGC to the Cabinet Office's profit while strengthening its grip on economic planning and strategy for infrastructures. They also mean that the Treasury and Cabinet Office have to cooperate in the control they exercise over projects. We turn to the modalities of this control in the following discussion.

Proceduralisation of Control

In 2001, OGC introduced the Gateway Process as a mandatory tool for project assessment. The process is designed as a performance management tool to allow the public sector to assess the effectiveness of projects, including PPPs/PFIs, throughout their procurement process. There is no legal basis for this assessment of projects. The basic principles are mentioned first here, before highlighting the distinction between local PPPs and major projects.

The aim is to spot any potential problems as early as possible and tackle them. Six 'gates' (from 0 to 5) are distinguished: strategic assessment, business justification, procurement strategy, investment decision, readiness for service and benefits evaluation.[152] For instance, Gateway 1 probes whether stakeholders have been identified and consulted and whether they support the option followed by the public

---

148 PAC, *Assurance for Major Projects* (384 HC 2012–13) conclusions nr 4.
149 NAO, *Planning for Economic Infrastructure*, 2013, 19.
150 Treasury, *Pre-Budget*, 2009, Ch 4, 65.
151 Ibid 65.
152 Treasury, 2003, 61.

authority.[153] Gateway 2 is concerned with the proper procurement route and its compliance with legal requirements.[154] The reviews are conducted on a confidential basis and lead to the review team agreeing on an overall project assessment of red, amber or green for inclusion in the Gateway report.[155]

The Gateway Process is carried out differently for major projects and local PPPs/PFIs. In the case of local PFIs, the Gateway Process is divided into two phases. Local Partnerships carry out an assessment and then convenes a 'project review group' (PRG). The PRG is set up to confirm the funding of the project. It is chaired by the Treasury and contains permanent representatives from Communities and Local Government (CLG) and Local Partnerships.[156]

In the case of major projects, the aim is to increase the review process continuously, leading to a layering of control. Firstly, a starting gate – or an additional step – has been added into the Gateway process for these major projects. This ensures control over the project as early as possible. Secondly, a sophisticated system of 'major project approval and assurance' has been devised following NAO recommendations.[157] This system involves the Treasury, with the Major Projects Review Group (MPRG)[158] and the MPA from the Cabinet Office. The MPRG selects specific issues and projects on the basis of criteria such as the whole life costs, complexity, novelty and replicability of the projects. All the chosen projects are non-standard but the aim is both to limit the risks a bespoke project may entail and to learn lessons to be replicated elsewhere.[159] Following this process, major projects should develop an integrated assurance and approval plan which puts forward the 'planning, coordination and provision of assurance activities' during the lifetime of the project.[160] This therefore extends control over projects from their negotiation stage to their implementation. However, this system has encountered problems. Some departments have not implemented the plan.

---

153 OGC Gateway™ Process, *Review 1: Business Justification*, 2007, 11–12.

154 OGC Gateway™ Process, *Review 2: Delivery Strategy*, 2007, 9–10, 11, 13–14.

155 Treasury, 2003, 61.

156 Treasury, 2008, 42, box 5.1.

157 NAO, *Assurance for High Risk Projects*, 2010.

158 Established following Treasury, *Transforming Government Procurement*, 2007, 17–18; Strassarino and Mollers (n 137 above) 149.

159 Treasury, 2008, 43.

160 Treasury and Cabinet Office, *Major Project Approval and Assurance Guidance*, 2011, 9.

Coordination between the MPA and the Treasury needs to be strengthened, as the latter decides on spending and the former reviews projects.[161]

Standardisation: From SoPC4 to PF2

Contractual documentation for PPPs has been standardised to some extent as have the projects themselves through the development of PPP programmes. The early PPP projects were highly exploratory – even if based on international techniques or previous peculiar projects delivered in the UK. PPPs would be used for projects such as air traffic management (NATS), a laboratory, IT systems in courts, LU etc. However, PPPs were increasingly standardised in two ways. PPP programmes were designed as a model for replication in different projects with minor adjustments. The cases of the LIFT, BsF and waste PFI programmes are discussed later.[162] This section shows how this increasing standardisation, under the form of 'Standardisation of PFI Contracts' (SoPC) or PF2, results in central government pre-selecting options and contractual terms for the public authorities involved in PPPs/PFIs. This, in turn, reduces public authorities' actual scope of discretion.

The most prominent standardisation of contractual documents is the SoPC. Since 1999, the Treasury has undertaken efforts of standardisation to suggest balanced contracts,[163] culminating in the SoPC Version 4 (SoPC4[164]) in 2007. SoPC4 upgraded SoPC3 following changes in policy,[165] law[166] and market demand/practice.[167] However, the key objectives of the standardisation remained similar:

- developing a 'common understanding of the main risks which are encountered in a standard PFI project';
- bringing consistency in PFI, especially regarding pricing in similar projects; and

161 PAC, *Assurance for Major Projects* (384 HC 2012-13) conclusions nr 1 and 2.

162 In the following section, pp 94–6 and in Chapter 5, pp 213–22.

163 *SoPC1* (1999); *SoPC2* (2002); *SoPC3* (2004): see *SoPC4*, para 1.1.1.

164 http://webarchive.nationalarchives.gov.uk/20100407010852/http://www.hm-treasury.gov.uk/ppp_standardised_contracts.htm

165 Treasury, *Standardisation of PFI Contracts – Version 4 – An Outline of Principal Changes*, 2007, 9 (market testing).

166 Ibid 35 (competitive dialogue).

167 Ibid 8 (changes in services), 14 (asset property).

- reducing the time and costs of negotiation.[168]

The SoPC4 considered itself guidance,[169] containing elements of a different nature. Variations existed on a departmental basis, such as for waste[170] or education.[171] Some parts of SoPC4 were explanatory, while other sections were recommended or suitable drafting.[172] Normally, not many amendments would be needed for those sections with specific drafting. A list of the sections that should not be amended was provided.[173] When the PFI project was large, complex or novel, changes might be contemplated.[174] Compliance with SoPC4 was enforced, as derogations from the SoPC4 needed to have been discussed properly with the department in charge of the projects and in due course accepted by the Treasury. If the procedures for derogations had not been followed, the final business case was not approved.[175]

After amendments with two addenda, SoPC4 was replaced by PF2 in 2012 when the Treasury issued a draft for the contracts governing the new version of PPPs/PFIs. PF2 basically builds on the SoPC4 logic in terms of standardisation. It also lists terms which have a required form of drafting.[176] It further seeks to 'fill in some of the gaps in contract standardisation, in particular providing new standard form service output template, a pro forma payment mechanism, and new PPP shareholder arrangement'.[177] As was the case between SoPC3 and SoPC4, the changes in the documentation reflect either new policy choices or adjustments following legal or market requirements to follow practice more closely (as emerged from SoPC4).[178] Most changes attempt to improve the *VfM* and risk allocation between public and private actors, the two recurring concerns in PPPs across any of their expressions. The technical differences between SoPC4 and PF2 are detailed in Chapter 3. SoPC4 and PF2, however, share the same approach in providing public

---

168 *SoPC4*, para 1.2.1.
169 Ibid para 1.2.1 and 1.4.1.
170 WIDP, *Residual Waste Treatment Contract – Consultation Draft*, 2009.
171 PfS, BsF, *Project Agreement*, 2007.
172 *SoPC4,* para 1.6.2.
173 Ibid para 1.4.1.
174 For the process: see Treasury, *Revision to Standardisation of PFI Contracts (SoPC)*, 2007.
175 Treasury, *Public Private Partnerships – Technical Update*, 2010, Annex B, para B 17.
176 *PF2* (draft), para 2.1.1.
177 Ibid para 1.2.1.
178 IUK, *PF2: A User Guide*, 2012.

authorities involved in PPPs/PFIs with contractual templates; they reduce the scope for discretion that public authorities exercise when they negotiate the contractual terms of their relationships with their private partners.

Conclusions

While PFIs were initiated as importing finance and skills from the private sector into the public sector, PPPs have been taken over as an internal means of transforming public infrastructure and services and their procurement. Change and transformation have thus always been linked to PPPs/PFIs. They were more than symbolic and originated in pragmatic reactions to financial needs and poor public infrastructures.

Over time, the PPP/PFI regulatory space has changed and the discretion exercised by public authorities has been structured differently: from an approach heavily influenced by market logic, the machinery has become more bureaucratic and public-centred. *VfM* and risk allocation, however, are wide pockets where market logic remains paramount as a structuring technique for public discretion across PPPs/PFIs and PF2. The reasons for this formalisation are to some extent contingent to market failures. In this sense, private discretion has not lived up to the initial expectations. This statement is also evidenced by the increasing presence of the law in structuring public discretion in the PPP regulatory space.

LEGALISM: ARCHITECTURE FOR PUBLIC DISCRETION

Where does the law fit in the state superstructure that has been expanding to support PPPs/PFIs? As PFIs developed as a financial solution to financial/economic issues, their legal treatment was not considered actively at first. However, PFIs/PPPs evolved. No general legislation has been passed to frame the overall legal treatment of PPPs/PFIs. Statutory solutions have been developed with respect to specific projects[179] or to bring answers as questions arise. Here, are surveyed, the most directly relevant legal answers regarding the public authorities' powers, PPP subject-matter, their elaboration procedure, their contractual framework and their terms as progressively clarified.

[179] E.g.: for the London Underground: GLA 1999, Ch VII or Severn Crossing Act 1992.

Firstly, the law grants necessary powers to enter into PFIs/PPPs. At the outset, PFIs built on financial creativity developed by public authorities. Therefore there was a risk that the contracts might be found *ultra vires*, following *Hammersmith*[180] and *Crédit Suisse.*[181] The Local Government (Contracts) Act 1997 removed this insecurity by establishing a certification process. Following this procedure, once a certificate was issued, the local authority could no longer claim the contract to be invalid or void. However, other bodies, such as audit ones, could still challenge the contracts. A similar mechanism exists for the NHS.[182] A series of other bodies have been granted powers to enter into PFI agreements on an ad hoc basis.[183] In this sense, the actors allowed into the PPP regulatory space are neatly defined through the legal framework and their contracting parties are assured that they have the required powers to enter into PPPs/PFIs.

Secondly, the law also grants the Treasury the power to guarantee private projects or PPPs/PFIs. The Infrastructure (Financial Assistance) Act 2012 intends to reassure international financial investors about the Treasury's powers. It thus parallels the Local Government (Contracts) Act 1997, which sought to give confidence to domestic financial market players that local government had the powers to enter into PPPs. Although financial guarantees do not require the government to pay anything upfront, they involve significant risks if the guarantee is called on, risks that the government does not always assess realistically.[184] In the past, guarantees have been provided, for instance, for the London Underground PPPs, High Speed 1 and NHS PFI hospitals, and these have been called or relied on. The 2012 Act thus provides for reporting by the Treasury to Parliament on arrangements connected to financial assistance, expenditures incurred and actual and contingent liabilities.[185] Although targeting a different legal issue, both the Local Government (Contracts) Act 1997 and the Infrastructure (Financial Assistance) Act 2012 address private investors' lack of trust in PPPs/PFIs. They ascertain public

180 *Hazell v Hammersmith LBC* [1992] 2 AC 1.

181 *Crédit Suisse v Allerdale BC* [1997] QB 306.

182 National Health Service (Private Finance) Act 1997.

183 Treasury, *Joint Ventures*, 2010, para 3.15, referring to regs 3(2) and 8(3) of, and Pt 2 of Sch 1 to, the National Health Service (Functions of Strategic Health Authorities and Primary Care Trusts and Administration Arrangements) (England) Regulations 2002, SI 2002/2375 for the powers of PCTs to enter into LIFT.

184 NAO, *Planning for Economic Infrastructure*, 2013, 34.

185 Infrastructure (Financial Assistance) Act 2012, s 3(3).

authorities' powers and organise the modalities under which discretion may be used so that trust in the use of taxpayers' money is maintained.

Thirdly, the law specifies how PPPs/PFIs have to be negotiated and elaborated. European procurement regulations include three main sets of texts. The first is for awarding public works contracts, public supply contracts and public service contracts (classic directive[186]). The second text is for utilities (utilities directive[187]) and the third one is for remedies (remedies directive[188]). These directives pursue three main goals: minimisation of the discretion of public bodies, maximisation of transparency in public procurement and prevention of discrimination (especially on the basis of nationality).[189] Therefore, procurement directives limit how public authorities can develop their policies through contracts with private contractors.[190] The Public Contracts Regulations 2006 implement European regulations on public works contracts and utilities, and the Public Contracts (Amendment) Regulations 2009 implement the remedies directive.[191] The public procurement procedure applicable in PPPs/PFIs, the competitive dialogue, is detailed in Chapter 3.[192] It follows a

---

186 Directive 2004/18/EC of the European Parliament and of the Council of 31 March 2004 on the coordination of procedures for the award of public works contracts, public supply contracts and public service contracts [2004] OJ L134/114. The Directive 2014/24/EU of the European Parliament and of the Council of 26 February 2014 on public procurement and repealing Directive 2004/18/EC [2014] OJ L 94/65 provides that the transposition period lasts until 18 April 2016 (art. 90).

187 Directive 2004/17/EC of the European Parliament and of the Council of 31 March 2004 coordinating the procurement procedures of entities operating in the water, energy, transport and postal services sectors [2004] OJ L134/1. The Directive 2014/25/EU of the European Parliament and of the Council of 26 February 2014 on procurement by entities operating in the water, energy, transport and postal services sectors and repealing Directive 2004/17/EC [2014] OJ L 94/243 provides that the transposition period lasts until 18 April 2016 (art. 106).

188 Directive 2007/66/EC of the European Parliament and of the Council of 11 December 2007 amending Council Directives 89/665/EEC and 92/13/EEC with regard to improving the effectiveness of review procedures concerning the award of public contracts [2007] OJ L335/31.

189 Davies, 2008, 124.

190 S Arrowsmith, 'The EC Procurement Directives, National Procurement Policies and Better Governance: The Case for a New Approach' (2002) 27 ELRev 3, 8–9.

191 Public Contracts (Amendment) Regulations 2009, SI 2009/2992; Public Contracts Regulations 2006, SI 2006/5.

192 See Chapter 3, pp 106–16.

period in which PPPs/PFIs were procured through a flexible negotiated procedure,[193] even though the legality of this procedure had been challenged in the legal scholarship.[194] Outside these legal requirements, the Gateway Process exercises close scrutiny of the elaboration process, helped by various guidelines, technical notes and the OGC/Treasury guidelines on competitive dialogue.[195] This system of public sector monitoring of the public partners of PPPs/PFIs is counter-balanced by few judicial challenges against public procurement in general, and certainly PPP/PFI procurement.[196]

Fourthly, public procurement regulations are in the main silent on the rules applicable to public contracts once they have been signed. Therefore, contract law applies as a starting point to the relationship between the private and public parties in the performance phase of PPPs/PFIs. The contract terms rely on standardised contracts negotiated or developed by industries and public authorities.[197] Chapter 3 details how contract law is adjusted in PPPs/PFIs and how the SoPC4 and PF2 developed specific solutions to delicate questions, especially those bearing on the financial terms of the relationship. Contract law does not, however, apply to two situations: SoPC4 and PF2 expressly exclude the application of the Contracts (Rights of Third Parties) Act 1999,[198] and the Construction Contracts Exclusion Order 1998[199] exempts PFIs from parts of the Housing Grants, Construction and Regeneration Act 1996.

Fifthly, the law may regulate the services performed by PPPs outside contract law. The Deregulation and Contracting Out Act 1994 sets limits regarding the missions transferrable to a private entity and the maximum duration of the transfer. Normally, the transfer lasts no longer than ten years. However, in the case of the PFIs covered by the Local Government (Contracts) Act 1997, the maximum duration is forty years.[200] In many cases, though, the service delivered relates to the maintenance of the assets and no specific public missions are transferred, resulting in there

---

[193] E.g.: European Commission, Decision no 264/2002, *London Underground Public Private Partnership* [2002] OJ C309/15.

[194] S Arrowsmith, 'Application of the UK Procurement Regulations to PFI Contracts: New Case Law' [2002] PPLR na84.

[195] Treasury/OGC, *Competitive Dialogue in 2008*, 2008; 4Ps, *A Map of the PFI Process Using Competitive Dialogue*, 2006.

[196] See Chapter 4, pp 170–73.

[197] S Furst and others, *Keating on Construction Contracts* (8th edn, Sweet & Maxwell 2006) 14–15 on PFI and Ch 14 on public procurement.

[198] *SoPC4,* para 30.5; *PF2* (draft), para 31.2.

[199] SI 1998/648.

[200] Local Government (Contracts) Act 1997, s 9.

being no direct legal relationships between the private contractors and the individual users. Chapter 4 develops the consequences of this for control over the public discretion used in PPPs/PFIs.

Finally, PPP/PFI projects have to integrate various legal requirements stemming from thematic policies, such as the normal regulation processes (e.g. health and safety, rail regulation etc.), freedom of information or planning.

In short, the law sets a framework that grants powers, sets processes and provides tools to organise the relationships between public and private partners in the PPP regulatory space. It also imposes a range of specific regulatory requirements. This excludes public bodies which did not get powers to make PPPs, constrains the ways in which public authorities choose their contracting parties, or brings them *a priori* into the opposing mindset of contracts. The law has been relied on to remedy problems of trust in public authorities' powers and of abuse of discretion. It formalises market logics (e.g. in procurement and contracts) or facilitates private investments (e.g. Local Government (Contracts) Act 1997 and Infrastructure (Financial Assistance) Act 2012) as ways to organise the solidarity between public and private partners. It also limits the policy goals that public authorities may pursue through contracts and their potential contribution to overall well-being (public procurement).

Overall, the legal techniques that shape PPPs/PFIs in the regulatory space do not allow a detailed understanding of how PPPs/PFIs work in practice or how PPP/PFI commitments and interests are structured. In particular, which principles should be followed by the public and private partners in order to fill in gaps (contractual or statutory) or to develop new solutions developed? How are public and private partners' interests coordinated, prioritised or balanced in PPP regulatory space? Do they take into account the purpose of PPPs/PFIs, namely a common project carried out to provide public infrastructure and services to users? The actual motivations in the heads of the public and private individuals deciding how to respect their commitments and (trying to) meet others' expectations is a matter of speculation. However, this monograph seeks to tease out some of the structural factors likely to affect how discretion is used. It is suggested that, among these factors, next to institutions and law, communities also play a role in structuring PPP/PFI relationships.

FUNCTIONALISM: COMMUNITY BRIDGING OF STATE AND MARKET

The complexity of designing and managing large investment projects delivering infrastructures and services requires that public bodies have the necessary experience to lead them. However, the English civil service has historically lacked such skills.[201] Problems of budget and time overruns in construction contracts, only confirm the need to address this. For this reason, the key function of PFIs when they were first created was to bring in to the public sector and its staff the discipline and expertise they supposedly lacked. Therefore, PFIs would contribute to the public sector's expertise. This function of PFIs as a vehicle for transforming public administration evolved, however. PPPs/PFIs drew attention to the need for public authorities to be advised on the projects, leading to the development of advisors arranging deals in innovative ways. PPPs/PFIs gather together private actors to finance and perform the projects, public actors to pay and control these projects, and advisors to provide support for designing, negotiating, performing and winding up PPPs/PFIs. This creates communities of actors involved in PPPs/PFIs. This section outlines how PPPs/PFIs rely on these various communities for their development, with a special role being played by expertise.

As mentioned, at the outset PFIs were supposed to bring market discipline and expertise to the public sector. This has remained a key contribution of PPPs/PFIs throughout their evolution[202] up to the PF2 policy.[203] However, public authorities face a problem here, namely the identification of the market and of private actors interested in developing and financing PPPs/PFIs. Such information requires not only expertise but also coordination among the potential interested private actors. This requires planning, organisation and representation of private sector interests, while being respectful of competition among private actors. Financial institutions are key here, as evidenced by the Labour government's explicit good will towards business and the City of London.[204] The

201 Lord Fulton, *The Civil Service,* vol 1 (1968 Cmnd 3638) Ch 1.

202 E.g.: Treasury, 2006, Box 3.1, para 3.48–50.

203 Treasury, 2012, Foreword, 6–7, para 1.20.

204 M Hellowell, 'The UK's Private Finance Initiative: History, Evaluation, Prospects' in G Hodge and C Greve (eds) *International Handbook on Public–Private Partnerships* (Edward Elgar 2010) 307, 308–13.

coalition government also seeks to encourage investors.[205] PUK and then IUK have been instrumental in organising this cooperation with private actors.

However, public authorities also have to match needs for public infrastructures and services with private actors' interests. Specific expertise and commercial skills are required. PPPs/PFIs have recurrently highlighted the need to address the weakness of public bodies in these respects.[206] Developing PPPs/PFIs mainly relies on an extended community, especially revolving around experts such as lawyers, public administrators, bankers, auditors etc. advising on their complex technicalities. These experts have been widely used in PPPs as a method of cross-fertilisation between the public and private sectors and across projects.[207] However, this dependency of the public sector on external expertise has also been criticised.[208] For a while, this problem was addressed through secondments from the public sector to the private sector, thus supporting mutual learning as well as triggering potential conflicts of interest.[209] The setting up of the MPA was then supposed to alleviate this weakness in technical expertise.[210] The government has also kept open the possibility 'for the greater centralisation and improved professionalism of public sector procurement'.[211] Finally, in wider terms, the Civil Service Reform Plan, which includes the MPA, has announced measures such as training to transform these aspects of the civil service in order to improve the delivery of major projects such as PPPs/PFIs.[212]

PPPs/PFIs therefore create specific expertise that public authorities have sought to harness within the UK, where PPPs/PFIs can be seen as a laboratory for testing ideas and techniques thereafter exported to other parts of public procurement or public services.[213] Expertise has also been

---

205 Treasury, 2012, box 8.A; *PF2* (draft), paras 1.4.1 and 1.4.2.

206 Treasury, 2012, 8; NAO, *Commercial Skills for Complex Government Projects*, 2009, passim.

207 NAO, *PFI Contract for the Redevelopment of West Middlesex University Hospital*, 2002, para 2.10; *PFI: The Contract for the Defence Fixed Telecommunications System,* 2000, 56.

208 E.g.: Cabinet Office, *Accelerating Government Procurement*, 2011, 6–7.

209 E.g.: PAC, *M25 Private Finance Contract* (651 HC 2010–11) recommendation 8; PAC, *Equity Investment in Privately Financed Projects* (1846 HC 2010–12) Q50–52.

210 NAO, *The Efficiency and Reform Group*, 2013, para 2.20.

211 Treasury, 2012, 9.

212 HM Government, *The Civil Service Reform Plan*, 2012, ch 3.

213 E.g.: Treasury, *Public Services: Meeting the Productivity Challenge*, 2003, 16.

harnessed in relation to international audiences. We saw that PFIs were developed in a context of economic crisis in 1992–93. At the time, one of the following strategies, alongside boosting the construction industry, was to develop jobs which could compete with low-income countries, jobs to which the UK could bring high added value, such as legal or financial skills.[214] These two fields of expertise are at the core of PPP/PFI projects. Following this, official documentation has been issued to promote PPPs/PFIs and export PPP/PFI expertise abroad.[215] IUK even has a team dedicated to this exportation abroad.[216]

Therefore the PPP regulatory space encompasses communities of experts in PPPs/PFIs comprised mostly of public and private partners. These communities influence how public authorities exercise discretion in PPPs/PFIs. Expertise is key to their decision making in order to develop PPP/PFI projects that attract financial investors and private contractors. They also express concerns for solidarity and trust. Indeed, relationships of dependency on this expertise or interdependency between the interested actors have been highlighted. Securing private actors and investors' confidence in public projects does not happen out of the blue. Extended preparation and mutual understanding are needed to foster a general climate of trust. The extent to which communities contribute further to autonomy, solidarity and trust in PPPs/PFIs is explored in later chapters, especially Chapter 5.

ILLUSTRATIONS FROM ENGLISH PPPs

The previous sections show how PPPs/PFIs oscillate in policy terms between market-analogue and state-analogue models. The same hesitation can be seen at the project level. At the outset, many one-off deals were signed in transportation, prisons, defence, hospitals and schools. From 2000, once PUK was set up, a series of PFI programmes were developed in schools, social housing, healthcare and waste. However, single PPPs/PFIs went on being designed to tackle highly idiosyncratic situations (e.g. LU, NATS). This section illustrates these experiments

---

[214] A Davies, *Perspectives on Labour Law* (2nd edn, CUP 2009) 15 and 29.

[215] E.g.: World Bank and others, *Attracting Investors to African Public–Private Partnerships – A Project Preparation Guide* (Washington 2009) ix; C Greve and G Hodge, 'A Transformative Perspective on Public–Private-Partnerships' in T Christensen and P Laegreid (eds), *The Ashgate Research Companion to New Public Management* (Ashgate 2010) 265, 271.

[216] IUK, *Creating Public Sector Capacity – The UK Experience*, 2012, 7.

with PPPs/PFIs and the different structures involved in the relationships between public authorities, private contractors and individual users with three case studies: firstly, the Private Sector Resource Initiative for the Management of the Estate (PRIME) and Strategic Transfer of the Estate to the Private Sector (STEPS), early accommodation PFIs restructuring the office estate of central government; secondly, the London Underground PPPs (LU PPPs) aiming to finance the upgrade of the LU infrastructure; and thirdly, Local Improvement Finance Trust (LIFT), a PPP programme supporting the building and refurbishment of general practitioners' premises.

The case studies are mainly built on the *VfM* reports issued by the NAO. Constituting the best sources of information about PPPs/PFIs,[217] the NAO findings help us reconstruct their most important features. The three PFIs detailed here, accommodation PFIs, LU and LIFT, were chosen for the different perspectives they offer on the links between factual settings (innovative, complex and high value), contractual arrangements and prominent performance issues.

Firstly, accommodation PPPs/PFIs, here PRIME and STEPS, rely mainly on contractual relationships between central departments and private partners. No direct contact exists between the contractor and individuals. The main questions which they prompt can be framed in clear contractual terms: *VfM*, risk allocation, changing circumstances, choice of private partners, scope of the assets and the services bundled in the PFI. Few other issues interfere in the overall analysis, laying bare the structure on which PFIs rely. As they were signed more than ten years ago, they represent a good basis for a longer-term perspective on PFIs. Secondly, the LU PPPs achieved supreme refinement in contractual terms. They also were one of the rare cases in which two PFIs share many factual features, allowing for more fine-tuned comparisons. Finally, LIFT has been mainly developed through an external structure set up at central level and in charge of streamlining PFIs. Here, small projects of refurbishing general practitioners' premises are bundled together and procured through the LIFT local structure. If adjustments to individual circumstances are needed, the scope for these adaptations is limited. LIFT has also kick-started similar programmes in schools, waste and housing.

---

[217] T Prosser, 'The Powers and Accountability of Agencies and Regulators' in D Feldman (ed), *English Public Law* (2nd edn, OUP 2009) 241, para 5.20. Compare with the challenging view on the NAO reports in A Pollock and D Price, 'Has the NAO Audited Risk Transfer in Operational Private Finance Initiative Schemes?' (2008) Public Money and Management 173.

Market-Analogue Model in Accommodation: PRIME[218] (1998) and STEPS[219] (2001)

Designed as market-analogue models, PRIME and STEPS illustrate the first PFIs. Negotiations for PRIME started in 1996, at the time when the first PFIs were also elaborated in highways,[220] prisons[221] and hospitals.[222] In PRIME and STEPS the operation was close to a real estate/financial operation.[223] The NAO issued four reports on these two PFIs and a couple of other reports on similar operations, allowing for a grasping of their overall working. These PFIs mainly focus on *VfM* and risk allocation. They illustrate how the contract evolves in the long term, with few disturbing factors such as a complicated social, organisational or regulatory environment. Therefore, they can be seen as paradigms for market PFIs, where the issues are mostly contractual in nature, for instance the extension of the contract or changes of circumstances. However, the scope of these contracts and the necessary balance to be found between public and private interests structure how public discretion is framed.

Features: Innovative, high value, services

Both PRIME and STEPS developed innovative and large-scale contracts to rationalise government accommodation.

Under PRIME, the Department of Social Security transferred nearly all of its estate ownership and management to Trillium, a private partner, in 1998. This was then 'the biggest ever property transaction by a UK Government department'.[224] Signed for twenty years, the contract sought to address problems that the department encountered with its estate, that is, its extensive refurbishment and maintenance, its large vacant space and its fragmentation across more than a hundred service contracts. The PFI would be innovative in two respects. Firstly, the PFI would bundle in one single contract the right for the department to occupy the estate with

---

218 Private Sector Resource Initiative for the Management of the Estate.

219 Strategic Transfer of the Estate to the Private Sector.

220 NAO, *The First Four Design, Build, Finance and Operate Roads Contracts*, 1998.

221 NAO, *The PFI Contracts for Bridgend and Fazakerley Prisons*, 1997.

222 NAO, *The PFI Contract for the New Dartford & Gravesham Hospital*, 1999.

223 NAO, *PFI: The New Headquarters for the Home Office*, 2003; *Redevelopment of MOD Main Building*, 2002; *Innovation in PFI Financing: The Treasury Building Project*, 2001; *The New British Embassy in Berlin*, 2000.

224 NAO, *PRIME*, 1999, summary, para 1.

the provision of services to the Department such as cleaning, maintenance, catering or security. This bundling of assets and services has been the subject of many discussions. In other PFIs signed at the same time as PRIME, such as the Newcastle PFI, that option was not followed.[225] The issue of including soft services in PFIs has recurred ever since.[226] Secondly, PRIME would also be innovative in that the Department would have rights to share in the profit or savings generated by Trillium.[227]

STEPS refers to a twenty-year contract signed in 2001 between two departments, the Inland Revenue and HM Customs & Excise, and Mapeley. With that contract, the Departments transferred the ownership and management of nearly 60 per cent of their estate for an overall value of £220 bn.[228] The transfer of the rented properties was actually a virtual assignment.[229] The legal tenant remained the Department because the change of tenant was unlikely to be accepted by landlords. Mapeley only manages on behalf of the Department.[230] However, instead of dealing with numerous contractors, the Department only dealt with Mapeley.

When PRIME and STEPS were negotiated, financial innovation was highly emphasised.[231] In STEPS, this led to the contractors being partly located offshore.[232] This actually provided only limited benefits for the contractors and strained the relationships between the public and private partners. This led to Treasury guidelines specifying that such mechanisms should be banned in the future.[233]

---

225 NAO, *The Newcastle Estate Development Project*, 1999.

226 Treasury, 2003, 83; Treasury, 2006, para 1.23 and paras 5.57–5.73, especially para 5.69; Treasury, 2012, 48.

227 NAO, *PRIME*, 1999, summary, para 2.

228 NAO, *STEPS,* 2004, summary, para 3, 132 freehold properties were transferred and leased back. Another 459 properties rented from third parties were also transferred to Mapeley for management.

229 Landlords are not legally obliged to accept the rent paid by third parties, here Mapeley or Trillium (C Edwards and P Krendel, *Institutional Leases in the 21st Century* (Estates Gazette Ltd 2007) 158).

230 NAO, *STEPS Eight Years On*, 2009, para 3.6.

231 For the financial innovation in terms of funding competition, see NAO, *Innovation in PFI Financing: The Treasury Building Project*, 2001, recommendation 12; *PFI: The New Headquarters for the Home Office*, 2003, recommendation 7.

232 NAO, *STEPS*, 2004, summary, para 12-14.

233 NAO, *PRIME Expansion*, 2005, summary, para 10.

Flexible structuring: VfM and risk allocation

PRIME and STEPS both seek to structure flexible contractual relationships between the public and private partners, translated into *VfM* and risk allocation, two notions at the core of the relational nexus detailed in Chapter 3.[234] Here we illustrate their significance in PRIME and STEPS.

Firstly, *VfM* allowed the possibility of vacating or adding new offices, as well as of rationalising these offices and the many fragmented[235] service contracts linked to them, depending on the needs involved.[236] The aim was indeed that the Department would focus on its core functions and not on estate management, which was reportedly poor.[237] However, once the property was transferred, issues still came up requiring further negotiations and Departments were not necessarily free of all estate management questions.[238] The contract relies on the possibility of the Department vacating certain office areas or adding areas with or without incurring additional costs, depending on an agreed classification of assets (core, intermediated or flexible). *VfM* is thus reached in practice as far as the Department is able to make the best use of these terms (e.g. thanks to long-term planning).[239]

Secondly, the principle of risk allocation in these two PFIs has been put as follows:

> [o]ne of the principal reasons for undertaking a property deal such as PRIME or STEPS is that the risk of managing property in line with general movements in the economy and financial and property markets is transferred to the private sector contractor.[240]

In the past, the contractors benefited from positive movements in these markets. Innovative benefit-sharing mechanisms were indeed used.[241] After the 2008 financial crisis, the contractors have been facing market downfalls. In STEPS, risks seem to be poorly managed and not jointly tackled, while defaulting by Mapeley would result in costs for the Department.[242] The question of actual risk transfer may be asked, as the

---

234 See Chapter 3, pp 116–29.

235 NAO, *PRIME*, 1999, para 1.8; NAO, *STEPS*, 2004, fig 5 and para 1.8 ff (e.g., single point of access).

236 NAO, *STEPS Eight Years On*, 2009, para 2.5.

237 NAO, *PRIME*, 1999, summary, para 4; NAO, *STEPS*, 2004, para 1.11.

238 NAO, *STEPS*, 2004, para 1.11.

239 NAO, *STEPS Eight Years On*, 2009, summary, para 10.

240 NAO, *STEPS*, 2004, para 3.10.

241 NAO, *PRIME Expansion*, 2005, paras 2.10–2.18.

242 NAO, *STEPS Eight Years On*, 2009, para 3.5 ff and recommendation c.

contractor has approached public authorities with concerns related to its difficulties in finding new tenants. According to the NAO, the Department should not make concessions to Mapeley but explore alternatives, for instance in committing to some buildings or working with other bodies to occupy space.[243]

Changes and difficulties

During the implementation of the PFIs, the contractual relationships evolved due to mergers. In STEPS, the existence of a single contract for the whole estate was reported to be positive for the merger.[244] In PRIME, the 2001 merger resulted in a contractual expansion to additional assets.[245] However, the most striking performance feature relates to differences in the general management of the contracts. From the first few months the contracts followed different courses. In PRIME, Trillium's management was overall satisfactory. This led the contract to be expanded without competition.[246] By contrast, Mapeley soon had cash flow difficulties in STEPS, tackled by setting up a working group.[247] The situation improved due to changes in the property and financial markets (external factors) and the appointment of a financial director at Mapeley (internal factor). Regarding contractual performance, STEPS is noteworthy for the fact that the performance measurement system designed by Mapeley did not work properly.[248] The system had to be renegotiated during the contract's performance. The system was introduced in 2005 but by 2009 it was not yet formally incorporated in the contract.[249]

In conclusion, PRIME and STEPS represent market-analogue PFIs as they only rely on contracts negotiated between the public and private partners. The two contracts aimed to rationalise government accommodation: public authorities would gain more autonomy in terms of both focusing on their core missions and improving flexibility regarding office use. Market mechanisms and competitive pressure have been used but not

---

243 Ibid para 2.20.

244 Ibid para 2.7 ff.

245 NAO, *PRIME Expansion*, 2005.

246 Ibid 8–9 and 13 (partnering agreement in development).

247 NAO, *STEPS*, 2004, para 3.3 ff.

248 Ibid summary, paras 17 and 18.

249 NAO, *STEPS Eight Years On*, 2009, para 1.8. Other elements such as additional buildings have not been integrated in the contract, with the result that correlative advantages in terms of vacation allowances may not be used. The reason for non-integration is due to the offshore structure of the contractors combined with the weak estate market (para 2.15).

to their fullest logic. In PRIME, no competition was run for expanding the contract. Specific internal structures were needed in STEPS to address early cash flow issues. However, structures built into the contracts do not always work, as the poor implementation of performance measurement in STEPS shows. *VfM* and risk allocation are related to flexibility in the contracts, for instance through benefits sharing. However, their results depend on the possibility of public authorities learning from previous relevant experiences and planning for the long term. In this respect, STEPS gives a contrasting picture. It has consciously learnt from the experience built up in PRIME,[250] for instance to pool resources regarding information gathering on the state of the estate. However, *VfM* in STEPS depends on the concrete long-term strategy of the Department, which is still unclear. Risks have not been fully transferred in STEPS. In any case, some cooperation between the parties is needed to mitigate supervening risks. Interdependence between parties directs how they may use their autonomy with flexibility. Returning to this issue, Chapter 3 builds on STEPS and PRIME as background illustrations.

London Underground PPPs (2003–10)

While STEPS and PRIME provide services directly to public bodies, London Underground (LU) illustrates PPPs directly connected to the provision of public services to individual users. Often used to illustrate English PPPs/PFIs,[251] LU has been extensively reported on: four reports have been issued by the NAO, along with reports by the Public Account Committee (PAC), the Transport Committee of the House of Commons and the London Assembly. Among the wealth of available data, three key issues are investigated here: the contractual set-up, the discretion used in performing the PPP and the relationships with commuters. These points show that the public authorities remained strongly involved in the delivery of the LU PPPs, making it a state-analogue PPP.

A complex contractual setting

Part of the central/local relationship reorganisation, the LU PPPs illustrate the technical, financial and political complexity of PPP contracts. Unusually for PPPs, a statutory framework sets the key features of the

---

250 Ibid summary, paras 2.5 and 3 and Pt 2.

251 For a detailed account of LU PPPs: Harlow and Rawlings, 2009, 425 ff.

LU PPPs (key system assets, land, insolvency of the private contractors and the PPP Arbiter[252]).

To upgrade the LU, three LU PPPs were negotiated from 1998 to 2002–03 and signed between London Underground Limited (LUL), a subsidiary of Transport for London (TfL), and three Infracos owned by private consortia, known as 'Metronet'[253] (for two contracts) and 'Tube Lines'[254] (third contract). The contracts were signed for a period of thirty years. Due to uncertainties about upgrading over such a long period (especially as the state of some assets was not known at the time of the negotiations), the price was only fixed for seven and a half years. A mechanism for revision was built into the contracts, relying on the intervention of the PPP Arbiter. The LU contracts were so designed that the trains, tracks, tunnels etc. came into private ownership, while the trains were run by LUL. Commuters were still purchasing their tickets from LUL. The tickets did not cover the costs of running LU and a yearly grant from the central government had been secured for a period of 10 years. Four periodic payments were made to the Infracos each year. These were a function of three main performance criteria: availability, ambience and capability.[255] The LU PPPs thus illustrated a combination of public and user funding of the provided infrastructure. However, the Infracos were fully paid by LUL. LUL was supposed to organise the financial streams needed to pay the Infracos; in this sense, the Infracos did not incur risks linked to the number of commuters.

The LU PPPs were complex to create due to their technical, financial and political intricacy. The contracts were novel because of the specific splits between infrastructure and service and the complexity of the incentive mechanisms.[256] Complexity also arose from the unknown state of the grey assets. Finally, there was also complexity because of the political reluctance of the Mayor of London.[257] It is difficult to isolate a contract from its context. Yet the context alone does not explain why Tube Lines and Metronet arrived at different results: Metronet faced outright failure in 2007, while Tube Lines succeeded for longer.

---

[252] GLA 1999, s 210 ff.

[253] The legal contracting parties were Infraco BCV Limited and Infraco Sub-Surface Limited.

[254] The legal contracting party was Infraco JNP Limited.

[255] For an illustration of the complexity of the formulas used: Harlow and Rawlings, 2009, 429.

[256] NAO, *London Underground – Successfully?*, 2004, summary, para 4.

[257] Transport Committee, *The London Underground and the Public–Private Partnership Agreements* (45 HC 2007–08), para 26.

Discretion in contractual performance

Metronet did not succeed in performing the contracts as required, and went into administration in 2007. Its assets were brought back into public ownership. Meanwhile, Tube Lines seemed to achieve its contractual aims and to deliver *VfM*. When the periodic review to define the works and the price for the period 2010–17, starting in 2009, Tube Lines was in a strong bargaining position, reinforced by the pressure to complete specific refurbishments and extensions for the London Olympics in 2012. In June 2010, however, its assets were transferred back to public ownership.

The LU story highlights the difficulty of achieving the right contractual mechanism. It suggests that contracts do not guarantee success. Metronet and Tube Lines were not entirely similar: for instance, their supply chains were organised differently.[258] Tube Lines used open tenders or general competition. In Metronet, the main suppliers were also the shareholders of the consortium ('tied supplied chain'), which led to a conflict of interest.[259] Metronet's failure discredited tied supply chains, now discouraged for new PFIs.[260]

A closer examination of the process leading to the extraordinary review and the subsequent failure of Metronet highlights another issue: the use of discretion by LU and how Metronet and Tube Lines tackled it. Metronet faced major cost overruns related to the station refurbishment programme. The contracts allowed TfL to set standards for station refurbishment and those standards were higher than anticipated for both Metronet and Tube Lines.[261] This meant problems of interpretation, delays and higher costs.[262] However, Metronet and Tube Lines reacted differently to the issue. Metronet failed to implement solutions developed with Tube Lines and LU.[263] Tube Lines decided to standardise the works, designed solutions applicable to more than one station, lobbied to decrease the standards etc. It kept the programme under control and encouraged TfL to reconsider its own organisation so that contract decisions relating to Tube Lines were made quickly.

Metronet's failure sheds light on contractual and organisational factors in PPPs/PFIs. It underlines the importance of commitment to the PPP/PFI

---

258 Ibid para 13.

259 A similar supply chain had however been used successfully for the Channel Tunnel Rail Link (NAO, *Metronet*, 2009, 55).

260 Ibid 8–9.

261 Ibid 49.

262 Ibid para 2.8.

263 Ibid para 2.9.

from both parties. Tube Lines seemed determined to find solutions. Problems in defining the works to be carried out by the Infracos came back in the periodic review for Tube Lines. The specificity of the process is detailed in Chapter 3 as it illustrates how the PPP Arbiter structures its discretion.

LU and commuters

Commuters are related to the LU PPPs in different respects: through fares, safety and the service performed. Commuters were not involved in the definition of the outputs. They were indirectly present in the contractual performance through the ambience criterion being part of the periodic payment. Public bodies remained responsible for safety[264] and for deciding on fare increases.[265] Specific statutory provisions had been inserted in the Greater London Authority Act 1999 (GLA 1999) to ensure that the continuity of the service would be maintained if one of the Infracos went into administration.[266] Disruption to LU operations was kept to a minimum when TfL took over from Tube Lines in 2010. If commuters were not directly involved in service definition or monitoring,[267] they might be represented. TfL did not represent commuters. TfL mainly implemented the mayor's transport strategy.[268] Commuters' interests were represented by the London Transport Users Committee,[269] which had to be consulted in transport matters and handled complaints against transport entities in London. Its members were appointed by the London Assembly, not elected. Commuters' representation was thus indirect. The London Assembly Transport Committee then represented commuters in a more direct way, for instance when it investigated LU overcrowding.[270]

In conclusion, the LU PPPs illustrated a complex and innovative contract in which local and central government were involved. They were state-analogue models in many respects. These respects included the

264 NAO, *London Underground*, 2000, App 1.

265 For a recent illustration: TfL, *Business Plan 2009/10 – 2017/18*, 82.

266 GLA 1999, ss 220–224.

267 There were regular consumer satisfaction inquiries up to 2008, however.

268 GLA 1999, s 154.

269 GLA 1999, s 247 ff. The Committee is known as 'London TravelWatch'.

270 E.g.: Transport Committee, *Too Close for Comfort: Passengers' Experiences of the London Underground* (LA 2009).

interface that LUL placed between commuters and Infracos, the commuters' representation by public bodies regarding the defining and monitoring of the service performed under the PPPs, and the promptness with which they came back into public ownership.

Incremental Programmes: LIFT[271] (2000)

While the LU PPPs were unique contracts tackling a specific backlog of investment in the Tube, LIFT was developed as a programme to tackle underinvestment in community-based healthcare. LIFT aims to transform the primary care sector through innovative ways of procuring specific long-term infrastructure.[272] The Department of Health started LIFT in 2000 to support primary as well as social care services and facilities in England. LIFT was started as a programme for empowering local government.[273] Later, the Treasury took it over to disseminate innovative ways of procuring long-term infrastructure.[274] LIFT thus evolved into a state-analogue model in which supporting institutions were required to develop and manage the programme. Such a programme approach to PPPs was then broadened to include waste, schools (BsF) and social housing. Here, the key points of LIFT are detailed in terms of how local and central levels are connected thanks to techniques used within the programme itself. They illustrate how institutions, law and communities of actors may interact to provide public investments.

At the central level, the Department of Health and PUK set up a national joint venture in 2001, called Partnership for Health. It was renamed Community Health Partnership (CHP) in 2007. It is now wholly owned by the Department of Health.[275] By 2013, CHP has established 49 LIFT companies (LIFTCos), local joint ventures delivering services to tenants and patients. CHP coordinates and develops LIFT projects. It provides procurement expertise and direction for the projects,[276] transfers expertise across them,[277] develops standardisation[278] and adapts documentation

---

271 Local Improvement Finance Trusts.
272 Treasury, 2008, 16.
273 ODPM, *Strategic Partnering Taskforce – Final Report*, 2004.
274 Treasury, 2008, 21.
275 www.communityhealthpartnerships.co.uk/about-chp
276 Treasury, 2006, 41.
277 Ibid, 41.
278 NAO, *LIFT*, 2005, 1.

related to LIFT. It also encourages best practices, for instance with yearly awards in different categories.[279]

At a local level, Primary Care Trusts (PCT) had powers to enter into LIFT.[280] Following the dissolution of PCTs in 2013, CHP took over the role of PCTs.[281] LIFTCos are the owners of the GPs' premises they build and refurbish. LIFTCos get income from leasing space to PCTs, healthcare professionals, nurses and other interested social care or voluntary sector tenants.[282] It was thus decided to give priority to the convenience of having a broad range of services at the same location.[283] A strategic partnering board representing public bodies such as strategic health authorities and local authorities exercises oversight on the LIFTCo.

At a technical level, three points may be noted relating to how connections between entities are set up in LIFT: firstly, through joint ventures; secondly, through a partnership ethos; thirdly, through express LIFT.

Firstly, LIFTCo, joint ventures between local PCTs, private partners and CHP carry out the investment programme and some health planning functions.[284] LIFTCo enjoys the exclusivity to provide new services or facilities commissioned in an area. Such exclusivity should be a factor in 'continuous improvement through successive stages of work which is facilitated by the accumulating experience of working together'.[285]

Secondly, LIFT develops a partnership ethos between the participants in the LIFTCos. On this basis, a strategic partnering board assesses local needs in care and issues a yearly strategic services development plan.[286]

Thirdly, LIFT illustrates continuous innovation and the creation of a community of actors. CHP developed 'express LIFT', a version of LIFT where streamlining is refined and procedures shortened. One of the main

---

279 For 2010: http://www.communityhealthpartnerships.co.uk/article/2010-lift-awards-short-list-announced (including categories such as 'best Local Government Project Team', 'best LIFT Company' and 'best community/user involvement in a project').

280 Regs 3(2) and 8(3) of, and Pt 2 of Sch 1 to, the National Health Service (Functions of Strategic Health Authorities and Primary Care Trusts and Administration Arrangements) (England) Regulations 2002, SI 2002/2375.

281 http://www.communityhealthpartnerships.co.uk/property-and-asset-management.

282 NAO, *LIFT*, 2005, 2.

283 Which fitted with the 'Patient Choice' policy (Ibid 10).

284 4Ps, *A Map of the LIFT Process*, 2004, 9.

285 Treasury, 2008, 21.

286 CHP, *LIFT – Enabling Integrated Services, Co-location and Partnership Working*, 2007, 7.

features is that CHP has used the new framework procurement process to choose seven contractors. When taking part in express LIFT, the local bodies run a competition open only to these seven contractors, who are assumed to have the necessary experience to carry out a LIFT project and deemed to have demonstrated *VfM*.

In sum, LIFT represents a systematic innovation in which projects are bundled together in programmes for a given territorial area. In 2000, the approach was new, breaking with a range of one-off deals. Yet the system remains complex because of the many local actors involved in delivering the project. The governance structure (e.g. the strategic partnering board) becomes intricate. LIFT aims to develop a community at different levels: as a project for a deprived area focused on health, by bringing public and private actors together to develop the works to be carried out, and by promoting a partnering ethos between the parties. This community development relies on the articulation of central and local institutions. Running through the monograph, these features of LIFT are amplified with BsF and waste PFIs. The interplays between institutions, law and communities are especially discussed with respect to BsF and waste PFIs in Chapter 5.

DISCRETION IN THE PPP REGULATORY SPACE

This chapter gave an overview of how English PPPs are organised at a general level. Three main structures in the regulatory space were highlighted: institutions, law and community. How do these three main structures contribute to coordinating the public, private and individual interests involved in PPPs/PFIs? Answering that question leads us to suggesting an account of how discretion structures these interests in the PPP regulatory space.

To suggest such a narrative, the following analytical scheme is used. We saw in Chapter 1 that PPPs are hybrid in multiple senses because of the legal and non-legal techniques on which they rely and the public and the private logics they bring together.[287] Hybridity is translated into the discretion exercised in PPPs. Discretion results from statutory provisions and prerogative powers[288] and is exercised and controlled through public and private techniques such as financial guarantees, procurement,[289]

---

[287] See Chapter 1, pp 14–16.
[288] See above this chapter, pp 46–60.
[289] See above this chapter, pp 77–81.

contracts[290] and *VfM*.[291] PPPs are also embedded in a community gathering together key public and private actors.[292]

These three structures – institutions, law and community – appear at first to be relatively independent from each other, following their own logics and requirements. Law grants powers and establishes contracts and procurement. Institutions set processes for negotiating PPPs/PFIs (e.g. OGC and the Gateway Review) or develop policies to promote them (e.g. IUK and PF2). The Treasury issues standardised documents related to SoPC4 and then PF2. *VfM* becomes a refined control technique in PPPs/PFIs and is disseminated across the public sector. PPP expertise is exported. The LU PPPs and LIFT case studies highlight the role that public bodies play in organising PPPs/PFIs, funding them and implementing them. Cohesion across the structures seems to happen thanks to the specific project focus institutions give to PPPs/PFIs, not thanks to any legal conceptual glue.

However, a closer look at the interactions between institutions, law and communities is needed. How are these three main structures related to each other when it comes to the exercise of discretion in developing and performing PPP/PFI projects? How is discretion shaped by these structures in decisions related to particular sets of circumstances? Are these structures excluding of each other, mutually reinforcing or factually coexisting? How do they evolve and transform each other over the course of a project?

A provisional hypothesis is thus suggested: as hybrids, PPPs/PFIs exist within tensions between the three structures of institutions, law and community. It is suggested that each of the three structures expresses conceptions regarding autonomy, solidarity and trust. When there are tensions between these three structures and the conceptions of autonomy, solidarity and trust they are associated with, discretion is used to articulate these three concepts and to coordinate and integrate the competing interests affected by decisions related to PPPs/PFIs.

To account for this process, legal techniques need to be supplemented by narratives. The starting point is that the law provides vantage points for constructing narratives regarding PPPs/PFIs and who does what for whom under which (changing) conditions. Between what legal techniques facilitate and limit a range of possibilities are opened up for which the law does not account. Narratives may account for these possibilities,

---

290 See above this chapter, pp 75–7.
291 See above this chapter, pp 58–9.
292 See above this chapter, pp 82–4.

with either a strengthening or a weakening effect on the legal techniques. Narratives are developed and conveyed by communities of actors or users in the PPP regulatory space. For instance, the LU PPPs were not only provided for in the GLA 1999 and the contractual documents. Reports from the NAO explicitly asked whether they had been good deals and whether they were likely to be successful.[293] Their potential success and subsequent failure have been shaped by the PPP Arbiter's reviews and the tensions between LUL, the public body, and Metronet and Tube Lines, the private contractors, when it came to the actual implementation of LUL's discretion in requiring refurbishment specifications in the stations.[294] A series of PPP actors thus developed the narrative of the LU PPPs. It is therefore suggested that law and community supplement each other in order to structure relationships in the PPP regulatory space. Law and community thus contribute to an account of the relationships involved in PPPs/PFIs based on legal techniques and narratives. A common ground develops between the three concepts of autonomy, solidarity and trust as expressed differently in institutions, law and community. This leads us to ask to what extent this process applies in any other English PPPs/PFIs.

While this chapter has mainly highlighted the sources of discretion and the extent to which public bodies enjoy autonomy in their decision-making, the next chapters turn to how relationships in PPPs/PFIs are organised to coordinate the public, private and individual interests involved in PPPs/PFIs. Chapter 3 focuses on the relationships between PPP/PFI partners and Chapter 4 on the relationships with external bodies and third parties. Both chapters detail how PPP/PFI relationships are organised according to market-analogue and state-analogue models and how these models evolve in practice. While formalisation can be stated to some extent, informality mushrooms around it. Trust indeed needs both formality and informal personal relationships in order to develop among the PPP partners. Intermediaries, social groups or communities are needed for PPP users and third parties to trust in how accountability and regulation are implemented in PPPs/PFIs. Therefore, Chapter 5 brings together these two needs for trust and communities in the coordination of public, private and individual interests in PPPs/PFIs. It suggests that it

---

[293] NAO, *London Underground PPP: Were They Good Deals?*, 2004; NAO, *London Underground: Are the Public Private Partnerships Likely to Work Successfully?*, 2004.

[294] See above this chapter, pp 90–94.

may be possible to develop a community-analogue model for organising these interests and to offer a structure for discretion and ethical regulation that supplements the law.

3. Organising long-term relationships between PPP/PFI partners

INTRODUCTION

Public–private partnerships/Private Finance Initiatives (PPPs/PFIs) are long-term public contracts relying on cooperation between public and private entities to provide public infrastructures and services, while allocating risks between them. In materially delivering specific infrastructures and services, PPPs/PFIs connect public authorities, contractors and individual users in the regulatory space. In setting up PPPs/PFIs, public authorities have to make a whole range of choices, accentuated by the polycentric issues PPPs/PFIs involve: the likely but unknown changes necessary over their long duration and the various third parties affected as users, taxpayers or otherwise. This chapter maps how the public and private actors within a PPP/PFI relate to each other and according to which legal or non-legal principles discretion is exercised in the PPP regulatory space.

PPPs/PFIs need to coordinate the interests pursued by each partner, i.e. the public interest and the private contractors' economic interests. In the exercise of discretion linked to this coordination, three different moments are relevant: the elaboration, signing and performance of the PPPs/PFIs. For each of them, a basic set of techniques is identified: public procurement, relational nexus and contract. When present in these techniques, the law starts from the logic of competition or opposition. Therefore PPPs/PFIs are basically organised according to a market-analogue model. However, this only tells part of the story, as dialogue and cooperation are also needed. These latter elements ensure that PPPs/PFIs are developed and implemented in such a way that the agreed public infrastructure or service is delivered over time to meet the public needs it was intended to provide for. Such communication requires PPP/PFI parties to trust in the others' mutual goodwill. Trust needs thus to be fostered beyond market logic. Two main options are open to protect the interests involved in PPPs/PFIs: formalisation and better understanding of the other parties following practical demonstrations of reliability with a cooperative mindset.

This chapter suggests that formalisation increasingly features in the relationships between public and private partners. The evolution of English PPPs/PFIs from financially free-standing contracts in the 1990s to the Standardisation of PFI Contracts (SoPC) Version 4 (SoPC4) in the 2000s and Private Finance 2 (PF2) in 2012, illustrates this formalisation and the changing role of market logic in providing public infrastructures and services. However, as public authorities have incrementally gained more control and direction over the projects, cooperation between public and private actors has developed in parallel to become an equally central feature of PPPs/PFIs. Therefore, the techniques used by public authorities to exercise their discretion in PPPs/PFIs are structured by these tensions between formalisation and cooperation and by their influence on how autonomy, solidarity and trust interplay in PPPs/PFIs. Depending on their emphasis, PPPs/PFIs follow thus a more or less market-analogue or state-analogue model, where legal techniques and non-legal techniques or narratives supplement each other.

This chapter starts from the principle that English PPPs/PFIs are formalised long-term contracts, building on relational theory. It then turns to each of the three significant moments in PPPs/PFIs: elaboration, signing and performance. During their elaboration, formalisation relies mostly on public procurement procedures, where competition has been subsumed into a competitive dialogue. The relational nexus formalises, in contractual terms (payment/service), the managerial balance achieved between parties in terms of value for money (*VfM*) and risk allocation. During PPP/PFI performance, formalisation depends on contractual processes and governance mechanisms. In each case, the law only sets a basis that needs to be filled in with cooperation. Such cooperation could become embedded in the PPP/PFI relationships thanks to communities developing narratives of complexity, innovation and partnering. Yet the mainly economic focus of these communities limits their success. Therefore the protection of public and private interests in the PPP regulatory space may call for the development of ethical principles of behaviour in order to structure PPP/PFI commitments in the long term.

PPPs/PFIs: FORMALISED LONG-TERM CONTRACTS

Enforceable contracts under private law,[1] PPPs/PFIs are classified as relational contracts.[2] This section looks at how the tenets of relational theory need adjusting when translated from a purely economic sphere of exchange into relationships involving public and private entities pursuing the delivery of a public infrastructure or service.

Relational theory highlights the difference between day-to-day contractual behaviour and classical contract law. It explains why parties do not act on a pure cost-benefit analysis basis but choose to preserve a contractual relationship. Parties to a long-term relationship refrain from using their full discretion, requesting strict contract compliance or exiting a contract opportunistically. They accept shared risks and benefits. They develop solidarity and cooperation with the other party and even with the common endeavour in order for the project to succeed. Such contracts are often linked to loose formal planning and little litigation.[3]

A difference appears between contract and contractual behaviour, between a paper deal and a real deal. The literature debates the relevance of the distinction. However, PPPs/PFIs are complex multi-layered paper documents. They do not just exist in the written word: they bring about sophisticated relationships between (at least) two organisations over a long duration. From a 2008 survey, it appears that:

> [j]ust over a third of contract managers say they or their colleagues have referred to the PFI contract frequently in the last 12 months – that is, at least once or twice a week (35%). Around half have referred to it occasionally [...] and a further 15% say they have rarely referred to the contract [...]. Three per cent say they have never looked at the contract.[4]

The paper deal is not where PPPs/PFIs end but where they begin – with all the structures enabling the various protagonists to integrate (or not) the spirit underlying the negotiated agreements, which reflect a given balance of interests between the partners at that time.

---

[1] Davies, 2008, 10; Vincent-Jones, 2006, 31.

[2] E.g.: M Freedland, 'Government by Contract Re-Examined: Some Functional Issues' in P Craig and R Rawlings (eds), *Law and Administration in Europe* (OUP 2003) 123, 126.

[3] S Deakin and others, '"Trust" or Law? Towards an Integrated Theory of Contractual Relations between Firms' (1994) 21 JLS 329.

[4] Ipsos/Mori, *Investigating the Performance of Operational PFI Contract – A Research Study Conducted for PUK on behalf of HM Treasury*, 2008 Survey of Operational PFI Projects, sd, 39.

Autonomy and Solidarity: Contractual Starting Point

That parties' autonomy lies in their equality and freedom to exercise their discretion is questionable under private law. It is even more problematic in relation to public persons. Public authorities have different powers and duties from contractors, so they need to obey different rules and principles (e.g. non-fettering).[5] In any given PPP/PFI, a public authority may endorse conflicting functions. For example, it may be simultaneously the contracting party and the planning authority (e.g. the local authority may be the contractual party in a PFI school and issue planning permits for developing a swimming pool at that school). It may also be the contracting authority and the overseeing body (e.g. the Department of Health being the contracting party in PFI hospitals and setting and implementing the norms for the governance of hospitals or for the classification of hospitals and their specialised fields). Further, it may be the funding body and the regulating body (e.g. the department which co-finances a waste PFI and sets the pollution or health and safety norms to be respected). Specific rules on spending public money apply and public accountability should be ensured. In PPPs/PFIs, the questions of bounded rationality, asymmetry of information, free-rider techniques and opportunism are even more present because public and private – nearly by nature – do not share the same knowledge.

With this autonomy as a starting point, parties enter a contract with opposing interests. The contract represents, then, a compromise arising from this opposition. Autonomy finds different expressions during contractual performance. Self-interest and maximisation are often exercised from a long-term perspective.[6] Vincent-Jones[7] and Craig[8] present PPPs/PFIs from this perspective, stressing their competitive side. However, parties in a PPP/PFI are also highly interdependent under the model highlighted by relational theory. This is mostly due to the high levels of investments sunk in idiosyncratic assets. To unlock this practical interdependence and neutralise part of the power held by the contractor, the public authority resorts to inventiveness in creating competitive tension with notional models.[9]

---

[5] Davies, 2008, 64 ff.

[6] D Campbell and D Harris, 'Flexibility in Long-Term Contractual Relationships: The Role of Co-operation' (1993) 20 JLS 166–91.

[7] Vincent-Jones, 2006, 175.

[8] Craig, 2012, para 5-017.

[9] When negotiating with one single corporation, public authorities create artificial competitive tensions, for instance through the use of a PSC or a

Law, especially contract law, plays different roles in organising public and private commitments in relation to interdependence and solidarity. For Vincent-Jones, the law is one technique for ensuring that parties reach joint-utility maximisation.[10] However it may also disturb it. Davies is, by contrast, cautious about defining the respective roles and responsibilities of the parties neatly, emphasising law and the specific missions with which public authorities are endowed. She would understand the contract, as a whole, as being public in nature: the outcome of this contractual relationship between public and private should contribute to the public good. One difficulty in long-term contracts is deciding when to shift from pragmatic problem solving to enforcing contractual rights.[11] However, contract law is not a panacea as it may focus more on the value of each performance than on its quality.[12] Alternative techniques such as partnering may be used, entailing their own sets of issues, most notably in terms of accountability. We return to partnering as a narrative used in PPPs/PFIs at the end of this chapter.[13]

Interdependence and solidarity structure the public and private commitments of PPP/PFI parties and thus lead them towards either joint utility maximisation or the common good. Assessing the extent to which PPPs/PFIs coordinate public and private interests over time in such a way that the parties are able to achieve their objectives requires us to consider trust between PPP/PFI partners and its contributing factors.

Trust, Cooperation and Formalisation

As the previous chapters highlighted, hybridity is a key feature of PPPs/PFIs. PPP/PFI parties have distinct objectives, namely delivering public services and making profit. Moreover, PPPs/PFIs are long-term contracts where a balance between stability (obtaining the contractual performance that the parties had hoped for when agreeing to their own commitments) and flexibility (adaptation to changing circumstances) needs to be organised. The question is thus how these distinct objectives, which drive discretion and frame autonomy, are articulated in a joint project where parties need to have confidence that they will be able to achieve their long-term objectives. This requires some form of (mutual)

---

should-cost model and alternative commercial models: see NAO, *PRIME Expansion*, 2005, 19.

10 Vincent-Jones, 2006, 29–30.

11 Davies, 2008, 37.

12 Ibid.

13 See below this chapter, pp 144–46.

trust. How is trust created, though? Vincent-Jones and Davies underline that, next to the law, non-legal techniques regulate parties' relationships. Vincent-Jones suggests non-legal techniques for addressing (personal) trust issues in contracts. For instance, partnering encourages 'joint development for separate but complementary benefits'.[14] Achieving basic contractual values builds flexibility into the contract. Davies emphasises the law as the solution to fostering trust in the contractual system as a whole.[15] In the past, however, lesser degrees of formalisation have been suggested, for instance limited to some questions[16] or to standard forms.[17]

Trust matters significantly in PPPs/PFIs because of the advantages it carries: it reduces cost[18] and complexity and allows flexibility in the face of contract incompleteness. When parties trust each other, they do not have to detail minutely how changes to the contracts will be processed if risks supervene. They trust they will find solutions through cooperation. This trust in the other partner entails a risk of disappointment. Trust is built through incremental communication and processes for getting to know each other, as business parties, throughout negotiations, adjustments in the planning, joint training and meetings. The setbacks are loss of time and high costs. Two options can be used to overcome these setbacks. On the one hand, formalisation is used as a shortcut. It frames how parties seek control, which may foster trust in the contractual partner. However, formalisation may also undermine trust. On the other hand, concrete cooperative actions and personal factors, such as highly skilled staff, may give strong signals to partners that one is committed to sustaining constructive relationships in the long term. However, building this human process is time-consuming and costly, leading to practical barriers to building trust only on this ground.

Through this contractual paradigm, the law shapes parties' interests in autonomy or interdependence terms, organising how parties may use their discretion according to a market-analogue model. However, it requires additional ways of organising public and private parties' commitments, such as cooperation and trust. If the law helps build trust, it

---

14 Vincent-Jones, 2006, 195.

15 Davies, 2008, xxi.

16 H Street, *Governmental Liability: A Comparative Study* (CUP 1953) 104–5.

17 C Turpin, *Government Procurement and Contracts* (Longman 1989) 114.

18 S Deakin and J Michie, 'The Theory and Practice of Contracting' in S Deakin and J Michie (eds), *Contracts, Co-operation, and Competition – Studies in Economics, Management, and the Law* (OUP 1997) 20.

may not impose it. Developing trust requires a context of shared meaning and goals developed, for instance, among communities. Trust depends on both law and communities, and on stability and flexibility. The following sections highlight this tension between formalisation and cooperation with three techniques (procurement, relational nexus and contractual performance) and their supplementing narratives of complexity, innovation and partnering.

ELABORATION OF PPPs/PFIs: ORGANISED COMPETITION

In the 1990s, many budget and time overruns in public projects had been linked with the poor contractual terms of construction procurement.[19] Therefore, attention shifted to the careful drafting of terms, entailing an even longer procurement process for PPPs/PFIs. The average duration of the tendering process in PPPs/PFIs was estimated at 34 months in 2009.[20] The Treasury is seeking to reduce this lengthy, and thus costly, elaboration phase to 18 months between the project tender and the appointment of a preferred bidder.[21] The elaboration process is paved with discussions and meetings between the contracting authority and the bidders, which should ensure that PPPs/PFIs reach an internal balance of interests between their would-be partners. This first phase of the PPP/PFI relationship is left outside the traditional reach of the legal techniques of contract law.[22] This section details how PPPs/PFIs came to receive tailored treatment in the otherwise highly formalised procurement framework.

Public procurement is mostly a legal process setting formal requirements for the choosing of a successful bidder thanks to competition and transparency. Due to the specificity of PPPs/PFIs in terms of their complexity, duration, invested money and social issues tackled, competition may not result in a solution meeting a public authority's needs. Conversely, lack of competition, maybe due to the high negotiation costs of PPPs/PFIs,[23] may lead to poor terms for the public authority or taxpayers. For these reasons, the EC classic directive introduced a specific procedure in 2004: the competitive dialogue. For complex public

---

[19] NAO, *Modernising Construction*, 2001, 41.

[20] NAO, *Lords*, 2009, 53.

[21] Treasury, 2012, 13.

[22] For implied contracts during the elaboration phase of public contracts, see Arrowsmith, 2005, paras 2-88–2-93.

[23] Treasury/OGC, *Competitive Dialogue in 2008*, 2008, para 5.1.6.

projects, '[c]ontracting authorities shall open, with the candidates selected [...], a dialogue the aim of which shall be to identify and define the means best suited to satisfying their needs'.[24] The preferred procurement route for most English PPPs/PFIs,[25] this competitive dialogue opens up discussions on any aspects of the contract. Selection of the contractor operates on the basis of the most economically advantageous tender[26] (MEAT) and not the lowest bid. MEAT allows public authorities to take non-economic considerations into account while awarding the contract.[27] Scope for discretion thus arises.

This section retraces the evolution of public procurement techniques in relation to PPPs/PFIs in terms of both their legal aspects and their practical implementation: while formalisation creeps in in various guises, flexibility also resurfaces to coordinate public and private interests in the PPP regulatory space.

From Competition to Competitive Dialogue

In the early days of the PFIs, three types of projects were identified: financially free-standing projects, joint ventures between public and private sectors and services sold to the public sector. Financially free-standing projects did not expose public money and therefore could be excluded from the scope of public procurement. The other projects, however, were tied in with competition.

Public procurement needed adjustments to attract private actors into PFIs by transferring various rights to surplus assets or by allowing innovative financing structures. The tendering process needed flexibility to adjust to the various possible bids. The negotiated procedure offered such prospects. However, technical questions arose.[28] The negotiated procedure was only open under narrow conditions, most of them more flexible in the case of services than of works.[29] In the case of mixed

---

[24] Classic directive, art 29(3) as transposed in the Public Contracts Regulations 2006, SI 2006/5, reg 18 (PCR 2006).

[25] Treasury, 2008, 40. The negotiated procedure should only be applied in 'truly exceptional' cases: Treasury/OGC, *Competitive Dialogue in 2008*, 2008, 9 (box 3.1).

[26] PCR 2006, reg 18(27).

[27] C Bovis, 'Public Procurement in the European Union: Lessons from the Past and Insights to the Future' (2005–06) 12 Colum JEurL 53, 94.

[28] J Skilbeck, 'The Private Finance Initiative and Public Procurement' [1996] PPLR 148.

[29] S Arrowsmith, 'Public Private Partnerships and the European Procurement Rules' (2000) 37 CMLR 709, 721–23.

(works and services) contracts, European law was rather arcane, so it had been possible to construe PFIs as public procurement for (operational or financial) services,[30] displacing the onus of PFIs from the works and assets. English contracting authorities were, however, structuring the negotiations so that only a limited number of bidders were invited to negotiate and their numbers were narrowed down following the bidding stages.[31]

Building on this practice, the UK government pushed forward the introduction of the competitive dialogue in the 2004 EC directives as a possible solution for complex projects, PFIs included.[32] However, the formalisation in the law of a practice developed to structure market competition is not neutral. The next sections highlight the tensions between formalisation and discretion and between legal techniques and their practical implementation. The competitive dialogue is a key technique framing the PPP regulatory space. When it was introduced in European law, it was a close copy of the English practice developed in the context of PFI procurement. However, its further implementation in England triggered legal uncertainty and further constraints on how public authorities exercise their discretion in the PPP regulatory space.

Formalised Process, Complexity and Legal Gaps

If a project is objectively complex, the competitive dialogue is allowed. '[A]ll aspects of the contracts' are open for discussion.[33] The final selection is based on the MEAT.[34] This creates a large space for discretion, especially for the public authority. Would this situation then be close to a purely contractual one? The competitive dialogue is not a watertight pocket of full discretion. PPPs/PFIs are actually the result of a cooperative endeavour between public and private entities (joint efforts, questions and comments, meetings etc.) through a formalised dialogue. The law sets limits to safeguard competition: complexity, transparency and technical limitations to the dialogue. However, in each case, this formalisation makes new legal issues arise.

---

[30] Ibid 714–16; Skilbeck (n 28 above) 149.

[31] Arrowsmith and Craven, 2012, 213.

[32] Ibid 191; compare: NAO, *Improving the PFI Tendering Process*, 2007, para 1.7.

[33] Classic directive, art 29(3).

[34] PCR 2006, reg 18(27).

Firstly, the competitive dialogue is opened for particularly complex contracts. Article 1(11)(c) of the classic directive defines the notion of a complex contract as follows:

> a public contract is considered to be 'particularly complex' where the contracting authorities:
> – are not objectively able to define the technical means [...] capable of satisfying their needs or objectives, and/or
> – are not objectively able to specify the legal and/or financial make-up of a project.[35]

While complexity should not be accepted too lightly,[36] it is open to interpretation. On the one hand, recital (31) of the classic directive highlights that competitive dialogue is only available when public authorities 'find it "objectively impossible" to define the means to satisfy their needs' or to assess market solutions in technical, legal or financial terms. On the other hand, English practice interprets complexity in more subjective terms, relating it to a public authority's ability to determine the best solution to meet its needs.[37] To establish this ability, specific circumstances and (lack of) previous own experience with complex projects might be taken into account.[38] So far the European Commission has not challenged any decisions to proceed with the competitive dialogue.[39] Furthermore, English public authorities have been strongly encouraged to use it by central funding providers,[40] in practice leading the competitive dialogue to be considered the default procurement route[41] far beyond PPPs/PFIs and infrastructure projects. Therefore the ambiguity between objective and subjective complexity has led to a legal uncertainty resulting in a wide discretion for public authorities to use the competitive dialogue.

---

[35] Slightly reworded in PCR 2006, reg 18(1). The condition of complexity has been removed from the Directive 2014/24/EU of the European Parliament and of the Council of 26 February 2014 on public procurement and repealing Directive 2004/18/EC, art. 30.

[36] P Trepte, *Public Procurement in the EU – A Practitioner's Guide* (2nd edn, OUP 2007) para 7-189. European Commission, *Explanatory Note – Competitive Dialogue – Classic Directive*, CC/2005/04, rev 1, 2005, para 2.

[37] Arrowsmith and Craven, 2012, 206.

[38] Ibid 210.

[39] S Arrowsmith and S Treumer, 'Competitive Dialogue in EU Law: A Critical Review' in S Arrowsmith and S Treumer (eds) *Competitive Dialogue in EU Procurement* (CUP 2012) 3, 40–41.

[40] Arrowsmith and Craven, 2012, 205.

[41] Treasury, *Review of Competitive Dialogue*, 2010, para 2.35.

Secondly, transparency is required. Before starting the dialogue, the public authority needs to plan the dialogue process carefully and to disclose information related to the way in which it will use its discretion to formalise the dialogue. It should publish its needs and requirements[42] and the planned successive stages to reduce the number of solutions discussed during the dialogue,[43] as well as communicating the award criteria and their relative weighting or importance.[44] Furthermore, further elements are expected to be communicated to the bidders in practice, such as the communication process, access to information, the timetable of the dialogue etc. This sets milestones for steering future discussions. From a legal perspective, the procuring authority itself fully controls these milestones. The Office of Government Commerce (OGC)[45] and Local Partnerships[46] have issued guidelines suggesting how this discretion could be exercised.[47] However, they left it legally uncertain if and how the dialogue can be adapted to changing circumstances once it has been launched.[48]

Thirdly, formal requirements need to be respected during the competitive dialogue. Cherry picking – or the mixing of different bids by the public authority – is not allowed.[49] Time limits need to be fixed, taking into account the circumstances and complexity of the contract.[50] All participants need to be treated equally.[51] Transmission of information needs to be tailored to the matter.[52] All these requirements aim to maintain competition during the dialogue. Fair competition is also fostered, as negotiations after closing the dialogue need to be limited to

---

42 PCR 2006, reg 18(5).

43 PCR 2006, reg 18(6).

44 PCR 2006, reg 18(18)(d).

45 Treasury/OGC, *Competitive Dialogue in 2008*, 2008.

46 E.g.: 4Ps, *A Map of the PFI Process Using Competitive Dialogue*, 2006.

47 S Arrowsmith, 'Implementation of the New EC Procurement Directives and the Alcatel Ruling in England and Wales and Northern Ireland: A Review of the New Legislation and Guidance' [2006] PPLR 86, 105 commenting on the influence of previous guidelines less detailed than the 2008 ones.

48 OGC, Procurement Policy, *Practical Guidance on the Use of Competitive Dialogue*, Information Note 04/06, 31 July 2006, 5; Arrowsmith and Craven, 2012, 259.

49 Treasury/OGC, *Competitive Dialogue in 2008*, 2008, para 5.2.12; European Commission, *Explanatory Note – Competitive Dialogue – Classic Directive*, CC/2005/04, rev 1, 2005, para 3.2.

50 PCR 2006, reg 18(8).

51 PCR 2006, reg 18(21)(b).

52 Treasury/OGC, *Competitive Dialogue in 2008*, 2008, para 5.3.3.

clarification, specification or fine-tuning of tenders.[53] After the preferred bidder has been chosen, the discussions are limited even further. This is important because the preferred bidder at that stage is in a powerful position, as he is 'virtually guaranteed the contract'.[54] At the same time, this is the moment when financial arrangements are set and supervening circumstances (such as planning requirements) may also have to be taken into account. Therefore adjustments may be needed. However, here again legal uncertainty has crept in over ascertaining the completeness of final tenders to be submitted, acceptable clarifications to the final tender and the changes allowed to the bid.[55]

The competitive dialogue is thus a formalised procedure in which public authorities' discretion to tailor the process in a suitable manner is left wide open within the regulatory space that the competitive dialogue contributes to frame. However, it is surrounded by legal uncertainty, which narrows down the actual flexibility of the dialogue and the extent to which discretion can effectively be used. Authoritative legal scholarship calls for guidance to clarify these legal uncertainties.[56] However, bearing in mind that the competitive dialogue is an optional legal technique for public authorities, it has been heavily used, especially in PPPs/PFIs, IT projects and the health sector.[57] Faced with this practical use of the competitive dialogue, the Treasury and the Cabinet Office have reacted by delimiting further the regulatory space within which public and private interests need to be coordinated.

Practical Issues and Informal Answers

As mentioned above, the procedure of the competitive dialogue had been explained with official guidelines supporting its use by public authorities. The apparent success of the competitive dialogue led to concerns related to its potential use outside its legal remit:[58] genuinely complex projects. The Treasury and the Cabinet Office have become more concerned with

---

53 PCR 2006, reg 18(26).

54 NAO, *Improving the PFI Tendering Process*, 2007, 21, para 3.18.

55 Arrowsmith and Craven, 2012, 235 ff.

56 Ibid 271.

57 S de Mars and R Craven, 'An Analysis of Use of Competitive Dialogue in the EU' in S Arrowsmith and S Treumer (eds) *Competitive Dialogue in EU Procurement* (CUP 2012) 144 ff.

58 Cabinet Office, *Accelerating Government Procurement – Management Summary of the Findings of a 'lean' Study to Investigate Waste and Inefficiencies in Government's Procurement Process*, 2011; Treasury, *Review of Competitive Dialogue*, 2010.

practice than with legal techniques[59] and have taken initiatives to tackle two practical issues arising from the intensive reliance on competitive dialogue: duration and costs. They have also sought to reassure private actors regarding the skills and good preparation of public authorities engaged in the competitive dialogue so that delays in the negotiation process can be limited. This section illustrates again that coordinating public and private interests in PPP regulatory space involves tensions between formalisation and flexibility, however here in the official guidelines related to public procurement.

The first measure is concerned with time reduction in public procurement. In 2012, the Cabinet Office issued a policy note which sets a presumption against competitive dialogue and emphasises market discussions before procurement starts.[60] In principle, procurement should be completed within 120 days and not used as a means for negotiating with the market. It seeks to apply management principles known as LEAN principles into procurement in order to improve *VfM*.[61] While the note trumpets a presumption against competitive dialogue, it mainly seeks to identify complex procurements for which it would be suitable, namely infrastructure procurements, private finance projects or joint ventures. The note therefore reminds public authorities of complexity as a legal requirement for the competitive dialogue and rephrases it in terms of the foreseen duration of the procurement (i.e. longer than 120 days). In parallel, it seeks to address complexity by displacing the onus of the negotiations outside the formal framework of the dialogue towards the pre-procurement phase, where few formal requirements apply.[62] The note recommends engaging with the market to resolve further potential difficulties in procurement. For instance, it suggests boot camps involving intensive discussions for several weeks, physically gathering bidders around an information room and across various streams of discussions (e.g. commercial, technical, financial).[63] This strategy intends to ensure innovation as well as opportunities for suppliers to have informal

---

59 Treasury and IUK, 2013, para 5.6.

60 PPN, *Procurement Supporting Growth: Supporting Material for Departments*, Action Note 04/12, 9 May 2012. It is mandatory for central government departments and all other bodies are encouraged to adopt it (p 5).

61 The LEAN principles refer to a managerial 'process that sets out the most efficient path for getting from the required business outcome to the award of a contract.' (http://ccs.cabinetoffice.gov.uk/about-government-procurement-service/lean-capability/lean-sourcing)

62 Appendix B.

63 Treasury, 2012, box 3.D.

discussions among themselves.[64] Therefore, the formalisation of a principled time limit to procurement reinforces the connection between the competitive dialogue and privately financed projects and emphasises informal pre-procurement as a solution to complex issues.

Alongside time concerns in procurement, the Treasury has engaged in systematic cost reduction in PPPs/PFIs and the competitive dialogue. In its 2010 review on the competitive dialogue, the Treasury recommended more formalisation of the dialogue by public authorities themselves, for instance in establishing their own procedure before starting the procurement[65] or producing a guide to their evaluation approach.[66] It also highlighted the need for good planning and preparation, especially in pre-procurement, the 'most challenging and influential stage of the competitive dialogue procurement'.[67] Following these recommendations, the Treasury issued a detailed procurement routemap in 2013. In sharp contrast to the Cabinet Office's policy note, this routemap aims to provide 'a structured approach' to procurement.[68] Non-prescriptive and reflective, it sets out tools for implementing behavioural changes in procurement.[69] It therefore presents managerial frameworks for authorities to ask questions throughout the procurement process, most notably an assessment of complexity. Here the various factors contributing to lengthy procurement are mapped, accounting for the interconnectedness of people, organisational cultures, goals and practices or procedures.[70] It considers legal issues in relation to complex procurement and the competitive dialogue, actually repeating the Cabinet Office's note and absorbing its content to put it in its wider context of infrastructure procurement.[71] Flexible in its method for assessing complexity, this routemap illustrates another approach to formalisation; not through presumption but with sophisticated managerial tools of assessment and decision making. The concrete implementation of this tool by public authorities is, however, not articulated, thus leaving space for practical uncertainty.

---

64 PPN, *Procurement Supporting Growth: Supporting Material for Departments*, Action Note 04/12, 9 May 2012, Annex B.

65 Treasury, *Review of Competitive Dialogue*, 2010, para 3.29.

66 Ibid para 3.48.

67 Ibid para 13.

68 Treasury and IUK, 2013, Preface.

69 Treasury and IUK, *Infrastructure Procurement Routemap: A Technical Note on Application*, 2013, 4.

70 Treasury and IUK, 2013, chart 2.B and p 10.

71 Ibid 32.

Both initiatives agree on good preparation for procurement by procuring authorities as a way forward, yet they illustrate extreme approaches related to formalisation and flexibility towards the coordination of public and private interests during the elaboration stage of PPPs/PFIs. On the one hand, the Cabinet Office's note proclaims a straightforward principle against the competitive dialogue in which implementation mostly relies on informal pre-procurement discussions with market actors. It considers complexity only as a duration issue. On the other hand, the Treasury's routemap elaborates a sophisticated framework for the questions that public authorities should answer when they use their discretion. Complexity is here an analytical and multifaceted tool for decision making. Yet solutions to this complexity have to be developed on a case-by-case basis by each contracting authority.

These two initiatives of the Cabinet Office and the Treasury seek to flesh out the coordination of public and private interests within the PPP regulatory space. They frame the autonomy of public authorities to exercise their discretion in this regulatory space in terms of complexity and good preparation, as well as expertise within the procuring authority. The key phase for structuring relationships and creating solidarity between the public and private parties in the regulatory space is the pre-procurement phase, away from the legal requirements. Yet transparency and non-discrimination in the procuring stage should help foster trust that the chosen bidder will deliver the best available solution.

Formalising Discretion and Ever-elusive Certainty

Public procurement is a way to ensure competition across the European market and to limit state protectionism. At a micro level, public procurement is a technique combining the market/competition with legal processes and requirements. It regulates the use of public money for meeting social needs and pursuing the common good. Competition thus needs to be organised to ensure that public money achieves that common good. For this reason, time and budget considerations in the elaboration phase of PPPs/PFIs have been important. A certain degree of foreseeability and confidence in the projects, their negotiations and their modalities is required to keep the time, budget and risks taken by contracting authorities, and particularly bidders, as limited as possible during the bidding process. An evolution from market-analogue to state-analogue models follows, highlighting how autonomy, solidarity and trust are conceived in PFIs/PPPs.

Firstly, autonomy is not meant here as equality and freedom without constraints. Procurement relies on competition, and the competitive dialogue opens up a large space for negotiations regarding the project and assessing the chosen bid. However, the whole process must be formally planned and staged (number of candidates, bid requirements etc.). The legal procurement framework does not operate in a void. Institutions, especially the Gateway Process and the government guidelines on public procurement, are relied on: advice and approval are needed from external bodies, for instance, limiting further the autonomy of public authorities.[72] The effective autonomy of procuring authorities depends on their skills in navigating the technicalities of public procurement and good preparation. The law does not provide for these behavioural attitudes on its own.

Secondly, solidarity as a way to address interdependence between the parties is expressed in different ways, such as pooling resources or developing mutual interests in the success of a PPP/PFI. Little pooling of resources is present during the elaboration process. Information communicated to candidates should be equally transmitted between the competitors but cherry picking is not allowed, even if this might result in a better fit with the public authority's needs. By contrast, solidarity understood as a movement towards mutual interest is more present in the competitive dialogue: the formalised framing in the different stages leads to a jointly developed shared project. The public authority adapts its position, allowing for a convergence towards a jointly acceptable solution with bidders.

Thirdly, trust is (or should be) created thanks to the specific procedures followed to ensure transparency, non-discrimination and fair competition. Minimum requirements are imposed on the bidders (technical, financial etc.), which should ensure that they have the basic abilities to perform the contract properly. Trust is also fostered by the prohibition of cherry picking. However, trust in achieving a potentially successful project may come mostly from non-legal techniques, such as the assessment process developed by PPP expert bodies[73] and the professional skills of the partners.

Therefore, structuring and planning issues build the sense that the procedure is conducted in a professional way without impeding equal treatment of the competing candidates. Formalisation occurs in the law and in the official guidelines issued to address the competitive dialogue. Yet key notions such as complexity or fine tuning are open to informal understanding. Complexity is legally defined but official guidelines

---

72 See Chapter 2, pp 70–75.

73 Treasury and Cabinet Office, *Major Project Approval and Assurance Guidance,* 2011; OGC, *Annual Statement*, 2009, 18–19.

interpret the notion in different ways. Yet across all the definitions of complexity third parties are mainly understood as taxpayers whose money needs to be well spent thanks to the public procurement process. Concrete individuals' needs for the PPP/PFI in procurement are not taken into account at this stage of PPPs/PFIs.

These aspects of autonomy, solidarity and trust highlight how discretion is shaped during the elaboration of PPPs/PFIs, in tension between formalisation and flexibility, to coordinate public and private interests in PPP regulatory space. Similar tensions in the evolutions occurring in PPPs/PFIs are underlined in the next sections, starting with the relational nexus of PPPs/PFIs.

RELATIONAL NEXUS: EXCHANGE, VALUE FOR MONEY (*VFM*) AND RISK ALLOCATION

Exchange, in the form of payment for works and services, is at the junction between procurement and contracts. Exchange in PPPs/PFIs can be approached from both legal and public management perspectives. The former highlights the mutual obligations of the parties – the payment and the works and services provided. The latter underlines *VfM* and risk allocation. These approaches are closer to each other than appears at first. *VfM* is translated into the relationship between the price and the works and services obtained. Risk allocation also links price with service: the more risks are transferred, the higher the price. Balancing price, works and services, *VfM* and risk allocation is part of PPP/PFI complexity: legal and economic perspectives may not use the same concepts to refer to the same reality. In short, exchange is a way for the public and private parties to coordinate their respective interests in the regulatory space. *VfM* and risk allocation are modalities of this coordination.

The mutual commitments of the parties under PPPs/PFIs are approached in terms of payment first. *VfM* and risk allocation are then discussed in turn as two mechanisms through which the rational maximisations of parties might find their full expression. However, from an ideal definition and quantification of parties' commitments, the practice of PPPs/PFIs brings forward a more entangled picture, where relationships are spread over time and across different parties, qualitative factors are taken into account and joint management mechanisms are set up. Formalisation of *VfM* and risk allocation in contractual terms is only partial. Formalisation occurs outside the contractual agreements and the contractual exchange mostly relates to procedures for managing listed risks, not to substantial solutions.

PPPs/PFIs as Frameworks for Exchanging?

Relational theory highlights the idea that contracts build relationships over time, extending beyond the mere on-the-spot economic exchange analysed by (neo-)classical contract theories. PPPs/PFIs are frameworks for long-term commitments, setting the service (standards) and subject matter of the contract for an agreed duration.[74] These three elements reflect how parties understand autonomy and solidarity in PPPs/PFIs. Here the focus is laid on payment.

Payment in PPPs/PFIs can take different forms. Especially relevant is how PPPs/PFIs are commonly structured around a 'special purpose vehicle' (SPV) dedicated to a specific PPP/PFI project. All the financial streams concern only this specific project. No liability or income is linked to the SPV other than that generated by the service or infrastructure as temporally and geographically delineated in the contractual documents.[75] There is thus no cross-subsidy or solidarity with other projects (to either's benefit).[76] From this starting point, financial streams can be structured in three ways: financially free-standing projects, a more transactional model such as SoPC4 or an institutional model such as PF2. They all start from a market-analogue approach but actually deviate from it: financially free-standing projects and SoPC4 because of practical needs and the PF2 because of its public shareholding. In practice, PPPs/PFIs blend straightforward payments for services with other income and finance streams.

Firstly, in financially free-standing projects, the private sector is paid for its investment through charges or payments falling on users (i.e. the individuals or the corporations using the service or infrastructure), not by the public authority commissioning the service or infrastructure. There is no direct exchange between the public and private entities. Normally the main sanction for defaults by the contractor should be translated into users exiting.[77] The market is the sanctioning mechanism. Financially free-standing projects were supposed to be the flagship of PFIs. However, PPP/PFI users are unlikely to be able to exit due to a lack of other service providers. Therefore the market is unlikely to work as a sanctioning

---

74 Treasury, 2006, 8.
75 *SoPC4*, para 12.2.
76 NAO, *Lords*, 2009, para 1.2.
77 E.g.: *SoPC4*, para 7.4.1.

mechanism. Given this user vulnerability, financially free-standing projects are rare.[78] Alternative sources of funding[79] are used, such as the sale of redundant assets with profit sharing to the benefit of the public authorities, generating third-party revenues through the use of the assets by specific users[80] (such as the paramedical services available in the Local Improvement Finance Trust (LIFT)), or payments by public authorities funding the project or paying themselves for the (services connected to) assets (such as waste PFIs). Therefore, different streams of money are often bundled together to finance PPPs/PFIs: from users, specific sales, third-party users and public authorities (local, central and European). The various streams of money and services are not necessarily correlative in time or space.

Secondly, SoPC4 is mostly based on a mechanism through which the public authority pays for assets and services. A transactional model is far more present. SoPC4 is clear: 'no service, no payment'.[81] PFIs/PPPs are distinctive regarding both construction contracts and public procurement. In these contracts, advance payment is usually made throughout the works, after an architect certifies them.[82] In PPPs/PFIs, once the works are completed, the assets are not paid at once but their price is spread over the full duration of the contract, under the form of an availability payment for instance. This delays the payment to the constructor and requires even more financial structuring of the project.

progress ?

Thirdly, PF2 applies the same principle of 'no service, no payment' as SoPC4.[83] However the financial engineering behind the investment in the project is more complicated as it aims to gather investments from a broader range of participants. In SoPC4, private contractors bring equity

78 Financial Reporting Advisory Board, *Accounting for PPP Arrangements Including PFI Contracts*, FRAB (89) 02, 2007, 2. The Second Severn Bridge and the Queen Elizabeth II Bridge at Dartford are usual illustrations of free-standing PFIs. Both projects were developed in the early days of PFIs.

79 The question is limited to how the service or infrastructure can be paid for; it does not cover how corporations may be able to generate profit for themselves on the basis of PPPs/PFIs but outside the performance of the projects themselves. Refinancing is not discussed here.

80 For the various possible streams of third-party revenues: *SoPC4*, para 7.4.

81 *SoPC4*, para 3.7.4.

82 Housing Grants, Construction and Regeneration Act 1996, s 109; S Furst and others, *Keating on Construction Contracts* (8th edn, Sweet & Maxwell 2006) para 1-024; 4-005 and 17-051 ff; P Trepte, *Regulating Procurement – Understanding the Ends and Means of Public Procurement Regulation* (OUP 2004) 333–4.

83 *PF2* (draft), para 7.9.5.

through bank borrowing. PF2 aims to attract equity from institutional investors such as pension funds and insurance funds. To this end, the English government – and not the contracting public authority (i.e. in many cases a local authority) – intends to act as a minority shareholder, holding equity invested in the project.[84] Financial streams will thus be even more spread and entwined across actors and relationships, notably between the government as shareholder and the contracting public authority.

Therefore, whatever the PPP/PFI structure chosen, payment mirrors the parties' (inter)relationships, not necessarily as parallel commitments but often in differing or displaced ones. Parties are caught up in a web of relationships framing the choices available to them in the PPP regulatory space. In structuring their relationships, parties need to take into account two further requirements for PPPs/PFIs: *VfM* and risk allocation. Those two notions structure discretion and parties' autonomy. They are now detailed.

VfM: Factoring Trust?

PFIs and *VfM* have always been closely linked together. In PPPs/PFIs, '[t]he standard rationale is *VfM*: achieved through private-sector innovation and management skills delivering performance improvement and efficiency savings'.[85] Part of the 'contract culture' and the 'audit society',[86] *VfM* applies to any public spending[87] in requiring economy, efficiency and effectiveness. No specific legal definition is otherwise provided. *VfM* is an underlying legal obligation for the government, which may be sanctioned for improper use of public money and, even in more extreme cases, held to have committed criminal offences. The National Audit Office (NAO) assesses *VfM* and its reports are debated in the Committee of Public Accounts (PAC), ensuring parliamentary control.[88]

VfM and its external control aim to ensure that taxpayers' money is used properly. However, the three notions of economy, efficiency and effectiveness are too broad to achieve this. More objectification or

---

84 *PF2* (draft), Ch 5.

85 Harlow and Rawlings, 2009, 414 (footnote omitted).

86 Ibid respectively 57 and 59.

87 See National Audit Act 1983, s 6; Treasury, *Managing Public Money*, 2007.

88 See Chapter 2, pp 58–9 and Chapter 4, pp 160–64.

systematisation is required to build trust in how these notions are used to assess public spending. *VfM* has been developed in two ways to strengthen confidence, especially so that contractors know how their bid is tested: a quantitative way and a qualitative way. As a quantitative tool, *VfM* brings more self-understanding by public authorities in formally assessing the costs of a project. As a qualitative tool, *VfM* communicates information, either by demanding or processing it. It also processes qualitative considerations (such as long-term or parallel policies) and creates a mechanism through which public and private partners cooperate in coordinating their interests in developing the project within the PPP regulatory space.

Autonomy: VfM *as an answer mechanism*

As a benchmark for developing a PPP/PFI, *VfM* is by origin a market mechanism[89] assessed throughout the Gateway Process. The public authority thus needs to convince the funding providers that its method for assessing *VfM* is sound and that *VfM* is indeed satisfied in the project. However, *VfM* has undergone various reshapings since its inception in PFIs. Different techniques have been used to reach an objective assessment of the economy, efficiency and effectiveness a project may bring: from general competition to the Public Sector Comparator (PSC) and checklists, *VfM* has been formalised.

At the outset, *VfM* was defined by nothing more than reference to competition.[90] From 1997 onwards, *VfM* was assessed with a PSC. 'The PSC describes the option of what it would cost the public sector to provide the outputs it is requesting from the private sector by a non-PFI route'.[91] Representing a financial model of the project, the PSC included a quantification of the risks transferred and the risks retained by the government.[92] For each PSC, the authority had to decide which factors and risks would be taken into account, and how to price them. The necessary speculative part of the exercise and the wish to secure PPPs

[89] Treasury, Procurement Guidance no 2, *Value for Money in Construction Procurement*, 1997, para 1.4.

[90] Treasury, 1993, 8.

[91] Treasury, 1997, para 3.10.

[92] Ibid para 3.12.

when/as no real alternative was open led to misuse.[93] Both the PAC[94] and the NAO[95] criticised the method.

In 2003, the PSC was reformed to 'inform [...] a wider value for money assessment'.[96] A factor accounting for bias optimism was also introduced in 2003.[97] This refers to the fact that public decisions overestimate the positive sides of projects and underestimate the negative sides. Optimism bias was only applied to the PSC, not to the PFI bid, therefore giving advantage to the latter. Normally, the fixed price in PFIs should sufficiently motivate the private contractor to deliver on time and on budget.[98]

The construction of the PSC requires the public authority to understand how it works differently. The PSC is a speculative exercise because it compels the taking into account of uncertain factors. It requires tracing back services public authorities rely on for free as part of the general context in which they operate: staff are assigned to different projects, IT systems and databases are used for different purposes etc. The addition of the optimism bias factor goes in a similar direction towards grasping factors better: here, they are psychological ones linked to the functioning of public services. Once a contractor is asked to provide similar services, they need to find out how to provide the service and price it. The comparison between PFIs and the PSC was strongly structured in 2011 as 'a decision-support' for public authorities.[99] This assessment relied on both filling in Excel spread sheets with pre-determined factors and assumptions and assessing the sensitivity and specificity of each project.[100] However, this tight canvassing of public discretion could not be fully isolated from a more encompassing appraisal of the project. Therefore, in 2012 it was announced that the quantitative assessment of *VfM* would be integrated within a qualitative assessment:[101] the quantitative assessment should not be interpreted as a pass or fail test.

---

93 Arrowsmith, 2005, para 2.16 and 2.18.

94 PAC, *Delivering Better Value for Money from the Private Finance Initiative* (764 HC 2002–03) summary.

95 NAO, *The Laganside Courts*, 2003, recommendation d); NAO, *Examining the Value for Money of Deals under the Private Finance Initiative*, 1999, 18.

96 Treasury, 2003, 81.

97 NAO, *Note on Optimism Bias – Lords*, 2009.

98 Treasury, *Quantitative Assessment – User Guide*, 2011, para 1.71.

99 Ibid para 1.12.

100 Ibid passim and Treasury, 2012, para 7.28.

101 Treasury, 2012, paras 7.28–7.31.

Solidarity: VfM *as question-raising*

Looking inside public authority organisation, the PSC is only a limited part of assessing *VfM*.[102] *VfM* is more open-structured, with a floating definition. In the PPP/PFI framework,[103] *VfM* triggered the elaboration of the notion of the 'whole-life-cycle'. Appearing in 1998, the notion referred to 'the optimum combination of whole life cost and quality to meet the customer's requirements'.[104] With some fluctuations, it has been reproduced since then.[105] It entails the partners adjusting their interests and goals during the project, over its whole life. It does not take into account users' needs, however, an issue to which Chapter 4 returns. Yet *VfM* is transformed from a quantitative one-time assessment to an ongoing assessment over the life of a project.[106] The NAO contributed to this ongoing assessment of *VfM* in PPPs/PFIs in 2006 by issuing an evaluative framework.[107] This sets out questions to ask across the successive stages of PPPs/PFIs in order to assess the potential *VfM* of a project.[108] However, developing a qualitative assessment of *VfM* is contentious as it reveals political choices about the factors allowed to bear on the *VfM* assessment. In 2012, the coalition government announced its intention to revise the *VfM assessment guide,* dating back to 2006 and New Labour.[109]

In this qualitative sense, *VfM* operates in two different ways: firstly, it constrains the free decision making a public authority theoretically has when deciding on a project; secondly, it establishes a communication framework with contractors to develop PPPs/PFIs. Taking the first point, *VfM* adds a requirement to those set under the public procurement regulations. Public procurement regulations impose only the MEAT as a criterion. They mention that the assessment is to be made on the basis of set criteria points and weighing. *VfM* is more detailed and stretches out to before and after the bid assessment. Secondly, *VfM* helps communicate the grounds for choosing a bidder on an understandable and more

---

102 NAO, *Lords*, 2009, para 4.10.

103 C Pasquire and L Swaffield, 'Life-cycle/whole–life costing', in J Kelly, R Morledge and S Wilkinson (eds), *Best Value in Construction* (Blackwell 2002) 139.

104 Treasury, Procurement Guidance no 2, *Value for Money in Construction Procurement*, 1997, para 3.1.

105 E.g.: Treasury, 2008, box 3.1.

106 Treasury, *Value For Money Assessment Guidance*, 2006, 5.

107 NAO, *A Framework for Evaluating the Implementation of Private Finance Initiative Projects*, 2 vol, 2006.

108 E.g.: OGC, *Value for Money Evaluation in Complex Procurements*, 2002.

109 Treasury, 2012, 12.

objective basis. The whole elaboration process of the project around *VfM* may be seen as an attempt to gather information from the other party and to construct the necessary techniques enabling such gathering. The point is especially clear in PPPs/PFIs, where little actual competition is achieved because of the lack of bidders. In the Private Sector Resource Initiative for the Management of the Estate (PRIME), for instance, public authorities achieved *VfM* through the construction of a 'should cost' model, benchmarking the only private contractor's proposal and directing questions at him about his costing of the project.[110]

In getting these questions and answers, better mutual knowledge is developed, creating a basis for further trust and cooperation. In PPPs/PFIs, *VfM* becomes a joint effort, even if discretion remains in the process.[111] A similar pattern can be deciphered in the other key feature of PPPs/PFIs: risk allocation.

Risk: Clarification as Optimum?

Risk allocation and management convey the idea that risks are price-tagged and brought into a risks matrix under the headings 'public', 'private' or 'shared', and therefore clinically transferred and taken care of. Three main questions arise in relation to risks:[112]

- *risk identification*: what are the risks a specific project entails?[113]
- *risk allocation*: who bears the final – economic, social, financial – consequences if the risk supervenes? Who decides on and pays the potential insurance? Who receives the rewards or losses associated with a risk?[114]
- *risk management*: how is the risk integrated in the working of the entity? What measures are taken to avoid or reduce the risk or its financial consequence if it occurs?

The complexity of risk mapping needs both a formulaic, standardised approach to risks and adaptation to the contemplated project. Translating material risks into contractual terms involves discretion. The risks matrix

---

110 NAO, *PRIME Expansion*, 2005, 19.

111 PAC, *The Procurement of the National Roads Telecommunications Services* (578 HC 2007–08) recommendation 3.

112 TTPF, Technical Note no 5, *How to Construct a Public Sector Comparator*, 1999, 3.

113 Ibid 28.

114 NAO, *Lords*, 2009, Pt III.

may be read in combination with the contractual terms dealing with each category of risks (e.g. changes in law, in service, contractor distress, strikes etc.). Each PPP/PFI has a basic set of risks common to any construction project, then some specific to the PPP/PFI contractual or financial design. Common risks such as construction risks or budget overruns may already need interpretation (e.g. the starting point or expiry of deadlines). Additional risk categories are added depending on the sector. Then, maybe to address specific situations, supplementary risks are identified (such as technical risks involved in waste PFIs[115] or complex engineering works for infrastructure projects).

In so far as the three questions can be distinguished from each other in practice, risk identification relates to autonomy in PPPs/PFIs, risk allocation to solidarity and risk management to trust. We detail each in turn here. The process of risk identification-allocation-management takes place in a context of discretion and uncertainty where parties search for further clarification from one step to the next. Formalisation, control and trust interplay here.

Autonomy: identifying risks

How far are parties autonomous in calculating risk? Risk identification needs to be set against the background of the limited information and knowledge of the future parties have when elaborating a PPP/PFI. The more idiosyncratic the project, the trickier the risk identification becomes and the riskier the funding of the project. Regulatory risks (e.g. health, safety etc.) need to be listed and translated into matrices and priced so that the *VfM* of the PPP/PFI can be assessed. This complex process requires expertise and communication between the parties.

To some extent, there are always non-chartable risk areas in any project. However, PPPs/PFIs are especially vulnerable as they rely on innovative techniques. In waste PFIs, for instance, technology has been a major hurdle. By contrast, the law expressly takes risks outside the negotiation sphere of the parties; for example, the Local Government (Contracts) Act 1997 prevents local authorities from escaping bad bargains. The private sector is very reluctant to take risks in an uncertain environment and needs reassuring techniques and institutions.

Solidarity: allocation and sharing risks/benefits

How is solidarity expressed through risk allocation between PPP parties? In theory, PPPs/PFIs rely on the allocation of risks to the party who is

---

[115] E.g.: NAO, *Waste PFI*, 2009, App 3.

best able to manage them.[116] Contract law assumes that risk allocation is the outcome of the parties' opposing interests.[117] Between two private contractors, the 'legal rules of contract facilitate the efforts of bargaining parties to minimise and allocate optimally the risks of [future regret] contingencies'.[118] However, public authorities struggle with this risk allocation: they tend to exercise tight control over the specification of what is expected from the contractor or they may be in a weaker position and tempted to shoulder more risks than agreed when facing the prospect of disrupted public services.[119] While risk allocation may at first imply a distinct separation of risks between the parties, in practice, solidarity appears in the techniques used to organise this allocation. It ends up as a more or less extended sharing of risks. This trend is here illustrated with SoPC4 and PF2.

Under SoPC4, PFIs were constructed in such a way that the SPV should bear all the risks transferred under the contract. The SPV had very low capital and limited personal financial room. The risks borne by the SPV needed to be carefully listed and strictly limited. SoPC4 contained terms for identifying risks (e.g. changes in law or changes due to supervening events) which would be shared between the parties and influence how they would be borne.[120] Conversely, benefit sharing was organised in SoPC4.[121] In cases of financial trouble, however, the contractor was in a position of power, as the public sector maintained the responsibility for keeping the public infrastructure or service running[122] regardless as to whether or not public authorities had given a formal guarantee to the creditors of the SPV.[123] The interdependence between the parties resulted in factual solidarity. Cases of failing PFI hospitals illustrate this point, where public authorities had to step in to wipe out the debts of the PFI hospitals to keep the services running.[124]

By contrast, PF2 starts from the principle that solidarity binds the parties, as public authorities are equity shareholders along with the

---

116 Treasury, 1995, 12.

117 S Boyron, 'The Public–Private Divide and the Law of Government Contracts: Assessing a Comparative Effort' in M Ruffert (ed), *The Public–Private Law Divide: A Potential for Transformation* (BIICL 2009) 221, 238–39.

118 C Goetz and R Scott, 'Principles of Relational Contracts' (1981) 67 Va LRev 1089, 1090.

119 Davies, 2008, 36.

120 *SoPC4*, para 14.2.3 and 14.8.4; *SoPC4*, para 5.1.2.

121 *SoPC4*, para 34.5.

122 NAO, *Managing the Relationship*, 2001, 10.

123 E.g.: London Underground or NHS PFI hospitals.

124 See Chapter 5, pp 235–42.

private contractors and investors. This should ensure that both risks and benefits are shared between the public and private parties. PF2 retains the SoPC4 principles of risk sharing in the case of supervening events and benefit sharing for refinancing.[125] It modifies SoPC4 solutions in the case of changes in the law, however. PF2 specifies that public authorities should bear risks in a series of cases (e.g. long construction periods).[126] Even then, however, a form of solidarity remains as both parties have to discuss the changes required in the service, the contracts and the financial structure of the contracts. A procedure is set to steer the discussions around the reasonable endeavours taken by the contractor following the required changes.[127]

Risk allocation helps to define which party is the primary bearer of risks and organises how to deal with them within its autonomy. However, whether in the contractual elaboration of the terms related to specific risks or in the implementation of PPPs/PFIs, solidarity needs to be organised. The factual or contractual interdependence between the partners implies that the discretion of the one affects the other, and mechanisms for dealing with these consequences need to be developed. Here comes risk management.

Trust: management and formalisation

How do parties trust their counterparts to manage risks? Long-term contracts face a high likelihood of unforeseen/unforeseeable circumstances, so contracts are incomplete and need flexibility. The aim of fostering trust and solidarity within the relationship would be to prevent opportunism/free riding.

To prevent risk allocation becoming purely formal, risk management is required. Early on it was assumed that: '[o]nce it has been decided which risks to transfer, the private sector supplier should be left to manage those risks in the best way possible in the interests of achieving efficiency'.[128] SoPC4 and PF2 equally underline that too much public intervention in risk management (for instance of the supply chain) needs to be avoided, for fear of reversal of the risk transfer.[129] However, the NAO emphasised

---

125 *PF2* (draft), Ch 15 and para 28.5.
126 Ibid para 16.6.1 and 16.6.3.
127 Ibid para 16.6.
128 Treasury, 1995, 16.
129 *SoPC4*, para 16.1.2 and *PF2* (draft), para 7.25.1.2.

the need to solve problems together,[130] which entails a more cooperative management approach.[131]

SoPC4 and PF2 therefore suggest places where cooperation between the parties may be agreed on. In practice, there is a role allocation between the public and private entities regarding risk management: the contractor manages risks and needs to transmit information to the public authority[132] in a position of control. Documenting the payment procedures with regard to the reached performance[133] and setting up the channels to ensure the risks are properly managed inside the contractor contributes to ensuring that contractors manage risks. Ensuring that the risks are manageable and that they may be monitored during PPP implementation may, however, affect their identification and allocation. This takes place within an overall process of formalisation and trust building. Trust, indeed, is based on internal control, on constant reassessment of the grounds on which one trusts. The risk matrix allows parties to objectify whether their trust in the other one is justified through verifying if the other's behaviour meets the agreed standards of behaviour and process, falls short or exhibits commitment to extra effort. Similarly, if one party wants to show its reliability and good will, the risk matrix may serve as a comparison. Such goodwill may be of importance in the overall interplays of relationships as they unfold in the PPP regulatory space. SoPC4 and PF2 acknowledge this regarding the consequences of delays. If the private contractor suggests acceptable alternatives to running the services, the sanctions may be mitigated.[134]

Formalising Discretion: Gaps in Implementing Efficient Rationality

The exchanging of services against a price over twenty to thirty years is a legal technique on which the whole negotiation process and implementation of PPPs/PFIs turns. The legal framework gives few indications of how public and private partners should coordinate their interests at the time of this exchange in the regulatory space. Contract law as applied

---

130 See below this chapter, pp 144–46.

131 OGC, *Risk Allocation Model for Project Strategy and Procurement*, 2006; OGC, *Best Practice: Risk Allocation in Long-Term Contracts*, 2002; Treasury/OGC, *Managing Risks with Delivery Partners*, 2005, 5.

132 TTPF, Technical Note no 5, *How to Construct a Public Sector Comparator*, 1999, para 4.8.3.

133 4Ps, *A Guide to Contract Management for PFI and PPP Projects*, 2007, 31.

134 *SoPC4*, para 4.2.6; *PF2* (draft), para 8.2.6.

relates far more to on-the-spot exchanges. It starts from a wide freedom between parties with opposed interests, who are free to allocate risks as they deem fit, adjusting services and prices accordingly. As PPPs/PFIs are far from this paradigm, and as relational contracts are more a theory than a practice, other concrete tools are used to structure the PPP relational nexus. *VfM* and risk allocation/management are two ways to rely on a common language for mechanisms leading to definitions of the contractual obligations of payments and services between the public and private parties. They help one understand how public authorities exercise their discretion in the PPP regulatory space, while the law leaves a wide range of options available with few indications of how to choose among them. These non-legal techniques thus also articulate concerns around autonomy, solidarity and trust.

Firstly, autonomy balances objectification and subjectivity in *VfM* and risk allocation. Both techniques bring a lens through which to analyse the project with objectivity. However, they allow for subjectivity as well, preserving some autonomy in the design and construction of the PSC, the qualitative assessment of *VfM* or the risk matrix. Both the objective and subjective aspects call for a high level of technical expertise expressing an efficient rationality. This rationality does not extend to assessing the human or social needs that the PPP/PFI intends to address in a systematic way or to integrating concerns relating to the practical implementation of PPPs/PFIs.

Secondly, solidarity is constructed through the enabling of communication in *VfM* and is related to parties' interdependence in risk allocation. It is close to joint maximisation by each party as no specific space is left for identifying public interest, outside what *VfM* expresses. Parties identify a shared goal which is mainly negative in the sense that their focus is to address the risks that their joint endeavour would face. The positive and rewarding aspects of their common objective for themselves, the users relying on the infrastructure/service or the wider community are left uncharted. In this sense, PPPs/PFIs constitute a community of interests limited to the respective interests of the public and private partners in the regulatory space. This community does not extend to third parties' interests and needs. These third parties are only included in the process in terms of their capacity as taxpayers.

Thirdly, trust is fostered through both *VfM* and risk allocation setting parties' expectations. Parties trust that once a risk is allocated to one party, this party will take care of its own obligations. This trust is not a blind trust but is mostly based on rational calculativeness and on the formalisation of *VfM* and risk matrices. This trust does not contribute much to the actual cooperative behaviour needed to develop and implement this *VfM* and risk allocation.

In this section, tensions between market mechanisms and formalisation have appeared again, as in public procurement. The specificity here, however, is that these tensions appear largely without direct interference from the law but within the large discretionary space opened up by contract law (and the competitive dialogue) in the PPP regulatory space. Formalisation of the *VfM* and risk allocation, the two requirements applied to discretion in PPPs/PFIs, is constantly ongoing, with permanent refining of *VfM* (from competition, to checklists and revision of the qualitative assessments) and adjustments to risk identification, allocation and management. The transition from SoPC4 to PF2 shows the hesitations relating to this risk allocation and management. This recurring adaptation of formalisation weakens the potential stability in the coordination of public and private interests in PPPs/PFIs and their regulatory space. The role of cooperation and mutual trust in this coordination becomes blurred even if ever present in some form (e.g. in addressing legal changes). Similar tensions are also present in the concrete implementation of PPPs/PFIs, as the next section explains.

PERFORMANCE OF PPPs/PFIs: ADJUSTING COMPLIANCE

PPPs/PFIs are long-term processes. Good communication about potential expectations helps with innovation, savings and planning investments in these idiosyncratic assets. *VfM* may then be achieved,[135] even if this will always stay uncertain by want of systematic evaluation.[136] Legal techniques (such as SoPC4 or PF2) and market-based techniques (such as competition) are brought in during the performing of PPPs/PFIs. The logic of the process shifts from competition to cooperation, from public procurement process to contract law, from construction to implementation. Projects adapt to circumstances. Risk materialises. Public authorities need to ensure that contractual commitments are complied with. Yet they also need to ensure that the PPP/PFI achieves the objectives set with regard to the public interest. A discrepancy between these initial contractual commitments and evolving public interests may appear and need to be tackled. Contract law is highly unsatisfactory here. It only knows two possibilities: frustration of the contract or maintaining the contract as

135 OTF, Note no 2, *Project Transition Guidance*, 2007.
136 NAO, *Lords*, 2009, para 4.2.

agreed if the extreme conditions of frustration are not met. Parties may then organise their commitments in a different way: formalisation and cooperation will be needed to preserve their relationships and protect their interests.

Preserving the Relationship and Protecting Parties' Interests

This need for the parties to organise their commitments in the regulatory space can be illustrated by looking at the practical implementation of this organisation. Starting from strict role delimitation between public authorities and private contractors,[137] cooperation is required on practical grounds, for instance regarding payment mechanisms and changes to the contract. In these cases, an annual review is recommended, even if changes require the agreement of both parties. In other cases, cooperation is due to a statutory duty, such the one in LIFT where the PCT and the SPV have to cooperate under health and safety regulations.[138] If innovation has to benefit the PPPs/PFIs, a constructive attitude of sharing information and solving issues is necessary to ensure that the contract brings *VfM*. This requires using discretion in the direction of cooperation between the parties. Effective management of the relationships builds on this dynamic between discretion and cooperation. Here we look first at the limits to the legal solutions.

The law, whether it is contract law or administrative law, does not provide satisfactory answers. Contract law does not deal well with cases of discretion.[139] English law rejects the idea of good faith as a general principle.[140] A good faith principle for renegotiating the contract in case of changes in circumstances cannot be invoked to set collaboration in motion, even on the basis of an express term. Indeed, from this traditional perspective, contracting parties are supposed to have opposing interests.[141] Contract law does not offer suitable solutions for addressing

137 *SoPC4*, para 3.2.1; *PF2* (draft), para 7.2.1.

138 HSE, *Safety by Design in the Construction of Public Healthcare Estate*, SIM 07/2005/12, 2006, para 9. Both the Trust and the SPV have duties under health and safety legislation, including the duty to cooperate and coordinate their activities (Management of Health and Safety at Work Regulations 1999, SI 1999/3242, reg 11).

139 D Oliver, 'Review of (Non-Statutory) Discretions' in C Forsyth (ed), *Judicial Review and the Constitution* (Hart 2000) 307, 315.

140 S Smith, *Atiyah's Introduction to the Law of Contract* (Clarendon Press 2005) 164–166.

141 The 'adversarial ethic' governing English contract law: R Brownsword, *Contract Law* (2nd edn, OUP 2006) 115.

Superficial referencing on these points!

practical needs for cooperation in either performing the contract or negotiating new terms to adjust to circumstances.

Like contract law, legitimate expectations, borrowed from administrative law, only offer limited solutions. The contractor may expect that its expectations will not be disrupted by its partner public authority (e.g. changes of circumstances such as new elections or financial crises). Contractors' expectations under a clear contract indeed seem stronger than those based on 'a representation by the public authority',[142] as is now accepted in the legitimate expectations doctrine. Legitimate expectations may offer solutions in cases where public authorities try to get out of a bad bargain. They can limit the use of public discretion but it may be more difficult to rely on them to ensure evolving coordination of the public and private interests in the long term, for instance to adjust to changing political and financial circumstances. Legitimate expectations are also less likely to provide solutions to day-to-day issues demanding decisions but without immediate drastic consequences.

For these day-to-day decisions, discretion is needed and parties may organise the coordination of their interests during the implementation of the PPPs/PFIs, through either contractual terms[143] or a partnering agreement. This section looks at how, in PPPs/PFIs, preserving the relationship between the public and private sectors by maintaining both flexibility and stability[144] takes on a different sense from in purely private contracts for two reasons. Firstly, the public authority needs the service. It is often politically, if not legally, required to ensure the service is delivered to the users. Secondly, the contractor invests only limited funds in the highly expensive and often idiosyncratic public infrastructure. Financial institutions are supposed to ensure that the contractor delivers the service properly, so that periodic payments pay back the loans. These banks are thus theoretically highly incentivised to monitor the contractor's performance. Yet external control by financial institutions has not proven to be a good way to ensure that public authorities' interests are effectively protected. Therefore more systematic public control has had to be devised while maintaining flexibility in PPPs. Here, the two logics of market and state again come together.

Clearly starting from this market logic, PPP/PFI performance developed into formalised control and cooperation during implementation. Illustrations taken from SoPC4, the PPP Arbiter set-up in the London

---

142 Davies, 2008, 183.

143 E.g.: *SoPC4*, para 15.3.2.5 (benchmarking).

144 E.g.: *SoPC4*, para 5.1.1.

Underground (LU) PPPs and PF2 all show this incremental evolution from market-analogue to state-analogue, while the tension between formalisation and cooperation endures.

Payment: From Automatism to Monitoring

The payment mechanism (or 'unitary charge') reflects risk allocation through the price paid. Highly complex, it establishes the necessary incentive for the delivery of a service.[145] It is key in organising the subtle balance of penalties and rewards.[146] The starting point is that the payment mechanism helps make the contract self-enforcing. However, sanctions are formally calibrated in the contract. Concrete difficulties in applying the payment mechanism arise, as performance needs to be monitored on the ground. Formalisation, expertise and ultimately cooperation between the parties are needed. Contract sets the necessary framework. Market mechanisms thus work differently depending on the two main phases of performance: construction and operations.

PPPs/PFIs seek to reduce cost and time overruns during construction. Normally the reimbursing of the loan falls at the same time as the work delivery and the start of periodic payments by the public authority. Through paying the contractor only at the time when the asset is delivered, the construction risks are transferred to the contractor: the first penalty for late delivery is non-payment.[147] In this way, PPPs/PFIs are self-enforcing.[148] There is no space for discretion or subjectivity. Market mechanisms take care of the problem.

This rather uncomplicated use of market mechanisms does not work for the operational phase. Here, the most straightforward sanction for defaults is adjusting service charges according to the quality of the performance. This requires monitoring of the contract performance, thus making the public authority aware of how well the contract is (or is not) performed. However, some flexibility is required: the public authority has to weigh the relevance of compliance with the importance of a specific matter.[149] Subjectivity can creep in to the monitoring system through the interpretation of performance indicators,[150] as well in the diversity of

---

[145] *SoPC4*, Ch 7.

[146] NAO, *Lords*, 2009, para 5.20.

[147] Ibid para 2.14.

[148] *SoPC4*, paras 4.1.2–4.1.3; *PF2* (draft), para 8.1.2 and 8.1.4; Collins, 1999, 116.

[149] NAO, *Managing the Relationship*, 2001, 28.

[150] NAO, *Lords*, 2009, para 5.20: What 'clean' really means?

ways – formal and informal – in which the performance is assessed (e.g. monthly management reports and meetings, face-to-face discussions, key performance indicators and audits, day-to-day monitoring, complaints received[151]). SoPC4 suggests a formal method of monitoring, the 'Quality Management System'.[152] Cooperation to gather information on performance from both the public and private sectors is needed,[153] extending to arranging 'for joint training and development of Authority and Contractor staff to encourage partnership'.[154] However, differences may arise between the agreed system and the system as used on the ground.[155] Mindful of this problem, PF2 suggests simplifying the payment mechanism and standardising it when possible.[156]

This illustrates the constant ambiguity between the need to foster cooperation and partnership on the one hand, and control and formalisation on the other hand. Cooperation is helpful because it eases relationships and reduces costs (of monitoring) but is also dangerous as it may give rise to occasions for opportunism. Control is required because public authorities need to know if contractors are trustworthy and will deliver what they are paying for. However, control diverts energy and is costly. It may lead to adverse effects if the contractor is so tightly constrained that it does not try out new solutions, fearing sanctions for relatively minor defaults, while taking the risk of securing improvements in the long term. Therefore, penalties may be 'offset for other services rendered or suspended as part of a plan to work together to improve performance'.[157] However, control and cooperation need each other. Cooperation needs a rational ground on which some autonomy for the contractor is recognised, and control is a way to gain such rational grounds. Control needs cooperation because cooperation makes control less expensive and enables it to be carried out in such a way that both parties learn how to address the issues the control underlines. In practice,

---

151 Ipsos/Mori, *Investigating the Performance of Operational PFI Contract – A Research Study Conducted for PUK on behalf of HM Treasury, 2008 Survey of Operational PFI Projects*, 2008, sd, 19.

152 *SoPC4*, para 10.4.

153 Ibid para 10.4.3 and 10.6.1.

154 Ibid para 10.4.4.

155 Treasury, *Making Savings in Operational PFI Contracts*, 2011, para 1.13.

156 *PF2* (draft), Ch 19.

157 NAO, *Lords*, 2009, para 2.15 and 5.22.

PPPs/PFIs evolve from a system of pragmatism in contract management[158] to a system where the contract is performed as agreed.[159]

Changes: Balance between Stability and Flexibility?

As Chapter 1 discussed,[160] PPPs/PFIs seek to address the tension between a need for stability in the parties' expectations and interests and a need for flexibility in order to keep the PPP/PFI relationship alive despite changing circumstances. To ensure that *VfM* is maintained during the long duration of PPPs/PFIs, techniques need to be devised to address these changing circumstances.[161] The extreme complexity of these issues, however, pinpoints the limits of formalisation and the need for cooperation between parties in order to bring about the balance between stability and flexibility. This section looks at the general approach to changing circumstances over time and then turns to two extreme illustrations. The first illustration is the LU PPP, where a sophisticated contractual governance mechanism was designed to integrate changes in the determination of the price paid for the services. The second illustration involves soft services (e.g. catering, cleaning), which have now been excluded from PF2 because of the difficulties that they triggered in relation to changes.

In principle, PPP/PFI contracts would address the issue of changes; this is, however, a typical case of planning under considerable uncertainty because of the long duration and high-risk profile connected to innovation. Formalisation and incremental adaptation of SoPC[162] have been used to address the point that the contractor might be in a power position when the public authority requires changes.[163] SoPC4 required including a change protocol that the parties had to develop in order to organise the negotiation process related to changes during the contractual performance.[164] For large value changes, cooperation between the public and private partners is required throughout the process of requesting

[158] Treasury, Private Finance Panel, *Further Contractual Issues*, 1997, 10 quoted in M Elsenaar, 'Law, Accountability and the Private Finance Initiative in the National Health Service' [1999] PL 35, 39.

[159] Treasury, 2006, 65; *SoPC4*, para 7.2.5.

[160] See Chapter 1, pp 16–17.

[161] NAO, *Changes*, 2008.

[162] OTF, Note no 3, *Variations Protocol for Operational Projects* (entered into prior to SoPC4), sd, para 1.4.

[163] *SoPC4*, para 5.25.

[164] For a typology of possible changes in services, see *SoPC4*, para 13.2.3.

changes.[165] PF2 does maintain the change protocol for changes which cannot be anticipated during the elaboration process of the PPP/PFI.[166] It even goes further in suggesting that departmental PPP Units standardise the applicable change protocols.[167] A tension between formalisation and cooperation is present; however, the whole process should be kept to a limited bureaucracy[168] and the supply chain should not be an obstacle preventing flexibility.[169] This implies that, beyond the formal processes, a cooperative mindset might be needed to ensure smooth adaptation to circumstances.

The practical difficulties of devising an appropriate change procedure to adapt the PPP/PFI to their long duration and the new information gained during their implementation can be illustrated with the LU PPPs aiming to upgrade the LU infrastructure.[170] Part of the complexity in these PPPs was linked to the state of the grey assets and the uncertainty regarding the works to be carried out over a thirty-year period. More specific information was to be obtained regarding the scope of the works to be carried out as the contracts were performed. The price could thus not be agreed for the whole contract duration and specific events might make a price revision necessary. To deal with both possibilities, a PPP Arbiter was appointed.[171] He had two main functions: issuing directions to adapt the contract in case of an extraordinary event and defining the price during the seven-and-a-half-year periodic reviews. These two powers had far-reaching (financial) consequences. They have both been used. An extraordinary review led to Metronet's failure. The periodic review led to Tube Lines' assets being bought back by TfL.

For both reviews, a similar chain of general and specific decisions can be underlined. The PPP Arbiter issued documents on both the procedures[172] and the substantial[173] elements. Parties were consulted.[174]

---

165 *SoPC4*, para 13.3.3.

166 *PF2* (draft), para 11.1.8.

167 Ibid para 11.3.1, also referring to a 2007 note on *Change Protocol Principles*.

168 *SoPC4*, para 13.5.3.

169 *PF2* (draft), para 11.1.

170 See Chapter 2, pp 90–94.

171 The official name is 'Public–Private Partnership Agreement Arbiter', Greater London Authority Act 1999, s 225(3).

172 PPP Arbiter, *Procedural Approach to Periodic Review*, 2009.

173 PPP Arbiter, *Reference for Guidance from London Underground Ltd*, 2008.

174 PPP Arbiter, *Analytical Approach to Calculating ISC – Consultation Draft*, 2009, para 1.2.

International benchmarks were requested so that they could be integrated into the business standards/industrial good practice the PPP Arbiter was supposed to apply when defining the contractual price.[175] The PPP Arbiter framed his own discretion through its own guidelines, supplemented by the parties' views.[176] Once this framework was shaped, there was a subsequent process of communication between the parties[177] in which the timing and planning were precisely defined but with safety valves to allow for negotiations or adjustments.[178] Discretion was built into the whole process[179] but cooperation among the PPP parties (e.g. through communication and the transmission of information) was also required for the success of these reviews.

Overall, the PPP Arbiter represented an attempt to entrust an entity with the discretion to adapt the PPP contracts over time and to make the coordination of the public and private interests evolve in the PPP/PFI relationship. Yet it failed to provide the balance between stability and flexibility that the parties needed to maintain their relationships.

Another illustration can be given with the solutions devised for changes related to soft services, namely services such as catering, cleaning and porterage. Soft services are subject to many changes and their market prices may fluctuate strongly over time. SoPC4 had devised a benchmarking and market-testing process based on market techniques. In the case of benchmarking, payments to sub-contractors needed to be adjusted according to market prices,[180] while in the case of market testing the contract was re-tendered and the payment incurred by the public authority needed to be adjusted accordingly.[181] The procedure granted

---

[175] PPP Arbiter, *International Benchmarking of the Costs and Performance of Maintaining and Renewing Metro Systems*, 2010.

[176] Tube Lines was consulted on matters relating primarily to Metronet's agreements (PPP Arbiter, *Treatment of Investment at an Extraordinary Review: Initial Guidance*, 2006, para 3.23).

[177] PPP Arbiter, *Reference for Directions and Guidance from London Underground Ltd in Respect of the Periodic Review of Tube Lines' PPP Agreement – Draft Direction on Costs and Related Matters and Initial Thoughts on ISC Setting and Financing*, 2009, 1–3.

[178] PPP Arbiter, *Updates Timetable for Periodic Review Reference*, 2009.

[179] Ibid para 1.9 or PPP Arbiter, *Reference for Direction and Guidance from London Underground Ltd in Respect of the Periodic Review of Tube Lines' PPP Agreement – Direction on Financing Impossibility*, 2010, para 2.40.

[180] OTF, Note no 1, *Benchmarking and Market Testing Guidance*, 2006, 5.

[181] Ibid 5–6; Add PUK, *Benchmarking and Market Testing – Help Pack*, 2007; DH PFU & PPP Forum, *Benchmarking and Market Testing in NHS PFI projects – Code of Best Practice*, 2006.

discretion to the public authority[182] and required cooperation between the public and private partners.[183] Indeed, the parties needed to discuss the available modalities for these processes.[184] However, parties faced practical problems: benchmarking and market testing are disruptive of contractual relationships, their process is time consuming, comparable data may be lacking, and they may lead to adjusting the service rather than reducing the price.[185]

To address these problems, PF2 removed soft services from PPPs/PFIs as a principle.[186] Public authorities themselves or third parties appointed by public authorities will provide these soft services. While this solution addresses the issue of benchmarking and market testing, it mostly displaces the issue of formalisation and cooperation. Indeed, the interactions between the various actors (authority, contractor, authority service providers and contractor sub-contractors) need to be coordinated,[187] if not more. PF2 expects 'that service delivery will be enhanced if all parties cooperate with each other and act in a manner so as not to impede the others in the carrying out of their activities'.[188] Therefore, it provides for contractual terms encapsulating that duty of cooperation and for an interface protocol between the public authority and its private contractors. This illustrates the complexity of finding adequate solutions to the intricate web of relationships involved in PPPs/PFIs. Removing soft services from PPPs/PFIs solves the practical issues of benchmarking and market testing; processes which are supposed to happen every couple of years. However, it also requires day-to-day cooperation in the managing of all actors involved with the PPP/PFI site and the formalised interface protocol in PF2. The contracting authority gains direct control of soft services instead of their previous arm's length involvement in the market exercise.

Changes have thus become incrementally formalised: from techniques based on market techniques public authorities have gained increased control over their handling. Yet the concrete implementation of these interface and change protocols may rely on active cooperation from all parties involved in PPPs/PFIs.

---

182 *SoPC4,* para 15.3.2.5.
183 See Ibid para 15.4.4.
184 Ibid para 15.3.2.6 and 15.4.5.
185 NAO, *Benchmarking and Market Testing*, 2007.
186 Treasury, 2012, Ch 4.
187 *PF2* (draft), para 7.11.2.
188 Ibid para 7.11.4.

PF2: Formal Public Control from Inside

The previous sections have shown how formalisation and cooperation interplayed in SoPC4 and how difficulties, mainly in the actual implementation of payments, the management of suppliers and changes to contracts, resulted in poor *VfM*. Acknowledging these issues, PF2 seeks to foster flexibility in the contractual relationships while providing more control for the public authority over the actual performance and management of infrastructures and services. This section considers how this next step revolves around formalisation and joint decision making: PF2 illustrates a new form of the state-analogue model.

PF2 develops a standardised framework for projects in which the government becomes a minority shareholder and holds an equity share of 30–49 per cent.[189] The system is primarily devised to address funding problems that PPPs/PFIs face following the financial crisis.[190] New sources of finance, such as institutional investments provided by pension funds and insurance funds, are sought in light of these problems. However, these institutional investors are reluctant to take up the same level of risks as banks, prompting the government to inject finance into the projects directly.[191] To manage these public investments in PPPs/PFIs, a specific central unit, located in the Treasury and staffed with specialists, has been announced.[192]

PF2 thus formalises close interplays between public and private parties within the ownership of the projects. Indeed, public authorities bear greater risks in the projects than previously, as they may lose their investment in the equity if the projects fail to deliver their obligations. However, public authorities may also benefit from any profits that the projects make.[193] The English government will thus be involved in the project's decision making through board membership. Contracting authorities will not have a director on the board but will be represented by an observer, appointed by central government. This person will represent local concerns but will not vote or participate in the decision-making process.[194] The benefits of this public presence inside the governance of the projects are summed up as 'better partnership working between the public and private sector as the public sector will have

---

[189] Ibid para 5.3.1.1.
[190] Treasury, 2012, 10–11.
[191] *PF2* (draft), para 5.1.1-2.
[192] Ibid para 1.4.1.
[193] Treasury, 2012, para 2.1.
[194] *PF2* (draft), para 5.5.3.

greater visibility of project information and will be involved in strategic decision making.'[195] It should also give public authorities access to financial information related to the project.

PF2 thus brings public authorities to the core of the decision making of PPPs/PFIs to give them more control and direction in the project. This relies on legal techniques[196] formalising how economic power will be exercised.

Cooperation as Reclaiming Control over Performance

Cooperation is an issue for contract law. However, in long-term contracts, it is inevitable. Planning is likely to be more procedural than substantial, especially in PPPs/PFIs as flexibility is needed and innovative techniques give rise to unforeseen/unforeseeable circumstances. Discretion is expressed on various occasions, in applying sanctions, monitoring performance, managing specific risks such as those generated by sub-contractors or changing circumstances. As concluded in the previous discussions on payment, tensions mushroom between formalisation, control and trust. The evolution from market-analogue to state-analogue affects how autonomy, solidarity and trust are expressed in PPP performance.

Autonomy is the starting point for the parties as SoPC4 defines clearly parties' roles and responsibilities. In PF2, public authorities' powers are expressed not only within legal techniques but also economic techniques, leading to increased public control and direction of the strategic decision-making of the project.

However, solidarity in the success of PPPs/PFIs leads to interdependence between the parties and requires cooperation to implement the contract successfully at a day-to-day level and adjust it. Again, this solidarity is expressed in direct economic terms in PF2, where public authorities may lose their equity share if the project fails, on top of shouldering other financial issues. This interdependence, however, applies only to the public and private partners. Third parties are only marginally involved in ensuring that the contract is well performed; for instance, through user-satisfaction inquiries. In PF2, local interests are only represented by an observer to the board, lacking voting rights. The

---

195 Treasury, 2012, para 2.4.

196 PF2, *HoldCo/ SPV Shareholders' Agreement Consultation Draft,* 2013.

extent to which these local interests will be genuinely integrated within the decision-making process will depend on factors other than their legal protection.

Therefore how far the cooperation between the public and private partners in the PPP/PFI will achieve the original or developing public interest goals will depend on the level of trust that the parties generate towards each other throughout the contract implementation (e.g. thanks to training and good communication). Trust is needed to avoid time consuming and costly procedures. However, trust can only flourish if there is concrete evidence that parties perform their contractual commitments in a satisfactory manner. This trust is, however, the product of a constant tension between formalisation and cooperation. Formalisation provides a stable framework for assessing performance (objectives and procedures) but weakens the parties' ability to show their good will. Cooperation contributes to mutual understanding but may lead to distorted compliance.

Legal techniques and formalisation are therefore limited in the trust that they foster. Two other elements, narratives and communities, may contribute to it, however. These lead to tailored solutions to common problems and coordination of public and private interests in the PPP regulatory space. The next section examines them to highlight how far the move from competition to cooperation is a practical challenge.

COMMUNITIES AND SHARED NARRATIVES

In the PPP regulatory space, three main techniques are used to structure the commitments and interests of public and private partners: public procurement, the relational nexus and contract. In each case, the legal aspects of these techniques are primarily linked to competition and the opposition of interests. In a subsequent move, however, cooperation is slowly integrated within the legal techniques; for instance through the competitive dialogue. This moves away from legal techniques towards managerial techniques seeking to coordinate the interests of public and private actors. Behavioural changes are then necessary. These managerial techniques are also incrementally formalised and generate new occasions for control. Such a process may foster trust in settling parties' expectations. However, it may also stifle trust. This section underlines the point that PPPs/PFIs are also connected to narratives, which promote trust on grounds other than formalisation.

Three narratives are pinpointed here: complexity, innovation and partnering. Each is connected to one of the three main techniques of

PPPs/PFIs: complexity with the competitive dialogue, innovation with the relational nexus and partnering with cooperation outside contracts. However, these narratives are not the only alternative ways of shaping how discretion is used in PPPs/PFIs. Communities also extend trust and cooperation beyond formalisation.

The Problem: A Narrative of Complexity

As Chapter 1 detailed, PPPs/PFIs are complex because of the polycentric issues they entail.[197] This complexity is also underlined in the ways in which PPPs/PFIs are established. The Treasury has long-listed factors contributing to complex procurement, stretching from scale, duration, internal and external interfaces, technology, financial structure and market capacity to delivery risks.[198] It has even developed a complexity assessment tool in this respect.[199] This narrative of complexity justifies the reliance on non-legal techniques, especially trust.

Underlining complexity helps us to suggest ways to tackle it.[200] Next to institutionalised and external expertise, formalisation and law help to reduce complexity, to instil trust that suggests solutions have been tested successfully or result from past experiences. Public procurement has been adapted to the specific needs of PPPs/PFIs so that, in theory, the autonomy of public authorities will not be unduly curtailed when it comes to sophisticated projects, which is necessary for the collectivity. PPPs/PFIs objectively reach a certain degree of complexity so that the formal condition of complexity opens up the competitive dialogue. Complexity is both the problem and the reference the law takes to provide a tailored solution. While one might have expected that complexity would entail a distinct regime limited to the circumstances triggering complexity, the Treasury generalises the solutions to complexity as a source of inspiration for any other procurement.[201] Solutions to complex problems become the norm. Indeed, their formalisation is needed to simplify their implementation not only in complex procurement but in any procurement. Luhmann's assertion that new complexity emerges from attempting to reduce complexity seems confirmed here.[202] In

[197] See Chapter 1, pp 17–20.

[198] Treasury, 2008, 14–15.

[199] Treasury and IUK, 2013, Ch 2.

[200] Complexity is a theme developed in project management: see e.g. K Remington and J Pollack, *Tools for Complex Projects* (Gower Publishing 2007).

[201] E.g.: Treasury and IUK, 2013; Treasury, 2008, para 2.3.

[202] N Luhmann, 'Trust' in *Trust and Power* (John Wiley & Sons 1979) 57.

contrast, however, to this trend, the Cabinet Office seeks to contain complexity and to identify complex procurements with lengthy procedures (i.e. longer than 120 days).[203]

Once a project is labelled complex, a narrative offers a solution: innovation.

The Solution: A Narrative of Innovation

Given the complexity in PPPs/PFIs, contractual, financial or technical innovations are key to reaching *VfM*. Innovation in PPPs[204] can be related to new outcomes (e.g. technologies used in waste PFIs), new legal or delivery processes (e.g. the competitive dialogue as first introduced in 2004), new ways to deliver public services or infrastructure (e.g. increased use of concessions), or new organisational structures in the relationships between public and private actors (e.g. PF2). The Treasury's documents repeatedly underline the importance of innovation to delivering *VfM* in long-term infrastructure.[205] Innovation is linked to trust, as trust allows parties to foster expectations of cooperation in contractual performance. Useful information and suggestions for innovation are then shared between the parties.[206] PPPs/PFIs can be seen as a laboratory where innovation is experimented with and then disseminated into other public services. The evolution of the win-win logic into cooperation illustrates this best.

In detailing the origins of English PFIs, Chapter 2 explained that innovation was, at the outset, mostly conveyed under the motto of 'win-win'.[207] PFIs would trigger contractual innovation, breaking the history of antagonism between public and private entities due to CCT or previous poor procurement management. PFIs would bring benefits to both parties: public authorities would gain projects otherwise not developed, and contractors would have new markets and opportunities for

---

[203] See above this chapter, pp 111–14.

[204] For an overview of innovation in public management: C Pollitt, 'Innovation in the Public Sector: An Introductory Overview' in V Bekkers, J Edelenbos and B Steijn (eds) *Innovation in the Public Sector – Linking Capacity to Leadership* (Palgrave 2011) 35.

[205] Treasury, 2012, 1, 6, table 1.A; Treasury, 2008, box 1.3. For the link between innovation and financial risks regarding financing infrastructure, see Treasury, 2010, para 4.11.

[206] Collins, 1999, 112.

[207] See Chapter 2, pp 62–7.

profits.[208] Innovation and creative skills have been mentioned repeatedly as important elements for bringing these mutual benefits.[209] Recent legal scholarship still underlines that:

> [t]he idea is that the government decides between competing objectives, defines the standards required and safeguards the wider public interest. The private sector brings the discipline of the market place, a focus on customer requirements, management expertise and innovation.[210]

However, this win-win idea has been put in the background of recent official policy guidelines.[211] Indeed, win-win logic did not secure the immediate success of PPPs/PFIs. One of the main issues related to the prospects that a win-win situation would be achieved was that it could be at the expense of staff as there were less favourable working conditions in the private sector. This led to remedial actions such as the extension of TUPE protection to staff transferred under PPPs/PFIs,[212] diffusing at least some personal distrust of PPPs/PFIs. Also, secondments between public and private partners have been promoted to overcome potential culture clashes and distrust.[213] Furthermore, the importance of breaking away from adverse relationships between the public and private sectors has been emphasised. These behavioural changes are promoted in PPPs and other forms of procurement.[214] This indicates the close connections between levels of cooperation, between individuals and between organisations.

Shifting away from the opposition to the win-win approach, this focus on cooperation between staff members has been generalised to all PPP partners. Cooperation between staff fosters trust. Conditions are then set for steering PPPs/PFIs through changing contexts thanks to joint working

---

208 Treasury, 1993, 6.

209 Treasury, 2012, 6; Treasury, 2000, para 10-12; Treasury, 1997, Foreword; Treasury, 1995, Foreword.

210 Craig, 2012, 120 (footnotes omitted).

211 Neither the 2003, the 2006, the 2008 nor the 2012 Treasury policy documents, explicitly mention 'win-win' logic as a key feature for PPPs. However, the idea is still floating (e.g.: Treasury, 2012, 6; Treasury, 2008, 3; Treasury, 2006, Ch 7; Treasury, 2003, 1).

212 Treasury, 2000, 38–9.

213 PAC, *The Operational Performance of PFI Prisons* (904 HC 2002–03) recommendation 2.

214 Treasury and IUK, 2013, 4.

and cooperation: the so-called 'partnership ethos'.[215] We turn to this narrative of partnering as a means of reaching innovation.

The Means: A Narrative of Partnering

Cooperation has been a key word used to explain the issues arising in PPPs/PFIs, such as managing risks. In terms of performance, cooperation and formalisation are interrelated in technical terms. For instance, the above discussions on payment during PPP performance have underlined how cooperation has been required to monitor performance and has relied increasingly on formalisation. Alignment between public and private interests or objectives replaces the traditional opposition between them.[216] Here, the narrative of partnering connects the need for innovation and a means of achieving it by building on cooperation and more especially on the supply chain and its techniques. It goes beyond the supply chain, however, to encompass a 'whole business approach'.[217] This non-legal narrative is paramount as it may be the feature which encapsulates the distinctiveness of PPPs/PFIs in coordinating public and private interests in a tailored way.

Legal scholarship often refers to joint working or partnering or partnership arrangements[218] as key features of PPPs/PFIs. During the 1990s, the Latham[219] and Egan[220] reports promoted partnering agreements in construction contracts. Such agreements emphasise developing a 'shared vision'[221] for a project. Partnering has been presented as a 'paradigm shift' regarding supply chain management[222] towards more equality across the supply chain participants. Present in PFIs since 1999, it was reiterated[223] and even neatly developed in the Building Schools for

---

[215] Treasury, 2008, 33; NAO, *Allocation and Management of Risk in Ministry of Defence PFI Projects*, 2008, 40.

[216] Treasury, 2012, 7.

[217] NAO, *National Savings and Investments' Deal with Siemens Business Services, Four Years On*, 2003, recommendation 1.

[218] Vincent-Jones, 2006, 175; Harlow and Rawlings, 2009, 413.

[219] Sir Latham, *Constructing the Team*, 1994.

[220] Sir Egan, *Rethinking Construction*, 1998 going as far as advising against contractual agreements. M Hirst, 'Shared Risk and Reward' (2009) Cons Law 20.

[221] Treasury, 2006, para 5.49.

[222] N Fisher and R Morledge, 'Supply Chain Management', in J Kelly and others (eds), *Best Value in Construction* (Wiley-Blackwell 2002) 219.

[223] OGC, *The Integrated Project Team – Teamworking and Partnering, Achieving Excellence in Construction Procurement Guide*, 2005; OGC, *Best*

the Future (BsF) programme's 'strategic partnering agreement'.[224] The absence of legal bindingness is underlined on a recurring basis.[225] Despite the absence of any legal rights, this kind of agreement 'fulfils a communicative purpose about the mutual rights and duties for the parties' and draws attention to the 'special concerns' the parties may have.[226] In terms of PPP-related mechanisms, the 'partnering ethos' is rendered similarly as:

> [it] describes the behaviours and techniques aimed at promoting effective communication between local government and its partners to achieve openness and trust, better mutual understanding, earlier identification of problem areas in projects, and increased value for money in complex procurement projects.[227]

However, the relationships need to balance partnership and 'a proper system of rewards and penalties for good and bad performance, and satisfactory procedures for dealing with change.'[228] In short, partnering needs both flexibility and bindingness, both legal or contractual underpinning and trust.[229] Partnering is put forward as a principle enabling autonomy to be directed softly in the direction of a commonly developed solidarity thanks to the trust partnering can foster. However, surveys on the practical implementation of partnering agreements show reluctance to use them.[230] Partnering is used only in a very limited number of cases,[231]

Practice, Forming Partnering Relationships with the Private Sector in an Uncertain World, 2004; *SoPC4*, para 13.4.4.11.

[224] On BsF and its changes, see Chapter 5, pp 213–22.

[225] OGC, *The Integrated Project Team – Teamworking and Partnering, Achieving Excellence in Construction Procurement Guide*, 2005, 6.

[226] Goetz and Scott (n 118 above) 1117.

[227] ODPM, *Strategic Partnering Taskforce – Final report*, 2004, Annexes to Final Report, 76. Additionally, NAO, *Managing the Relationship*, 2001, recommendation 5.

[228] PAC, *Delivering Better Value for Money from the Private Finance Initiative* (764 HC 2002–03) recommendation 4.

[229] The NAO also underlines the connection between 'trust-based relationships and effective collaboration […] but also building in contractual protections.' (NAO, *The Radiocommunications Agency's Joint Venture with CMG*, 2000, recommendation 4.)

[230] J Mason, 'The Views and Experiences of Specialist Contractors on Partnering in the United Kingdom' (2009) 25 Const LJ 206.

[231] E.g. (outside PFIs): UK-Nottingham: Construction work 2013/S 094-159978, *Contract notice*, OJ/S S94, 16/05/2013, 159978-2013-EN (available at http://ted.europa.eu/udl?uri=TED:NOTICE:159978-2013:TEXT:EN:HTML).

even though more than ten years of repeated efforts by official[232] and professional[233] bodies have highlighted its benefits.

This relationship between bindingness and flexibility is also present in PF2. This new structure of public–private relationships based on public shareholding is designed to lead to a greater alignment of interests and objectives between public and private actors. This leads to 'ensuring a collaborative approach by both the private and public sector to improving project performance and managing risk' and creating 'a more genuine partnership', 'allowing for a better understanding of perspectives between the public and private sectors'.[234] Presented as a 'true' long-term partnership, PF2 also plays on the ambiguity between the legal and non-legal aspects of partnership and partnering. PF2 indeed relies on shareholders' agreements but this does not mean that the relationships between the public and private actors will necessarily be more cooperative, especially as one of the main aims of the government is to gain increased access to commercial information held by its private counterparts. Maybe for this reason, PF2 emphasises that the government's PF2 directors will have the 'appropriate professional skills' to take commercial decisions, thus shifting trust away from techniques to personal managerial skills.[235]

In a nutshell, partnering is frequently emphasised as providing an appropriate ethos for structuring public and private commitments. As a non-legally binding solution, partnering could provide solutions to weaknesses in contract law, especially for changing circumstances, resolving issues or needs for renegotiation. However, partnering is not used on any large scale. There is a discrepancy between the need to move out of contract law and the need to use non-legal techniques and narratives to address gaps in contract law. Indeed, the uncertain legal treatment of partnering backfires. When things go wrong, legal techniques are needed. This monograph underlines, however, that between the contractual techniques for structuring parties' relationships and the contractual techniques for resolving disputes, there is a space for non-legal techniques and narratives. This space enables parties to organise their commitments and interests, building trust in each other and making contracts necessary only as a last resort. Communities may also contribute to trust and cooperation among parties.

---

232 E.g.: Treasury and IUK, 2013, para 1.15; Business and Enterprise Committee, *Construction Matters* (127-I HC 2007–08) para 132.

233 Construction Industry Council, *A Guide to Partnering Workshops*, 2005 and *A Guide to Project Team Partnering*, 2nd edn, 2002.

234 Treasury, 2012, 29.

235 *PF2* (draft), para 5.2.1.

Communities: Embedding Generalised Cooperation?

We have seen that three narratives are used in PPPs/PFIs: complexity, innovation and partnering. PPPs/PFIs are also used to disseminate these narratives across public and private sectors for other types of projects. In this sense, a 'PPP community' develops a recognisable identity and shared meanings articulated around complexity/innovation/partnering. It builds on legal techniques and institutions, such as the Office of Government Commerce (OGC), Partnerships UK (PUK) and Infrastructure UK (IUK),[236] and on professional organisations[237] and experts.[238] This section queries the extent to which their cumulative effects may embed cooperation across PPPs/PFIs and their partners in the PPP regulatory space.

The presence of communities and institutions paints a hybrid picture of the regulatory space surrounding PPPs/PFIs.[239] The relational distance between them may be understood with the help of the network literature. Indeed, networks fit the graphic representation of PPPs/PFIs as designed, for instance, in NAO reports.[240] Thinking in terms of networks may provide insights into the tensions between public and private interests and between cooperation and competition. Although the network literature does not discuss PPPs/PFIs expressly, it highlights the importance of generalised reciprocity between network actors as a justification for developing a balance between flexibility and the stabilisation of expectations arising from networks.[241] Accordingly, part of the distinctiveness of networks lies in trust and confidence, which sets them apart from contractual mechanisms. Yet these communities and institutions do not necessarily coordinate public and private interests. They may coexist next to each other or be in tension.

Many communities may be distinguished over the course of the development and implementation of a PPP/PFI. Firstly, a procurement

---

236 E.g.: Treasury and IUK, 2013, Box 1.A and 24 on the role of construction and consultancy industry.

237 E.g.: CBI, *Building Strong Foundations: Financing UK Infrastructure*, 2011.

238 E.g.: PwC, *Is PFI Working? Buying Excellent, Settling for Average*, 2011.

239 Compare Vincent-Jones, 2006, 298–309.

240 E.g.: NAO, *M25 Private Finance Contract,* 2010, fig 1; NAO, *PFI in Housing*, 2010, fig 2.

241 G Teubner, *Networks as Connected Contracts* (H Collins (ed), Hart 2011) 74, 161, 165, 220.

community between purchasing departments and their main suppliers[242] can be traced, underlining the interdependence of public and private actors. This procurement community may be strengthened in PPPs/PFIs because often there are only a limited number of potential candidates for a project. High investments and specific technologies mean that only large firms – to the factual exclusion of SMEs – are likely to be able to participate. Secondly, PPPs/PFIs entail large amounts of idiosyncratic assets and sunk investments. Payment mechanisms have been developed into sophisticated financial tools which aim to isolate the risks borne by the PPPs/PFIs from other projects. In this way, PPPs/PFIs can be seen as an autonomously operating community, governed by the contracts mapping the risks and setting the framework for assessing *VfM* in future decisions. Finally, the supply chain combined with the possible use of partnering may also develop into a community focused on the delivery of a PPP/PFI project. These communities isolate PPPs/PFIs from other projects but remain silent on the possible solidarity or trust that parties develop.

Beyond PPPs/PFIs as a community comprising only two entities, namely a public authority and a contractor, further communities are developed with the support of institutions. For instance, the government seeks to structure industry involvement in infrastructure through industry expert groups.[243] Public authorities may actively seek to develop a sector so that more candidates are available or to attract new private finance.[244] The law may also shape these communities. A legal novelty such as the remedies directive may modify the overall consensual approach to accepting the public authority's choice in public procurement.[245] Legal techniques such as the competitive dialogue may make issues arise. Legal communities are then officially called on to advise on possible interpretations.[246] Legal techniques such as public shareholding in PF2 may bring about a distinct public–private entity. Yet more than legal techniques is required to achieve the proclaimed aim of aligning public and private

242 C Turpin, *Government Procurement and Contracts* (Longman 1989) 258–9.

243 Treasury and IUK, *Infrastructure Cost Review – Implementation Plan,* 2011, 10.

244 For instance in PF2.

245 P Braun, 'Strict Compliance versus Commercial Reality: The Practical Application of EC Public Procurement Law to the UK's Private Finance Initiative' (2003) 9 ELJ 575.

246 Treasury, *Review of Competitive Dialogue*, 2010, box 3.A.

objectives in the PPP regulatory space. Commercial skills and professional effective management are necessary as well.

This short overview of communities involved in the relationships between PPP/PFI partners highlights their limits. Each of these communities is strongly anchored in an economic rationality. They seek to develop market opportunities in, for instance, developing the narrative of innovation. They highlight the complexity of procurement and the legal certainty needed for market actors to bid. They seek to give confidence to institutional investors to invest in PPPs/PFIs and they foster a narrative of partnering to move beyond a 'behavioural legacy' and 'lack of trust' throughout the supply chain[247] etc. Although these narratives of complexity, innovation and partnering might also be applied to the concrete social and human needs that PPPs/PFIs seek to address for the sake of common welfare, these communities leave PPP/PFI users and third parties aside completely.

FORMALISATION, COOPERATION AND PROTECTION

This chapter analysed the coordination of the public and private interests in PPPs/PFIs and how the relationship between PPP/PFI partners has been transformed from market-analogue to state-analogue, from competition to ongoing control. At first, discretion was supposed to match market logics of self-interest, competition and economic exchange. However, discretion had to be formalised and choices pre-selected in order to simplify the procurement and management of the projects. This led to an increased need for cooperation between PPP/PFI partners. Non-legally binding documents have quickly arisen. Therefore both more formalisation and new informality contribute to coordinating public and private interests in the PPP regulatory space.

This tension between formalisation and cooperation is present in the elaboration, signing and performance of PPPs/PFIs. Regarding the elaboration of PPPs/PFIs, the competitive dialogue formalised previous practice. Yet, it triggered legal uncertainty in relation to complexity and legal gaps regarding the modalities of the formalisation of the competitive dialogue. Informal guidance and policy notes were then elaborated to reduce the costs and time needed to develop PPPs/PFIs. However, the practical implementation of these changes again requires more than the

---

247 Treasury and IUK, 2013, para 1.15.

formalisation of decision making. Behavioural changes and improved skills in contracting authorities are also needed.

In the relational nexus, two market techniques, *VfM* and risk allocation, have been formalised. Yet they keep a subjective dimension. *VfM* is continually revisited and fine-tuned. Risks are constantly shifted and re-allocated between public and private parties. While *VfM* and risk allocation are the linchpins of PPPs/PFIs, their modalities appear to be highly unstable and elusive.

In PPP/PFI performance, the opposition of self-interest that underpins the contractual commitments relies on the development of standardised solutions and on increasing fine-tuning to match practical needs. This constant search for improved control from public authorities over the concrete implementation of PPPs/PFIs leads to complex and rigid solutions (e.g. in payment mechanisms and change protocols), yet cooperation is still required to secure efficient solutions (e.g. in the interface protocols).

Overall, therefore, the coordination of public and private interests in long-term relationships such as PPPs/PFIs requires discretion in such a way that parties may preserve their relationships and seek to obtain the benefits that they were expecting from the PPPs/PFIs in terms of either economic return or the provision of the common good. However, a market-analogue model of PPPs/PFIs based on competition requires formalisation to give direction to how discretion may be used, to give stability and to protect parties' expectations and interests. Increased control follows, weakening flexibility and adaptability to changing circumstances. Alternatives to formalisation and control may be sought through trusting the cooperative mindset of the other parties to fill in gaps in the legal techniques. Developing shared narratives such as complexity, innovation and partnering also allows competition to transform into cooperation. Yet the communities highlighted in this chapter give these narratives purely economic logics benefitting only the public and private partners directly involved in PPPs/PFIs, to the omission of users or other third parties.

In this chapter, the law was the starting point. Discretion was strongly focused on two well-delineated entities for a rather well-defined project. In Chapter 4, we turn to the coordination between third parties' interests and PPPs/PFIs in PPP regulatory space, where formalisation of the relationships between individuals and PPPs is far less prominent. Following the hypothesis suggested in Chapter 2,[248] alternative techniques or

---

[248] See Chapter 2, pp 96–9.

narratives would structure these relationships on the basis of a community bringing individuals and PPPs close to each other. However, the law is still there, although more as an extreme endpoint. Protection of these third parties' interests also leads to tensions between formalisation and informality, and between law and community. Chapter 5 elaborates on these.

4. Lacking relationships with third parties

INTRODUCTION

As a long-term method of cooperation between public and private actors, public–private partnerships/Private Finance Initiatives (PPPs/PFIs) deliver infrastructures or services to the public at large (e.g. London Underground (LU)), to specific categories of users (e.g. pupils in BsF,[1] patients in LIFT[2]), or to a public authority (e.g. office accommodation such as PRIME[3] and STEPS[4]). Public authorities have to decide which schools will be refurbished first when PFIs are delivered in waves, such as in the BsF programme. They also have to decide which PFI hospital will go ahead for which catchment area. PPPs/PFIs are thus means of allocating resources among various categories of individuals. Public authorities exercise their discretion as a means of ensuring coordination and balance between competing interests for scarce resources over time. Control over how such discretion is exercised is needed. Parents may want to be involved in the educational projects and refurbishment plans for the schools attended by their children. They may want to understand how the private contractor's contractual performance matches the contractual agreements or how the theatre and sport facilities or computers can be best used and adapted to the changing needs of education and the career prospects of their children. They may thus want to access contractual and financial information or be consulted to express their satisfaction or concerns with the education provided by the school and its PFI. This chapter maps the roles that the law plays in organising the relationships between PPPs/PFIs and third parties and more especially in providing third parties with ways to control how public authorities use their discretion in PPPs/PFIs through regulation or accountability techniques.

---

1 Building Schools for the Future programme.
2 Local Improvement Finance Trust.
3 Private Sector Resource Initiative for the Management of the Estate.
4 Strategic Transfer of the Estate to the Private Sector.

This chapter suggests that the legal techniques used to organise the relationships between PPPs/PFIs and third parties rely on a state-analogue model where accountability is key to controlling whether public authorities exercise their discretion in the public interest. There is indeed, as a rule, no contractual relationship between PPPs/PFIs and users. However, a range of other elements borrowed from market logics (such as value for money (*VfM*), efficiency, competition, self-interest etc.) have been integrated in the legal techniques regulating PPPs/PFIs. This leads to a highly hybrid design for the regulation and accountability of PPPs/PFIs where *VfM* becomes the most prominent standard for assessing whether public authorities pursue the common good when they develop and implement PPPs/PFIs. In short, the efficient spending of public money is the main factor used to assess the infrastructures and services provided through PPPs/PFIs. Other factors, such as adequate or sustained fulfilment of social and human needs, are not captured by this *VfM* standard. Concerns related to maintaining continuing access to education, health or mobility without undue complexity or despite financial distress (such as London Underground (Public-Private Partnerships) (LU PPP) or PFI hospitals) fall outside the rationality of *VfM*. The techniques of control that the law provides to third parties therefore reduce the standards against which public discretion is used in PPPs/PFIs and strongly limit the actual legal relationships between PPPs/PFIs and third parties.

This lack of an integrative relationship between PPPs/PFIs and third parties may also result in disconnecting public authorities from individuals' needs and interests, although the former are supposed to serve the latter through PPPs/PFIs. To try to address this issue and suggest ways to organise the relationships between PPPs/PFIs and third parties, means such as narratives developed by communities could be relied on. Communities develop narratives, particularly to describe relationships of trust. These narratives would address the moral distance between individuals and the PPP system and create 'social bonds of integration, order, communication, and interaction'[5] between PPPs/PFIs and third parties. Such an alternative form of regulation stumbles, however, over the weakness and diffuseness of the potential communities. Taken together, these communities only convey ambiguous and contested narratives that fail to provide an integrative framework for supporting third parties and

[5] R Cotterrell, *Law's Community – Legal Theory in Sociological Perspective* (Clarendon Press 1995) 305.

PPP/PFI partners, leading not to shared but to disputed and partial understandings of projects, interests or values.

This chapter starts by explaining the standard position of users and third parties in PPPs/PFIs and the contribution of accountability and regulation to controlling how the public discretion used in PPPs/PFIs pursues the common good. It then turns to three types of control over public discretion. The first type is concerned with the control that public bodies such as Parliament or the central government exercise over PPPs/PFIs through either political accountability or regulation. Both of these are based on the *VfM* standard. The second type of control is judicial: courts review mostly procedural issues related to the use of public discretion and have, for instance, reviewed the termination of PFI funding in the case of BsF. The third type of control is more diffused across a multitude of regulatory techniques and extended accountability supporting user involvement in the design or performance of PPPs/PFIs. The analysis of these three types of control shows that the law plays a marginal role in protecting individuals' interests in PPPs/PFIs and that their interests are barely coordinated through legal techniques in the PPP regulatory space, therefore leaving *VfM* as the main standard for assessing PPPs/PFIs overall. Finally, this chapter turns to non-legal techniques, namely narratives and communities, to state that these equally fail to coordinate individuals' interests and the common good in PPPs/PFIs more comprehensively; they also fail to integrate the social dimensions that PPPs/PFIs involve in seeking to provide for users' and third parties' needs, beyond spending taxpayers' money.

FRAMING CONTROL OVER PPPs/PFIs

As PPPs/PFIs are used for allocating rights and resources within society, they require the coordination of the interests of a wide variety of third parties, as Chapter 1 has explored.[6] Before turning to the details of legal techniques combining state and market models in the relationships between PPPs/PFIs and third parties, this section introduces the issues related to users' and third parties' interests, starting with their lack of contractual rights under PPP/PFI contracts as a rule. Alternatives in the form of regulation and accountability techniques are thus required to control how public authorities exercise their discretion in coordinating the interests involved in the PPP regulatory space.

---

6 See Chapter 1, pp 17–20.

No Contract: Looking for Alternative Relationships with Users and Third Parties

Individuals' needs and interests regarding the infrastructure or service provided with the PPPs/PFIs may in theory be integrated in PPP/PFI contracts or regulated by contract law. This would match the contractual dynamic of autonomy and empowerment of citizens.[7] However, users do not enjoy directly enforceable rights in PPP/PFI contracts, even though users' interests may be taken into account indirectly.

PPPs/PFIs do not open enforceable rights at private law to individual users. Such a contractual approach would have highlighted an economic (or exchange-based) underpinning to the relationships between users and private contractors. However, there is a difference between what is theoretically possible and how PPPs/PFIs are structured, especially in the Standardisation of PFI Contracts (SoPC) Version 4 (SoPC4) and Private Finance 2 (PF2). In most cases,[8] the contractor contractually performs a service to the benefit of the public authority paying for it. PPPs/PFIs are usually no longer designed for performing frontline services.[9] There is no contract between the prisoner and the corporation operating the PFI prison, between the social tenant and the operating PFI contractor, between the LU commuter and Tube Lines. It is then difficult to construct a legal relationship between the contractor and individuals on the basis of a contract. It may be tempting to construct a contractual benefit for third parties through the contract between the public authority and the contractor. However, standard terms in SoPC4 and PF2 exclude the application of the Contracts (Rights of Third Parties) Act 1999.[10] SoPC4 and PF2 do, however, integrate users through the payment mechanism, which includes user satisfaction to a limited extent through calculating deductions for poor performance or deciding on remedial action.[11] However, no entitlement is granted to users and this constitutes only a weak translation of the true market logic, where consumer dissatisfaction is converted into financial pain for the private contractor.

Although the relationship between PPP users and PPPs/PFIs is not contractual as a rule, there are cases of PPPs/PFIs where users may be

---

[7] Davies, 2008, 233; C Donnelly, *Delegation of Governmental Power to Private Parties* (OUP 2007) 350.

[8] More generally on the absence of 'contract-like' arrangements between individuals and private contractors: Donnelly (n 7 above) 331.

[9] Harlow and Rawlings, 2009, 415.

[10] *SoPC4,* para 30.5; *PF2* (draft), para 31.2.

[11] *SoPC4,* para 7.9.

regarded as consumers on an equal footing with any market player with the option to refuse to enter into the relationship and to use the PPP/PFI (the so-called exit option). This would be the case for users paying tolls for crossing PFI bridges. Yet techniques based on private law, price and exit are not enough to regulate the relationships between users and PFIs.[12] Indeed, exit or non-use may be impossible in practice, for instance when only a bridge can be used to cross a river in a safe and speedy way. Moreover, interests other than those of the direct PPP/PFI users, such as the local economy served by the bridge, may need to be accounted for regarding the fixation of the price or the maintenance of the bridge.

If contractual relationships are absent to protect users and third parties, the law may use techniques other than contract to organise the coordination of interests in the PPP regulatory space. The first way is to consider third parties in their capacity as taxpayers, as members of the collectivity who financially contribute to the infrastructures and services provided by PPPs/PFIs. In this sense, third parties may be involved in the decision-making process pertaining to the use of PPPs/PFIs or ask for accounts of how policies are decided and then implemented.

The second way to organise this coordination of interests related to PPP users and third parties is for the law to take into consideration the vulnerability and dependency of some users, such as prisoners, patients or pupils in the implementation of PPPs/PFIs. Indeed, PPPs/PFIs perform specific functions when delivering public infrastructures and services and specific duties may be imposed on PPPs/PFIs or their partners to ensure a given level of protection for these individual users. PPPs/PFIs would then be accountable to these users and/or to public authorities (contracting authorities or regulators) for the ways in which they discharge their duties.

Finally, the law may take into consideration specific groups benefiting from PPPs/PFIs as well as contributing to their success, for instance, sports or theatre societies using BsF schools out of hours. These groups may contribute to community development and generate third-party revenues for the school and possibly neighbouring shops. In this case, the law does not offer one single framework but public participation procedures may be organised to ensure a connection between the PPP/PFI project and such third parties.

---

[12] E.g.: Welsh Affairs Committee, *The Severn Crossings Toll* (506 HC 2010–11) 7–15.

Given the above, the relationships between PPPs/PFIs and third parties may be based on public or private law or have a more procedural nature. More or less emphasis can then be put on finding formal techniques to protect third parties, for instance, from damage that they may suffer from PPP/PFI shortcomings,[13] or on developing techniques based on the consumer interest.[14] In short, gaps in accountability may be addressed through formal solutions voted on in Parliament or through procedural and informal regulation.[15]

Accountability, Regulation and Participation

Since their inception, PPPs/PFIs have drawn attention to their purposive regulation and uncertain accountability.[16] Accountability and regulation are multi-faceted concepts which partially overlap.[17] They are concerned with 'standard setting, monitoring and enforcement'[18] operations. They both seek to develop a framework to control how public authorities exercise their discretion. On the one hand, public authorities are limited in this by the accounts that they have to give regarding how they set standards, monitor and enforce them. On the other hand, legal provisions impose conditions on how public discretion is used and require public authorities to take into account certain economic, social or environmental interests.[19] Accountability developed from command and control techniques within a hierarchical state model which pursued the common good. Regulation, by contrast, has developed as a way to address market failures and then integrated a range of social, environmental, procedural or democratic values that actors need to be mindful of in their behaviour. Therefore both regulation and accountability shape how public discretion

[13] Davies, 2008, 248 ff and 257–8.

[14] Vincent-Jones, 2006, 334.

[15] Ibid 333.

[16] E.g.: M Freedland, 'Public Law and Private Finance – Placing the Private Finance Initiative in a Public Frame' [1998] PL 288.

[17] M Dowdle, 'Public Accountability: Conceptual, Historical and Epistemic Mapping' in M Dowdle (ed) *Public Accountability – Designs, Dilemmas and Experiences* (Cambridge Studies in Law and Society, CUP 2006) 1; R Mulgan, '"Accountability": An Ever-Expanding Concept?' (2000) 78 Public Administration 555; M Lodge and L Stirton, 'Accountability in the Regulatory State' in R Baldwin, M Cave and M Lodge (eds) *The Oxford Handbook of Regulation* (OUP 2010) 349.

[18] A Davies, *A Public Law Analysis of Government by Contract* (OUP 2001) 91 ff; Vincent-Jones, 2006, 69.

[19] Prosser, 2010, Ch 1.

is controlled in terms of conditions and procedures as well as the values that public discretion needs to take into account.

Accountability and regulation partially overlap in seeking to control public discretion. Yet they also rely on trust: trust in those holding to account or regulating as well as trust in the information processed in the accountability and regulation techniques.[20] To secure this, accountability and regulation often require supplementation with participatory procedures that involve users and third parties more systematically in the regulatory and accountability processes.

Next to detecting abuses of discretion, accountability mechanisms offer a series of benefits: they open up a sphere of discussion, of learning, of feedback and possible reflective adjustments to the standards set or the accountability process itself. In having a pedagogic effect, accountability also indirectly makes public decisions understandable and accessible to parties outside the accountability process. These may then be in a position to comment on and contribute to the decision-making process. Potentially, accountability thus provides a legitimating effect for the decisions taken and the decisions to follow.[21] It strengthens trust in public processes.

Yet accountability possesses some limits. For instance, accountability may only address extreme circumstances of crisis or illegality. It only provides particular solutions to narrowly delineated administrative issues, while the overall administrative machinery may present systemic dysfunctions. Furthermore, it reflects on past situations, making thus a more systematic framework for directing upcoming public decisions necessary.[22]

Regulation may then be used to address these limits of accountability. Vincent-Jones, for instance, suggests moving from the narrow accountability under public law towards an extended accountability and the 'wider context of regulation'.[23] This includes upwards accountability (to parliaments and courts), horizontal accountability (to parallel institutions and grievance handlers) and downwards accountability (towards lower level institutions, such as consumers or markets).[24] Yet regulation stretches beyond pure control, being also policy-driven and purposive. It

20 Davies (n 18 above) 76.

21 Ibid 79–80.

22 P Cane, *Administrative Law* (5th edn, Oxford 2011) 406–8.

23 Vincent-Jones, 2006, 75.

24 P Vincent-Jones, 'Book Review: Regulating Government by Contract – Towards a Public Law Framework' (2002) 65 MLR 615; C Scott, 'Accountability in the Regulatory State' (2000) 27 JLS 38.

extends beyond the law to encompass a range of tools such as information, persuasion and financing. In that sense, PPPs/PFIs have been actively promoted as a tool for changing the provision of public services[25] and the behaviours of individuals and socio-economic actors, be they private constructors, doctors establishing their surgeries or local authorities investing in waste PFIs etc. In order for this regulatory system to fill the accountability vacuum, citizens are crucial actors. They should participate in the organisation and delivery of public services so that issues arising in public services can be pragmatically resolved. Regulation should indeed improve the responsiveness of public authorities. For instance, consultation or involvement exercises in schools with parents and pupils may bring issues requiring training or better information to the attention of the private contractors. These issues might include room cleaning, improvements to the food or lack of awareness among teachers about the possibilities of lighting or computer systems, requiring training or better information. Normally, once these problems have been flagged up, processes should ensure that they are addressed quickly.

Presented in these forms, accountability and regulation therefore both imply interactions with users and information exchanges with them. They both strengthen trust and both lead to an understanding that the relational distance between public authorities[26] and third parties relies on procedural participation techniques. Participation helps to call discretion-holders to account and informs them about the factual situations they have to address, so that they take more responsive decisions.[27]

Discretion in PPPs/PFIs is embedded within these accountability and regulatory techniques. Three elements are taken forward to map how control over discretion is concretely exercised in PPPs/PFIs. The first is the way in which the spending of taxpayers' money is controlled through political accountability and regulation. Secondly, is the way in which courts formally protect individuals' interests. Thirdly, is the extent to which alternative techniques have been developed to organise how individuals can voice their needs and expectations of PPPs/PFIs.

---

[25] Freedland (n 16 above) 297 ff.

[26] R Baldwin, M Cave and M Lodge, *Understanding Regulation: Theory, Strategy and Practice* (OUP 2011) 352.

[27] T Prosser, *Nationalised Industries and Public Control – Legal, Constitutional and Political Issues* (Blackwell 1986) 112 and Chs 8 and 9, 151 ff.

CONTROL OVER SPENDING TAXPAYERS' MONEY: POLITICAL DISCONNECTION

Public discretion in PPPs/PFIs is first and foremost limited through accountability and regulatory techniques assessing whether taxpayers' money is being spent according to the *VfM* standard. Indeed, PPPs/PFIs have the potential to leverage large investments and strategic planning in delivering specific policy goals. They have brought market logic into spending on public infrastructures with their features of risk allocation and *VfM*. The extensive use of taxpayers' money in order to provide public infrastructures and services triggers issues of political accountability. This section shows how *VfM* became the overriding standard for making PPPs/PFIs accountable and controlling public discretion in PPPs/PFIs, leading to the marginalisation of other considerations of public interests.[28]

Accountability through Multi-centred Conversations

As a starting point, the public law framework of accountability shapes scrutiny of how the public interest is pursued. Parliament has a range of techniques available to call the departments to account for their decisions related to PPP/PFI policies, programmes and projects. For instance, it does so in authorising, by statute, the secretary of state to enter into PPPs/PFIs. It also does so through oral questions, written questions or adjournment debates.[29] These techniques, however, can be either too specific or too general, which limits their capacity to control or influence departmental action related to PPPs/PFIs. However, PPPs/PFIs have benefited from sustained attention from Parliament, in the form of more or less interdependent circles of conversations involving the same key players: Parliament, the Executive and audit bodies. While expertise and specialisation trigger disconnection between the different conversations going on in parallel, *VfM* is the unifying element across these mechanisms.

PPPs/PFIs have given rise to a large number of interactions between the National Audit Office (NAO), the Public Accounts Committee (House of Commons) (PAC) and the Treasury, with different departments involved depending on the specific case. The NAO built a strategy to

---

[28] I am grateful to Nikiforos Meletiadis for our discussions on the relationships between accountability and audit in PPPs/PFIs.

[29] HC Deb 23 June 2011, vol 530, cols 143–94.

investigate PPPs/PFIs[30] and reports on the savings its work on PPPs/PFIs has helped to achieve.[31] By June 2013, the NAO had issued 84 *VfM* reports on PPPs/PFIs;[32] most of them debated in the PAC. Most PAC's reports regarding PPPs/PFIs are conversely based on the NAO *VfM* reports.[33] The Comptroller and Auditor General and NAO staff are in attendance when the PAC hears witnesses related to NAO's investigations and intervene in the examination of witnesses to clarify issues.[34] Finally, the Treasury responds to PAC's recommendations, working in cooperation with the department investigated.[35]

Alongside the PAC's reports regarding PPPs/PFIs directed at the core of the Treasury,[36] NAO's reports also affect Treasury's policy as the Treasury builds on NAO's findings in its official guidelines.[37] The key standard used throughout these conversations to assess PPPs/PFIs is *VfM,* which has thus been developed and interpreted through this conversation between the Treasury, the PAC and NAO. The merits of the policies, programmes or projects fall outside the NAO's remit.[38] However, these routinised conversations intersect with other conversations, held partly among other actors, and have influenced the standards used in them. The LU case and the 2009 Lords' Inquiry illustrate this expansion of *VfM* throughout the actors involved in political accountability.

The first illustration of parallel conversations relates to the reviewing of individual PPP/PFI projects such as the LU. The NAO and PAC had

---

30 NAO, *Lords,* 2009, para 1.10 ff.

31 In the NAO's analysis of *VfM* and the savings the NAO activity generates, a specific heading relates to the gains from scrutiny on PFIs (e.g.: NAO, *Annual Report*, 2009, 108).

32 NAO, *Lords*, 2009, Foreword numbered them to 72. By June 2013, twelve further reports had been issued.

33 PAC, *150 Years of the Committee of Public Account Holding Government to Account* (HC 2007) 23.

34 E.g.: PAC, *Department of Health: The Franchising of Hinchingbrooke Health Care Trust and Peterborough and Stamford Hospitals NHS Foundation Trust* (789 HC 2012–13) especially Q202–203 (C&G and NAO director); PAC, *Financing PFI Projects in the Credit Crisis and the Treasury's Response* (553 HC 2010–11) Q110.

35 For a discussion of the partnership between the Treasury and the NAO, A Page and T Daintith, *The Executive in the Constitution – Structure, Autonomy and Internal Control* (OUP 1999) 195 ff.

36 Treasury, *Annual Report and Accounts 2008–09*, 2009, 141.

37 E.g.: Treasury 2012, box 1.B; box 1.C; box 1.D; box 4.A; Treasury, 2008, box 1.1; para 2.7; para 3.17; para 4.1; box 4.2; box 5.3.

38 National Audit Act 1983, s 6(2).

investigated the *VfM* of LU in the early stages.[39] When Metronet failed, three further parliamentary reports were issued: two by the transport committee in 2008 and 2010 and one by the PAC in 2010. They all sought to analyse how Metronet failed to deliver *VfM* in the modernisation of the LU. However, they emphasised different issues with the LU. In its first report, the transport committee focused on the reasons behind Metronet's failure, mainly identified as the tied supply chain used by Metronet.[40] Although the term '*VfM*' was only used a few times, the main line of investigation related to its various aspects, such as risk transfer, the efficiency or economic performance of Metronet and the costs for the public purse. The report thus recommended an extension of the PPP Arbiter's powers. It also managed to squeeze in a chapter on staff and passenger safety as an add-on.

The further two reports built on this previous report. In 2010, the transport committee drew on Metronet's failure in terms of the relationships between Tube Lines and Transport for London (TfL) and on the performance of the former Metronet lines, now run by the publicly-owned London Underground Ltd. The report unequivocally concluded that the LU PPP was not delivering *VfM* and that London Underground Ltd was also failing in this respect.[41] The 2010 PAC's report also looked at the lessons to be learnt from Metronet's failure in terms of the relationships between Tube Lines and TfL and highlighted the importance of granting more powers to the PPP Arbiter. Yet it took a far more critical stance over the Department of Transport's handling of the situation. Indeed, 'the responsibility for safeguarding taxpayers' interests rested firmly with the Department'.[42] It was considered 'naïve' to expect the lenders to perform their tasks due to the financial safeguard that the Department had granted to these lenders.[43]

This case illustrates how the two parliamentary committees build on each others work, with *VfM* being their common focus. All in all these reports shed a different light on *VfM* and the financial burden for the

---

[39] PAC, *London Underground Public Private Partnerships* (446 HC 2004–05); NAO, *London Underground – Successfully?*, 2004; NAO, *London Underground – Good Deals?*, 2004; NAO, *London Underground*, 2000.

[40] Transport Committee, *The London Underground and the Public–Private Partnership Agreements* (45 HC 2007–08).

[41] Transport Committee, *Update on the London Underground and the Public–Private (PPP) Partnership Agreements* (100 HC 2009–10) para 56–7.

[42] PAC, *Department for Transport: The Failure of Metronet* (390 HC 2009–10) conclusion 2.

[43] Idem conclusion 5.

taxpayers. Only occasionally have other concerns, such as safety, been mentioned by the transport committee.

The second illustration of parallel conversations brings us to the inquiry into PPPs/PFIs as a matter of policy by the House of Lords in 2009.[44] Different bodies made submissions and were heard: financial experts, academics, PPP expert bodies, departments involved in PFIs, non-profit organisations, professional bodies and the NAO. Individual submissions on behalf of civil society groups did not lead to hearings. Moving the place of debates regarding PPPs/PFIs from its usual PAC at the House of Commons to the House of Lords changed the roles of the participants. The NAO was called on to account for its actions so far concerning PPPs/PFIs. Its submission reached beyond the direct questions asked as it drafted a fully autonomous paper, not respecting length limits. The NAO's report brought its long-standing work into a coherent narrative of assessing the *VfM* of PPPs/PFIs.[45] Building on these submissions, the House of Lords departed from the House of Commons/Treasury/NAO conversations. Apart from relabelling PPPs/PFIs as 'private finance projects' (PFP)[46] and questioning the innovation linked to PPPs/PFIs,[47] the House of Lords also redirected how PPPs/PFIs might be used to secure *VfM* in two ways. Firstly, it recommended bundling more core services provided to users within the PPPs/PFIs.[48] Secondly, it emphasised that exceptionally complex projects may not be suitable for PPPs/PFIs.[49] This illustrates that shifting the core of the conversation altered the NAO's story line towards more reflexivity and affected the possible evolutions PPPs/PFIs faced following the 2008 financial crisis. However these changes were all recommended on the basis of *VfM* but assessed in a different way from how the conversations between House of Commons/Treasury/NAO usually do so.

These illustrations show that the classical model of political accountability has integrated a market element, *VfM,* as a benchmark for assessing PPP/PFI policies and projects. Furthermore, from being a tool for assessing PPP/PFI projects, *VfM* has become a goal of the policy developed in relation to the PPPs/PFIs. The presence of *VfM* in the

---

44 SCEA, *Private Finance Projects and Off-Balance Sheet Debt* (63 HL 2009–10).

45 NAO, *Lords*, 2009, Pt 2.

46 Ibid abstract.

47 Ibid para 180.

48 Ibid para 186.

49 Ibid para 187.

conversations supporting political accountability has also spread within the regulatory system, to which we turn in the following lines.

Regulation through *VfM* Expertise and Fragmentation across Social Values

Chapter 2 explained how English PPPs/PFIs have been developed alongside the institutionalisation of expert bodies dedicated to PPPs/PFIs (and public procurement): Partnerships UK (PUK), the Office of Government Commerce (OGC), Infrastructure UK (IUK), Local Partnerships and Departmental PFI Units.[50] Matching the idea of a 'centre' in central government,[51] the Treasury's prominence among these PPP expert bodies was clear. We also saw that the successful development of PPPs/PFIs relied on an extended community revolving around external experts, such as lawyers, public administrators, bankers, auditors etc.,[52] where secondment across actors was often used. This helped cross-fertilisation between the public and private sectors and across projects.[53] The role of experts advising the public authority in the exercise of its public interest function raises questions about the standards used to assess PPPs/PFIs.

A specific logic emanates from these expert bodies and their interrelationships. As in other regulatory bodies,[54] various tensions between social and economic logics are faced in the PPP expert bodies. However, more than other public bodies, PPP expert bodies are isolated from the needs expressed by users under any of their possible labels, such as consumers, patients, pupils etc. This process can be related to three factors. Firstly, consultation exercises carried out by PPP expert bodies to develop their policies draw submissions mainly from public authorities, advisory firms (such as legal firms and consultancies), industry actors and their representative organisations,[55] all using *VfM* as the relevant standard for assessing PPPs/PFIs, rather than other social values.

---

50 See Chapter 2, pp 70–73.

51 Page and Daintith (n 35 above) 54.

52 See Chapter 2, pp 82–4.

53 NAO, *PFI Contract for the Redevelopment of West Middlesex University Hospital,* 2002, para 2.10; NAO, *PFI: The Contract for the Defence Fixed Telecommunications System*, 2000, Pt 4.

54 T Prosser, 'The Powers and Accountability of Agencies and Regulators' in D Feldman (ed), *English Public Law* (2nd edn, OUP 2009) 241 para 5-68.

55 E.g.: Treasury 2012, App A; OGC, *Consultation Document 2nd Consultation on Implementing the New Remedies Directive (Includes Draft Regulations)*, 2009, para 18.

Secondly, *VfM* has slowly become the main focus for PPP expert bodies. When suggesting the creation of the OGC, the Gershon Review did not mention *VfM* among the OGC's responsibilities.[56] *VfM* then permeated into all OGC key goals.[57] PPP/PFI negotiation follows a mandatory formal assessment through the Gateway Process developed by the OGC and now taken over by the Major Projects Authority (MPA) at the Efficiency and Reform Group (ERG).[58] The process aims to assess *VfM* in PPPs/PFIs across their whole development, from the early stages of project development towards an ongoing assessment of a project's performance during its lifetime.[59] The lack of a counterbalancing goal may be linked to the absence of a statutory basis for the OGC and the MPA[60] and the very wide statutory mandate that the PUK had.[61] These bodies are left to set their own goals and they spread them. Other regulatory bodies, by contrast, have mission statements or statutory duties where individuals are often seen in both their economic and non-economic capacities.[62] This focus on *VfM* at the expense of other benchmarks isolates PPP bodies from social needs.

Thirdly, *VfM* tries to integrate quantitative and qualitative factors and concerns about taxpayers' money and about wide-ranging goals of sustainability or consumer protection. However, the ultimate benchmark remains the good use of taxpayers' money, absorbing other social concerns.[63] *VfM* represents deeper values reflecting the ethos or 'shared culture' of the community of PPP/PFI experts, which is not, for the most part, reflected in legal rules.[64]

However, there is a strong discrepancy between the mechanisms available to ensure *VfM* in the elaboration phase compared to those available during the implementation phase. No real systematic assessment of *VfM* has been carried out during project implementation for a

---

56 P Gershon, *Review of Civil Procurement in Central Government*, 1999, Annex 1.

57 E.g.: OGC, *Annual Statement*, 2009.

58 Treasury and Cabinet Office, *Major Project Approval and Assurance Guidance,* 2011, 3. See Chapter 2, pp 73–5.

59 Treasury, *Major Project Authority – Integrated Assurance*, 2012, para 2.2.

60 Ibid App A.

61 Government Resources and Accounting Act 2000, s 16.

62 E.g.: Office of Fair Trading: Fair Trading Act 1973, s 2; for the Office of Rail Regulation: economic functions in the Railways Act 1993 and safety functions in the Railways Act 2005, and in the Health and Safety at Work etc Act 1974; H Wade and C Forsyth, *Administrative Law* (10th edn, OUP 2009) 125.

63 See Chapter 3, pp 119–23.

64 Comp K Yeung, *Securing Compliance* (Hart 2004) 10.

long time, although many surveys have been carried out on the topic.[65] *VfM* is difficult to assess during the implementation of PPPs/PFIs because PPPs/PFIs are subject to regulators other than the PPP expert bodies, all with their own regulatory aims. For instance, various regulators monitor health and safety issues. In the LU, the Office of Rail Regulation issued prohibition notices to Tube Lines for safety issues entailing serious risks of personal injury.[66] While the Care Quality Commission, for instance, monitors safety issues in hospitals and highlights the importance of coordination between care services, it has never issued guidelines dedicated to PFI hospitals and how safety concerns may be worked out in *VfM* terms. Such decisions are apparently left to be balanced in each PPP/PFI by their members. The fragmentation of the regulatory system monitoring PPPs in relation to specific non-financial issues leads to unclear messages for PPPs/PFIs, as the sources of these messages are institutionally and functionally different.[67]

Fragmented or integrated, PPPs leave out third parties' interests. The experts (bodies) work at securing *VfM* in the sense of making good use of taxpayers' money. Third parties' needs became subsumed in the concept without detailing how these needs have been taken into account or represented by PPP expert bodies. This concurs with Cotterrell when he notes that:

> policy is often a response to social problems as perceived by the particular political constituencies of policy-makers. Where policy-making is highly centralized it may reflect, sometimes in very direct ways, values grounded in social experience wholly different from that of the particular populations affected by policy-guided regulation.[68]

The remoteness or separation between policy and expectations[69] is not addressed in the ways in which control of PPPs is carried out. A dynamic of fragmentation of social values across various regulators cleared the way for the *VfM* standard to become recurrent across the political accountability techniques and made it possible for the PPP expert system to use it as the predominant standard.

---

65 E.g.: Ipsos/Mori, *Investigating the Performance of Operational PFI Contract – A Research Study Conducted for PUK on behalf of HM Treasury*, 2008 Survey of Operational PFI Projects.

66 http://www.rail-reg.gov.uk/server/show/nav.1585.

67 In regulation in general, R Baldwin and J Black, 'Really Responsive Regulation' (2008) 71 MLR 59, 63.

68 Cotterrell (n 5 above) 304.

69 Ibid 305.

Limits of Expertise in *VfM*

The evaluation of the public interest by public authorities in the PPP system creates a community of experts spread across public and private entities and bound together by their expertise in *VfM*. Through their conversations, the PPP bodies reflect on the issues, draw lessons and issue recommendations for adjusting the system, which are more or less implemented in subsequent projects or guidelines. The accountability of the PPP system works on the basis of a circularity between a limited number of players around the *VfM* concept used as the benchmark to control public spending. *VfM* is the standard used in both the accountability and the regulatory techniques, a bridge between state and market logics. The PPP system mirrors how autonomy, solidarity and trust are conceived between the main players. Similar concerns regarding users seem barely noticeable.

Firstly, there is autonomy for the different bodies involved in the PPP system, in as much as no formal oversight powers are exercised. As a mandatory process in order to get funding, the Gateway Process is, however, an institutional means of paving the way in which discretion is used. The Gateway Process checks that the interested stakeholders have been consulted on specific projects.[70] Yet, this does not affect how the PPP system works as a whole. The Lords' inquiry has been one rare occasion on which individuals could be involved in debates on PPPs/PFIs. However, the technicality of the questions limits the possible dialogue with non-specialists, who have not been heard by the House of Lords. At barely any point in the overall PPP system are individuals' needs for autonomy directly taken into account.

Secondly, solidarity in the PPP system exists in the form of joint working, sharing of information[71] and secondment mechanisms to transfer expertise between the public and private sectors or within the public sector. The different bodies share a common language with the notion of *VfM* and the question lists and reviews with which it is associated. Again, *VfM* refers to individuals as abstract taxpayers, not as persons with particular interests for whom the collectivity needs to provide specific protection. However, such a process encounters weaknesses regarding how the information is coordinated and made relevant for all subsequent bodies. The main expert bodies have little direct knowledge of how PPPs/PFIs are conducted on the ground. They depend on reported cases,

---

[70] E.g.: OGC Gateway™ Process, *Review 1: Business Justification*, 2007, 11–12.

[71] NAO, *BsF*, 2009, summary para 16; para 4.8.

specific crises and the personal expertise of their members. There is no formal structure or principle organising how the different conversations held in the House of Commons' select committees and in the House of Lords need to be articulated between themselves or concerning the outcome of controls performed by regulators. In this sense, the overall outcome is not the product of a carefully debated discussion but of the factual quantitative predominance of *VfM,* used as the most common standard across the accountability and regulatory systems.

Thirdly, trust in the PPP system is built through the expertise and specific skills the PPP bodies attempt to develop. Trust is developed through increasing the predictability of the system with routine processes such as the Gateway Process, whilst still being open to adaptations, for instance in the case of major projects. The small number of experts available and their regular interactions in various capacities may also ensure that trust is built up among the members of the PPP system. Practical limits to accessing and aggregating information on specific projects leave gaps in the accountability of the system,[72] limiting how far the system may be trusted.

Overall, a sharp distinction emerges between the system developed regarding policy measures and individual PPP/PFI projects. There is a dynamic of connection between the various players and their supplementary expertise at a general level. Yet, disconnection emerges between this general level and project specificities and their users' needs. Individuals are only conceived in their abstract capacity as taxpayers in this part of the system. The next two sections investigate two legal techniques available to individuals to protect their actual interests in PPPs/PFIs. They can use two means of controlling how public discretion is used in the PPP regulatory space: firstly, courts, as detailed in the next section and, secondly, extended accountability, which is explained in the following one.

COURTS: LIMITS TO THIRD PARTIES' LEGAL PROTECTION

As a second control over how public authorities use their discretion in PPPs/PFIs, courts offer a space for aggrieved third parties to challenge public decisions and obtain legal protection of their interests. Judicial

---

[72] Liaison Committee, *Parliament and Government Finance: Recreating Financial Scrutiny* (426 HC 2007–08).

control over PPPs/PFIs is, however, problematic for three reasons. Firstly, PPPs/PFIs may cause private parties to exercise public power. The extent to which judicial control reaches such private parties is uncertain. Secondly, PPPs/PFIs not only suppose the involvement of private parties in the exercise of public powers but their arrangements also lead to a diffusion of power across multiple local and central, public and private actors. This diffusion is spread over long periods of time, both for the contractual negotiations and the contractual performance of the PPPs/PFIs. Thirdly, PPPs/PFIs are a tool for allocating resources and the judiciary has traditionally exercised a high level of self-restraint in these matters.[73] These difficulties explain why there are only very few cases reported on PPPs/PFIs. On the basis of the limited relevant case law available, this section analyses the limits of judicial control and assesses how courts represent their own roles in the judicial protection of individual interests involved in PPPs/PFIs.

An analysis of the case law related to PPPs/PFIs and similar legal issues shows that the judiciary has not developed any innovative approaches when deciding on cases involving PPPs/PFIs. The analysis mostly illustrates that the public law techniques available to courts are inadequate for controlling the provision of public benefits and services. Yet courts frame key directions to address how dilemmas between individual and collective aims have to be balanced. In this sense, the case law revolving around PPPs/PFIs helps to elucidate how autonomy, solidarity and trust are understood in public decisions related to PPPs/PFIs.

The overall emerging picture of judicial control shows that challenges to the public discretion involved in PPPs/PFIs may target four different types of issues. Firstly, decisions involved in the procurement process are challenged by bidders and third parties. Secondly, decisions taken during contractual performance could in theory give rise to legal challenges by individual users and third parties, albeit such a challenge has yet to reach any courts. Thirdly, courts may be called on in cases involving access to information related to PPPs/PFIs or their supporting techniques. Finally, courts have decided on cases where central funding to local authorities has been ended. This section takes each of these possible issues in turn in order to identify the beneficiaries of the available legal techniques of judicial control and to highlight the obstacles that they face to seeing their claim accepted.

---

73 J King, 'The Justiciability of Resource Allocation' (2007) 70 MLR 19.

Procurement: Self-interest as the Norm and Public Interest as the Exception

The discretion and public decisions involved in the procurement process may be challenged through either the procurement remedies available to bidders[74] or the judicial review available to third parties. Remedies are intended primarily to offer means for candidate bidders whose bids have been rejected to have the procurement process reviewed by a judge. If the court finds that the duties owned to economic operators under the Public Contracts Regulations 2006 (PCR 2006) have been breached, they have the duty under certain circumstances to make a declaration of ineffectiveness of the contracts awarded.[75] In this sense, the remedies directive primarily aims to police individual procurement processes but also to decentralise the controlling of the implementation of the EU procurement directives to market players. English courts have long endorsed such a position. Under the 2007 remedies directive,[76] courts have maintained caution in relation to public procurement remedies and judicial challenges launched by third parties.

In England, procurement litigation has been historically low, turning over around two cases a year up to 2006.[77] Recently, procurement litigation has increased.[78] Yet the overall level of procurement litigation remains low, amounting to approximately twenty cases a year.[79] However, as PPPs/PFIs follow the competitive dialogue, with its many legal uncertainties[80] and high bidding costs, they may become more contentious, especially in high profile cases. For instance, Sita UK challenged the rejection of its bid for the Greater Manchester Waste Disposal Authority, a contract estimated to be worth more than £3 bn. The *Sita UK*

---

[74] Public Contracts Regulations 2006 (PCR 2006), SI 2006/5, reg 47.

[75] PCR 2006, reg 47K as amended.

[76] Implemented in the UK through Public Contracts (Amendment) Regulations 2009, SI 2009/2992.

[77] C Pedder and A Fletcher, 'Courts Main Drivers on Public Procurement' (2012) 23:6 Construction Law 17.

[78] P Craig and M Trybus, 'Angleterre et Pays de Galles/England and Wales' in R Noguellou and U Stelkens (eds) *Droit comparé des contrats publics – Comparative Law on Public Contracts* (Bruylant 2010) 339, 358.

[79] Pedder and Fletcher (n 77 above) 17. Although no figures for individual cases are available, data from the European Commission suggest that the level of litigation across Europe is significantly higher: see Commission Staff Working Document, *Annual Public Procurement Implementation Review 2012*, Brussels, SWD (2012) 342 final, 31 ff.

[80] See Chapter 3, pp 111–14.

case highlights one key issue with the procurement remedies in the UK, namely the limitation period in which to start proceedings and the starting point from which the time starts to run.[81] The judges keep the time window for starting proceedings limited, avoiding creating uncertainty or the cancellation of a procurement for an infringement long past, with all the costs and delays that this implies.[82] Yet in 2013 the Ministry of Justice proposed reducing the time limits in procurement cases even further to thirty days, following the industry's preferences.[83]

If the courts take a cautious approach to procurement remedies legally open to bidders, they take an even more cautious approach towards judicial reviews that third parties launch against the decisions taken during the procurement leading to PPPs/PFIs. The traditional position of courts in this regard has been spelt out in *Kathro,* where the judge stated that compliance with procurement regulation is a primary concern for economic actors, not for third parties who would use the regulation as 'a fall-back way of trying to stop [a] project'.[84] In short, rejected bidders looking after their self-interests are supposed to best represent the general interest of securing compliance with public procurement.[85]

This traditional position is, however, evolving. Courts repeat the principle following which procurement is first a matter of private interests. However, when a breach of the PCR 2006 involves a public interest, courts recognise exceptions justifying making judicial review available to third parties: firstly, when the failure to comply with the PCR 2006 has a particularly adverse effect on the claimant and secondly when it constitutes a particularly grave departure from public law obligations.[86] These exceptions open up more space for challenging procurement decisions by third parties. The concrete application of these exceptions

---

[81] *Sita UK Ltd v Greater Manchester Waste Disposal Authority* [2011] EWCA Civ 156 [26] (test applied by the High Court) and confirmed [31] and [38].

[82] Such negative consequences of re-running the procurement are mentioned in *R (Law Society) v Legal Services Commission* [2010] EWHC 2550 [131].

[83] Ministry of Justice, *Reform of Judicial Review: the Government Response*, 2013, para 33, giving a clear preference to the position of public authorities and especially business actors (para 16) over the concerns mentioned by the legal profession, those responding from representative bodies, and members of the public all strongly opposed to the proposals (para 18).

[84] *R (Kathro) v Rhondda Cynon Taff Country BC* [2002] Env LR 15.

[85] S Arrowsmith, 'Application of the U.K. Procurement Regulations to PFI Contracts: New Case Law' [2002] PPLR na84.

[86] *R (Chandler) v Secretary of State for Children, Schools and Families* [2009] EWCA Civ 1011.

reveals, however, the enduring caution that courts harbour about opening up too many cases and weakening the procurement process.

Recent cases where the factual situations are similar to PPPs/PFIs suggest that judicial reviews would not be allowed if the judge felt that the breach of PCR 2006 was used only as a way to oppose the project as such, even if the breach of the PCR 2006 was as serious as complete non-compliance with it.[87] Furthermore, if the public authority had been following practice spread over the board or governmental guidance, claimants would be unlikely to succeed as the court would be extremely cautious in this case.[88] In most areas there now exists guidelines related to the procurement process for PPPs/PFIs or the competitive dialogue, which would make courts reluctant to accept claims against the project.

However, when professional organisations have been involved in the consultation process and argue that there have been failures in the procurement process affecting the wider public,[89] they may meet with more clemency both in terms of standing and in the extension of time limits.[90] PPPs/PFIs also relate to the provision of infrastructure and services to vulnerable people, such as patients or prisoners, and the irregularity of the procurement process may prevent them benefitting from certain services or services of a given standard. Therefore, professional bodies representing them and which have been involved in the PPP/PFI policy or programme might benefit from this more favourable approach to standing even if individuals may not.

Overall, procurement decisions are subject to judicial control mainly through procurement remedies relied on by bidders and in a highly ancillary way through judicial reviews started by third parties. However, in every case, courts choose to limit such challenges, either in taking a strict approach to time limits or in imposing a high threshold for standing. In this sense, judges have not taken the opportunity of creatively welcoming the new remedies directive or the recently emerging challenges in exercising a higher level of scrutiny of procurement

---

87 *R (Chandler) v Secretary of State for Children, Schools and Families* [2009] EWCA Civ 1011 [78]; *R (Unison) v NHS Wiltshire Primary Care Trust* [2012] EWHC 624 (Admin) [15].

88 *R (Unison) v NHS Wiltshire Primary Care Trust* [2012] EWHC 624 (Admin) [16].

89 *R (Law Society) v Legal Services Commission; Dexter Montague & Partners v Legal Services Commission* [2007] EWHC 1848 (Admin) (appealed but not with regard to standing).

90 *R (Law Society) v Legal Commission* [2010] EWHC 2550 (Admin) [126].

decisions. Finally, third parties are not welcome to challenge procurement decisions. Therefore, to the extent that judicial control over procurement applies, it mainly hinges on the self-interest of private contractors, either directly in the legal challenges or in the time limits on challenging a decision, set in accordance with the declared preferences of private contractors.

Unlikely Safety Net for Contractual Performance

During the contractual performance of PPPs/PFIs, courts may also be called on in order to control public discretion. If individual users or third parties identify a violation of their human rights by the public authorities involved in PPPs/PFIs or a ground for judicial review against a decision taken by these public authorities, then they are able to go to court. However, PPPs/PFIs may pose hurdles for individuals and third parties. As a rule, indeed, SoPC4 and PF2 exclude the possibility that rights could be directly created to the benefit of third parties.[91] So far, no reported case deals directly with these issues. The main grounds for challenging how public discretion has been exercised during PPP/PFI performance, namely breach of human rights, judicial review, breach of legitimate expectations and breach of statutory duties, all present difficulties for third parties.

Applicants relying on human rights and judicial review encounter a first obstacle in locating a public element in the contractor-individual relationship,[92] bringing it under the public law framework. Case law is indeed reluctant to recognise this element widely. The 'public function' test is used restrictively in case law in relation to the direct application of the Human Rights Act 1998 (HRA 1998) to contractors.[93] Judicial review is opened when the contractor exercises coercion or decides on entitlements.[94] This may be difficult in practice. As PPPs/PFIs are organised around SoPC4, the main interface with the individual remains the public authority. Finding a spot where the private contractor or the special purpose vehicle (SPV) is either actively deciding on entitlements or exercising coercion (such as expulsion from housing estates) may be rare, although possible in theory. Judicial review against decisions taken by

---

91 *SoPC4*, para 30.5; *PF2* (draft), para 31.2.

92 Davies, 2008, 80.

93 *YL v Birmingham CC* [2007] UKHL 27, overturned in the Health and Social Care Act 2008, s 145(1); less restrictive: *R (Weaver) v London and Quadrant Housing Trust* [2009] EWCA Civ 587.

94 Davies, 2008, 236 ff.

public authorities in PPPs/PFIs is also rarely successful. For instance, the speed with which a challenge has been launched has been assessed with regard to the factual background of a PFI, especially the huge amounts of money at stake. This element, among others, justified the rejection of the claimants' challenge.[95]

Arguing in terms of legitimate expectations that the public authority's conduct has created may be a second route for individuals to use to protect their interests or needs. Substantial (such as remaining in a care home 'for life', having permanent social housing) or procedural (such as being consulted)[96] legitimate expectations can be protected through judicial review. PPPs/PFIs may be a case where, due to the circumstances (high financial commitments, energy and time devoted to designing tailored solutions, sharpness of needs, specific vulnerability of the individuals), legitimate expectations regarding the delivery and maintenance of a service may have been created to the benefit of users of the privately financed infrastructure or service. However, public discretion to deliver, change or terminate infrastructures or services provided through PPPs/PFIs may be constrained by financial elements outweighing individual users' legitimate expectations. SoPC4 or PF2 contracts include detailed terms for calculating the financial compensation that the public authority has to pay in cases of voluntary termination.[97] These financial terms primarily aim to protect financial institutions' investments. They may also deter public authorities from cancelling the PPP/PFI and thus indirectly protect individual users, making judicial protection redundant in many cases.

Such cost/benefit analyses regarding maintaining an infrastructure or a service and terminating it are likely to take place in a climate of financial, economic and political pressures. A series of cases of financial distress or reorganisation in PPPs/PFIs has arisen, for instance in PFI hospitals. They have been primarily addressed through a range of statutory or pragmatic techniques. Chapter 5 will detail how the complexity of the PFIs cushions the PFI users in some ways but transfers the financial burden onto other services.[98] Furthermore, in the cases where

---

95 *R (Enfield BC) v The Secretary of State for Health* [2009] EWHC 743 (Admin).

96 Harlow and Rawlings, 2009, 224 ff.

97 E.g.: *SoPC4*, para 21.5; *PF2* (draft), para 23.5.

98 See Chapter 5, pp 235–42.

funding had been ended and procedural legitimate expectations recognised by the courts, the claimants were all local authorities, not individual users.[99] Therefore, all in all, courts have not offered legal protection to individual users and their substantial or procedural expectations.

Finally, the breach of a statutory duty by public authorities may offer a remedy. Yet again such a remedy is not widely open to individual users or third parties. Strict requirements apply before a tort may be accepted. These include the category of the beneficiary of the duty, the legislative intention to confer an action, the direct link between the damage and the breach, and the nature of the damage. Mostly, if there is any other remedy, like a complaint, the action for damage is often excluded.[100] The government favours non-legal redress, as the next section shows. It is thus likely that such an alternative remedy exists, limiting the ability to use a statutory duty to protect individuals' expectations.

If these judicial controls over the use of discretion during the contractual performance are theoretically possible, there is not much evidence that users' interests are actually protected in this way in PPPs/PFIs. However, it may be suggested that the very existence of such judicial control may in itself offer prophylactic protection when PPP/PFI partners negotiate or implement PPPs/PFIs. Furthermore, users and third parties may use the threat of litigation to secure concessions from the public authority or obtain satisfaction through settlements.[101]

Limited Access to Information

During the elaboration of the PPP/PFI programmes or projects, or during their contractual performance, individual users or third parties may wish to gain access to information related to that elaboration or performance. One may think about expert reports on technologies used in waste PFIs, about strategies for procuring transport PPPs, financial evaluations of available options to refinance projects, monthly reporting of contractual performance against contractual targets etc. Making this information available would contribute to developing more transparent decision-making and provide means of assessing how public discretion is used in PPPs/PFIs. Two cases involving PPPs/PFIs or the techniques on which

---

[99] See below this chapter, pp 177–81.

[100] O Hood Phillips and others, *Constitutional and Administrative Law* (8th edn, Sweet & Maxwell 2001) para 31-025.

[101] In general, see: V Bondy and M Sunkin, 'Settlement in Judicial Review Proceedings' [2009] PL 237.

they rely show, however, that judicial challenges in this area have met with mixed success.

The first case relates to access to the information generated through the Gateway Review. The Gateway Process treated PFI/PPP cases with confidentiality.[102] Only very limited information was released. However, the administrative court decided that the Freedom of Information Act 2000 (FOI Act 2000) applied to reviews carried out through the Gateway Process in a case where a Member of Parliament sought disclosure of those reviews.[103] It was, however, unclear whether all future gateway reviews should be disclosed or whether each request for information should be considered on an individual basis.[104] Following that decision, some Gateway Process reports have been made available. The Ministry of Justice has been adapting its working assumptions regarding what information has to be made public under the Gateway Process.[105] For instance, the purpose and conduct have to be released but the name of the review team members and the conclusions, findings and recommendations are withheld. This illustrates the difficulty of balancing the interest of the wider public to access information with the commercial interest of the parties involved in PPPs/PFIs and the need to secure a space during policy formulation where confidentiality is maintained. Access to substantial information related to the Gateway Review and *VfM* assessment thus remains limited.

The second case involves the disclosure of information related to the operation of a local waste PPP/PFI by Veolia, where a local elector sought to gain access to the contract, invoices related to it and their appendices (rates, various formulae, deductions, performance scorecard), exposing all the contractual mechanisms for calculating payments. The local elector relied on the Audit Commission Act 1998, s 15(1), which entitles any interested person to:

(a) inspect the accounts to be audited and all books, deeds, contracts, bills, vouchers and receipts relating to them; and
(b) make copies of all or any part of the accounts and those other documents.

---

102 Treasury, 2003, 61.

103 *Office of Government Commerce v Information Commissioner* [2008] EWHC 774 (Admin).

104 [90]–[91].

105 http://www.justice.gov.uk/information-access-rights/foi-guidance-for-practitioners/working-assumptions/foi-assumptions-gateway-reviews.

The first instance judgment took great care in assessing the scope of application of this provision and granted access to the documents asked for by the local elector.[106] Veolia challenged the decision on the grounds of commercial confidentiality. The Court of Appeal made a narrower interpretation of section 15(1) to protect the confidentiality of the commercial information, pursuant to art 8 ECHR and art 1 First Protocol of the ECHR; namely the right to respect for private life and the right to peaceful enjoyment of possessions.[107] The court thus implied an exception to the right to access documents which was not mentioned in the Audit Commission Act 1998.

Overall, therefore, the court has given priority to the commercial interests of the private contractor over the interests of the local electors in calling public authorities to account for the ways in which local taxpayers' money is being spent. Users and third parties are only given limited access to the information related to PPPs/PFIs, namely the contractual documents generated during their implementation, and therefore have few ways to ensure that the private contractor performs the contract as contractually agreed.

Termination of Funding: Deference as a Principle

A specific issue arises in PPPs/PFIs when central government changes the funding of local PPPs/PFIs. The government change in 2010 illustrates this issue powerfully. The prominent BsF programme was cancelled, the conditions for waste PFIs to be centrally funded were reformulated and the methodology for calculating annual funding was revised. Local authorities have challenged all of these three changes on several grounds partly overlapping across the cases. These grounds included irrationality, fettering of discretion, frustration of substantial and procedural legitimate expectations and breach of the public sector equality duties (PSED). In all cases, the judges have taken a deferential approach to controlling resource allocation as a matter of principle. Only limited procedural requirements to consult and to have regard to equality were accepted as limiting ministerial discretion. The room for discretion thus remains broad when it comes to the balance between the need for change and a minimum level of stability.

---

106 *Veolia ES Nottinghamshire Ltd v Nottinghamshire CC* [2009] EWHC 2382 (Admin) [72].

107 *Veolia ES Nottinghamshire Ltd v Nottinghamshire CC* [2010] EWCA Civ 1214.

Luton is the most comprehensive case in which public discretion to end central funding has been discussed. In July 2010, the Secretary of State (SoS) for Education decided to end BsF funding for all projects which had not reached the final business case (FBC) stage by January 2010. PFI projects which had only reached a preliminary stage (namely the outline business case (OBC)) would not be provided with central funding. As this applied to them, Luton and other local authorities challenged the decision taken by the SoS. Some of the claimants were so close to reaching the FBC stage that they had planned to start building the schools in the upcoming weeks. Holman J rejected claims that the decision was irrational, that the discretion had been fettered and that substantive legitimate expectations had been frustrated. Indeed, he explained his understanding of his constitutional role in the context of the broad discretion that the government enjoys to 'balance a number of complex, and perhaps conflicting, social and economic variables in order to determine what he believes is the fair, effective and efficient solution to the central issue in question'.[108] Thus, the SoS is politically responsible for the decisions made in such a context and courts should not usurp the minister's political role.[109] Taking a deferential approach to ministerial discretion, the judge clearly affirmed the principle of political accountability as being the primary means of controlling such discretion. Judges would only intervene to sanction extreme cases.

Luton illustrates two of such extreme grounds. The first one is an unfair use of such discretion. Here, the abrupt change in funding after years of intensive discussions between the local authorities and Partnership for Schools (PfS) amounted to unfairness and abuse of power. Even in the absence of promised or usual consultation, such a consultation should have been held to mitigate the drastic consequences of the change. The 'pressing' economic problems of the financial crisis did not constitute an overriding public interest justifying not holding such a consultation.[110] The second extreme ground enabling the judge to exercise scrutiny of ministerial discretion is the breach of the duty to have regard to the position of specific groups such as minorities and the disabled

---

108 *R (Luton BC) v Secretary of State for Education* [2011] *EWHC 217* (Admin) [47].

109 *R (Luton BC) v Secretary of State for Education* [2011] EWHC 217 (Admin) [48]. For a critique regarding such a restrictive conception of judges' constitutional role, see E Palmer, 'Resources Allocation, Welfare Rights – Mapping the Boundaries of Judicial Control in Public Administrative Law' (2000) 20 OJLS 63, 74.

110 [96].

under the PSED. Here the complete absence of any kind of reference to the PSED during the decision-making process made the judge's appreciation of the breach relatively straightforward.[111]

In *Luton*, therefore, the autonomy of the SoS is recognised for its wide discretionary powers, limited primarily in terms of political accountability. Judges only intervene to ensure a degree of trust. Here trust was breached due to an abrupt rupture following extensive discussions over time. Even the pressing economic climate did not justify shattering such basic trust in being given a 'cushion against change'.[112]

Building on *Luton*, *Dudley* confirms the ancillary role of the judiciary with regard to ministerial discretion.[113] In 2011, the SoS for Communities and Local Government changed the system by which PFI credits were paid to a local authority, Dudley, for its PFI project pertaining to information and communications technology in schools. The change from a 'declining basis' to an 'annuity system' meant that the local authority would not be fully reimbursed for the financial costs that it had incurred in the PFI and would stop getting funding after a few more years. The court limited its control and rejected substantive legitimate expectations,[114] again for constitutional reasons to do with the accountability of the Crown to the House of Commons[115] and the impossibility of a government binding its successor. However, as in *Luton*, procedural legitimate expectations of consultation had been created.[116] In the circumstances of the case, it was found that the change fundamentally altered the commitment made to Dudley and that Dudley had enjoyed an advantage under the previous system. This meant that fairness required offering it the possibility to make representations before losing that advantage.

In this case, therefore, a similar broad discretion to change funding modalities was recognised as belonging to the SoS while actually there

---

[111] According to the judge, all the documents focused '*entirely on different stages in the procurement process and what savings had to be made*', with no '*single reference to disability, race or gender need/impact anywhere in them*' ([112]).

[112] [89] quoting *R (Bhatt Murphy) v The Independent Assessor (also, Niazi)* [2008] EWCA Civ 755 [49].

[113] *R (Dudley MBC) v Secretary of State for Communities and Local Government* [2012] EWHC 1729 (Admin).

[114] [72]–[73].

[115] [74].

[116] [53]–[61].

was already a commitment to finance a PFI project. Considerations of trust again needed to be taken into account in framing this discretion, however.

In *Cheshire*,[117] ministerial discretion was even less constrained than in *Luton* or *Dudley.* The SoS for Environment, Food and Rural Affairs had decided not to provide PFI funding to Cheshire for its waste project. The project had received its OBC in 2005 but there were conditions appended to the approval and the project met with delays, notably due to the internal reorganisation of the local authority. Various steps were taken such as the approval of financial close and of the preferred bidder by the Department for Environment, Food and Rural Affairs (Defra) in August 2010, although the funding was still made conditional. However, in view of the Comprehensive Spending Review (CSR) due in October 2010, Defra decided to reduce the number of projects that it funded. It developed a methodology to decide which projects would go forward. The application of this method meant that Cheshire did not get PFI funding.

Here again, no substantive legitimate expectations had been created. Indeed, the government is entitled to reformulate its policy time and again, even more so when decisions lie in the macro-political. Then the court's supervision should be less intrusive.[118] Furthermore, the claimant had been reminded of the conditions and qualifications throughout the process. Finally, the judge also rejected procedural legitimate expectations for Cheshire to be consulted. Indeed, the upcoming CSR justified the difficulty of consultation given its timing and the desirability of identifying the projects which would be stopped by it.[119] Therefore the factual circumstances of the economic crisis and the financial pressures on the budget were assessed differently in *Luton* and *Cheshire.* According to Langstaff J, the emergency around the CSR made it 'an urgent priority to secure economic stability',[120] so departments needed to have wide discretion. As courts were 'ill-equipped to resolve such issues',[121] '[j]udges must be particularly slow in entering the politically sensitive area of allocations policy'.[122] In this case, therefore, the department was

---

117 *R (Cheshire East BC) v Secretary of State for Environment Food and Rural Affairs* [2011] EWHC 1975.

118 [57]–[58].

119 [78].

120 [90].

121 [90].

122 [104] quoting Nicholas Blake QC.

recognised as possessing wide autonomy to decide not to undertake consultation.

This overview of three cases dealing with terminations of funding highlights the constant reluctance of courts to interfere with resource allocation. They have only agreed to limit ministerial discretion on procedural grounds of consultation or PSED. Even then, they are ready to interpret exceptions based on public interest in favour of wider ministerial discretion. Finally, the breach of PSED in *Luton* represents an extreme case where no single trace of regard for equality could be found.

Judicial Control, Intermediation and Extremes

The previous section highlighted the limited degree of judicial control over the public discretion involved in PPPs/PFIs, especially with regard to the protection that individuals enjoy in relation to PPPs/PFIs. Overall, judges take a deferential approach to issues arising from PPPs/PFIs, either explicitly as in the cases related to termination of funding or implicitly as in the procurement cases. It is, however, possible to extract a general picture of how courts articulate concerns for autonomy, solidarity and trust in the matters arising in connection with control over the use of discretion in PPPs/PFIs.

Firstly, a high level of autonomy is recognised as belonging to public authorities when they decide upon matters arising in procurement, contractual performance, access to information or the termination of funding. Indeed, in all cases, courts have been cautious to exercise scrutiny of public discretion, imposing, for instance, high thresholds for the standing of third parties (in public procurement) or taking a deferential approach towards politically sensitive decisions related to the allocation of financial resources (in terminations of funding). However, such a wide discretion attributed to public authorities has limits in terms of solidarity and trust.

Secondly, solidarity is normally expressed in mechanisms conveying values important to the social group and the protection recognised for specific needs and vulnerabilities. Here solidarity is bare under these terms. Regarding the curtailing of the factual (if not legal) power that PPPs/PFIs exercise over vulnerable individuals, courts appear as an ultimate recourse when other techniques of extended accountability or regulation do not provide solutions. Courts seek to retain this subsidiary role of a minimal safety net in extreme cases. Complex issues of balancing social and political factors, assessing how spending cuts have to be spread over various projects etc. are all matters expressing social values relating to sharing the burdens of the economic crisis. They belong to the discretion of the government, with judges taking a deferential approach to them without issuing any guidelines as to what solidarity or common values in society might demand. Judges consider that such a distribution of tasks results from constitutional principles. Yet they slightly depart from this approach when it comes to the requirement to have due regard to PSED. PSED highlights a minimum level of interdependency across individuals in a society in a way that Chapter 5 explores further.[123]

Thirdly, trust as a factor that public discretion needs to take into account is mostly expressed by courts when they recognise that procedural legitimate expectations have been frustrated. Here the issue turns around balancing needs for policy change for the common good as identified by central government on the one hand, and a minimum stability in the ways in which local authorities organise their own affairs on the other hand. In this case, procedural legitimate expectations of consultation are protected. Any drastic change would amount to unfairness and abuse of powers as there have often been extended discussions over long periods of time with central government, and local government has incured expenses related to the PPP/PFI projects for which funding has been terminated. Therefore the protection of legitimate expectations allows for a minimum threshold of trust to develop. Such minimal trust is needed to balance the concern for adaptation to political and economic changes and the administrative organisation of complex negotiations and contractual performance like the ones present in PPPs/PFIs. In this sense, the law comes in to create a minimal framework for how the balance between the interests of different groups in society is struck, both in general and over time.

Overall, these cases involving PPPs/PFIs highlight how extreme are the instances decided by the courts and the role played by intermediate groups in representing individual interests. There have always been intermediaries, such as local government in the case of funding termination or economic actors in procurement litigations. Courts exhibit high levels of distrust towards claimants who come up to oppose PPP/PFI projects. Nothing indicates that courts would be inclined to adopt a more welcoming stance towards individual claims seeking the protection of interests or needs in the context of PPPs/PFIs. Therefore we turn to alternative techniques available to individuals and third parties to protect their interests: extended accountability in the context of wider regulation.

---

[123] See Chapter 5, pp 224–7.

GAP-FILLING: THIRD PARTIES' VOICES

We have seen that the PPP system mostly works on its own through its specific logic, where taxpayers' money or *VfM* is distinctively important, and that courts offer only limited protection to users and other third parties. Neither of these two techniques ensures that public discretion in PPPs/PFIs is used to meet users' needs or third parties' interests. However, regulatory techniques relying on extended accountability may have been developed in a move to empower citizens.[124] This section considers the subsidiary role that the law attaches to third parties' voices and its reliance on intermediaries in order to fill in this gap between political and judicial controls over the use of public discretion in PPPs/PFIs.

Mapping the different techniques available for protecting individuals' concerns outside political and judicial accountabilities stumbles over the wide diversity of available techniques, depending on each regulatory issue for which different techniques have been developed over time. Such diversity leads to the possibility of redundancy and conflicts between the available techniques. While the regulatory literature is divided about the benefits of redundancy,[125] a cause for concern may be the lack of a single focal point for organising and monitoring how individuals' concerns are met.

This section considers two techniques to illustrate the more or less active role given to individuals and the greater or lesser consideration that PPP/PFI partners give to individuals' concerns. The first is active participation through consultation, where consultees need to take active steps but lack any guarantee that their views will be properly reflected in the final decision. The second comprises redress techniques where individuals' complaints may lead to public authorities reconsidering their decisions. Across these two techniques, the law is weak in its formal and binding requirements, leaving a broad scope of discretion for public authorities to factor in to their decisions how autonomy, solidarity and trust need to be balanced against each other in the coordination of third parties' interests in PPPs/PFIs.

---

[124] PASC, *From Citizen's Charter to Public Service Guarantees: Entitlements to Public Services* (411 HC 2007–08); HM Government, *Building Britain's Future*, 2009, 62 and 64.

[125] C Scott, 'Accountability in the Regulatory State' (2000) 27 JLS 38, 57; contra: R Baldwin, M Cave and M Lodge, *Understanding Regulation: Theory, Strategy and Practice* (OUP 2011) 350.

Involvement and Consultation

Public involvement in PPP/PFI matters is another way in which individuals' needs or satisfaction with PPP/PFI infrastructures or services can be channelled towards public authorities. Involving users in the PPP/PFI decision-making process or in assessing PPP/PFI performance may take an array of modalities. These range from mere information gathering to real power sharing in taking decisions on PPPs/PFIs or monitoring performance,[126] from involving groups affected throughout the contractual negotiations and performance to getting limited views on specific issues such as the minimisation of work disturbances or setting fees for car parks attached to the PPP/PFI. Often, programme or project specificities are taken into account through the involvement of a person representing these particular features. For instance, local authorities have an observer on the PF2 board to represent local needs.[127] In school PFIs, former head teachers are seconded to the PFI team of the local authority to bring their expertise in the field.[128] These observers and seconded head teachers may bring valuable expertise to the issues addressed by the PPPs/PFIs but they may also filter and misrepresent users' and third parties' concerns. In these cases, such involvement fails to integrate individual needs into the service/infrastructure delivery properly. Participation by users or affected third parties may also happen during PPP/PFI implementation, according to the modalities set out in the PPP/PFI contract. For instance, this may happen through residents' steering groups,[129] consumer satisfaction inquiries, helpdesk reporting systems and total quality management.[130] While involvement aims, in theory, to bring service delivery and users' needs closer, the law gives little guidance on how public authorities should seek to organise public participation and leaves space for intermediation by groups and representatives. This section illustrates this wide public discretion over consultation, one particular modality of public involvement.

Consultation is used in a patchy way in PPPs/PFIs. Yet PPPs/PFIs offer an outstanding occasion to embed an opportunity for users to appraise

---

[126] S Arnstein, 'A Ladder of Citizen Participation' (1969) 35 JAPA 216.

[127] Treasury, 2012, para 2.6; *PF2 (*draft), para 5.5.3.

[128] L-M Foo, D Asenova, S Bailey and J Hood, 'Stakeholder Engagement and Compliance Culture' (2011) Public Management Review 707 (relating the Scottish experience, which the authors consider similar to the English one).

[129] E.g.: http://www.newham.gov.uk/Housing/PrivateSectorHousing/HousingPFI/ForestGateandChatsworthresidentsteeringgroup.htm.

[130] E.g.: *SoPC4*, para 7.9.

their needs realistically, communicate them and monitor how they are met within the contractual negotiations and performance techniques. As PPPs/PFIs put forward a long-term structure, decisions on investments and adjustments may be defined and planned incrementally, with ideas incorporated within the design and redirected according to changes made. Furthermore, consultation may be beneficial for its own sake,[131] even if its influence on the actual decision is difficult to assess as it depends on the methodology used. However, consultation faces three difficulties within the English framework: firstly, in terms of statutory underpinning; secondly, in terms of modalities; and thirdly, in terms of its limits.

Firstly, there is no general statutory duty to consult in common law.[132] Consultation depends on specific statutes,[133] which makes it difficult to organise participation for PPPs/PFIs according to a common pattern. Depending on the specifics of each policy area,[134] consultation takes different forms at different moments and with different legal consequences. For instance, in cases they determine, local authorities have the duty to inform, involve and consult representatives of local persons identified as affected by or having an interest in a function that they carry out.[135] The implementation of the duty remains largely at the discretion of the public authorities themselves and a collective approach to consultation is emphasised.[136] The Public Sector (Social Value) Act 2012 (PS(SV) Act 2012) also introduces a duty for public authorities to 'consider whether to undertake any consultation as to the matters' related to the economic, social and environmental well-being of their area during the pre-procurement stage of service contracts.[137] This also leaves discretion to the public authority to organise the consultation.

---

[131] *R (Cheshire East BC) v Secretary of State for Environment Food and Rural Affairs* [2011] EWHC 1975 [80].

[132] Davies, 2008, 114–18.

[133] Ibid 114.

[134] E.g.: For NHS: Health and Social Care Act 2001, s 11(1), then the National Health Service Act 2006, s 242, followed by the Local Government and Public Involvement in Health Act 2007, s 233 etc.; for social housing: CLG, *Tenant Involvement in Housing Management: Supplementary Guidance*, sd.

[135] Local Government and Public Involvement in Health Act 2007, s 138. HM Government, *Creating Strong, Safe and Prosperous Communities Statutory Guidance*, 2008, 20.

[136] P Vincent-Jones and others, 'New Labour's PPI Reforms: Patient and Public Involvement in Healthcare Governance?' (2009) 72 MLR 247–8.

[137] PS(SV)Act 2012, s 1(7).

Secondly, fundamental requirements apply to the modalities of consultation in general, regardless of its statutory or voluntary basis.[138] They have been summed up as follows:

> To be proper, consultation must be undertaken at a time when proposals are still at a formative stage; it must include sufficient reasons for particular consultation to allow those consulted to give intelligent consideration and an intelligent response; adequate time must be given for this purpose; and the product of consultation must be conscientiously taken into account when the ultimate decision is taken.[139]

Following these legal constraints, consultation in PPPs/PFIs requires answering a series of questions related to its modalities. Who is consulted? On which matters? When? For what purpose? The answering of these questions differs at policy and project levels. In the first case, the Department for Business, Innovation and Skills issued a code of practice on consultation,[140] which especially drew attention to the need to target interested parties,[141] if necessary by relying on intermediary bodies and appropriate trade, community or third sector organisations.[142] The code of practice was replaced by *Consultation Principles* in 2012. Lacking any legal force,[143] the *Consultation Principles* highlight proportionality between the type and scale of consultation and the impact of the decision considered. Consultation thus depends on the matters considered, with little transparency or consistency specified. The House of Lords especially raised concerns regarding these new principles, asking the government to clarify its 'commitment to wider engagement with vulnerable and hard-to-reach groups' and recommending that the departments 'publish a timely Government response to a consultation process'.[144]

The Treasury's consultation leading up to the PF2 illustrates the House of Lord's concerns regarding the ways in which the government took into account the answers submitted during the consultation. The consultation

---

[138] C Donnelly, 'Participation and Expertise: Judicial Attitudes in Comparative Perspective' in S Rose-Ackerman and P Lindseth (eds) *Comparative Administrative Law* (Edward Elgar 2010) 357, 369.

[139] *R v North and East Devon HA Ex p Coughlan* [2001] QB 213 [108].

[140] HM Government, *Code of Practice on Consultation*, version 3, 2008.

[141] Ibid 4.

[142] Ibid 10.

[143] Cabinet Office, *Consultation Principles,* 2012, last sentence.

[144] Secondary Legislation Scrutiny Committee, *The Government's New Approach to Consultation – 'Work in Progress'* (100 HL 2012–13) para 50 and 56.

related to the PF2 mainly attracted answers from 136 organisations, most of them drawn from public authorities and the PPP/PFI community (such as Balfour Beatty, BAM PPP UK Ltd, CBI, Ernst and Young). Three MPs also submitted answers and only sixteen individuals.[145] The Treasury published a summary of the extensive answers received, yet it is a matter of guesswork to trace how each answer contributed to the policy finally adopted, if at all.[146]

If consultation organised at policy level seems not to directly engage with individual users, consultation organised at the level of PPP/PFI projects may be the outcome of a sophisticated strategy developed by the public and private partners while carefully pondering the timing and methods necessary to engage users and affected groups.[147] In practice, assessing its success is delicate: it may differ between projects, among participants or between the public authorities and the users and affected parties.[148] The dynamics behind consultation remain little understood[149] but the overall result may depend on users' perception of the motivation underlying the consultation process and their sense of being genuinely listened to in their needs and particular situations.[150] Poor consultation with the users and the local community may cause trouble and make a project capsize due to lack of public confidence. For instance, the development of the Paddington health campus had to be cancelled because it had not been designed with sufficient input from doctors and nurses from the outset. This lack of information and consultation with the people affected by the redevelopment resulted in their repeated opposition. This led to delays in the project and ultimately to its cancellation.[151]

Finally, consultation has limits in the extent to which it contributes to informing public authorities about individuals' needs. Firstly, individuals may face difficulties in articulating their needs. Secondly, little public participation may in fact be secured, or it may have to be secured through

---

145 Treasury, 2012, App B.

146 Treasury, 2012, App A.

147 L-M Foo, D Asenova, S Bailey and J Hood, 'Stakeholder Engagement and Compliance Culture' (2011) Public Management Review 707, 711.

148 Ibid 707.

149 T Brannan, P John and G Stoker, 'Active Citizenship and Effective Public Services and Programmes: How Can We Know What Really Works' (2006) 43:5/6 Urban Studies 993.

150 Foo, Asenova, Bailey and Hood (n 147 above) 707.

151 PAC, *The Paddington Health Campus Scheme* (244 HC 2006–07), recommendation 1; NAO, *The Paddington Health Campus Scheme,* 2006, paras 2.28–2.29.

the self-interest of participants.[152] Defining service standards or controlling discretion would then be fragile. Furthermore, targeting the right group for participation may be difficult: taking the example of LIFT, would participation need to involve individual (groups of) users with specific needs but limited in numbers on the one hand, or GPs more aware of the average needs of the wider local population on the other hand?[153] Probably both but then the polycentric challenge arises of balancing the various expressions of needs. Room for appreciation opens up. Justification may be given but rationality difficult to fathom. Finally, even if the 'right' persons are targeted by the consultation, assessing their satisfaction with how the service provides for their needs may be difficult. Practical issues appear – such as the definition of satisfaction, the subject matter of the satisfaction (e.g. service as a process or the actual benefit gained from the services), the balance between short-term satisfaction and overall longer term or wider satisfaction factors etc.[154]

Overall, consultation is not enshrined systematically in a legal technique tailored to PPPs/PFIs on the level of either principles or modalities. It is difficult to define who should be consulted or how and with what kind of means to identify or express needs. Therefore, public involvement is likely to rely on proxies such as seconded staff, local representatives or groups representing specific interests in the consultation process. If individuals are not in a position to signal their needs or interests before an issue arises, they may well voice their concerns through complaints and redress techniques, to which we now turn.

Complaints and Redress

As a matter of principle, users of infrastructures and services delivered through PPPs/PFIs may be protected without any legal entitlements through administrative redress or ombudsman intervention. However they may also face obstacles, starting with identifying the entity responsible for the issue that they want to complain about.[155] Each PPP/PFI project is

---

[152] A Davies, 'Foundation Hospitals: A New Approach to Accountability and Autonomy in the Public Services' [2004] PL 808, 819.

[153] Outside the LIFT application: A Davies, 'A Tangled Web? Accountability and the Commissioning Role in the "New" NHS' (2007) King's Law Journal 387, 402.

[154] PASC, *From Citizen's Charter to Public Service Guarantees: Entitlements to Public Services* (411 HC 2007–08) paras 29–36.

[155] Commission for Local Administration in England, *Special Report: Local Partnerships and Citizens Redress – Advice and Guidance*, 2007.

part of a different contractual and regulatory framework and each situation may give a different answer. Once the public or private entity has been identified as the responsible entity, then new obstacles arise: firstly, the labyrinthine redress system; secondly, the limits to the complaints system.

Firstly, in principle, administrative redress enjoys the government's favour over judicial review.[156] There is a systematic resistance to diverting money from the actual delivery of services towards techniques of redress.[157] Therefore the government seeks to minimise costs and uses non-legal redress in core public services, especially 'forms of redress which trigger immediate improvements in services and avoid having to go through complex court processes'.[158] Yet the modalities of administrative redress are particular to each policy domain, lacking a general coherence.[159] Remedying this does not seem likely to happen soon.[160] The users' position is no different in PPPs/PFIs from in other public infrastructures or services. The usual complexity of the redress system remains, with added uncertainty regarding who from the public authority or the private corporation should have acted differently. This uncertainty weakens the assumption that private corporations may be disciplined by users' voices.

Secondly, ombudsmen offer protection against maladministration committed by public authorities or the bodies acting on their behalf which, in case of PPPs/PFIs may, in context, cover contractors. They investigate cases of maladministration and may issue non-binding recommendations to the public authority if appropriate. This protection is, however, dependent on a range of factors which limit its efficiency. The users need to identify the competent ombudsman. For instance, local residents may complain to the Local Government Ombudsman for local issues but

---

[156] Harlow and Rawlings, 2009, Ch 10; P Craig, 'Access to Mechanisms of Administrative Law' in D Feldman (ed), *English Public Law* (2nd edn, OUP 2009) 757, para 17.91.

[157] P Birskinshaw, 'Grievances, Remedies and the State – Revisited and Re-appraised' in M Adler (ed) *Administrative Justice in Context* (Hart 2010) 353, 354.

[158] PASC, *From Citizen's Charter to Public Service Guarantees: Entitlements to Public Services: Further Government Response to the Committee's Twelfth Report of Session 2007–08* (1147 HC 2007–2008), Appendix 2 – Government Response, para 5.

[159] V Bondy and A Le Sueur, *Designing Redress: A Study about Grievances against Public Bodies* (Public Law Project 2012) 4.

[160] Law Commission, *Administrative Redress: Public Bodies and the Citizen* (2010 HC 6, LC no 322) para 1.3.

school issues or contracts related to public transport are excluded from the Local Government Ombudsman's remit.[161] In some cases, complaints cannot be made directly to the ombudsman but need to be passed on to it by an MP[162] or other designated persons.[163] Finally, some ombudsmen may only investigate whether the public authority carried out its duties. When there is a fragmentation of the service provision between public and private providers, the private provider's conduct falls outside the remit of the local ombudsman.[164] Such an issue could very easily arise in PPPs/PFIs.

Individuals may benefit from non-legal techniques to protect their interests. Although this may provide for quick redress, this makes individuals vulnerable to the discretion of the public authorities. There are no guidelines or official documents laying out how redress or ombudsman mechanisms need to be included in PPPs/PFIs or how redress and ombudsmen need to approach PPPs/PFIs. For instance, annual reports of ombudsmen such as the Local Government Ombudsman, the Parliamentary Ombudsman or the Prison Ombudsman do not mention whether the complaints they handled related to PPPs/PFIs. It is thus difficult to assess whether there have been no problems in PPPs/PFIs, whether the ombudsman did not find PPPs/PFIs relevant to his/her investigations, or if the user in PPPs/PFIs never found the relevant forum to see her complaint handled. This makes the redress and ombudsman system blind to PPPs/PFIs and prevents the integration of lessons related to maladministration into PPPs/PFIs: redress and ombudsmen may not ensure adequate coordination of individual needs and third parties' interests in PPPs/PFIs.

Intermediaries: A Reliable Alternative to Individual Protection?

The previous section mapped how techniques of extended accountability help to control public discretion when it comes to the protection that individuals enjoy in relation to PPPs/PFIs. In most PPPs/PFIs developed under SoPC4 and PF2, no main direct relationship exists between the PPP/PFI and users. Nonetheless, decisions taken in PPPs/PFIs affect individuals, either as users or as third parties. The question is then how the interests of PPPs/PFIs and of these individuals are coordinated through the discretion that public authorities use in PPPs/PFIs, and how

161 Local Government Act 1974, Sch 5(3)(1)(a) and (5).
162 Parliamentary Commissioner Act 1967, s 6.
163 Localism Act 2011, s 180.
164 Local Government Ombudsman, *Annual Report*, 2011–12, 36.

concerns for autonomy, solidarity and trust are expressed in the control exercised over this use of discretion. This is assessed here.

Firstly, public authorities enjoy autonomy as none of the techniques of extended accountability analysed here impose strict constraints on them. For instance, consultations are not statutorily required as a rule and their modalities are often left to public authorities' discretion. Yet, individuals' autonomy is a concern running through these techniques of extended accountability, in the form of empowerment and voice. Users' and third parties' voices are factually considered through the categories they form (e.g. local residents likely to pay parking fees in PPPs, pupils) and not in terms of their individual circumstances or needs.

Secondly, solidarity is expressed in mechanisms conveying values important to the social group, such as public involvement and consultation. Also, public involvement is likely to rely on proxies such as local representatives and interests groups. These techniques illustrate that self-interest is not the only value pursued in PPPs/PFIs. Other values and collective aims such as the pursuit of economic, social and environmental well-being may be part of an extended accountability bridging the gap between the PPP system and individuals. Chapter 5 analyses the specificity of their collective dimension.

Thirdly, trust in the protection of and respect for individuals' needs met through PPPs/PFIs relies on the adequate designing of public involvement procedures tailored to the specificities of PPP/PFI projects and programmes, as well as effective redress that is provided when needed. However, all the cases explored here are patchy and no detailed data are available to assess how the techniques of extended accountability actually work in PPPs/PFIs. This statement should lead to caution regarding how far these techniques provide adequate means for individuals and third parties to express their needs. The law (e.g. PS(SV) Act 2012) and the *Consultation Principles* put blind faith in the possibility of individuals finding groups channelling and voicing their needs. Yet such trust in the existence of these groups is not articulated in a general message, at least not one embedded in any legal technique, thus leaving space for a narrative to do so.

Attention has been drawn to how individuals may put forward their needs and interests to the public and/or private partners cooperating in PPPs/PFIs. There is a range of processes such as redress and procedural rights of consultation, often exercised through intermediation, with legally protected rights as a last resort. This overview pictures a patchwork of techniques organising the relationships between individuals and PPP/PFI partners and systems. Combined with the assessment of how the PPP system is disconnected from individuals' needs, a qualitative gap is formed. The following section highlights a possible way, notably narratives conveyed by communities, to bridge this gap.

NARRATIVES AND COMMUNITIES: TENSIONS

So far this chapter has mapped the legal techniques for exercising control over public discretion and their limits. To coordinate the interests of PPPs/PFIs with those of their users and other third parties in the PPP regulatory space, narratives and communities may supplement the legal techniques used in political and judicial accountability or extended regulation. This section probes three narratives to account for this coordination in its three aspects of problem (narrative of public service), solution (narrative of responsiveness) and means of developing a solution (narrative of transparency). However, each of these narratives presents weaknesses: the narrative of public service is contested; the narrative of responsiveness is too narrow and imprecise; the narrative of transparency is ambiguous. Furthermore, these narratives face difficulties in their implementation as the communities likely to convey them do not converge towards a shared aim.

Problem: Public Services as a Narrative beyond the Contracting State's Shortcoming?

In *The Contracting State*, Harden clearly spells out the problem of relying on markets and contracts for the delivery of public services. Contracts present two features. Firstly, they pursue specific political objectives without necessarily referring to a clear legal framework. Secondly, they could contribute to the promotion of constitutional values in enhancing individual rights and government accountability for policy decisions. However, contracts do not lead on to that result on their own. They need to be embedded in a broader legal and constitutional framework for public services which, he noted at the time of writing in 1992, 'does not exist'.[165] Since then, state failure to deliver public services has been reiterated.[166] From this statement, experiences such as the PFIs have been developed to tackle this state failure.[167] Scholarship has attempted

---

[165] I Harden, *The Contracting State* (Open UP 1992) xi.
[166] E.g.: Vincent-Jones, 2006, 29–30.
[167] See Chapter 2, pp 62–7.

to develop a conceptual approach to public services[168] but no constitutional or legal framework has emerged so far. The market and regulation have taken over. Yet they have also brought disappointment: they do not automatically ensure that public infrastructures or services are delivered with *VfM* or match individuals' needs. Therefore, public services feature on the political agenda and transformation has been promised in diverging directions.

To address these failures, one solution would be to transform how public services are delivered and to suggest a narrative related to these public services. Yet developing such a narrative for public services and backing it up with legal techniques and financial means is at the core of recurring structural tensions in England. These tensions revolve around the role of the state in general, the relationships between central and local government, and the interplays between public institutions, economic actors and wider social actors as part of various communities.

PPPs/PFIs illustrate these tensions, as a brief comparison of the New Labour and coalition government positions evidences. Under New Labour, PPPs/PFIs played a prominent role in the transformation and modernisation of public services and the investments required to achieve them. The Treasury recurrently presented this modernisation in the form of a challenge[169] 'to deliver efficient and responsive services, which meet public expectations throughout the country'.[170] The coalition government reaffirms the link between PPPs/PFIs and public services, between its policy related to PPPs/PFIs and its *Open Public Services – White Paper,*[171] in which it sets out its plans for modernising public services.[172] Despite this clear connection in principle, its modalities have changed in a range of ways. Firstly, the coalition government emphasises that PPPs/PFIs are only one of the numerous ways in which the private sector delivers public infrastructures and services, next to privatisation or procurement. Secondly, before 2010 public infrastructures were supposed to support the delivery of public services. By contrast, the coalition

---

[168] On public service as a legal technique and a seedbed for cohesion when the market fails, see T Prosser, 'Regulation and Social Solidarity' (2006) 33 JLS 364.

[169] Treasury, 2003, para 1.2 or Treasury, 2008, para 1.1. This takes place in an even broader political message of government modernisation (see Harlow and Rawlings, 2009, 72).

[170] Treasury, 2003, para 1.2. Repeated in Treasury, 2006, para 1.5, under amended form in Treasury, 2008, para 1.5.

[171] HM Government, *Open Public Services – White Paper* (2011 Cm 8145).

[172] Treasury, 2012, executive summary, first sentence.

government distinguishes public *infrastructures* which may be provided through PPPs/PFIs from public *services* to be provided by non-public sector entities such as charities, mutuals and social enterprises. This may imply that PPPs/PFIs are limited to the provision of public infrastructures to the exclusion of public services. However, while a 'fundamental reassessment' of PPPs/PFIs was announced following the Treasury Committee's recommendations,[173] long discussions led to PF2, which confirms the contribution of private finance to the delivery of public services.

Legal scholarship also underlines that 'PFI represents both an alternative to and, since the public sector is not generally the owner and operator of the assets, a transformation beyond the traditional paradigm of government contract'.[174] Vincent-Jones echoes these transformations when he points out the challenge of discovering 'how to connect the citizens and consumers with the purchaser and provider functions that have been separated as a result of quasi-market organisation'.[175] He suggests a narrative of responsiveness that the following section sums up.

Solution Revisiting Contracts: A Narrative of Responsiveness

As an answer to the contracting state's failures to deliver modern public services, Vincent-Jones suggests the development of a *New Public Contract*, a solution to the problems linked to the ways in which government contracts work in practice (the so-called *New Public Contracting*). This *New Social Contract* would be based on responsiveness, a combination of effectiveness and legitimacy.[176] This should help connect the regulatory system to individuals and coordinate PPPs'/PFIs' way of functioning with individuals' needs.

For Vincent-Jones, legal contracts explain only part of social relationships, while exchange explains the other part.[177] He conceives the social contract as 'a claim on the part of citizens and consumers *not to be excluded from* processes of decision making by public agencies in regard to a broad range of public service issues'.[178] To this end, the *New Public Contracting* should be made more responsive. Responsiveness relies on

---

173 G Osborne, 'Press Release: Government Plans to Reform PFI Model', 15.11.2011; TC, *Private Finance Initiative* (1146 HC 2010–12).

174 Harlow and Rawlings, 2009, 413.

175 P Vincent-Jones, 'Citizens Redress in Public Contracting for Human Services' (2005) 68 MLR 887, 898.

176 Vincent-Jones, 2006, 87.

177 Ibid 7.

178 Ibid 359 (original emphasis).

relational and institutional conditions such as trust and cooperation, fairness and reciprocity, institutional morality, public participation and transparency.[179] Developing the conditions for responsiveness relies on hybrid reforms or a mixture of law and regulation, public and private, processes and institutions.[180] In this mixture, Vincent-Jones underlines that the law should also be responsive in its structuring of discretion. Proceduralisation relies on available information to foster transparency and public deliberation.

As the previous sections of this chapter illustrated, the general architecture of PPPs/PFIs, their system and their relationships with individuals fit with what Vincent-Jones describes as responsive, i.e. in terms of processes for collecting information, adapting the system, offering transparency, and building first resort non-legal redress mechanisms and last resort legally enforceable ones. Through their interactions, institutions – such as the OGC, PUK, IUK or individual PPPs and local authorities – would, under Vincent-Jones's approach, develop the proper structures and staff to learn from others' mistakes and good practice. They would have the time and resources to look for what they need to know and they would solve information issues. If they could not succeed alone, supplementary means such as databases, training, soft law mechanisms and Gateway Processes would bring the relevant knowledge to properly skilled staff, and the decision-making process would be based on sound information. In an ideal world this would, should or could lead to the responsive system portrayed by Vincent-Jones. However, according to his own assessment, this is not the case, as relational and organisational norms are not present to ensure this responsiveness. Indeed, the overlayering of these varying mechanisms may render individuals' needs invisible, hidden behind the screen of regulation and its processes.

Responsiveness presents a series of issues. Firstly, responsiveness needs to be defined. To what must public services be responsive: individual needs, political and financial circumstances, institutional frameworks, statutory requirements or changes in them?[181] Secondly, it

---

[179] Ibid 348 ff.

[180] In further works related to patient involvement, Vincent-Jones moves towards emphasising deliberative democracy to develop responsiveness in public services (C Mullen, D Hughes and P Vincent-Jones, 'The Democratic Potential of Public Participation: Healthcare Governance in England' (2011) 20 SLS 21).

[181] Compare with responsiveness in regulation: Baldwin and Black (n 67 above) 68–76.

may be questioned whether responsiveness is always intrinsically valuable and may not have to give way to other social values or requirements[182] such as consistency, stability, solidarity or fairness. Thirdly, the institutional structures behind responsiveness are not mapped in terms of their relationships to each other.

Questions thus arise regarding how the *New Social Contract* ensures its own cohesion. The *New Social Contract* relates responsiveness, relationality or reciprocity to joint maximisation[183] of the entities as a guideline. However, it is difficult to assess how this joint maximisation is developed. Even more, responsiveness or reciprocity does not have to be grounded in joint maximisation. They may imply that one tries to understand the other party in the relationship, not assuming that one knows his/her wishes or that they both want the same outcome out of the relationship.[184] Commenting on this assumption, Fuller notes that '[t]here is no automatic corrective for this kind of error, which is probably as common as any that men are subject to'.[185] Here again, thus, a specific place may be required for techniques assisting with correction – either the law or ethics. Chapter 5 seeks to map out how institutions, the law and community interplay so that an ethical framework for discretion may be developed.

Overall, the *New Social Contract* and responsiveness seek to connect individuals with the system surrounding them. PPPs/PFIs echo the main organisational structure, as responsiveness suggests, in terms of hybridity between public and private, formal and informal. Vincent-Jones assesses the gaps and failings of PPPs/PFIs. He then suggests filling these gaps in by developing a *New Social Contract* as a cohesive mechanism connecting individuals and the system. It seems, however, that the moral underpinning of the *New Social Contract,* and the need to deepen the modalities of enforcement and compliance in the implementation phase of PPPs/PFIs, may potentially need mechanisms supporting this narrative. Hence, we turn to these potential mechanisms: first transparency and then communities.

---

182 P Cane, 'Administrative Law as Regulation' in C Parker, C Scott, N Lacey and J Braithwaithe (eds) *Regulating Law* (OUP 2004) 207, 218.

183 E.g.: Vincent-Jones, 2006, 29.

184 Tronto, 1993, 136.

185 L Fuller, 'The Forms and Limits of Adjudication' (1978–79) 92 HarvL-Rev 362.

Ambiguous Means: A Narrative of Transparency

From early on, critiques have been made of the poor accountability in PPPs/PFIs due to the lack of transparency in their contractual set-up, in the delivered services and in the financial streams between the public and private parties.[186] This has led to PPPs/PFIs being extensively documented with NAO reports in a way that few other policies have. The Treasury website also lists ongoing PFIs.[187] However, scepticism about their opaqueness and huge financial liabilities has continued. For instance, the House of Commons asked for more transparency on the financial justifications for PFIs[188] and on the benefits that the private investors reaped during the contracts,[189] especially when selling their shares in PFIs.[190] The House of Lords also recommended more transparency in the accounting of PPPs/PFIs and the gathering of comparable data.[191] This repeated call for transparency related to public finances has been at the heart of political efforts endeavouring to improve the accountability of PPPs/PFIs. The coalition government acknowledged the concerns about opaqueness in PPPs/PFIs when it launched its reform of PPPs/PFIs.[192] However, transparency as a form of accountability requires further specification as it means different things in different contexts. While transparency efforts have targeted financial opaqueness, they have focused on the *VfM* as a standard, while transparency concerns also arise with respect to the objectives pursued with PPPs/PFIs, the machinery supporting them, the level and quality of the services they provide to individual users and the benefits they deliver to third parties. This section highlights this ambiguity of transparency.

While agreement exists on the need for improving transparency, and more especially access to information on PPPs/PFIs,[193] the modalities for

---

186 Freedland (n 16 above) 296–97.

187 https://www.gov.uk/government/publications/pfi-projects-data; previously available on PUK's website: http://webarchive.nationalarchives.gov.uk/20110512094755/http://www.partnershipsuk.org.uk/PUK-Projects-Database.aspx.

188 PAC, *Lessons from PFI and Other Projects* (1201 HC 2010–12).

189 HC Deb 23 June 2011, vol 530, cols 143, 169 and 189.

190 PAC, *Financing PFI Projects in the Credit Crisis and the Treasury's Response* (553 HC 2010–11) recommendation 7.

191 SCEA, *Private Finance Projects and Off-Balance Sheet Debt* (63-i HL 2009–10) paras 165, 168.

192 Written Ministerial Statement, 15 November 2011 quoted in TC, *Private Finance Initiative: Government, OBR and NAO – Responses to the Seventeenth Report from the Committee* (1725 HC 2010–12) 3.

193 Vincent-Jones, 2006, 315 ff; Davies, 2008, 221 ff.

more openness are debated. We have seen that the main legal techniques used to attempt to gain access to information in PPPs/PFIs have been the FOI Act 2000 and the Audit Commission Act 1998. These have, however, delivered only limited access to information related to PPPs/PFIs. According to Vincent-Jones, making transparency an 'essential element' of a responsive system of government contracting[194] requires changes not only in law but also in administrative practice and in the culture within government.[195] In practice, these concerns for transparency have found an echo in the coalition government's transparency agenda, which links better accountability, better *VfM* in public spending and cutting the deficit.[196] However, actual changes in practices can pose challenges, as the following three cases illustrate.

The first major change follows the publication of Whole of Government Accounts (WGA) for the first time[197] for 2009–10[198] and then for 2010–11.[199] These aim to provide an accurate overview of the accounts of all bodies possessing a public nature or entirely or substantially funded from public money in order to give the Treasury a tool for developing its policies.[200] The 2009–10 WGA eventually disclosed the value of PFI assets (£30.9 bn), the associated liability for capital repayments (£28.1 bn) and the value of future obligations such as service charges and replacement costs (£131.5 bn).[201] The audience for the WGA was identified as Parliament[202] and a 'wide range of users', for whom the accounts were presented in an understandable way.[203] These financial disclosures triggered discussions in the PAC over PPPs/PFIs as a whole

---

194 Vincent-Jones, 2006, 312.

195 Ibid 320.

196 HM Government, *The Coalition: Our Programme for Government*, 2010, 20.

197 Although the duty had existed since the Government Resources and Accounts Act 2000, s 9(1).

198 Treasury, *Whole of Government Accounts – Year Ended 31 March 2010* (1601 HC 2011).

199 Treasury, *Whole of Government Accounts – Year Ended 31 March 2011* (687 HC 2012).

200 D Heald and G Georgiou, 'The Macro-Fiscal Role of the U.K. Whole of Government Account' (2011) 47 Abacus 446, 447.

201 Treasury, *Whole of Government Accounts – Year Ended 31 March 2010* (1601 HC 2011) 23.

202 Ibid 8.

203 Ibid 8.

policy.[204] In its financial sustainability report,[205] the Office for Budget Responsibility (OBR) then reported on these figures and highlighted uncertainties related to the ways in which PFI liabilities are or are not put off-balance sheet for planning public spending in the long term.[206] All these efforts resulted in quantifying issues which had long been raised for PPPs/PFIs.[207] However, no general strategy for analysing and using these data in the actual decision making of policies and projects has been developed,[208] which leads to the question of whether the first potential user of these data, the Treasury, benefits from them or is expecting other audiences – but then which ones? – to give direction to its financial policies.

The second change related to public finances follows the coalition government's transparency agenda, which aims to make public as much data as possible in order to make public services more accountable.[209] The *Open Data White Paper 2012,* which seeks to implement this transparency agenda, especially addresses the question of the MPA in its chapter on 'building trust'. It suggests that the MPA should report annually on its projects and programmes. However, the White Paper shies away from detailing the modalities of these reports and the level of expertise required to understand them, the extent of the information and the analysis of the information that these reports are expected to bring. Furthermore, the White Paper highlights the need to find a balance between transparency and confidentiality, 'to protect formulation of government policy or commercial interests where their protection is also in the public interest'.[210] In doing so, the White Paper mostly reiterates the solution developed in the *Office of Government* case regarding the balance to be struck between public interest in disclosure and public interest in non-disclosure when it comes to information related to policy formulation.[211]

---

[204] PAC, *Whole of Government Accounts 2009–10* (1696 HC 2010–12) para 4.

[205] E.g.: OBR, *Fiscal Sustainability Report*, 2011, box 2.2.

[206] Ibid box 3.3.

[207] E.g.: NAO, *Lords,* 2009, Pt 3.

[208] PAC, *HM Treasury: Whole of Government Accounts 2010–11* (867 HC 2012–13) conclusion 1.

[209] HM Government, *White Paper – Open Public Services* (2011 Cm 8145) 35.

[210] Cabinet Office, *Open Data White Paper – Unleashing the Potential* (2012 Cm 8353) para 3.9.

[211] *Office of Government Commerce v Information Commissioner* [2008] EWHC 774 (Admin) [78].

Finally, in a more general way, the transparency agenda is connected to the ongoing reform of the local audit system. Here, the armchair auditor is supposed to use the raw data and audit reports made available to challenge how local public services are provided. Following the *Veolia* case, where the judge did not accept the idea that the Audit Commission Act 1998 gives direct access to a series of contractual documents,[212] the Local Audit and Accountability Bill suggests extending the right of any interested person to access a series of documents pertaining to local audit. This would allow any interested persons to 'inspect the accounting records for the financial year to which the audit relates and all books, deeds, contracts, bills, vouchers, receipts and other documents relating to those records'.[213] Yet the practical use of such documents by armchair auditors to challenge the negotiation or performance of services provided through complex contractual relationships such as PPPs/PFIs remains unclear. It may be highly costly and time consuming for public authorities to provide information respecting commercial confidentiality. The information then provided may need either very specific expertise to be understood or a lot of further investigation to unpack the overall picture of service provision through a single PPP/PFI. Therefore the overall process may be off putting. Another option may be that specific groups could specialise in targeting particular public bodies, contractors, issues or projects. The overall effect across the provision of public services, through PPPs/PFIs or otherwise, in terms of quality, standards or ethos, remains to be seen over the long term.

Overall, the narrative of transparency does not succeed in connecting individuals to the PPP system. It leads to a series of questions. Firstly, transparency is not necessarily good in its own right and needs to be analysed in the context of the particular values and concerns it seeks to promote or address.[214] The changes reported here highlight how the focus is set purely on communicating financial information in a relatively one-sided way, with minimal contextualisation and analysis. For instance, no effort is made to explain the scope of the financial disclosure in the WGA. The possible context and wider benefits of PPPs/PFIs are totally set aside as no narrative is provided for the actual services and infrastructures that are financed with them. Hence, if there is indeed transparency, a constructive communicative ethos is lacking, something which

---

[212] See above this chapter, pp 175–7.

[213] Local Audit and Accountability Bill, s 25(1)(a).

[214] E Fisher, 'Transparency and Administrative Law: A Critical Evaluation' (2010) 63 CLP 272, 274.

should underpin transparency for it to be meaningful to the actors receiving the information.[215]

Secondly, implementing transparency within the public sector requires institutions to change their operations and behaviour and to develop systems to make transparency effective.[216] Yet the narrative for transparency applied to the MPA does not seem to bring much change to the previously reached legal solutions. In the case of local audit, transparency may well bring new documents within the public domain but here questions related to the institutional machinery within local government for implementing such new requirements have not been clarified.

Thirdly, the narrative of transparency requires a definition of the users and uses of the disclosed information. Would the user be first of all the public body who was required to gather, collect and process the information so that it could develop a better informed policy? Would it be Parliament so that it could exercise more relevant control? Would it be the public at large or specific groups within the public? Is transparency a way to swamp specific audiences with information? Is transparency allowing policy making to be challenged through constructive analysis of data? Is transparency a means of strengthening trust in policy-making and service delivery? Answering these questions would involve contemplating the objective of transparency and the legal consequences to be drawn from transparency requirements.[217] No clear answers are provided in relation to PPPs/PFIs, however.

In any case, transparency is ambiguous. It may lead to more careful reasoning by the administration. More conflicts may arise, however, because there are competing visions of what constitutes good administration.[218] If more financial data are available, and therefore a higher level of transparency organised on that account, it is unclear how this higher level of financial transparency can contribute to improving transparency about the means and aims of PPPs/PFIs or the webs of accountability and regulation in which they are embedded. Here again, the main standard which stands out is *VfM*, as well as expertise in accessing, understanding and using financial data, and the idea that in making data available to market actors (as well as the wider audience) innovative solutions for the

---

215 O O'Neill, 'Transparency and the Ethics of Communication' in C Hood and D Heald (eds), *Transparency – The Key to Better Governance?* (Proceedings of the British Academy, no 135, OUP 2006) 75, 81–2.

216 Fisher (n 214 above) 279.

217 Ibid 288–95.

218 Ibid 302.

provision of public services and their responsiveness will emerge. However, transparency highlights the importance of matching the information made public to its intended audiences and communities. Even if it seems uncontroversial that information is intended to be read, understood and processed by given audiences, the identification of the relevant communities may be a key issue across these narratives.

Communities without Shared Aims

As explained in the framework developed in Chapter 1, narratives and communities interplay in the sense that a community of actors may be distinguished thanks to its shared narratives or values. Conversely, communities convey or adapt narratives. In the relationships between PPPs/PFIs and third parties, there is no obvious legal contract to connect individuals with PPPs/PFIs and their systems. Furthermore, the narratives of public services, responsiveness and transparency give a patchy and contested picture. If public services seem to be consensual at a high level of principles, their implementation is subject to deep changes: while private finance seems to be a key means of financing infrastructures, public services are provided through economic and non-economic actors. Responsiveness suggests immediate and osmotic relationships between users and PPPs/PFIs that do not take into account the institutional and statutory frameworks within which these relationships are embedded. It also discounts the possible tensions between various categories of users with conflicting needs competing for scarce resources. Transparency only has meaning against the backdrop of the purpose for which it is developed: common good or self-interest? These tensions across narratives between the common good and self-interests, between market and public logics, are reflected in the communities carrying them.

Firstly, public services and infrastructure are at the centre of many concerns: government,[219] Parliament,[220] think tanks,[221] professional organisations[222] and the construction industry. They see public services with different lenses, more or less connected to their organisational objectives – being the common good, private interests or collective

---

[219] E.g.: Treasury, *Public Services: Meeting the Productivity Challenge*, 2003.

[220] E.g.: PASC, *Choice, Voice and Public Services* (49 HC 2004–05).

[221] E Cox, 'We Need an Infrastructure Strategy beyond the M25', 27.06.2013 (IPPR website).

[222] E.g.: CBI, 'CBI Reaction to Government Infrastructure Plan', 27.06.2013 (CBI website).

interests – more or less strongly linked to economic growth. This gives the sense that public services may be invoked on pragmatic or strategic grounds more than out of concern for the actual satisfactory delivery of common welfare or for their intrinsic potential to foster solidarity and trust across groups in society.

Secondly, responsive regulation is often mentioned but has limits. Responsive regulation tends to focus more on the implementation of policies than their development, for instance. Designing frameworks for responsive regulation is complex and uncertain. A series of factors, such as the broader institutional environment, the different logics behind the regulatory techniques and their continual changes, have to be factored in to these frameworks.[223] In short, responsiveness to self-interest does not match the common good in a straightforward way. Communities may be a necessary link between the two. However, the narrative of responsiveness leaves them out. Vincent-Jones' responsiveness builds on the social contract and joint maximisation. The contractual relationship is the first community of interests and the *New Social Contract* endeavours to encompass the whole society within shared values of responsiveness. It does not seem that intermediary communities would find a place under this scheme. Both autonomy (under the form of 'maximisation') and solidarity (in the aspect of 'joint' maximisation) would be guaranteed thanks to responsiveness (under the form of regulation), with the law and the state setting only minimal requirements or standards.[224]

Thirdly, transparency has been advocated by two prominent MPs. One, Margaret Hodge, Labour MP and chair of the PAC, has repeatedly emphasised that the government needs to give greater access to the financial information related to PPPs/PFIs and their business case.[225] The other, Treasury Committee member Jesse Norman, a Tory MP and one of the architects of the Big Society,[226] succeeded in getting the only

---

[223] Baldwin and Black (n 67 above) 59.

[224] Vincent-Jones, 2006, 320.

[225] In the PAC reports and in the press releases when these reports were published (e.g. M Hodge, press release to the publication of PAC's Report of Session 2010–12, on equity investment in privately financed projects, 02.05.2012, PAC website). She submitted three PAC reports as her answer to the Treasury Consultation (namely, *Financing PFI Projects in the Credit Crisis and the Treasury's Response; PFI in Housing and Hospitals*; *Lessons from PFI and Other Projects*).

[226] J Norman, *The Big Society: The Anatomy of the New Politics* (University of Buckingham Press 2010).

adjournment debate on PFIs in 2011.[227] He set up a campaign, the *PFI Rebate,* which advocated for private firms sharing the profits from PFIs with public authorities. He submitted a contribution to the Treasury consultation on the new approach to PPPs[228] and later endorsed the PF2 system, emphasising mostly that PF2 had to be on-balance sheet and the need for greater transparency of data.[229]

Both Margaret Hodge MP and Jesse Norman MP have articulated a narrative for greater financial transparency in relation to PPPs/PFIs. However they have not developed a narrative for greater transparency in the techniques articulating individuals' expectations and needs in PPP/PFI policies and projects. *VfM* in PPPs/PFIs provides a standard for calling public authorities to account. It refers to individuals in their taxpayer capacity. Although this aspect of public accountability matters, it only focuses on the means of delivering infrastructures and services. It does not help with mapping which infrastructures and services are required to meet individuals' needs or whether these needs are adequately met and their provision protected. These aspects of PPPs/PFIs would also need to be integrated in a narrative of greater transparency.

HYBRIDITY, FRAGMENTATION AND INTERMEDIATION

This chapter sought to assess the role that the law plays in organising the relationships between PPPs/PFIs and third parties, and more especially in the legal techniques available to third parties to control how public discretion has been used to coordinate users' and third parties' interests in the PPP regulatory space. There is no contractual relationship between PPPs/PFIs and third parties as a rule. Alternative relationships are thus based on a hybrid regime of accountability and regulation, where state-analogue and market-analogue models lack coordination. Throughout this chapter, a recurring dynamic has been the extent to which *VfM* has become the key standard for assessing whether public authorities pursue the common good with PPPs/PFIs. The law does not organise a specific relationship between PPPs/PFIs and third parties. Third parties are mainly understood in their taxpayer capacity, not in their capacity as users needing the infrastructure or service provided by PPPs/PFIs. The law only provides protection to individuals in extremely limited cases.

---

227 HC Deb 23 June 2011, vol 530, col 143.

228 Treasury, 2012, 97.

229 J Norman, *After PFI* (Centre of Policy Studies 2012).

Among the various techniques used to control public discretion, *VfM* has become the prominent standard for assessing PPPs/PFIs, mainly developed through conversations between PPP/PFI experts and the PAC/NAO/Treasury. Neither judicial review nor regulatory techniques like transparency or public involvement are designed to let users have a stake in the PPPs/PFIs and their development. For instance, parents are not systematically directly consulted in school PFIs to contribute to determining service specifications. Courts have rejected the idea that parents have the standing to challenge the procurement route that public authorities take to develop new schools. Judicial control does not plug the gaps in defining the balance between the individual and collective interests to be coordinated in PPPs/PFIs. Courts have indeed left a wide autonomy to public authorities to define the public interest that they want to pursue. Courts also take a deferential approach, relying on the principle of political accountability for ministerial decisions related to PPPs/PFIs. Here, the directing principle is mainly the standard of good use of taxpayers' money and the *VfM* test. Therefore, courts do not seek to integrate other interests or values into their control of public discretion. They only bring solidarity and trust in a limited way, in extreme cases such as abrupt changes or complete disregard of PSED. For the rest, *VfM* has become the key standard for assessing the political accountability of PPPs/PFIs. The public interest has thus not been developed into a consistent whole encompassing a well-organised integration of interests involved in PPPs/PFIs. Such integration would revolve, for instance, around a clear narrative of public services, assessed against their contribution to the common good in a transparent way (resource-wise, organisationally and need-based) under courts' attentive supervision, and at the request of users.

This lack of integration of the components of the public interest does not lead to full disintegration, however. The individual interests of users or third parties are protected thanks to groups representing them in either courts or the regulatory techniques. These processes contribute to defining the public good to some extent. The best illustrations of this are procurement and consultation. Compliance with procurement regulation and its contribution to the public interest is mainly devolved to disappointed bidders, who are assumed to be the best in place to protect their self-interests through courts. Individual judicial challenges are seen with caution but courts may more readily accept challenges introduced by professional organisations, evidencing how the protection of individual interests depends on collective representation. Consultation procedures related to PPP/PFI policies may in theory be open to any interested person. However, in practice, answers are mostly submitted by professional organisations, market actors or groups representing specific values such as labour conditions and environmental protection. Here again a market logic for how voices could become organised to protect individual interests is followed.

Therefore, the mix between state-analogue and market-analogue models results in the absence of a coordinated relationship between PPPs/PFIs and users or third parties. The most prominent relationship is based on individuals understood in their taxpayer capacity. This does not acknowledge either the variety of roles that individuals may play in relation to PPPs/PFIs or their vulnerability. If PPPs/PFIs were organised as state-analogue, then the users would be able to get accountability assessed through standards other than *VfM,* such as, for instance, standards expressing the importance of the services that meet their needs (e.g. access, continuity, quality). If PPPs/PFIs were organised as market-analogue, then there would be a multiplicity of providers to whom the users could turn and competition would influence the price and the quality of the services provided by PPPs/PFIs. Actually, in most PPPs/PFIs, we have a single provider who is not responsive to users' needs because the logic of the funding dictates the logic of the control mechanisms through the predominant *VfM* standard.

Overall, searching for coordination between individuals' interests and PPPs/PFIs highlights how institutions, the law and communities need to be combined with each other to start establishing such a connection. Legal techniques are mostly available as a last resort only. Communities are fragmented. Yet a space between the common good and private interests opens up between state and market techniques: collective interests surround PPPs/PFIs. Their specific coordination within PPP/PFI relationships is not explained by accountability and regulatory techniques. Chapter 5 explores these possible articulations by emphasising that a more encompassing standard to assess PPPs/PFIs needs to be developed, turning away from *VfM* in the spending of taxpayers' money to focus on an ethic of care in providing for users' needs.

5. Collective interests between public and private interests: From pragmatism to ethic?

INTRODUCTION

Chapters 3 and 4 have highlighted the economic rationality underpinning public–private partnerships/Private Finance Initiatives (PPPs/PFIs). Public procurement, competition and risk transfer featured predominantly in Chapter 3 and the limitations of these led us to highlight a narrative of complexity, innovation and partnering. Chapter 4 showed that accountability has been structured around expertise, self-interests and extended regulation. In both chapters, value for money (*VfM*) provided a key standard for coordinating the relationships between public authorities and individuals based on the notion of taxpayers' money. Due to the amounts of taxpayers' money at stake in PPPs/PFIs, spending needs to be accounted for and organised in ways acceptable in a given society. However, PPPs/PFIs have collective and social dimensions other than organising how taxpayers' money is used, for how long and to the benefit of which private contractors. They also address issues of poor, lacking or otherwise unsatisfying provision of public infrastructures and services such as transportation, hospitals, prisons or schools. They try to harness wider benefits for the community (in)directly. Pushed one step further, PPPs/PFIs may even organise projects so that citizens' potential to develop their identities can be supported thanks to the infrastructures and services provided in the context of the communities that they serve. This chapter suggests that PPPs/PFIs may be organised according to a community-analogue model: this model puts forward an ethic of care as a standard for assessing whether public discretion is used in order to support such individual transformation for the overall benefit in the collectivity.

This chapter moves beyond the market-analogue and state-analogue models used to analyse PPPs/PFIs in Chapters 3 and 4. It seeks to probe the intermediary layers between PPP/PFI policies and PPP/PFI projects, where collective interests are coordinated. Market-analogue and state-analogue models fail to explain how institutions, law and communities structure the options available to public discretion to coordinate these collective interests in the PPP regulatory space. Pragmatism would mainly focus narrowly on *VfM* as a way to inform both the means and the ends set for the spending of taxpayers' money that the coordination of interests involved in PPPs/PFIs. But an ethic of care would seek to provide a more encompassing answer to this coordination. It would seek to account for autonomy, solidarity and trust in such a way that each participant in a PPP/PFI sees himself as part of a collective project. In such a project, it is necessary at times to set aside self-interests in order to develop common interests in PPP/PFI projects over time and in order to allow the needs of all to be met.

This chapter first outlines communities and prioritisation of interests within an ethic of care. It then analyses three different ways in which communities interplay with institutions in developing PPPs/PFIs and especially in coordinating public, private and collective interests in PPP regulatory space. This highlights the contributions as well as the limits of the law in structuring these interplays. Therefore, this chapter suggests developing an ethical framework for coordinating collective interests in PPPs/PFIs. This framework tentatively suggests ways in which an ethic of care might provide a fruitful standard for comprehensively assessing how discretion is used when it comes to public–private relationships and their consequences for third parties and users taken as members of communities served by PPPs/PFIs.

SPOTLIGHT ON COMMUNITIES

Chapter 4 showed that the relationships between PPPs/PFIs, public authorities and users of PPPs/PFIs have not in the main created specific legal entitlements for individuals. Repeatedly, the legal and regulatory techniques process relationships in their collective dimensions and from the perspective of specific common needs shared among categories of users and third parties. The challenge then is to coordinate these collective interests. This pushes the role of the public authorities in relation to communities into the foreground. In setting priorities in favour of some collective interests over others, discretion faces dilemmas which need to be structured with the help of an ethical framework, such as that involved in an ethic of care.

Relationships between Institutions and Communities

Chapter 1 asked whether PPPs/PFIs could be understood as a community, as 'a comprehensive *framework* for social life'.[1] If this were so, the internal structure of decision making in PPPs/PFIs could have been a possible tool with which to coordinate the collective interests involved in the provision of public infrastructures and services. PPPs/PFIs would have developed their own identity and projects, detached from those of their actors, with their own values, interests, decision-making processes and purposes. The previous chapters have, however, shown that PPPs/PFIs do not process the integration of the interests involved in the provision of public infrastructures and services to such a high degree.[2] At most, they offer a focus allowing the various actors to articulate their interests, behaviours and commitments in relation to a particular project, carried out in a specific space and over a given long-term duration. PPPs/PFIs in this sense offer a framework for coordinating these interests in a relatively open-ended way. They are thus embedded in the longer English tradition of corporatism, where coordination of communities and institutions is a prominent matter.

As Chapter 2 explained, 'strong elements of latter-day corporatism'[3] feature in various mechanisms associated with PPPs/PFIs. Corporatism entails cooperation between specific interest groups and public authorities to develop policies and make them acceptable to a given constituency.[4] More broadly, public policies are influenced by various communities outside the parliamentary process (e.g. professional organisations, trade unions, the City etc.). Multiple sites of powers in society shape and constrain governmental action and discretion. The diversity among communities explains why group members may have multiple allegiances.

These multiple belongings to various communities may be delicate within the state. They may be beneficial to liberty and stability,[5] as they

---

[1] P Selznick, 'The Idea of a Communitarian Morality' (1987) 75 CalLRev 445, 449 (original emphasis).

[2] See especially Chapter 3, pp 114–15, pp 127–9 and pp 139–40 and Chapter 4, pp 167–8.

[3] Harlow and Rawlings, 2009, 419.

[4] Craig, 2012, para 1-034.

[5] P Craig, 'Theory, 'Pure Theory' and Values in Public Law' [2005] PL 440, 444.

offer frameworks for addressing complex issues.[6] Furthermore, communities are not necessarily homogeneous. Their different components in terms of beliefs, values, material interests etc. may interact in different ways, sometimes mutually reinforcing, sometimes conflicting.[7] Therefore, communities may contribute to living together in society and foster a transformative vision of their members; one akin, congruent with or supplementary to the one that public authorities develop. Communities may thus contribute to the overall coordination required in society to bring order and stability while offering a framework for accommodating, to some extent, flexibility, disagreements and diversity. Yet communities also challenge accountability processes: they create a grey zone of power, an intermediary level of intricate arrangements of interests where the law does not systematically penetrate.[8]

These collective dimensions call for the role of public authorities in relation to communities to be explored: how the state may want to identify and relate to such communities, either in facilitating them and entrusting them with specific missions or in controlling them and their competing powers and influences on their members.[9] Legal techniques may be used to do so, as may discretion, which will ultimately be exercised by prioritising some collective interests above others. Public law gives overall directions shaping this exercise of discretion. However, positive standards may also be needed; of a kind that an ethic of care may help develop.

An Ethic of Care: The Prioritisation of Interests within Relationships

Framing discretion within an ethical framework takes different shapes. For example, the theory of public choice offers one such possible ethical framework based on the assumption that civil servants will act in their own self-interests. It then derives a framework for how bureaucracies

---

[6] R Cotterrell, 'Rethinking 'Embeddedness': Law, Economy, Community' (2013) 40 JLS 49, 54–6.

[7] Ibid 57.

[8] P Birkinshaw, I Harden and N Lewis, *Government by Moonlight – The Hybrid Parts of the State* (Unwin Hyman 1990).

[9] For a typology of the possible interplays between social groups and the state, see S Chambers and J Kopstein, 'Civil Society and the State' in J Dryzek, B Honig and A Phillips (eds) *The Oxford Handbook of Political Theory* (OUP 2006) 363.

would need to be designed on the basis of such an assumption.[10] This section presents an alternative framework for assessing how discretion is shaped in PPPs/PFIs: an ethic of care.

Originally developed in feminist thinking, the ethic of care concept is now expanding from private relationships such as mother-child to reach collective relationships and to feed into political theories.[11] Indeed, similarities may be found between the actions and values involved in caring for children and their development towards autonomy on the one hand, and the attitudes and values involved in the relationships between the state and individuals in need within society on the other hand. As PPPs/PFIs are one tool for addressing these last needs, they may provide an interesting insight into how an ethic of care could operate to frame public discretion without falling into paternalism.

At the level of values, an ethic of care challenges the idea that individuals are entirely autonomous and self-supporting. Indeed, '[t]hroughout our lives, all of us go through varying degrees of dependence and independence, of autonomy and vulnerability'.[12] Care focuses on attending to the needs of particular others for whom we take responsibility, developing the relationships of caring that enable them to make progress in their physical and social development. Normally, those who consciously care for others are not seeking primarily to further their own individual interests. Indeed, their interests are intertwined with those of the persons they care for. 'The well-being of a caring relationship involves the cooperative well-being of those in the relation, and the well-being of the relationship itself'.[13] Therefore, an ethic of care builds on three key features: the importance of relationships with particular others, the transformation possible within these relationships, and the relationships between the practice of care and the values involved in this practice.

At the level of practice, four ethical components answer the question of how caring responsibilities should be met: attentiveness, responsibility, competence and responsiveness. Attentiveness implies the recognition of a need to be cared about. This means that '[o]ne needs, in a sense, to

---

[10] J Legrand, *Motivation, Agency, and Public Policy – Of Knights and Knaves, Pawns and Queens* (OUP 2003) 8.

[11] E.g.: V Held, *The Ethics of Care – Personal, Political, and Global* (OUP 2006); J Tronto, *Moral Boundaries – A Political Argument for an Ethic of Care* (Routledge 1993).

[12] Tronto, 1993, 135.

[13] V Held, 'The Ethics of Care', in D Copp (ed) *The Oxford Handbook of Ethical Theory* (OUP 2006) 537, 540.

suspend one's own goals, ambitions, plans of life, and concerns, in order to recognize and to be attentive to others'.[14] Responsibility looks beyond formal or legal obligations. Faced with a need to be taken care of, we are moved to act upon it, to take the responsibility to meet it either because we contributed to the need for care or because there is no other way for the need to be taken care of than us meeting it. Competence implies that the care is adequately performed, that there is concern about the end result of the care provided. The responsiveness of the care-receiver to the care highlights that care involves relationships of power, as well as that the vulnerability of the cared-for gives rise to inequality, relationships of authority, domination and subordination. Therefore opportunities for abuse abound and there is a need to balance the needs of the care-givers and care-receivers.[15] Importantly, Tronto distinguishes between reciprocity and responsiveness. Responsiveness suggests that we seek to understand the need of others. However, we should not do this as if we were in the others' shoes but as the others express their needs for themselves in their own ways.[16] The differences between care-givers and care-receivers need to be respected. Good care requires that all of these four elements are included within an 'integrated whole', what Tronto calls integrity of care.[17] Therefore, judgments have to be made about how care is provided: judgments about the needs to be met, conflicting needs, strategies to meet the needs, the responsiveness of care-givers etc.

These four components of an ethic of care offer a different approach to relationships from economic rationality based on the pursuit of self-interest in the longer term or accountability for the efficient spending of taxpayers' money. These components of an ethic of care may thus be useful for our understanding of how autonomy, solidarity and trust shape public discretion as used to coordinate collective interests in PPPs/PFIs, and especially to maintain relationships involving public authorities, private actors and individuals over time, even while they all need to change according to their circumstances and opportunities for transformation.

In order to investigate how such an ethical framework might contribute to assessing how public discretion is used in PPPs/PFIs, this chapter looks first at three interplays between institutions, law and communities. The first of these is a mutually reinforcing dynamic between institutions

---

[14] Tronto, 1993, 128.

[15] Ibid 135–6.

[16] Ibid 136. Compare with Vincent-Jones's definition in Chapter 4, pp 194–6.

[17] Ibid 136.

and communities. The second is an institutionalisation of collective interests within legal requirements. The third comprises tensions between institutions and communities. These show the limits of the law in organising the dynamics between institutions and communities according to the state-analogue and market-analogue models. Therefore, the last sections of this chapter highlight how an ethic of care may be used to supplement the law in coordinating further the relationships involved in PPPs/PFIs.

INSTITUTIONS AND COMMUNITIES: MOVING IN THE SAME DIRECTION?

Chapter 4 showed how a narrative of transforming public services thanks to PPPs/PFIs has been developed:[18] PPPs/PFIs have been built on institutions, allowing market-analogue relationships to develop. However, the development of PPP/PFI programmes supported by these institutions has also allowed communities to form around PPPs/PFIs. The Building Schools for the Future programme (BsF) and waste PFIs illustrate this dynamic.

This section looks at these interplays between institutions, law and communities in two ways. First, BsF and waste PFIs originally implemented a policy pursuing social transformations. The law has been instrumental in the interplays but has not driven the modalities of these transformations. Secondly, BsF and waste PFIs followed different courses after 2010, when the coalition government came into power and took drastic austerity measures affecting both programmes. On these bases, this section suggests therefore that neither institutions nor law make a community arise out of the blue but that they do influence elements (such as values, practices, patterns of material interests) which are important for starting, developing and maintaining communities.[19]

BsF and Waste PFIs: Balance Driven by Institutions

BsF and waste PFIs both brought forward a wish to transform a sector drastically. BsF emphasised educational transformation.[20] Waste PFIs emphasised diversions from landfill to meet landfill targets set in an EU

---

[18] See Chapter 4, pp 192–4.

[19] For this idea in another context: Cotterrell (n 6 above) 68.

[20] DCSF, *The Management of Building Schools for the Future – Wave 7 to 15*, 2008.

directive and thus avoid EU fines.[21] In both cases, local authorities played the predominant role as they were primarily responsible for delivering education and waste services.[22] However, they did not have the financial means to implement the policy developed at national level.

In both waste and schools,[23] PFIs had been previously used with limited success. Borrowing from the Local Improvement Finance Trust (LIFT),[24] BsF and waste PFIs streamlined the process of delivering bundles of PFIs thanks to standardised key features such as payment mechanisms,[25] adaptations to the Standardisation of PFI Contracts Version 4 (SoPC4) (the standard contractual documents developed by the Treasury[26])[27] and tailored solutions (e.g. for partnering,[28] or assessing *VfM*[29]). Dedicated central entities supported them: Partnerships for Schools (PfS)[30] and the Waste Infrastructure Delivery Programme (WIDP).[31] Both programmes relied on credit allocation in waves over a long period of time.[32] PfS and WIDP intervened in the assessment of projects through the Gateway Process. For instance, in BsF, the process

---

21 Directive 1999/31/EC of the Council 26 April 1999 on the landfill of waste [1999] OJ L182/1.

22 AC, *Responding to the Waste Challenge*, 2008, para 4. Local authorities had powers to enter into PFIs for schools on the basis of: Local Government Act 2000, s 2; Education Act 1996, s 14; Schools Standards and Framework Act 1998, s 22 and Local Government Act 1972, s 11 (see PfS, BsF, *Project Agreement*, 2007, 1).

23 AC, *PFI in Schools*, 2003.

24 See Chapter 2, pp 94–6.

25 Defra, *Waste Infrastructure Delivery Programme Residual Waste Procurement Pack Module 4 Part I: Payment Mechanism Principles*, 2008; Defra, *Waste Infrastructure Delivery Programme Residual Waste Procurement Pack Module 4 Part II: Payment Mechanism Drafting*, 2008.

26 See Chapter 2, pp 75–7.

27 Defra, *Standardisation of Waste Management PFI Contracts: Guidance on SoPC Derogations*, 2006.

28 PfS, BsF, *Standard Form BSF, Strategic Partnering Agreement*, 2008.

29 PfS, BsF, *OBC Appendix 3: VfM Guidance Note and Input Assumptions*, 2006.

30 A non-departmental public body coordinating delivery and supporting local authorities in the elaboration of PFIs.

31 In 2006, Defra set-up this departmental cell to speed investments to meet EU targets on landfill, following a NAO report.

32 BsF was built in 15 waves, stretching from 2005–06 to 2020–23. Waste PFIs were allocated on the basis of a wave of projects every six months.

was neatly mapped out, even including a template for the local authority's 'strategy for change'.[33]

Despite the commonalities in terms of legal backgrounds and institutional settings, the two programmes operated in different policy areas and required specific adjustments. In BsF, education was a public good to be shared, if possible by creating positive side effects; in waste PFIs, waste was a burden to be distributed while minimising negative side effects and possibly scratching positive externalities. Differentiation in techniques can be highlighted around similar issues of market attraction and integration of non-commercial aims in the project and public involvement.

Firstly, the institutions (PfS, WIDP) directly developed market techniques to deliver the PFIs with the use of the competitive dialogue. They also sought indirect market promotion as there were times when competition was scarce.[34] A distinct policy was carried out to attract construction corporations to a new waste PFI market.[35] A legal system of credit regarding landfill targets was set up to mimic market mechanisms and incentivise authorities in their waste management.[36] In BsF, this 'market attraction' focused on possible uses for a school and its facilities (e.g. swimming pool, sport facilities, hall, theatre) outside school hours. In waste PFIs, recycling of materials[37] and exploitation of energy and heat[38] needed to become part of the projects.

Secondly, Bsf and the Department for Environment, Food and Rural Affairs (Defra) both included communities as potential beneficiaries of PFIs thanks to the non-commercial aims of the PFIs. For instance, providing apprenticeships in the local area was a selection criterion in the procurement process.[39] Waste PFIs relied on the cooperation of third-sector actors during procurement[40] or in the creation of a secondary market for recycled material.

---

[33] PfS, BsF, *Strategy for Change, Guidance for Local Authorities in BsF Wave* 7–9, Version 10.

[34] NAO, *BsF*, 2009, 37.

[35] OGC, *Improving Competition and Capacity Planning in the Municipal Waste Market*, 2006.

[36] AC, *Responding to the Waste Challenge*, 2008, 33.

[37] Defra, *Waste Strategy for England,* 2007, Annex B: Delivery Landscape and Decision-Making Framework, para 10.

[38] Ibid para 4.

[39] NAO, *BsF*, 2009, para 3.16.

[40] Defra, *Waste Strategy for England*, 2007, para 36-37.

Thirdly, BsF and Defra had to involve further communities and convert the resistance and opposition that key players such as heads of schools[41] or local residents might express. In the case of waste, especially, the law organises participatory rights to the benefit of the public in terms of both access to information and public involvement.[42] However, public involvement was problematic because waste PFIs attracted planning objections from local residents, especially when they relied on incinerators. Organisations such as Friends of the Earth developed toolkits to explain how to block the whole process successfully.[43] Long procedures and delays jeopardised PFI planning. This led Defra to privilege more accepted technologies for its waste treatment plants.[44] Involvement was also needed because if the local residents did not sort their waste properly the system was likely to fail.[45]

By 2010, a balance between institutions and communities had developed in terms of efficiency in operating frameworks on the one hand, and legitimacy in dealing with communities affected positively or adversely by PFIs on the other. The law was used as a neutral tool regarding the delivery of the social transformations promised by BsF and waste PFIs. It was first considered as a source of the required powers for local authorities, secondly as a framework for planning consultation, and thirdly as a framework for organising competition through the competitive dialogue or market for landfill credits. In all this, the law does not formalise a specific policy aim. It grants powers or sets procedures. The only exception to this is the landfill targets set in the EU landfill directive. However, even in this case, the law remains neutral in the sense that it merely sets numeric targets which can be achieved in a variety of ways, some of which include behavioural changes. Institutions and communities were interplaying in a mutually supportive way, working towards similar purposes, although institutions were the main drivers

---

41 Needed to operate the payment mechanisms (*SoPC4*, para 10.1.3). The payment mechanism had 70 pages of documentation, raising the question of its usability (PfS, BsF, *PFI Agreement – Payment Mechanism*, 2008).

42 UNECE Convention on *Access to Information, Public Participation in Decision-making and Access to Justice in Environmental Matters*, 1998 (Aahrus Convention). For the implementation in England, see P Stookes, *A Practical Approach to Environmental Law* (2nd edn, OUP 2009) para 2.31 ff.

43 FoE, *Private Finance Initiative (PFI) Funding for Waste Infrastructure*, 2008.

44 Defra, *Waste Strategy for England*, 2007, Annex E: Summary Guidance on Energy from Waste (EfW) Technology, para 2: Defra opted for anaerobic digesting as its preferred technology.

45 AC, *Responding to the Waste Challenge*, 2008, para 41.

setting these purposes and the chief techniques for achieving them. The changes implemented in PPPs/PFIs when the coalition government came into power in 2010 challenged this mutual support between institutions and communities.

Shifts at the Centre: A Reconfiguration of Interplays

The spending cuts decided on by the coalition government from 2010 onwards highlight how coordination between institutions, law and community shapes public discretion. Both BsF and waste PFIs were prominent targets for the spending cuts. With its 2010–11 budget of £3.7 bn, BsF was 'the Government's single largest capital programme in any area'.[46] Its funding was ended for all projects which had not reached the final business case (FBC) stage by January 2010. In the 2010, as a result of the comprehensive spending review (CSR), the greatest cuts, bar the Treasury, were made in Defra. Defra decided to drop funding for seven of the waste PFIs under negotiation.[47] This section analyses how these changes have affected the interplays between institutions and communities and the role that the law has played in structuring discretion in BsF and waste PFIs.

The first step in reshaping the interplays between institutions and communities was marked by the judicial reviews that the local authorities submitted against the ministerial decisions ending funding for PFIs under negotiation. The *Luton* case relating to BsF and the *Cheshire* case relating to waste PFIs are relevant here. In *Luton*,[48] the judge rejected the grounds based on irrationality[49] but found that procedural legitimate expectations to be consulted and the duty to have regard to the public sector equality duties (PSED) had been breached. Therefore the Secretary of State (SoS) had to take the decision again, following these procedural requirements. In *Cheshire*,[50] the judge considered that no procedural legitimate expectations to be consulted could be found. Indeed, there was no practice or duty to consult. A difference appears here in how discretion is limited: in *Luton*, procedural requirements constrained discretion, while in *Cheshire* such procedural requirements did not apply.

---

46 S James, *Review of Education Capital*, 2011.

47 https://www.gov.uk/government/news/changes-to-pfi-programme.

48 *R (Luton BC) v Secretary of State for Education* [2011] EWHC 217 (Admin).

49 For the comments on this rejection, see Chapter 4, pp 177–81.

50 *R (Cheshire East BC) v Secretary of State for Environment Food and Rural Affairs* [2011] EWHC 1975.

The difference proceeds from different appreciations of the circumstances of the cases by the judges. In *Luton*, the judge considered that even a short consultation period could have been applied. The economic crisis was not a sufficient ground of public interest to set consultation aside.[51] However, in *Cheshire*, the judge considered that the CSR emergency was a sufficiently overriding public interest to justify the absence of consultation.[52] In short, the judges differed in their directions about the balance between public interests (the overall economic crisis or its consequences in the CSR) and the collective interests represented by BsF and waste PFIs. From here on in, BsF and waste PFIs would follow different courses.

The next steps in reshaping the interplays between institutions and communities resulted from the ministerial decisions taken after these judicial reviews. Regarding BsF, the decision to end funding was part of policy changes promoting academies. Carried out after that decision was taken, and published in 2011, the James Review questioned the criteria that BsF used to prioritise the areas funded, namely the level of deprivation of the local area and school attainment.[53] While building refurbishment was meant to be a key purpose of BsF, the actual state of the building was not taken into account in the funding allocation: BsF appeared more to pursue policy goals of transforming education than improving buildings.[54] The review therefore recommended simplifying school specifications and delivering school refurbishments through the Department for Education (DfE), acting directly with the construction industry. Therefore the DfE should no longer give out money but 'a building to meet local needs'.[55]

The changes recommended by the James Review were implemented: PfS, a non-departmental public body, was dissolved and its activities brought back within the DfE in an executive agency called the Education Funding Agency (EFA). EFA is in charge of the Priority School Building Programme (PSBP), the new school refurbishment programme, which draws on the lessons and documentation developed in BsF. There are, however, key differences between the two programmes. Firstly, PSBP documentation sets highly standardised technical specifications for

---

51 *R (Luton BC) v Secretary of State for Education* [2011] EWHC 217 (Admin) [96].

52 *R (Cheshire East BC) v Secretary of State for Environment Food and Rural Affairs* [2011] EWHC 1975 [90].

53 James (n 46 above) para 2.9.

54 Ibid 12–13.

55 Ibid 6.

school buildings, moving away from bespoke projects. Secondly, PSBP documentation does not include a strategy for change or partnering agreements. Thirdly, educational projects and their potential transformation are now a matter for academies' sponsors, outside PFIs or PSBP.

More than 200 schools will benefit from PSBP, through either capital funding or private funding. Local authorities keep the power to fund PFIs entered into for academies, based on s 6 of the Academies Act 2010.[56] The LEAN principles of procurement are followed and a boot camp during the pre-procurement process organised, here again under the competitive dialogue.[57] The first batch of schools to be privately financed, among which are the schools from Luton, was announced in the *Official Journal of the European Union* (OJEU) in June 2013.[58]

Therefore, despite a clear change of policy towards now promoting academies, key features from BsF remain: a dedicated institution but brought back within the Department, standard documentation with the exception of the strategy for change, and competitive dialogue. Public efforts have been refocused towards technical specifications, and educational projects are entrusted to sponsors and academies. The pre-procurement stage has become a key part of the process of designing the project. From this stage there may emerge a community comprised of the procuring authorities and the economic actors bidding for the projects. Institutions have reduced their missions, which may open opportunities for economic and educational communities to deliver innovative schools and education.

By contrast, waste PFIs have followed a different path. Policy has shifted towards a 'zero waste economy', which requires changes to both behaviours and infrastructures.[59] Defra seeks to foster coordination with the waste management industry[60] but has abolished the market for landfill credits. The reasons for these decisions lie in changes to the EU Waste Framework Directive.[61] Diversion from landfill and landfill targets have been superseded by waste prevention. The need to meet the EU's

---

[56] DfE, *Letter to Local Authorities – PFI Academies*, 2011.

[57] EFA, *Priority School Building Programme, Hertfordshire, Luton & Reading (HLR) Private Finance (PF) Batch – Bidders' Day*, 2013.

[58] UK-London: Building services, 2013/S 124-212992, Contract notice, Services, 29 June 2013 (http://ted.europa.eu/udl?uri=TED:NOTICE:212992-2013:TEXT:EN:HTML&src=0).

[59] Treasury and IUK, *National Infrastructure Plan 2011*, 79–83.

[60] Ibid 82.

[61] Defra, *Waste Prevention Programme for England – Call for Evidence*, 2013, 3.

2020 landfill targets has guided the technical methodology, leading to the first cancellation of waste PFIs in 2010.[62] This methodology was accepted in *Cheshire* without any requirement that the interested local government be consulted. Meeting the same requirement was again the only standard used in the 2013 report leading to Defra's decision to drop the remaining three PFIs (including two based on incinerators) under discussion.[63] As the three projects would have little effect on the probability of the UK meeting its landfill targets, WIDP would no longer provide financial support but would continue to advise on projects under negotiation. This report sets out a technical methodology[64] based on statistical probabilities and leaves no scope to discuss waste PFIs within the overall waste policy.

Overall, the zero waste policy still relies on cooperation between Defra, economic actors and voluntary organisations in terms of changing social behaviour.[65] However, PFIs play no role in this cooperation. In the end, the political shift from landfill diversion to waste prevention, technical reports focused on EU landfill targets and continuing public opposition to PFIs delivering waste incinerators[66] made new PFI projects redundant.

PPPs/PFIs: A Tool for Structuring Public–Private Relationships

BsF and waste PFIs illustrate the interactions between institutions and communities in developing an overall narrative of transformation to coordinate collective interests and PPPs/PFIs. By 2010, both programmes were fairly similar in terms of the overall state machinery supporting the development of the PFIs and communities involved in them. After 2010, this structuring role of PFIs disappeared. Institutions did not rely on PFIs as the primary vehicle for furthering policy transformations now pursued

---

[62] Defra, *Spending Review 2010 – Changes to Waste PFI Programme – Supporting Analysis*, 2010.

[63] Defra, *Forecasting 2020 Waste Arisings and Treatment Capacity*, 2013.

[64] Ibid.

[65] Defra, *Waste Prevention Programme for England – Call for Evidence*, 2013, 29–37.

[66] E.g.: TC, *Private Finance Initiative* (1146-i HC 2010–12) submission North Yorkshire Waste Action Group ev w 1; SCEA, *Private Finance Projects and Off-Balance Sheet Debt* (63-ii HL 2009–10) memorandum Shlomo Dowen on behalf of People against Incineration and the United Kingdom Without Incineration Network, 298; memorandum Mary Newton on behalf of Gloucester Friends of the Earth Network, 320; memorandum Jane Green on behalf of Coventry Friends of the Earth and CRACIN.

outside PFIs. PFIs were merely seen as financial tools for delivering school buildings and were no longer used for future waste infrastructures. This section highlights the limits of using market-analogue or state-analogue perspectives to analyse the concerns for autonomy, solidarity and trust in school PFIs and waste PFIs.

As a rule, autonomy was understood in both programmes in terms of expertise in developing documentation and innovative tools or reviewing the programme. In BsF, part of this expertise was held by PfS and part by consultants such as Price Waterhouse Cooper (PwC), commissioned in 2006 to review the scheme on a yearly basis.[67] The James Review brings part of this expertise back into the public sector: firstly, there is an officially authored review; secondly, PfS is replaced by EFA, located in the DfE. However, the practical implementation of PSBP relies on external consultants, as BsF did.[68] In waste, WIDP was the departmental unit in charge of funding. It remains in charge of advising on technical matters. Therefore, in both programmes, discretion heavily depends on expertise beyond financial matters and *VfM* assessments. It also relates to technical specifications regarding school buildings, technological issues involved in waste treatment and the probabilities of meeting EU landfill targets.

Both programmes relied on solidarity. Here, solidarity did not mean joint maximisation of self-interests by the public and private partners. It instead highlighted the interdependency of the actors involved in the programmes. In BsF, deprived areas were ranked as priorities, and in waste PFIs the involvement of third-sector actors expressed concern for solidarity. Solidarity between institutions and communities is also present in the form of subsidiarity. Indeed, institutions no longer define the content of educational projects in PSBP but leave it to the academies' sponsors. Financial provisions such as private initiatives have become ancillary means of providing the required school buildings.

Finally, both programmes expressed concerns for trust, away from calculativeness and means of counterbalancing risks. Partnering agreements, as non-legally binding techniques, were strongly linked to BsF. PSBP conveys the government's Big Society agenda, which is committed to the idea that community delivers public services in a more adequate way than state institutions. In waste PFIs, techniques fostering trust, such

---

[67] DCSF, *Evaluation of Building Schools for the Future – 2nd Annual Report – Final* Report, 2008, summary, para 2.

[68] E.g.: EFA, *Questionnaire for Legal Services Required in Connection with Privately-Financed Projects Procured through the Priority School Building Programme*, 2012.

as public involvement, were anchored in legal requirements. This public involvement caused much delay for waste PFIs because individuals and non-profit organisations were committed to opposing the technologies involved in PFI incinerators at all levels, as the evidence submitted in the Lords' inquiry reveals.

Overall, logics other than market- or state-analogue ones were relied on in school PFIs and waste PFIs. Users or affected third parties were not understood as taxpayers but as local residents or as people affected by the services delivered by the PPPs/PFIs. They were incentivised to sort waste, were part of the communities using the schools, benefited from jobs through linkages or the renewal of a special area around the PFIs, or expressed their opposition to waste PFI incinerators. The relationships between individuals and PPPs/PFIs were structured with an array of techniques, wrapped within a narrative of transformation. The role of the law was neutral here and instrumental in supporting the relationships between institutions and communities. It provided powers for public authorities (such as the Academies Act 2010, s 6) or set procedural limits to discretion, as the *Luton* and *Cheshire* cases showed. However, the law does not specify any transformation to be achieved. The only exception is the landfill targets but these were imposed by the EU and can be seen as external to the discretion exercised by English public authorities. The next section analyses cases where the law truly institutionalises collective interests to develop social transformations.

ETHICAL COMMITMENTS, LEGAL REQUIREMENTS AND SOCIAL CHANGES

Public contracting provides an opportunity to develop linkages to pursue policy goals thanks to the direct purchasing of goods and services. Linkages, also known as 'contract compliance',[69] are defined as the way in which 'government attempts to combine [...] three functions [...]: *participating* in the market but *regulating* it *at the same time*, by using its *purchasing* power to advance conceptions of social justice, particularly equality and non-discrimination'.[70] By imposing contractual terms encapsulating collective requirements related to social, environmental or equality conditions, public authorities firstly expressly declare the importance

---

[69] S Arrowsmith, 'Public Procurement as an Instrument of Policy and the Impact of Market Liberalisation' (1995) 111 LQR 235.

[70] See C McCrudden, *Buying Social Justice – Equality, Government Procurement and Legal Change* (OUP 2007) 3 (original emphasis).

that they attach to these conditions and secondly expect their contracting partners to comply with them. Linkages allow for consistency in public spending across public policies, which is 'an important value in public administration'[71] and helps to foster trust in public administration.[72] Linkages apply in PPPs/PFIs as in any other public contracts.[73] They connect PPPs/PFIs with far-off beneficiaries such as the community at large (e.g. terms linked to absence of corruption, environmental terms), groups of beneficiaries identified by specific features (e.g. non-discrimination terms and disabled workers) or classes of beneficiaries (employees and labour standards). The law thus encapsulates ethical commitments to advance collective interests on the basis that these communities share common features, vulnerability or territory. This section looks at two illustrations of linkages, namely the public sector equality duty (PSED) and the Public Sector (Social Value) Act 2012 (PS(SV) Act 2012). This is to highlight their potential in relation to changes but also the limits arising from their uncertain implementation.

From an historical perspective, the use of contractual linkages has been debated and their enforcement uncertain.[74] In the 1980s, local authorities used contractual linkages to thwart national policies, most notably compulsory competitive tendering (CCT).[75] For this reason, linkages were strongly limited: so-called 'non-commercial considerations' (e.g. terms and conditions of employment; promotion, training or other opportunities afforded to the workforce; the country of origin of supplies; any political, industrial or sectarian affiliations or interests of contractors) were excluded from the factors which could be taken into account by local government when awarding contracts following CCT.[76] Even though CCT was replaced by best value in 1999, the list of non-commercial considerations remained in force and still applies to public procurement. In procurement, human rights and social and environmental linkages are rooted in the creative scope the law allows with circumspection.[77]

---

71 Davies, 2008, 265.

72 Ibid 266.

73 NAO, *Sustainable Procurement in Government*, 2013, 11; CLG, *Local Government PFI Project Support Guide* (2008–09), 10; CLG, *Local Government PFI Project Support Guide* (2009–10), 15; CHP/SHINE, *Invitation to Go Green and Beyond – The Exemplar Sustainable Healthcare Buildings Programme*, sd.

74 McCrudden (n 70 above) 301 ff.

75 Ibid 336–43.

76 Local Government Act 1988, s 17(5).

77 Classic directive, art 26; Arrowsmith and Kunzlik, 2009, passim.

Overall, linkages integrate PPPs/PFIs within a given social and geographical environment. Linkages do not create individual rights for potential beneficiaries such as employees, disabled persons etc. They lack enforceability and adequate monitoring structures. They rely on their symbolic reach, on the discursive force of the law and on the ethical behaviour of public and private entities. Morality is tied in with linkages, as public authorities need to lead by example.[78] Linkages point out that moral obligations extend to 'distant strangers',[79] people whose lives are affected by our acts even if we do not know them. These moral obligations go beyond the reciprocity encapsulated in economic exchange because they are universal.

As a reaction to these limits of linkages, specific statutory duties have been progressively imposed on public authorities. These changes help to refine our understanding of the delicate interplays between ethical commitments, legal requirements and social changes, especially as PPPs/PFIs bring them into the light. The following sections detail two of these changes: the PSED and the PS(SV) Act 2012. Yet despite their legal sophistication being more developed than contractual linkages, both again feature significantly through the collective dimension of their beneficiaries: they do not create individual rights enforceable at private law.

PSED: Transforming Procedural Requirements into Substantial Equality?

The public sector equality duty (PSED) illustrates one way in which ethical commitments to equality can become formalised in legal requirements: public authorities have a duty to have regard to equality in taking their decisions. Therefore public decisions involving PPPs/PFIs have to implement the PSED. Judicial reviews based on breaches of the PSED in PPPs/PFIs have been submitted twice, once with success, once not. This section illustrates that legal requirements encapsulating equality potentially leave room for supplementation with an ethical commitment to equality in their concrete implementation and the coordination of collective interests involved in PPPs/PFIs.

The PSED results from the development of positive duties to promote equality imposed on public authorities over time. The Equality Act 2010,

---

[78] C McCrudden, 'Corporate Responsibility and Public Procurement' in D McBarnet and others (eds), *The New Corporate Accountability – Corporate Social Responsibility and the Law* (CUP 2007) 93, 97.

[79] O O'Neill, *Bounds of Justice* (CUP 2000) 189.

s 149 consolidated previously existing duties[80] and extended them to new grounds. Currently, public authorities have a duty, when they exercise their functions, to have regard to the need to eliminate discrimination, advance equality and foster good relations between persons sharing protected characteristics and persons who do not share them.[81] The relevant protected characteristics are age, disability, gender reassignment, pregnancy and maternity, race, religion, belief, gender and sexual orientation.[82] The PSED requires that public authorities consider the consequences of any of their decisions for categories of people sharing these protected characteristics. The PSED thus presents a strong collective dimension. The duty shifts from being mainly negative to positive. Public authorities have to do more than just ensure the absence of discrimination; they must also actively and positively promote equality of opportunity between different groups.[83] The PSED imposes a duty on public authorities, while no direct legal relationships between these public authorities and the protected categories can be identified. Behind the PSED lies the idea that change at the level of the social structure is required so that substantial equality is reached.[84]

The concrete implementation of the PSED presents several weaknesses, however. Firstly, the PSED only requires that public authorities have due regard to the grounds of discrimination and the consequences of their policies for these factors. There is no duty regarding the actual outcomes of decisions on equality matters. The second challenge for the PSED relates to enforcement. The PSED does not give rise to an individual and enforceable right. The main actors are the Equality Commission and the courts through judicial review. However, the Equality Commission has not been in a position to issue compliance notices due to spending cuts. Judicial review has become a first resort[85] but it mainly depends on non-governmental organisations' (NGOs) agendas. Furthermore, case law has been unpredictable in its results as the two judicial reviews relying on the PSED in PPPs/PFIs illustrate: firstly

---

[80] Namely through the Race Relations (Amendment) Act 2000, the Disability Discrimination Act 2005, s 49A and the Sex Discrimination Act 1975.

[81] Equality Act 2010, s 149(1).

[82] Equality Act 2010, s 149(7).

[83] C McCrudden, 'Equality and Non-Discrimination' in D Feldman (ed) *English Public Law* (2nd edn, OUP 2009) 499 para 11.156.

[84] S Fredman, 'Breaking the Mold: Equality as a Proactive Duty' (2012) 60 AmJCompL 265, 266.

[85] Ibid 270.

Dudley, where no breach of the PSED was found; secondly *Luton*, where the claim based on a breach of the PSED was successful.

In *Dudley*,[86] the SoS for Communities and Local Government had changed the system by which PFI credits were paid to a local authority, Dudley, for its PFI pertaining to information and communications technology in schools. Dudley argued that the SoS had breached the duty to have regard to the impact of the decision on protected persons. The judge rejected the claim as the PSED would apply more to local government than central government. The duty would only have to be carried out some years in the future as funding was being made available to the claimant for a few more years.[87] The judge also considered that the SoS's decision had only financial consequences[88] and that the local authority would have to make the decisions to cut or reduce a specific service or could find alternative funding arrangements. This may well have assumed a financial autonomy that local government may possess in theory but far less so in reality.

In this case, therefore, the SoS enjoyed a broad discretion to change funding modalities in a commitment to finance a PFI. However, the PSED should not be dismissed too quickly, as *Luton* shows. In the *Luton* case, the local authorities challenged the decision taken by the SoS for Education to end BsF funding for school refurbishments. The judge found that the SoS did not have regard to the PSED when taking the decision to end BsF. Indeed, some of the cancelled projects were special schools for disabled pupils or were situated in areas with significant populations of minorities. According to the judge, all the documents focused 'entirely on different stages in the procurement process and what savings had to be made', with no 'single reference to disability, race or gender need/impact anywhere in them'.[89] This absence was tied in with the lack of consultation.[90] Therefore the judge considered that the SoS's

---

[86] *R (Dudley MBC) v Secretary of State for Communities and Local Government* [2012] EWHC 1729 (Admin).

[87] Ibid [88]–[91].

[88] However, PSED has been accepted with regard to financial consequences of decisions, see T Hickman, 'Too Hot, too Cold or Just Right? The Development of the Public Sector Equality Duties in Administrative Law' [2013] PL 325, 332. The courts agree though that consideration of the impact of budgetary decisions may be deferred to a later stage of implementation as long as reallocation of funds is possible (p 343).

[89] *R (Luton BC) v Secretary of State for Education* [2011] EWHC 217 (Admin) [112].

[90] Ibid [114].

decision had been unlawful. An ex-post impact assessment of the cancellation of BsF was carried out, which concluded that:

> the stoppage of these school projects has inadvertently impacted more on children who can be seen to be disadvantaged in terms of social deprivation, and as having English as an additional language compared to national averages; and also as having slightly higher rates of minority ethnic people and on learners with [special education needs] compared to national average.[91]

Furthermore, an equality impact assessment was carried out in the drawing up of the schools listed for the PSBP.[92] As a result 'those schools in the very worst condition and all special schools included within the programme would be taken forward using capital grant'.[93] Equality duties thus have concrete effects.

PPPs/PFIs confirm that the case law involving the PSED is unpredictable.[94] *Dudley* illustrates the difficulty of identifying with precision the specific decision that needs to comply with the PSED within an intricate web of decision making. However, *Luton* illustrates that public authorities need to be aware of their duties, and not merely focused on issues related to procurement and *VfM* decided by decision makers completely disconnected from the reality where their decisions will take effect. It ensures a minimal awareness of the particular circumstances within which public decisions related to PPPs/PFIs are implemented.

Procedural Linkages: Social Value and Well-being

The Public Service (Social Value) Act 2012 (PS(SV) Act 2012) illustrates a second way to extend contractual linkages. It creates a new duty for public authorities to consider economic, social and environmental well-being in the pre-procurement stage of services contracts. It establishes a procedural connection between procurement and the purposes for which public authorities exercise discretion. This section highlights how this new duty is the (temporary?) outcome of long hesitations about the articulations between collective interests and market logic. This new legal technique embeds collective interests in contracting. Yet it leaves space for discretion about how public authorities implement it in general and in

---

91 https://www.gov.uk/government/publications/equalities-impact-assessment-building-schools-for-the-future.

92 HL Deb, 28 February 2013, vol 743, col 358WA.

93 HC Deb, 28 February 2013, vol 559, col 611W.

94 Fredman (n 84 above) 277.

PPPs/PFIs in particular. Public authorities may thus foster more or less collective interests through their decisions.

The PS(SV) Act 2012 requires public authorities to consider 'how what is proposed to be procured might improve the economic, social and environmental well-being' of their areas and 'how in conducting the process of procurement, it might act with a view to securing that improvement'.[95] The duty only applies in the pre-procurement stage of service contracts and is limited in its reach and bindingness. Indeed, the authority only needs to take into account what is relevant to the procurement, and not overall economic, social or environmental well-being.[96] It also needs to consider what is proportionate to taking these relevant matters into account.[97] The ways in which the duty will be applied are uncertain: it will be applicable in parallel with the best value duty already in force,[98] and it should not lead to the derogation of any legal obligations following the Public Contracts Regulations 2006 (PCR 2006).[99] If the extent to which the new duty affects the chosen contents may be limited, it may however give a ground for third parties to challenge public decisions in a case of breach of duty.[100] The new duty may face similar limits to its concrete implementation as the PSED, even more so because proportionality and respect for the PCR 2006 are explicitly mentioned in the PS(SV) Act 2012.

Even though the concrete implementation of this new duty is uncertain, this duty reveals the latest attempt to articulate the use of taxpayers' money (usually used as a proxy for the common good), collective interests and private interests. Indeed, it sets out how public contracting has to be designed so that the outcome of the competitive process, i.e. the procurement, can contribute to economic, social and environmental well-being. It can thus be considered especially relevant for PPPs/PFIs in three respects.

---

[95] PS(SV) Act 2012, s 1(3)(a) and (b).

[96] PS(SV) Act 2012, s 1(6).

[97] PS(SV) Act 2012, s 1(6).

[98] PPN, *The Public Services (Social Value) Act 2012 – Advice for Commissioners and Procurers*, information note 10/12, 2012. On the best value duty, see Chapter 2, pp 54–7 and Chapter 4, p 185.

[99] PS(SV) Act 2012, s 1(8) and (10).

[100] P Henty, 'Legislative Comment: Social Responsibility in Public Procurement: Public Services (Social Value) Act 2012' (2012) PPLR na193.

Firstly, the PS(SV) Act 2012 may signal that public authorities carry out different functions from private persons.[101] Their decisions are not taken in a void or with self-interest in mind: their impact needs to be factored into the decision-making process. Regarding public–private relationships, this may clarify the specific role that the public party performs within such arrangements to the benefit of the wider collectivity.

Secondly, the PS(SV) Act 2012 is the outcome of a private member's bill seeking to take a concrete step towards the realisation of the Big Society Agenda. It originally intended to use procurement to bring funding to social enterprises (e.g. community groups, cooperatives, charities) contributing to wider economic, social and environmental well-being as part of a national social enterprise strategy.[102] Yet the bill was only enacted after concessions were agreed between the government and the bill's author. One of these concessions required that the benefit of the Act would be open not only to social enterprises but also to any economic actors.[103] The ambiguity between economic and non-economic interests potentially benefiting from the spending of public monies appears strongly here. PPPs/PFIs may, however, be especially important in this regard. Indeed, they have the potential to organise cooperation between economic (providing for the infrastructure) and non-economic actors (delivering the services), which could especially be of value with regard to this new duty.

Thirdly, the PS(SV) Act 2012 may face many implementation problems.[104] It lacks direct enforcement mechanisms, although social enterprises may act in such a way as to secure compliance. The duty is limited to the pre-procurement stage. The outcome of these considerations of well-being and their integration in the contractual design, terms or performance is left uncharted in the statute. Well-being is a notion which may be difficult to quantify, although indicators are being developed by the Office for National Statistics (ONS) and Defra.[105] PPPs/PFIs may exacerbate the dilution of the possible impact of the pre-procurement

---

[101] Even though the Localism Act 2011, s 1 puts local authorities and private persons on an equal footing.

[102] *Public Services (Social Enterprise and Social Value)* HC Bill (2010–12) [6]; HC Deb, 19 November 2010, vol 518, col 1170.

[103] L Floyd, 'The Elephant in the Room: The Public Service (Social Value) Act 2012' (2013) 129 LQR 180, 181.

[104] Ibid 181–2.

[105] EAC, *Measuring Well-being and Sustainable Development: Sustainable Development Indicators: Government Response to the Committee's Fifth Report*

stage and project design on the economic, social and environmental well-being of a given collectivity. However, because of their institutional support, PPPs/PFIs may also leverage such an impact. The pre-procurement stage of PPPs/PFIs organises intense discussions and boot camps with market actors, as well as non-economic actors, interested in delivering public infrastructures and services. The indicators developed to assess well-being may become integrated in the *VfM* assessment. The Gateway Process and the major project approval and assurance process[106] may also enable a tracking down of whether the economic, social and environmental well-being that public authorities considered at the outset of their project is being delivered during the performance phase. The mere fact that this would be monitored may improve the understanding of how public spending impacts (in)directly on collective well-being.

Therefore PPPs/PFIs may be especially suitable vehicles in terms of having an impact on the economic, social and environmental well-being of a geographic area and making this trickle down the supply chain.[107] They may also provide an opportunity to monitor how the overall purpose of economic, social and environmental well-being is concretely implemented throughout the projects. This outcome is not guaranteed, however. It depends on the concrete implementation of the PS(SV) Act 2012 by public authorities and their partners in specific PPPs/PFIs.

PPPs/PFIs and Transversal Policies: Leverage or Dilution?

Institutions are increasingly required to take into account ethical commitments related to the protection of collective interests, such as equality or economic, social and environmental well-being. Legal techniques, such as contractual linkages, PSED and the PS(SV) Act 2012, allow public authorities to exercise their discretion according to these commitments. However, discretion remains broad and the legal requirements limited. Contractual linkages are only facultative when they are not prohibited. PSED only imposes a duty to have regard to equality. The PS(SV) Act 2012 requires public authorities to consider well-being at a pre-procurement stage. Furthermore, these requirements lack systematic enforcement mechanisms. However, the requirements all seek to ensure that institutions relying on market actors provide services, such as PPPs/PFIs, in order to fulfil transversal public policies such as equality or

---

of Session 2012–13 (139 HC 2013–14); ONS, *Measuring National Well-being: Life in the UK*, 2012.

[106] See Chapter 2, pp 73–5.

[107] In a similar sense: Henty (n 100 above) na196.

economic, social and environmental well-being in an area beyond market actors' interests, to ensure the delivery of collective benefits. Therefore, they inform our understanding of how autonomy, solidarity and trust can be balanced in public discretion according to logics other than state-analogue and market-analogue models.

Firstly, autonomy here refers to the faculty (contractual linkages) or duty (PSED, the PS(SV) Act 2012) of public authorities to fulfil their specific roles, distinct from the functions and interests pursued by private actors, when they exercise their functions. These roles are the protection of collective interests and the recognition of vulnerable groups within society. Even if they do not have the duty to guarantee the concrete realisation of this protection, public authorities need to have it in mind when exercising discretion. The legal requirements do not reach further at this stage. However, principles of consistency may inform public authorities' behaviours and attitudes to ensure that legal requirements are translated into practical steps towards the realisation of this protection, for instance in designing PPPs/PFIs.

Secondly, solidarity is illustrated here in the purposes that public authorities have when they spend taxpayers' money. Equality is needed not just for one given individual but for categories of people presenting protected features, as well as between these categories and between these categories and categories of people lacking these protected features. Solidarity is present in terms of economic, social and environmental well-being over a given area. In this sense, PPPs/PFIs are no longer a tool for delivering win-win outcomes for the public and private parties involved in them. They are instead directed towards structuring public and private relationships to deliver benefits for the wider community that they serve.

Thirdly, trust in public authorities by users and people affected by PPPs/PFIs, refers to the problem of transforming ethical commitments into daily practice. No dedicated institutional or legal frameworks support the implementation and enforcement of these legal requirements. No individual rights are created. Other actors, such as communities and NGOs, are informally entrusted with these. Equally, uncertainty applies in relation to the potential conflicts between various categories of protected persons, between the various components of economic, social and environmental well-being, and between equality and well-being. The legislator seems to accredit institutions or communities as sufficiently competent, fittingly resourced and adequately committed to implementing the legal requirements and to developing appropriate solutions to these issues. However, PPPs/PFIs require more attention in order for public authorities to leverage the high investments that PPPs/PFIs offer for their transversal policies and to not dilute these ethical requirements throughout the network of decisions to be taken and implemented.

These legal requirements institutionalising ethical commitments to collective interests seek to further social changes. Yet their concrete implementation relies on the assumption that institutions and communities will harmoniously support each other. However, the next section highlights the tensions that emerge between institutions and communities and the role that the law plays in policing them.

TENSIONS BETWEEN INSTITUTIONS AND COMMUNITIES

Public authorities are in charge of providing the common good. Communities have their own identities based on shared interests, values or beliefs. Institutions and communities may not share the same purposes for action. Tensions imply different perspectives but may trigger creativity from the protagonists to overcome them. Legal techniques may be useful for helping them find common ground throughout their interactions and disagreements. This section uses the case of NHS PFI hospitals to map out how tensions have been framed between institutions and communities and the role that the law has played in strengthening institutions' powers while clarifying communities' interests.

PFI Hospitals: Promotion and Resistance

In order to provide healthcare services across the country despite the financial pressures of the early 2000s, the Labour Government developed a policy relying on PFIs to finance major investments in hospitals. From the outset, PFI hospitals triggered opposition. Clearly, the actors involved in the organised institutional discussions did not share a common opinion on PFIs in principle. However, their involvement in these discussions moved them to develop a common language. This section maps out these disagreements in relation to PFI hospitals, starting with an early discussion of PFI hospitals and then distinguishing the main voices in the more recent debates on the issue.

In 2002, the Health Committee in the House of Commons investigated the policy in its early days and highlighted that the issue had led to a 'polarised debate' and antagonism, not least between the government and academics, most notably Professor Pollock.[108] For the proponents of PFI hospitals, they were the only available option for financing the state-of-art hospitals needed, moving beyond the traditional issues of time and budget that plagued conventional procurements. Overall the business community, including KPMG, the CBI and the Business Services Association, supported these views.[109] However, opponents argued that PFIs would reduce available beds, and challenged their *VfM* and risk transfer, the difficult access to documentation and the unfavourable staff transfer conditions. Overall, Unison, professional organisations such as the Medical Practitioners' Union and the NHS Confederation fell into this category. Similar levels of opposition could be found both at national and local levels.[110] Voluntary groups such as the Democratic Health Network and the Oxfordshire PFI Alert Group also expressed similar criticisms.[111]

Besides these debates related to PFI hospitals, the Health Committee noted two points which framed how institutions helped PFIs become embedded within a given community. Firstly, the Health Committee highlighted the need to learn from the first wave of PFIs when setting up the following waves. This led it to emphasise the role of a PFI Departmental Unit in facilitating the sharing of expertise.[112] The National Audit Office (NAO) built on such considerations to advocate the centralisation of data so that the Department of Health might leverage its bargaining power and deliver *VfM* projects. It also suggested that this Department promote PFI support clubs to foster exchanges of experience among trusts.[113] Such ideas would contribute to the development of a 'community of interests'[114] between trusts involved in PFIs, possibly developing a shared understanding of PFIs and a common strategy for dealing with contractual difficulties. However, the coalition government

---

108 Health Committee, *The Role of the Private Sector in the NHS* (308-i HC 2001–02) 20, 22.

109 E.g.: Ibid 20.

110 Ibid 21.

111 Ibid 31.

112 Ibid 31.

113 PAC, *PFI in Housing and Hospitals* (631 HC 2010–11), recommendation 7; NAO, *The Performance and Management of Hospital PFI Contracts*, 2010, recommendation para 21(a).

114 NAO, *The Performance and Management of Hospital PFI Contracts*, 2010, recommendation para 21(d).

disregarded these recommendations as they fell within the autonomy of local entities and were no longer its own responsibility.[115]

Secondly, the Health Committee was concerned about the impact that the PFIs might have on the 'local health economy'. This notion of a local health economy was not defined. However, the basic idea was that PFIs required the trusts to pay annual charges, which were ring-fenced and could not be allocated to other health projects and services required in the area. Therefore the trust would see its margin for dealing with upcoming needs and changing patterns of care limited.[116] The failures in PFI hospitals discussed in the next section illustrate this risk.

The debates related to the implementation of PFIs within the NHS remain. The recent inquiries into PFIs in both the House of Lords and the Treasury Committee have revealed sustained support for PFIs.[117] However, the opposition that the Health Committee pinned down has continued through four main groups: firstly, the medical community;[118] secondly, academics such as Pollock and Hellowell;[119] thirdly, trade unions;[120] and finally, civil society groups.[121] They all engage with the

---

115 Treasury, *Government Responses on the Fourteenth to the Eighteenth Reports from the Committee of Public Accounts Session 2010–11* (2011 Cm 8042) 8.

116 Health Committee, *The Role of the Private Sector in the NHS* (308-I HC 2001–02) 33.

117 TC, *Private Finance Initiative* (1146-i HC 2010–12) submission NHS Confederation ev 30; witness ev 16; submission Foundation Trust Network, ev w86; submission North Tees and Hartlepool NHS Foundation Trust ev w113; Treasury, 2012, 98.

118 Ibid submission BMA ev w9; SCEA, *Private Finance Projects and Off-Balance Sheet Debt* (63-ii HL 2009–10) memorandum BMA 251; witness 260.

119 E.g.: TC, *Private Finance Initiative* (1146-ii HC 2010–12) submission Professor Pollock, ev w130. Additionally: A Pollock and others, *Blaming the Victims: The Trust Special Administrator's Plans for South East London* (Centre for Primary Care and Public Health 2013); A Pollock, 'How PFI is Crippling the NHS' Guardian, 29 June 2012; M Hellowell and D Batty, 'Loss of Initiative' Guardian, 4 February 2009; D Price, D Gaffney and A Pollock, *The Only Game in Town? A Report on the Cumberland Infirmary* (Unison 1999).

120 SCEA, *Private Finance Projects and Off-Balance Sheet Debt* (63-ii HL 2009–10) memorandum Unison 255; witness 260; Unison, *Reform of the Private Initiative Response Template*, 2012; TUC, *Reform of the Private Initiative Response Template*, 2012.

121 TC, *Private Finance Initiative* (1146-ii HC 2010–12) submission Oxon PFI Alert Group ev w101.

discussion of the *VfM* of PFI hospitals[122] and the accountability of PFIs.[123] They also express their concerns about the consequences of PFIs for the local health economy.[124]

Starting with the 2002 inquiry into the role of the private sector in the NHS, a dynamic developed. The first parliamentary debates held by the Health Committee structured the debates related to PFI hospitals. Building on these, the NAO and the Public Accounts Committee (PAC) suggested the development of institutions to foster a community of interests among PFI actors and to improve *VfM*. Parliamentary debates and governmental discussions have enabled opponents and proponents of hospital PFIs to voice their opinions in a formatted way, even in template documents, revolving mainly around *VfM* and its components. Yet concepts such as 'local health economy' are shared across communities and institutions while being absent from the usual wording applicable to PPPs/PFIs. However, this shared recognition of the importance of local health economy has not been enough to address the tensions arising from the failing PFI hospitals.

Failing PFI Hospitals and their Knock-on Effects

These investments in PFI hospitals were 'the largest hospital building programme in the history of the NHS'.[125] However, they led NHS trusts to struggle with financial problems.[126] In two trusts especially, the South London Healthcare Trust (SLHT) and the Peterborough and Stamford Hospitals NHS Trust (Peterborough Trust), PFIs were identified as one of the main reasons for these financial difficulties. Specific systems were then organised to manage these failing trusts and the competing interests between individual patient care, care provision in a given area and public expenditure. Three features of these systems illustrate the tensions between institutions and communities and the role of the law in dealing

---

122 E.g.: Ibid submission BMA ev w9.

123 E.g.: Ibid submission Greg Dropkin and Sam Semoff on behalf of Keeping Our NHS Public ev w 43.

124 E.g.: Ibid submission BMA ev w9; SCEA, *Private Finance Projects and Off-Balance Sheet Debt* (63-ii HL 2009–10) memorandum BMA 251; witness 260.

125 Treasury, 2008, 5.

126 PAC, *Securing the Future Financial Sustainability of the NHS* (389 HC 2012–13); NAO, *Securing the Future Financial Sustainability of the NHS*, 2012.

with them.[127] Firstly, there is the development of the local health economy as a key standard for assessing decisions related to hospital PFIs. Secondly, there is the strengthening of the powers of the healthcare regulator, Monitor. Thirdly, there is the repeated combining of further formalisation and parallel informal solutions. This section maps these features emerging from failing PFI hospitals, starting with the SLHT case and then turning to the Peterborough case.

The SLHT

The SLHT has several hospitals across three London boroughs (Greenwich, Bexley and Bromley) and high level of debts. Attempts to address this, including the reorganisation of its hospitals through a PFI in 2009, did not improve its financial situation. In 2012, the SoS for Health decided to trigger the unsustainable provider regime introduced by the Health Act 2009.[128] This regime seeks to work out a solution for failing trusts thanks to the appointment of a trust special administrator (TSA) in charge of drafting recommendations to the SoS.

The SLHT illustrates how the statutory requirements and guidance[129] balance discretion for the SoS and the TSA to work out actions and recommendations with formal constraints. The principle is discretion granted to the SoS. Discretion is only limited by the purpose for which the SoS can exercise the power to appoint a TSA, namely the interests of the health service.[130] The guidance is clear that such an appointment should only happen as a last resort, when all other means of tackling financial distress have been exhausted.[131] The SLHT met these conditions: it had been facing a long-standing history of financial issues that a succession of reviews had not been able to adequately address. The trust was the most financially challenged in the country.[132] It depended on

[127] The law is here presented as relevant for the two case studies. However, the Health and Social Care Act 2012 has brought amendments to it. For a clear explanation of the changes brought by this act: A Davies, 'This Time, it's for Real: The Health and Social Care Act 2012' (2013) 76 MLR 564.

[128] Health Act 2009, s 16 introducing s 65A ff in the National Health Service Act 2006 (NHSA 2006).

[129] NHSA 2006, s 65N(2); DH, *Statutory Guidance for Trust Special Administrators Appointed to NHS Trusts*, 2012.

[130] NHSA 2006, s 65B(2); DH, *Statutory Guidance for Trust Special Administrators Appointed to NHS Trusts*, 2012 para 2.

[131] DH, *Statutory Guidance for Trust Special Administrators Appointed to NHS Trusts*, 2012, para 3–5; the explanatory note to the Health Act 2009 made also clear (para 35).

[132] HC Deb, 31 January 2013, vol 557, c1072.

weekly departmental support of £1m. This financial dependency on the Department of Health (DH) made it impossible for the trust to achieve NHS foundation trust status, in keeping with government policy. Therefore a TSA was appointed in July 2012.[133] Pursuant to ss 65F(1) and 65I(1) of the National Health Service Act 2006 (NHSA 2006), the TSA would provide the SoS with a draft report and final report stating the actions that the TSA would recommend that the SoS took in relation to the trust. The TSA issued a series of recommendations to the SoS, including the dissolution of the trust and the writing off of its debts. Parliament was informed throughout the process to ensure a minimum of political accountability.[134] However, TSA's discretion was constrained in two ways.[135]

The first constraint was related to the consultation and engagement procedure. The statutory requirements and guidance are clear: the TSA must hold at least one meeting with staff[136] and one other meeting 'to seek responses from any person who wishes to attend'.[137] It also has a duty to consult with strategic health authorities and any commissioners that may commission services from the provider if directed to do so.[138] However, the TSA must also exercise his judgement over 'who else it might be appropriate to consult' and he needs to ensure that the outcome of the engagement is 'meaningful and effective'.[139] The TSA made ample use of this discretion beyond the formal requirements. He engaged with public NHS providers and providers from other sectors.[140] Ipsos/Mori

---

133 The South London Healthcare National Health Service Trust (Appointment of Trust Special Administrator) Order 2012, SI 2012/1806 and The South London Healthcare National Health Service Trust (Extension of Time for Trust Special Administrator to Provide a Draft Report) Order 2012, SI 2012/1824.

134 E.g.: NHSA 2006, s 65B(5).

135 A third constraint related to the timing of each phase of the procedure is not detailed here. However, the SoS made use of the discretion the NHSA 2006 granted him to extend one of these phases due to the complexity of the situation (The South London Healthcare National Health Service Trust (Extension of Time for Trust Special Administrator to Provide a Draft Report) Order, SI 2012/1824, para 7).

136 NHSA 2006, s 65H(4).

137 NHSA 2006, s 65H(5).

138 NHSA 2006, s 65F(2).

139 DH, *Statutory Guidance for Trust Special Administrators Appointed to NHS Trusts*, 2012 para 53.

140 Ibid para 47; for an overview of the concrete steps and the breadth of the consultation, see *R (Lewisham and Save Lewisham Hospital Campaign Ltd) v*

organised a consultation and interpreted its answers.[141] This was a wide consultation, including online answers and petitions from various groups. Answers were received from political groups and individual politicians, as well as community and expert patient groups. Concerns were especially expressed regarding specific groups such as the elderly and children, for whom changes in the services provided could cause problems as they would lead to increased travel time.

The second constraint set on the TSA's mission related to his purpose, namely working out a solution for the organisation and the services to be delivered to the local health economy. This notion of a 'local health economy' is not mentioned in the statute but in the statutory guidance[142] and the order. The statutory guidance also indicates that the regime should seek to maintain the 'provision of safe and effective services during the time the regime is in progress'.[143] The order specifies that all the bodies consulted in order to trigger the regime have mentioned the need for the TSA to take into account the entire local health economy in his recommendations.[144] This purpose given to the TSA's mission directs the outcome of his efforts while granting him a wide scope of appreciation for how this purpose may be fulfilled.

The financial distress of the SLHT was such that a solution for the provision of health services across the south east of London required reorganising health provision beyond the territorial limits of the SLHT. The TSA therefore recommended the closure of services provided at Lewisham Hospital (notably its A&E and maternity units). Lewisham Hospital is located outside SLHT's territorial boundaries, in the neighbouring Lewisham borough.[145] Lewisham Hospital depends on the Lewisham Healthcare NHS Trust, an entirely different legal entity from the SLHT.[146]

Secretary of State for Health and Trust Special Administrator South London Hospital NHS Trust [2013] EWHC 2329, [140]–[143].

141 TSA Report, vol 1 para 38 ff, Ch 3 and vol 2, App G and App I.

142 DH, *Statutory Guidance for Trust Special Administrators Appointed to NHS Trusts*, 2012, para 15.

143 Ibid.

144 The South London Healthcare National Health Service Trust (Appointment of Trust Special Administrator) Order, SI 2012/1806 and The South London Healthcare National Health Service Trust (Extension of Time for Trust Special Administrator to Provide a Draft Report), SI 2012/1824.

145 For a map: TSA report, vol 2, App H, 5.

146 *R (Lewisham and Save Lewisham Hospital Campaign Ltd) v Secretary of State for Health and Trust Special Administrator South London Hospital NHS Trust* [2013] EWHC 2329.

The wider health economy frames the overall balance of service provision across the south-east of London and makes communities emerge within this territorial area, especially as all those affected by the Lewisham reorganisation expressed their strong opposition to the draft recommendations. They did so regardless of other affiliations (e.g. clinical commissioning group, local authorities, politicians, unions and staff) in the Ipsos/Mori consultation.[147] They demonstrated and launched a campaign to save their hospital. Such was the opposition that the SoS sought informal advice,[148] outside the process neatly organised for the unsustainable provider regime, leading him to amend the TSA's recommendations related to Lewisham and to maintain a free-standing midwife-led unit and a smaller A&E service at Lewisham Hospital. Lewisham Council and the Save Lewisham Hospital group challenged the SoS's powers to downgrade these services on the grounds that the TSA did not enjoy the powers to make recommendations outside the SLHT. The judge accepted this claim. As the TSA was only appointed to the SLHT, the TSA could only make recommendations related to the trust he was appointed to and not to other trusts.[149] The judicial review led to the quashing of the SoS's decision and the TSA's recommendations in relation to the Lewisham Hospital. Therefore the law comes in here to frame the limits to informal solution-making and to ensure that statutory powers and procedures are complied with when other options for expressing disagreements have been exhausted.

Overall, the SLHT shows that financial difficulties faced by PFIs require the development of an adequate regime helping to reorganise services across a given area. Broad discretion is required to deal with the specific circumstances of a case. Formal delineation of powers in terms of time, procedure and purposes needs to be implemented in a flexible way, leaving space to address the complexity of the situation, here the outcome of many unsuccessful attempts to deal with entrenched financial challenges. The formalism required here for speed and accountability reasons builds on open concepts such as the local health economy, allowing the identification of specific issues requiring an even more tailored approach. If discretion and a minimum formalisation of the

---

147 TSA report, vol 2, App G and App I.

148 SoS, *South London Healthcare NHS Trust: Notice*, 2013, https://www.gov.uk/government/uploads/system/uploads/attachment_data/file/156290/Notice-by-SofS-31-January-2013.pdf.

149 *R (Lewisham and Save Lewisham Hospital Campaign Ltd) v Secretary of State for Health and Trust Special Administrator South London Hospital NHS Trust* [2013] EWHC 2329, [76]–[94].

process are thus the starting point for defending the common interest in Parliament, experimentation, informal solutions and pragmatism fill in the gaps in dealing with tensions with local communities on the ground. Yet the law sets milestones to ensure support from the 'patients "most significantly affected"' by the decisions.[150]

Peterborough Trust

A similar logic of formalisation – and yet simultaneous informalisation – comes into play in the Peterborough case. The financial distress faced by the Peterborough Trust resulted from two strategic decisions which had been taken in parallel without coordination between authorities. First, the Peterborough Trust developed a PFI hospital between 2004 and 2006 and moved into it in 2010. Secondly, in 2009 a neighbouring trust, the Hinchingbrooke Health Care NHS Trust, sought to address ongoing financial problems by seeking a private partner to run it as a franchise. By 2012, it became clear that these parallel decisions had placed both trusts in further financial difficulties. The Peterborough Trust had the highest proportional deficit to turnover in the NHS in the financial year ending 31 March 2012. The Hinchingbrooke Health Care NHS Trust also remained in deficit.[151] Following NAO reports, the PAC concluded that:

> [t]he strategic management of health resources across the East of England SHA has failed. The Department is ultimately responsible for establishing systems that protect health service users and taxpayers. But the way that the health organisations involved exercised their responsibilities left *gaps* and meant nobody looked at the overall impact on the *local health economy*.[152]

Various issues have been identified with this case. A lack of Strategic Health Authority's (SHA) strategic control over healthcare provision was one issue. Another was the weakness of Monitor's powers. Indeed, in its advice on the PFI in 2007, Monitor concluded that it would not be affordable and communicated its decision to the Trust, the DH and the Treasury. However, after discussions, the PFI went forward. The diagnostic was that Monitor could only prevent such major investments if the financial situation of the trust was in financial breach of its obligations at

---

150 Ibid [133].

151 NAO, *The Franchising of the Hinchingbrooke Healthcare NHS Trust*, 2012.

152 PAC, *The Franchising of Hinchingbrooke HealthCare NHS Trust and Peterborough and Stamford Hospitals NHS Foundation Trust* (789 HC 2012–13) recommendation 1 (emphasis added).

the moment of the decision. As this breach was then only prospective, Monitor could not intervene further.[153]

The DH does not directly address PAC's conclusions on gaps in the overall oversight over the local health economy.[154] It mostly refers to the new powers granted to Monitor on the basis of the Health and Social Care Act 2012. This Act builds on the techniques already applied in the SLHT but refines the system applicable to NHS foundation trusts through three main differences. Firstly, Monitor is in charge of the oversight of NHS foundation trusts, stepping into the role previously played by the SoS regarding NHS trusts. Secondly, the condition under which Monitor intervenes is more technical: instead of triggering a regime failure in the interest of the NHS, as in the NHS trust case, Monitor should only trigger a regime failure when the foundation trust 'is, or is likely to become, unable to pay its debts'.[155] Thirdly, the purpose of a regime failure is to secure the continued provision of services at the level determined by the commissioners, in order to prevent any 'significant adverse impact on the health of persons in need of the service'.[156]

On this basis, Monitor developed guidance related to the TSA[157] and consulted on the development of a risk assessment framework (RAF)[158] and the identification of protected services.[159] These documents again show the interplay between formalisation and experimentation. The RAF distinguishes four levels of risk: normal, concern, distress or failure. When distress is diagnosed, a contingency planning team (CPT) is appointed to identify protected services. Appointing a CPT is not provided for in the statutory framework but is seen as a preparation for the mission of a possible TSA. In the Peterborough Trust, PwC was appointed as such a CPT.

In its guidance, Monitor also fleshes out the notion of the local health economy with the help of a minimum core of protected services that need

---

[153] Ibid recommendation 4.

[154] The notion comes back in the PAC report (e.g.: recommendation 5, p 8 and evidence).

[155] NHSA 2006, s 65D as substituted.

[156] NHSA 2006, s 65DA(3).

[157] Monitor, *Statutory Guidance for Trust Special Administrators Appointed to NHS Foundation Trusts*, 2013.

[158] Monitor, *Draft Risk Assessment Framework: Consultation Document*, 2013.

[159] These last two documents were still in draft form in June 2013.

to remain provided despite a provider's failure.[160] This minimum content departs from previous documentation in which the local health economy has been used in a more intuitive way. For instance, the TSA in the SLHT balanced the overall provision of healthcare services available over a given territorial area but did not act according to methods, assessments or standards previously developed for identifying the needs of the local health economy. By contrast, Monitor issued 62 pages of guidance on the continuity of healthcare services and commissioner-requested services.[161] Normally, Monitor expects that the services identified in the licence granted to foundation trusts as commissioner-requested services will be the same as those identified by the TSA should the provider fail.[162]

In the Peterborough Trust, therefore, Monitor is exercising its newly acquired powers and contributing to developing a minimum core of services to be maintained across the local health economy despite financial difficulties. As such, the law sets up procedures to deal with the aftermath of failing PFIs but does not develop techniques to prevent these failures from occurring, for instance in setting standards for implementing PFIs or in requiring a minimum of available financial resources before proceeding with a PFI.

PPPs/PFIs: Clarifying Institutions' Powers and Communities' Interests?

PFI hospitals illustrate the limits of state-analogue and market-analogue models. They show how the involvement of private actors within the NHS has been discussed within as well as outside Parliament. Market techniques have also shown their limits when PFIs have failed – although fairness requires mentioning that the trusts were already facing financial difficulties before entering into the PFIs. The legal techniques have been

[160] Monitor, *Guidance for Commissioners on Ensuring the Continuity of Health Care Services – Designating Commissioner Requested Services and Location Specific Services*, 2013, 3.

[161] Monitor, *Guidance for Commissioners on Ensuring the Continuity of Health Care Services – Designating Commissioner Requested Services and Location Specific Services*, 2013 and Appendix; Monitor, *Response to the Consultation on Guidance for Commissioners on Ensuring the Continuity of Health Care Services*, 2013. Monitor identifies this guidance as the guidance mentioned in NHSA 2006, s 65DA. It will also be used for the licence granted by Monitor (power based on the Health and Social Care Act 2012, s 97(1)(i) (p 7).

[162] Monitor, *Guidance for Commissioners on Ensuring the Continuity of Health Care Services – Designating Commissioner Requested Services and Location Specific Services*, 2013, 4, 8.

either general, such as the public law of political accountability, or specific, such as in the unsustainable provider regime. In all cases, practice has developed around the legal techniques. Institutions such as Monitor have gained strengthened powers, while minimum services are progressively identified and should contribute to the local health economy. A model other than state-analogue and market-analogue models, such as a community-analogue model, needs to be developed to inform more fully our understanding of how autonomy, solidarity and trust work when institutions and communities are in tension.

Firstly, autonomy relates to three aspects of the discretion that public authorities exercise in PFI hospitals. The first aspect of autonomy relates to how ministerial discretion is kept in check by political accountability, as both the promotion of PFIs in the NHS and the SLHT show. However, Monitor is now in charge of many of the decisions previously taken by the SoS, which weakens political accountability. The second aspect of autonomy refers to this power increase in Monitor, which also entails the development of specific expertise, especially when it comes to managing financial challenges relating to PFIs. However, part of the practical implementation of this expertise in concrete cases is delegated to specific units, such as the TSA or the CPT. The third aspect of autonomy concerns how public discretion relates to the vulnerability of patients in general and specific groups like women and the elderly. These need to be taken into account when solutions for failing PFIs are devised.

Secondly, solidarity is expressed in PFI hospitals through the development of identities and interests related to the geographical area covered by the services provided through the trusts. The Lewisham opposition is one example of such a spontaneous community, covering various groups affected by the closure of services at Lewisham Hospital. In the Peterborough case, no such clear-cut identifiable entity can be identified but the so-called local health economy had been jeopardised by the competition between Peterborough Trust and Hinchingbrooke Trust. Overall, this notion of the local health economy is gaining ground in highlighting the interdependency between services provided over a geographical area and over time. It relates to the physical proximity of the services to the patients needing them and catches practical issues such as travel time and travel means.[163]

Thirdly, trust expresses the reliability of the care services provided, even in cases of financial distress. This trust builds on statutory provisions, statutory guidance developed after consultations, the licensing

163 See the SLHT case.

powers of the health regulator (Monitor), the implementation of specific regimes triggered in extreme circumstances and, in even more extreme cases, on the public resistance of communities especially affected by the services identified for closure. Therefore the existence, access to and maintenance of specific services depend on a range of factors, highlighting the high value and interest that public authorities in general and communities in particular put on these services. These factors are interconnected. The statutory framework was developed at a time when financial failures in PFI hospitals called for solutions. Consultation has been used to develop the protected services and Monitor uses its licensing power to implement these protected services. The DH has attempted to reassure not only local communities such as Lewisham but also creditors that the unsustainable provider regime will not affect their contracts.[164] Therefore legal techniques have been incrementally supplemented by other techniques to build an overall sense of the reliability of healthcare services at a time when this reliability is being questioned. The next section turns to a way to supplement legal techniques in how discretion is used in PPPs/PFIs.

AN ETHIC OF CARE: A STANDARD FOR DISCRETION?

The previous three sections illustrated that institutions and communities shape public discretion in PPPs/PFIs through three different dynamics: mutual support, the institutionalisation of collective interests and tensions. In all cases, state-analogue and market-analogue models do not fully account for these dynamics, and the law only partly explains how discretion is used and limited. Therefore, an alternative model, a community-analogue model, needs to be suggested. In such a model, coordination of public, private and collective interests may be driven towards a given purpose: developing opportunities for individuals to transform their social identities (e.g. in terms of equality, well-being or healthcare). In such a model, an ethical framework, such as an ethic of care, may be developed as a potential standard for testing how discretion coordinates autonomy, solidarity and trust in PPPs/PFIs. Discretion is thus not only used in a pragmatic way, i.e. a way in which the means and aims constantly inform each other and where the law sets a framework

---

[164] DH, *NHS Trust and NHS Foundation Trust Special Administration – A Guide for Unsecured Creditors*, 2013.

where *VfM* is both the standard and the aim set for public action. An ethic of care may indeed provide a standard for assessing how public discretion supports the transformation of social identities when it coordinates public, private and collective interests. This section seeks to detail how such a standard based on an ethic of care might be used in PPPs/PFIs and how it might call for developments in PPPs/PFIs.

Law: Roles and Limits

Legal techniques provide a starting point for thinking about the coordination of collective interests and the interplays between institutions and communities. Legal techniques take various forms such as statutory provisions, judicial decisions or procedural requirements. Yet they do not offer a comprehensive account of how discretion is used and controlled in PPPs/PFIs. This leads us to briefly summarise their contributions and limits in relation to PPPs/PFIs.

The previous sections have shown that legal techniques are present in three main ways in PPPs/PFIs. Firstly, the law can be used as a neutral tool: it may be a mere technique which does not impose a given substantial solution. The differing appreciations by the judges in *Luton* and *Cheshire* of the circumstances providing a ground of public interest on which to set aside consultation show this neutrality in the legal techniques. Yet we also see that the outcome of judicial review is not so neutral. After the judge in *Luton* found that the SoS should have regard to the PSED and follow a consultation process, the SoS followed up this finding with an equality impact assessment of the cancellation of BsF and developed PSBP on this basis. As a result, schools with special educational needs were listed on the PSBP. Yet the confirmation of Defra's technical reasoning by the judge in *Cheshire* led the department to replicate a similar reasoning three years later, apparently without taking into account the different circumstances under which the decisions were taken. Therefore legal techniques may be neutral in that they do not prescribe a specific outcome at the end of a specific decision-making process. However, public authorities may take different courses of action in interpreting these outcomes and applying them in further cases or when following steps in the decision-making process.

Secondly, the law is used as a vehicle for advancing the collective interests of protected categories of people. The law formalises ethical commitments to equality, well-being or similar transversal policies. The PSED and the PS(SV) Act 2012 illustrate this point, as do contractual linkages. However, the actual furthering of these interests depends on the law only to a limited extent: these legal techniques have weak enforcement mechanisms, with either no dedicated agencies or dedicated agencies with only limited resources. The implementation of these ethical commitments is left to public authorities' discretion. Furthermore, the decision-making process between the moment at which these purposes need to be considered in the service design and the actual delivery of the service is so long and convoluted that the causal relationship between the two is weak at best. However, the existence of these legal techniques should not be dismissed. They ensure that public authorities are aware of these protected interests while exercising their discretion. They allow public authorities to act upon them even if they do not prescribe a specific result or give rise to individual entitlements. The extent to which public authorities really are in a position (resource-wise) or are committed to realising the protection of these ethical commitments informs the dilemmas inherent to the exercise of public discretion.

Finally, the legal techniques can also set a framework for organising discussions between institutions and communities. This framework can be general, as in the case of political accountability based on public law, or more specific and detailed, as in the case of the statutory framework now applicable to failing NHS foundation trusts. Yet in both cases, this legal framework does not encompass all interactions between institutions and communities, and informal techniques mushroom around it.

There is room for interpretation across these three functions that legal techniques perform to coordinate the collective interests involved in PPPs/PFIs and their regulatory space. We now need to depart from the state-analogue and market-analogue models to account on the one hand for the coordination between public and private interests, and on the other hand for the relationships between discretion and law. We highlight that communities contribute to this coordination of collective interests and develop 'webs of shared understanding about social relationships'[165] related to PPPs/PFIs. They may also develop a narrative based on an ethic of care as a standard set for the use of public discretion in PPPs/PFIs.

Ethic of Care: Contributions to Communities

Communities can have overlapping memberships, interests or values. They can be organised around factual elements or the coexistence of

---

[165] Cotterrell, 2006, 73.

people in a given space.[166] The SLHT case shows how services across a given area are tightly-knitted together. Communities can pursue shared interests, developing 'a shared understanding, e.g. an agreed project plan and performance measures',[167] or 'a "*shared vision*" about the objectives for the [project]',[168] as any other 'typical business community' would do.[169] Communities can also rely on a given ethos, interdependence and solidarity between their members.[170] The linkages used in PPPs/PFIs and the PSED convey this idea of a morality shared by the parties and extended to third parties. Communities may finally be based on mutual affection.[171] This type of community is found in PPPs/PFIs when there is a full commitment by the different parties not only to the nominal aim of the PPPs/PFIs but also to addressing the social issues related to the projects. For instance, BsF was developed as part of a 'strategic service delivery partnerships' programme designed to increase community involvement.[172] These different types of communities may develop their own narratives for the PPP/PFI project in terms of education, care or environment and in terms of their contribution to the transformative purpose that PPPs/PFIs may offer for individuals. These communities may also contribute to the ways in which the law organises and controls how public discretion may be used in PPPs/PFIs. Here comes an ethic of care, in that it is a set of values and practices against which discretion has to be exercised and shaped by institutions, law and communities. An ethic of care may supplement the legal techniques in shaping how discretion is exercised in PPPs/PFIs. Such a way forward is attractive but caveats also need to be mentioned.

Developing an ethic of care is appealing for its contribution to consistency and integrative dynamics. Firstly, it could apply equally to institutions and communities. Similar values and practices could hence apply both to public bodies and communities, representing collective interests when they act with a specific collective purpose (e.g. education for disabled children, care for elderly or protection of the environment). This purpose needs to fit within other collective interests. Professor Oliver follows a similar reasoning when she suggests that common values

---

166 Cotterrell, 2006, 68–9.

167 Treasury, *Project Governance*, 2007, para 7.14 (emphasis added).

168 Ibid para 1.2.1.

169 Ibid 69.

170 Cotterrell, 2006, 69.

171 Ibid.

172 CLG, *Strong and Prosperous Communities – The Local Government White Paper* (2006 Cm 6939-i).

apply across the public/private divide.[173] Secondly, an ethic of care could strengthen consistency in public policies by giving a positive content to discretion and not only a negative one, as the law does, or only an economically loaded one, as *VfM* does. Thirdly, an ethic of care could foster consistency and supplementation between formal and informal techniques. An ethic of care would not override legal requirements but provide a lens through which to reflect on legal requirements in terms of their implementation, development and adaptation when needed.

An ethic of care builds on the main features outlined at the beginning of this chapter: attentiveness, competence, responsibility, responsiveness and integrity. These features help develop standards against which to assess how autonomy, solidarity and trust shape discretion. We turn to each of them now, in turn.

Autonomy: Vulnerability and Expertise

Autonomy needs to be applied to the position of public authorities and private contractors, as well as to users and third parties involved in PPPs/PFIs. These entities involved in PPPs/PFIs are essentially different: on the one hand, PPP/PFI users and third parties are in a position of vulnerability; on the other hand, PPP/PFI partners are in a position of expertise. Using attentiveness and competence as drawn from an ethic of care helps to account for this vulnerability and expertise.

Attentiveness draws attention to the needs to be cared for. As the previous sections have illustrated, these needs can be identified through either the PPPs/PFIs or legal techniques. In the first case, BsF sought to address the dire state of school buildings and simultaneously to deliver schools in the most deprived areas of the country. By contrast, the James Review encapsulates the change between BsF and PSBP in clear terms: 'a philosophical shift in approach as it would mean that the DfE will deliver not money, but rather a building to meet local needs'.[174] In other PPPs/PFIs, the provision of healthcare or mobility is at the core of the project. However, the law also identifies categories of persons who need to be protected due to their vulnerable position within society. The PSED is probably the best illustration developed here, targeting vulnerability on the grounds of gender, race or disability, for instance.

---

[173] D Oliver, *Common Values and the Public–Private Divide* (Butterworths 1999).

[174] James Review (n 46 above) 6.

Therefore, PPP/PFI users in a vulnerable position can be affected in different capacities. The Ipsos/Mori consultation related to SLHT repeatedly brings forward concerns related to the weaker position in which women, not-often-heard-groups, the elderly and others are put when the provision of healthcare services is changed.[175] This fragmentation of various capacities and belongings to many communities calls for a more integrative approach to how PPPs/PFIs deliver infrastructures and services. Linkages may in this respect provide one way to implement such requirements in concrete projects. Such integration leads to complexity, hence the need for expertise among the PPP/PFI partners.

Competence contributes to an elaboration on this requirement for expertise. As Chapter 4 explained, specific expertise has been developed in PPPs/PFIs to assess *VfM*.[176] However, official documents from the Treasury,[177] the NAO[178] and the PAC[179] repeatedly mention the need to improve expertise in dealing with PPPs/PFIs and to address the challenges that public authorities face in providing public services. Indeed, the Peterborough Trust's failure was not prevented by the many experts involved at one point or another to advise on its financial distress.[180] The expertise relied on in the SLHT has also attracted criticisms in relation to its costs.[181]

An ethic of care calls for competence in the delivery of care or services in the sense that the care or service provided needs to be adequate, and that the needs are indeed met in practice once the service is delivered or the decision taken. Such an understanding would help to assess the suitability of expert bodies such as Deloitte carrying out equality impact assessments, for instance.[182] Equally, Defra's report leading to its decision to drop the waste PFI projects under negotiation in 2013 may be

---

175 TSA report, vol 2, App I.

176 See Chapter 4, pp 164–6.

177 Treasury, 2012, 8 and 39; Treasury, *Review of Competitive Dialogue*, 2010, 6; Treasury, 2006, Ch 6.

178 E.g.: NAO, *The Performance and Management of Hospital PFI Contracts*, 2010, recommendations 20–21.

179 E.g.: PAC, *M25 Private Finance Contract* (651 HC 2010–11) conclusions and recommendations 2, 3 and 7.

180 PAC, *Department of Health: The Franchising of Hinchingbrooke Health Care NHS Trust and Peterborough and Stamford Hospitals NHS Foundation Trust* (789 HC 2012–13) conclusion 5.

181 A Pollock and others, *Blaming the Victims: The Trust Special Administrator's Plans for South East London* (Centre for Primary Care and Public Health 2013) recommendation 5.

182 See the SLHT case: TSA Report, vol 3, App L.

revisited in this light. This decision seems highly technical, using statistical tools to address uncertainty issues. However, it narrowed down the problem of the role of waste PFIs in waste treatment to meeting EU landfill targets without including a range of other factors such as actual or realistic changes of behaviour towards waste, for instance.

Using competence in this sense does not challenge the technical, professional or instrumental skills of Deloitte, Defra and similar bodies. It may help us to conclude that these entities were indeed the most competent bodies available to carry out the job they were entrusted with in the manner they did. Yet competence under an ethic of care would then ponder such a conclusion and probably highlight the gap between the ideal of care for equality under legal techniques and its practical implementation. It may then suggest that the expertise required within public authorities and public staff is not, as such, the same expertise as that available in the private sector and among consultants. Instead, it is a specific and unique competence in understanding the limits of technical rationality and bridging the gap between sectorial – and in a sense narrow – knowledge of an issue and the concrete implementation of a solution on the ground with all its many interlinked aspects. This would also take into account the complex web of human constraints, political requirements and moral dilemmas.

In acknowledging the different positions of vulnerability of PPP/PFI users on the one hand, and the expertise of PPP/PFI partners on the other hand, an ethic of care breaks away from two kinds of assumptions. The first is an assumption of equality between all kinds of actors involved in PPPs/PFIs. The second is an assumption that the most important relationship between public authorities and individuals is anchored in the concept of accountability in spending taxpayers' money. An ethic of care does not necessarily neglect resource allocation per se but sees it as a means of providing services and infrastructures, not as defining institution-individual relationships. It looks at the other side of the coin: the purpose for which taxpayers' money is spent. Positively expressed, then, an ethic of care leads to a requirement that competent institutions or communities reach out towards vulnerable users, to help them become aware of their needs and vulnerabilities, articulate them and act upon them.[183] Vulnerability brings particular others to the attention and charge of both institutions and communities.

---

[183] D Engster, *The Heart of Justice – Care Ethics and Political Theory* (OUP 2007) 79.

Solidarity: Subsidiarity and Proximity

Solidarity needs to be applied to the relationships involved in PPPs/PFIs. It highlights the interdependency and interconnection among the parties involved in PPPs/PFIs. A decision affecting one of them is likely to affect the other participants either directly or indirectly. An ethic of care contributes to framing this interdependency between parties to a relationship in emphasising two requirements: responsibility and responsiveness. Applying these to the institutions and communities involved in PPPs/PFIs, two means of decision making can be distinguished: subsidiarity and proximity.

Subsidiarity relates to the identification of the person/entity responsible for taking charge of providing for needs once they are identified. This leads to a series of questions, such as the extent to which responsibility has to be taken, and the direct or indirect way in which the responsibility is to be discharged. In its original context, much connected to family relationships, an ethic of care requires one to provide personal and direct care for the needs of particular others. Applied to collective relationships, ethic of care implies that supporting institutions and policies are developed to sustain care and services. In this sense, Engster writes that: '[i]n care theory, government functions primarily as a collective moral entity that facilitates and extends our ability to care for ourselves and others'.[184]

Subsidiarity could be applied to decide how to allocate responsibility in different ways. It could contribute to framing the relationships between institutions and communities. For instance, subsidiarity could be applied to school PFIs to identify to what extent an institution is required to set educational transformation goals (the solution in BsF) or to decide that such goals are better left to communities (and their sponsors, as in PSBP). However, subsidiarity does not merely leave the option open but also requires that either institutions or communities actually take this responsibility and deliver the transformation promised to meet the identified needs. In this sense, subsidiarity may call for a transitional period or process ensuring that communities are equipped to deliver the goals with which they have been entrusted, not only in general but also practically across the country.

Subsidiarity also fleshes out the purposes and respective involvement of institutions and communities. Institutions may set an overall goal towards which communities organise themselves or communities may set their purpose with institutions only marginally intervening to police

---

184 Ibid 75.

extreme cases. It may well be that services have to be provided directly or indirectly by institutions. An ethic of care here draws attention to the problem of resources and may require that, even if a service is provided by one entity, another one takes the financial responsibility for it.[185] Subsidiarity in this sense can be fruitful in mapping the relationships between public and private partners in joint ventures (such as the ones used in LIFT, BsF or PF2) and in defining the particular role of each of them in decision making.

In defining the purposes of and relationships between institutions and the community, subsidiarity may also lead to the identification of core needs and services which have to be provided regardless of circumstances. Here exercises such as the one carried out to protect the continuity of health services may flesh out the baseline for institutions to provide finance or direct help, especially services. An ethic of care, however, would also help to flesh out the services to be maintained or adapted in order to ensure that identified needs remain adequately provided for.

Subsidiarity allows for a variety of interactions between institutions and communities. However, the distance between them remains to be specified. The face-to-face dimension between service provider and service receiver/user tends to become less important when an ethic of care is applied to collective interests. An ethic of care may even require intermediation by more professional and encompassing entities as long as the institution or community responsible is in a position to assess that the service is adequately provided and the needs met. In this sense, subsidiarity needs to be refined to avoid too wide an indeterminacy.

Based on responsiveness, proximity may be used for fine-tuning the actual implementation of subsidiarity. An ethic of care does not understand responsiveness in Vincent-Jones' sense. While Vincent-Jones uses responsiveness as a combination of legitimacy and effectiveness or as a form of joint maximisation between two equal entities,[186] an ethic of care uses responsiveness to probe the differences between service providers and service users. Responsiveness calls for listening to the needs of service users but also for being mindful of the needs of the service provider and the well-being of all those involved in the relationship.

---

[185] Ibid 79.

[186] See Chapter 4, pp 194–6.

Proximity means that we have special duties to those who are closest to us.[187] However, for those who are more distant from us, delegation to institutions providing care may be the best way to provide adequate care.[188]

Proximity would require that the service provider is sufficiently close to service users, in terms of space, identity, goals or otherwise, but both would need to remain distinct, especially avoiding any confusion of their identities, goals or aspirations, and one imposing his or hers onto the other. Proximity draws attention to two opposing problems. The first problem is 'extended distance'. In the case of the PS(SV) Act 2012, territorial proximity is key in considering the impact of the service being procured on the economic, social and environmental well-being of the area. However, distance between pre-procurement and actual implementation through the supply chain/contractual linkages has to be overcome. Extended distance is also illustrated in the Peterborough case and its gaps in strategic oversight. An ethic of care would call for strategies to avoid these gaps in the provision of services across the country. Strategic coordination is thus needed.[189]

The second problem is the reverse: closeness, confusion or parochialism, or the problem that institutions, communities or people become too enmeshed with the particular needs they are attending to and detach themselves from addressing broader needs and concerns for care.[190] In PPPs/PFIs, where multiple groups of needs may be identified, this closeness among the groups may need to be policed. In this respect, the separation of interests in joint ventures (such as the Local Improvement Finance Trust Company (LIFTCo) or PF2) may require sustained attention.[191] The claims regarding the maintaining or closing of services at Lewisham Hospital might also be assessed with such a risk of parochialism in mind.

Combined, subsidiarity and proximity contribute to our understanding of how PPPs/PFIs work in three ways. Firstly, they lead us to consider context-specific decisions and particular solutions. Standardisation of documentation and output specifications may be needed for considerations of time and costs but the concrete implementation of these standard documents may need to allow space for adjustments and tailoring in the way that the documents themselves are produced and

---

187 Engster, 2007, 72.
188 Ibid 75.
189 Ibid 73.
190 Tronto, 1993, 142.
191 E.g.: NAO, *Lift,* 2005, 7, recommendations.

designed. Secondly, subsidiarity and proximity may give indications about the possible need for and extent of formalisation through statutory requirements, guidance or other tools versus the possibility of communities taking ownership of the process. Thirdly, subsidiarity and proximity also highlight the need to listen genuinely to PPP/PFI users (and act on the information so obtained) and not only to consult and foster engagement, having 'due regard' and 'considering' specific grounds for protection.

Trust: Reliability and Integrity

Trust relates to the time dimension of the relationships involved in PPPs/PFIs, from the moment when needs are identified to the moment that the services are delivered in an adequate manner. The time dimension in the long-term relationships that PPPs/PFIs set-up brings two questions: changes and integration of all small and bigger-scale decisions. An ethic of care would call for specific efforts from public authorities to match values with practice: it calls for reliability when changes in services are required and for integrity across the decision-making process.

An ethic of care demands reliability through changes as a way to develop and maintain trust that the service will exist and be maintained at a level of standards and costs that is suitable for meeting needs over time and supporting the transformation of individuals as promised. Here, ethic of care can be seen as minimal: it only seeks to provide services and maintain them as suitable for transformations regarding identified needs. However, if the previous steps have been respected, and if integrity is indeed wrapping them all, this side of an ethic of care may reach endlessly further. By its very nature, an ethic of care applies to open-ended relationships with open-ended obligations for the parties providing the service to adapt to the needs of the PPP/PFI users as expressed and duly listened to. However, this may also lead to putting an end to the way a service is provided if more adequate or suitable alternatives have been developed. In short, an ethic of care leaves space for flexibility in the means of providing the services, while being more demanding regarding the stability of the outcome, namely concrete and adequate provision for users' needs.

The unsustainable provider regime in PFI hospitals illustrates such aspects of reliability through change and the extent to which change is appropriate. NHS foundation trust failures are now addressed by Monitor's statutory guidance on the continuity of services. The identification of these services extends beyond cases of failure to be brought forward within the terms and conditions required for licences to be granted. Yet Lewisham's opposition to the TSA's recommendations shows also that the determination of the modalities for the provision of services may be contentious. The SoS's decision to amend the TSA's recommendations after informal advice may signal a step towards listening to the needs expressed by representatives of Lewisham. However, Lewisham's judicial review also indicates that identifying the level of needs and the modalities to provide for them can be riddled with conflicts. An ethic of care may draw attention to the process through which this level and its modalities have been identified in asking the question: how could Lewisham's community and its members have been enabled to accept that the TSA's recommendations were not a back door service reconfiguration and to understand that their particular concerns and needs had been genuinely taken into account and the decision made with full awareness of their specificities?

In opening up a space for flexibility in the modalities for providing a service, an ethic of care also integrates the possibility that change is paced or that decisions are taken over time. Here, an ethic of care can provide indications for how changes have to be managed – openly but incrementally – both regarding the concrete implementation of change and the discontinuing of a service. PESD is a good illustration that concrete implementation of changes requires more than legal requirements and that statutory duties indeed evolve slowly, maybe calling for further statutory requirements. However, an ethic of care could also draw the attention of public authorities to the fact that these statutory requirements of 'having due regard' for protected features make sense and may bring about real change only if they are continuously mindful of these requirements throughout their decision-making process towards concrete implementation. This includes PPPs/PFIs and the leverage that their supply chain and contractual linkages offer. A snapshot of the need situation at one point in time is useful for assessing the extent to which equalities are at stake. However, situations change, conflicts between various protected categories happen, alternatives arise or disappear.

Regarding the discontinuation of services, an ethic of care would conform to the legal requirement of not using discretion unfairly, bringing about abrupt changes in decision making when addressees would expect to be shielded from such changes. In circumstances such as the one in the *Luton* case, an ethic of care would thus work pre-emptively, without the need to go through judicial review. The DfE, acting in a manner conscious of its obligations towards *Luton,* would have involved the local council before cancelling its funding. An ethic of care also leaves space for reallocation of resources among services, however, if this allows for users' needs to be suitably met, maybe even more suitably met.

If an ethic of care calls for reliability in the service provided, it also calls for integrity in the way in which decisions are taken in relation to this service provision. In this form, integrity means that the various steps of identifying vulnerability, gathering competent agents, and assessing the entity providing for the service at one point in time, and over time properly connect the needs for care or service with the practical provision for these needs and its follow up.

Such a bridge across the various decision-making phases takes different technical forms. Contractual linkages are one form as they aim to implement concrete broad policy ideals of equality and social and environmental concerns throughout contracting decisions. An ethic of care may here contribute to assessing when the scope of discretion given to public authorities is used in an appropriate fashion or is distorted from its purpose.

Consultation procedures could also provide such a technical bridge. An ethic of care could move institutions and communities to engage in a genuine listening exercise. This would mean more creativity in the deliberative process than compiling template answers on hundreds of pages, leading with little explanation to a new PPP/PFI policy (such as PF2). This would also mean that relying on narrowly scoped technical reports to decide on PPPs/PFIs would be discounted as a genuine listening exercise. This would further require communities to develop constructive strategies and not chiefly opposition to plans to deliver services through public–private relationships.

Another bridge may be the development of overarching concepts such as the 'local health economy', including current and future needs over a given area across vulnerable people and expert service providers. This could also articulate subsidiarity and proximity: a given territorial area can be identified, with various communities brought together with different values, needs or beliefs but a shared need for health services. Services are needed to provide for these needs but some flexibility in their modalities is built into the notion as long as the needs remain adequately and competently met. The operation of such a bridge, however, may require that such concepts become better framed – in their nature, status or boundaries, for instance.

Throughout reliability and integrity, an ethic of care shows its two aspects of practice and value. Reliability and integrity call for practical expressions so that trust can increasingly be built across the various PPP/PFI participants. Yet the various patterns of trust and layers of confidence that are developed incrementally over the long duration of

PPPs/PFIs contribute to the development of communities and to the interactions between institutions and communities, within and beyond the law.

AN ETHIC OF CARE: CAPTURING THE MISSING DIMENSION OF PPPs/PFIs?

This chapter has suggested an ethic of care as a standard for assessing how public authorities exercise their discretion in relation to the collective interests involved in PPPs/PFIs and their regulatory space. One key problem in PPPs/PFIs lies in the nature of the relationships between PPPs/PFIs and individual users. State-analogue and market-analogue models of PPPs/PFIs only consider users and third parties in their abstract capacity as taxpayers. However, it is possible to pinpoint categories of vulnerable users (e.g. hospital patients, pupils) and third parties (e.g. local residents in the surrounding of waste PFIs, disabled children) who are treated collectively due to their shared characteristics. PPPs/PFIs raise the question of the coordination of these users and third parties. A community-analogue model may organise this coordination within the PPP regulatory space. It would develop a narrative of a 'common project' pursued by PPPs/PFIs: the success of this common project would allow all parties involved, public authorities, private corporations and individuals, to further their interests.

In such a model, the relationships between individuals and communities are embedded in an ethic of care. 'The well-being of a caring relationship involves the cooperative well-being of those in the relation, and the well-being of the relationship itself'.[192] There would thus be prioritisation between and integration of competing interests during the decision-making process but this should not exclude or harm other interests definitively. A balance over time would be needed to ensure the welfare of PPPs/PFIs understood as a genuinely common enterprise, otherwise the project would fail and nobody would be able to benefit from it.

In short, this narrative of a common project would build on the example provided by the notion of a local health economy in PFI hospitals. The components and architecture of such an overarching notion bringing together public, private and collective interests would rely on

---

[192] V Held, 'The Ethics of Care', in D Copp (ed) *The Oxford Handbook of Ethical Theory* (OUP 2006) 537, 540.

the features that an ethic of care puts forward and that have been reworded here as expertise and vulnerability (autonomy), subsidiarity and proximity (solidarity), and reliability and integrity (trust). These features do not canvass how discretion has to be exercised but they give a framework against which discretion can be assessed when public, private and collective interests have to be balanced and priorities decided upon.

An ethic of care presents limits to how it works, however. Firstly, it may be criticised as being minimalist. The role of the state may have to go beyond providing for our individual needs to include means of developing our capabilities. However, at this stage, an ethic of care already gives some clues to what may need development. Further extension may be possible incrementally. Secondly, the identification of the vulnerability and needs to be provided for remains an issue. Under an ethic of care, this may be shared responsibility across public authorities and communities or may depend on concrete and specific circumstances. An ethic of care leaves this question undetermined. Finally, an ethic of care seems to suggest a self-regulating system where implementation of ethical values takes place spontaneously. A fully workable ethic of care should make enforcement redundant. However, realism would caution against a perfectly working ethical framework. Failure needs to be addressed. Overall oversight may then have to rely on institutional design. This chapter assumed that central institutions would do so. However, scholars discuss how an ethic of care could be best organised and communities may also become organised to provide suitable answers to addressing the integration of competing interests according to their specific circumstances.

Conclusions: Towards an ethic of care?

This monograph has investigated public–private partnership (PPPs)/ Private Finance Initiatives (PFIs), especially the role that the law plays in coordinating the relationships between public and private partners and between these partners and users within the PPP regulatory space. Within each set of relationships, the law shapes how public authorities exercise their discretion. It grants public bodies powers to enter into PPPs/PFIs in order to contribute to the public interest, for instance with safe public transportation in the London Underground, appropriate education (in the Building Schools for the Future programme (BsF) and the Priority School Building Programme (PSBP)) or healthcare (in PFI hospitals) across the country within budgetary constraints. The law also sets procedures such as the competitive dialogue to organise discussions between public authorities and market actors. It equally provides contracts to organise the obligations that market actors undertake and the risks that they take in the hope of being rewarded with profits. Overall, the law mainly contributes to making value for money (*VfM*) the key standard by which to assess how public authorities exercise their discretion in PPPs/PFIs. Yet the spending of taxpayers' money is only one side of PPPs/PFIs. PPPs/PFIs are also a means of providing infrastructures and services to the benefit of users and third parties. Users rely on the infrastructures and services provided through PPPs/PFIs to meet their needs for commuting to work, for developing proper professional qualifications or for getting treatments at a nearby hospital. Therefore, these needs have to be taken into account by public authorities when they coordinate the public, private and individual interests involved in PPPs/ PFIs. This book suggests that an ethic of care may contribute to a more encompassing assessment of PPPs/PFIs.

An ethic of care would emphasise the values and practice that should inform how public authorities, as entities in positions of power and trust, exercise their discretion in relation to the needs of individuals for whom they take responsibility. It would seek to encapsulate three dimensions of PPPs/PFIs. Firstly, the communities that may provide for stability in the coordination of the interests involved in the PPP regulatory space. Secondly, the flexibility that needs to be maintained over time among the commitments undertaken by the public and private partners and the expectations that these commitments create in the other participants involved in PPPs (such as users and third parties). Finally, an ethic of care encapsulates the various forms of trust that need to be developed in PPPs/PFIs in order for them to deliver appropriate services to individual users in the long term. Further research would, however, refine how values and practice informed by ethic of care could be brought into PPPs/PFIs and other public–private relationships.

COMMUNITIES IN THE PPP REGULATORY SPACE

In the PPP regulatory space, the law structures the relationships between public and private parties, public authorities and individuals as users, and individuals and private contractors, according to market-analogue and state-analogue models. It therefore tends to freeze these relationships at one moment in time, such as the agreement exchanged between the PPP partners at the signing of the contract. It singles out one relationship from among the others, that between the procuring authority and bidders, which is elaborated through the competitive dialogue without consideration for third parties and users. Indeed, in most cases, the law overlooks individuals' needs relating to PPPs/PFIs and focuses on *VfM,* taxpayers' money and economic rationality.[1] The law only develops techniques to protect individuals' needs in extreme situations[2] or through collective interests, as is the case in consultation procedures,[3] linkages, public sector equality duties (PSED) and the Public Services (Social Value) Act 2012 (PS(SV) Act 2012).[4] Therefore, a community-analogue model would contribute to accounting more fully for how public discretion is used to coordinate these collective interests in PPPs/PFIs. It would also highlight how an ethic of care may supplement the law in assessing how public authorities exercise their discretion in the common good, with individuals' needs included.

In drawing attention to the collective interests and communities that are involved in PPPs/PFIs and their dynamics in the PPP regulatory space, a community-analogue model highlights that communities and their memberships are variously spread across public and private entities. Communities provide narratives of the PPP/PFI as a project, so as to

---

1 See Chapter 3, pp 149–51.
2 See Chapter 4, pp 181–2.
3 See Chapter 4, pp 184–8.
4 See Chapter 5, pp 224–7.

make sense of the thousands of pages of contractual documents and the many minutes the project accumulates over its thirty-year contractual period. Communities develop reference points, shared values or thinking patterns on which these narratives rely when it comes to implementing the legal techniques used in PPPs/PFIs. Therefore, communities are also ways of coordinating public authorities, contractors and individuals within PPPs/PFIs: they may help them develop their association with the performance of PPPs/PFIs over time. However, a community-analogue model also highlights the difficulties encountered with communities, in terms of both identification and the actual scope of the coordinated interests. Yet whatever PPP relationship is examined – PPP relationships, PPP-individual relationships or relationships between PPPs and collective interests – an ethic of care would bring values and practices into PPPs/PFIs to help public authorities exercise their discretion in a way that includes more than just economic and *VfM* concerns.

In the relationships between public and private parties, a PPP community involving public and private bodies (such as Infrastructure UK (IUK), professional organisations and consultants) develops a distinctive identity alongside the narratives of complexity, innovation and partnering. At policy level, professional organisations have, for instance, contributed to the development of standardised documents (e.g. the consultation leading to Private Finance 2 (PF2)).[5] At project level, the supply chain forms a community between the main contractor and its sub-contractors. Overall, these communities may help coordinate the interests of their members, for instance in developing a narrative of innovation[6] or partnering.[7] However, they do not succeed in embedding generalised cooperation across all the interests involved in PPPs/PFIs as these communities are mostly driven by an economic rationality.[8] Yet the narratives of complexity, innovation and partnering could move beyond this economic rationality to reflect key features of an ethic of care. The first of these features is the complexity that public authorities face in prioritising interests and balancing individuals' needs with budgetary constraints. Second is the innovation requiring a change of mindset in how public and private partners enter into PPPs/PFIs, including a shift from thinking in mainly *VfM* terms to including broader considerations of social and human needs. Finally, there is partnering, which would consider a proactive attitude of cooperation between PPP partners as a

5 See Chapter 4, pp 186–7.
6 See Chapter 3, pp 142–4.
7 See Chapter 3, pp 144–6.
8 See Chapter 3, pp 147–9.

way of developing tailored expertise and adapting to necessary changes outside bureaucratic and rigid procedures minutely detailed in contractual documents.

In the relationships between PPPs/PFIs and third parties, an extended community of public and private bodies (e.g. IUK, Efficiency and Reform Group at the Cabinet Office) has developed a distinct expertise in PPPs/PFIs and spread the *VfM* culture, so distinctive of PPPs/PFIs, across the whole of public procurement. However, this community fails to coordinate individuals' needs and interests with PPPs/PFIs.[9] While professional organisations have been heard in parliamentary hearings related to PPPs/PFIs, no groups representing civil society have.[10] Yet such groups representing users or third parties (including environmental groups and trade unions) seek to challenge PPPs/PFIs in courts or to voice users' and third parties' concerns in submitting evidence in consultations related to PPPs/PFIs.[11] However, these communities of users and third parties only coordinate part of the public, private and individual interests involved in PPPs/PFIs. They do not work in a coordinated manner to achieve a shared goal, such as fostering the developmental capacities of users relying on the services provided by PPPs/PFIs.[12] It would be possible for them to develop common narratives for public services or for pressing for increased transparency in PPPs/PFIs, not only in terms of their financial make up but also in terms of the quality of services they deliver, so that the needs of individuals may be met in a way more in keeping with an ethic of care.

In the coordination of collective interests, 'community' refers to PPPs/PFIs themselves. PPP/PFI projects such as BsF, the Local Improvement Finance Trust (LIFT) and waste PFIs seek, indeed, to foster communities of local and central authorities, corporations, staff, neighbours, headmasters, non-profit organisations etc. To foster these communities, PPPs/PFIs rely on institutions and legal techniques with the distinctive aim of transforming public services at the level of communities. The challenge is then to ensure that the community develops its own narrative of a common project in terms of education, primary care or a sustainable environment etc. BsF and waste PFIs illustrate that reorganising the supporting institutions and legal techniques impacts on the communities that have developed.[13] However, communities may develop

---

[9] See Chapter 4, pp 202–4.
[10] See Chapter 4, p 163.
[11] See Chapter 4, pp 170–73.
[12] See Chapter 4, pp 202–4.
[13] See Chapter 5, pp 213–22.

and prosper without supporting institutions and outside specific legal techniques. Even more so, they may use legal techniques to express their opposition to public institutions. For instance, following the necessary restructuring of services due to the financial distress of the South London Healthcare Trust and its PFI hospital, the Save Lewisham Campaign gathered support from staff, doctors, patients, politicians etc. to oppose and demonstrate against the closure of services at the Lewisham Hospital. The campaign then brought a successful judicial review against the Secretary of State's (SoS) decisions and the trust special administrator's (TSA) recommendations made in relation to the failing trust and its PFI hospital.[14] In this case, interests other than mere economic interests and the public interest are thus fostered through such communities.[15]

Across these different relationships, communities may support the development of shared projects, practices, values or identity, which are needed to coordinate the private, individual and collective interests involved in PPPs/PFIs. Therefore they offer a more encompassing approach to PPPs/PFIs than a mere assessment of their *VfM*. All the same, the contribution of an ethic of care is limited. To begin with, these communities are highly fragmented: they only coordinate some interests. Furthermore, an ethic of care creates no individual rights, so that legal techniques mostly express moral concerns for specific interests such as those of the disabled or victims of discrimination and unfavourable labour conditions.[16] For the most part, an ethic of care becomes a background providing the values and practices that can help to ensure that public authorities implement their legal duties not as a useless tick-box exercise but mindful of the concrete circumstances of the people using and relying on the services provided by PPPs/PFIs.

Overall, communities have to be taken into account in the PPP regulatory space because they contribute to explaining how private, individual and collective interests are coordinated. They help shape expectations. The law, however, only encapsulates and promotes part of these communities and does not provide systematic effective enforcement mechanisms. Therefore, there is space for an ethic of care to contribute to the fostering of ethical behaviour among PPP partners.

---

[14] See Chapter 5, pp 236–40.
[15] See Chapter 5, pp 242–4 and 246–8.
[16] See Chapter 5, pp 222–32.

FLEXIBILITY

In the PPP regulatory space, public authorities, economic actors and individuals are interdependent: the common good entails meeting the needs of individual users but relies on the willingness and ability of economic actors to suggest projects that are also likely to bring them profit. The interdependency between these participants also highlights their different natures, and thus the potential conflicts between their interests. For these reasons, coordinating these interests is a complex, costly and time-consuming process. Market-analogue and state-analogue models focus on formal solutions to streamline this coordination, such as those developed in the contractual documentation (Standardisation of PFI Contracts (SoPC) Version 4 (SoPC4) and PF2) or in the official guidelines supporting the competitive dialogue.[17] These formal solutions pre-select the choices to be made by public authorities and limit how they may exercise their discretion. Formalisation therefore gives predictability and confidence to private contractors and investors in PPP/PFI projects. However, once set in motion, formalisation requires yet further formalisation. For instance, the competitive dialogue formalised practices that evolved from the negotiated procedure. It has been supplemented by official guidelines over time, leading to concurrent documents being issued by the Treasury and the Cabinet Office.[18] Further requirements, such as those laid down in the Gateway Process and major project approval and assurance, have also been added.[19] This layering of formal solutions and requirements is unsatisfactory as it may lead to redundancy, as well as to gaps. Therefore another approach, accepting the contribution of informal solutions to the coordination of the interests involved in PPP regulatory space is needed. It would highlight the flexibility needed among the techniques available for public authorities to exercise their discretion in this coordination of interests over time. An ethic of care may then help by informing how narratives may extend legal techniques and provide stable, yet flexible, patterns of thinking and approaching issues in PPPs/PFIs, therefore allowing for interests and expectations to be developed and adjusted according to these.

An ethic of care may help map how the nature and techniques of formalisation need to be related to the goals being pursued. Indeed, narratives provide a way of describing the processes used for identifying

---

[17] See Chapter 3, pp 108–11.
[18] See Chapter 3, pp 111–14.
[19] See Chapter 2, pp 73–5.

issues and solutions related to PPPs/PFIs. They contribute to a balance between the stability that formal solutions develop and flexibility in the use of these solutions. They help identify patterns of recurring or recommended practice according to which parties may decide to behave, and thereby they may contribute to the predictability of each party's behaviour.

Depending on which of the main PPP/PFI relationships are looked at, different balances have been drawn between formal and informal solutions to supervening issues of coordination. In the relationships between public and private partners, for instance, cooperation is needed to properly monitor performance and payment reductions[20] or to address interface issues related to the provision of soft services.[21] A narrative of partnering has been developed to address these issues.[22] In the relationships between individuals and PPPs/PFIs, a narrative of responsiveness has been suggested as a way to provide indications of how public authorities should integrate users' complaints about the services provided by PPPs/PFIs in their decision making.[23] When PPPs/PFIs are understood as structuring collective interests within themselves, then a narrative of a common project may be developed to account for how problems should be addressed over time so as to coordinate the interests of all participants to their overall benefit.[24]

Each of these three narratives of partnering, responsiveness and a common project seeks to address a specific issue within the relationships with which they are connected. Partnering seeks to move away from the adversarial logic of contract and competition, assuming that parties may share information, tackle changes and solve disputes if they are committed to making the project work. Responsiveness provides a way of delivering public services in an efficient, legitimate and transparent fashion. To this end, the norms produced through economic exchanges need to be broadened beyond a purely contractual setting. The common project narrative seeks to articulate the interests of public authorities, contractors and individuals together. It probes an alternative to economic rationality and self-interest in the exercise of discretion.

Each of the three narratives relies on the law to some extent but also leave space for an ethic of care to supplement the legal techniques in coordinating the interests involved in PPPs/PFIs.

---

20 See Chapter 3, pp 132–4.
21 See Chapter 3, pp 136–7.
22 See Chapter 3, pp 144–6.
23 See Chapter 4, pp 194–6.
24 See Chapter 5, pp 257–8.

Partnering is possible because contract law assumes parties are free to organise their economic relationships as they wish, with different strands of documents and commitments of various legal forces depending on the aspects of the relationships considered. Procurement, however, disturbs this freedom by setting formal processes through which to reach a common agreement. The narrative of partnering is characteristic here as it flows strongly from two other narratives, those of complexity and innovation. The narrative of complexity is anchored in legal requirements leading to the competitive dialogue. The narrative of innovation reduces also the negative side-effects of freedom of contract. Innovation in how public–private relationships are managed is needed to turn away from competition and adversarial relationships, abuse of power and thus lack of trust and dysfunctional markets. However, partnering is non-legally binding. The law does not attach clear legal effects to partnering, preventing partnering from developing further. Yet emphasising that parties need not only to behave as the law allows them to do but also according to other standards, such as those present in an ethic of care, would render partnering a useful way to organise parties' commitments and expectations in PPPs/PFIs, allowing for more flexibility in the face of concrete circumstances when risks supervene.

As part of a hybrid reform of public services, the responsiveness of public services needs legal norms, for instance to ensure transparency and accessible information regarding public services.[25] The law is required to set minimal standards of public services and to ensure that individuals are not excluded from either public services or the *New Social Contract.* However, in many respects, the law is limited: social norms are supposed to emerge from economic exchanges and joint maximisation. Law however, for instance public procurement law, may unduly constrain this process of emergence and prevent responsiveness from happening. Furthermore, responsiveness may be ambivalent and need to take into account the vulnerable position of users and not expect them to be fully equipped to express their needs and complaints in mere economic terms. Therefore, an ethic of care may embed key values and practices into responsiveness, helping to ensure that users' needs are not merely assessed under *VfM* or as if they had to be met as if they were subject to economic exchanges. This would foster trust in responsiveness, and trust mitigates the opportunities for free riding by public authorities, contractors or individuals.

---

[25] Vincent-Jones, 2006, 315–20.

The narrative of a common project also relies on legal techniques such as linkages or public consultation. The legal framework defines if and when linkages are allowed within the public procurement process. Thanks to linkages, public authorities use contracts to carry out their policies in a consistent manner and secure *VfM* in its qualitative meaning. However, linkages rely on how public authorities use their discretion and set their policy and moral requirements within the public procurement framework, as well as on the willingness of contractors to comply with the linkages. In both cases, the monitoring of how linkages are implemented escapes legal techniques (so far). These legal provisions make it possible for public and private partners and individuals to develop a 'common project'. However, the actual development of this narrative depends on institutions such as the Partnership for Schools (PfS) or the Waste Infrastructure Delivery Programme (WIDP) and on how the general aim of transforming public services is implemented with individuals and 'real' public authorities and corporations.[26] On this very transition, the law does not say much, while an ethic of care may direct public authorities' awareness to the concrete needs of PPP/PFI users and prompt them to use their discretion accordingly.

In all cases, we see that the law provides part of the explanation for how PPP relationships are structured. However, at some point, narratives are needed for explaining how the law is used, departed from, extended and filled in. Narratives highlight a positive disposition among the parties engaged in the PPPs/PFIs towards the other parties (including individuals) and towards the project itself. This disposition and readiness to go beyond the (minimal) legal requirements takes varying forms: finding common solutions, joint maximisation, conveying policy benefits to their intended beneficiaries and suspending one's self-interest. They always rely, in one form or another, on the trust that PPP participants may have in the others involved or in the projects.

TRUST

Discretion is at the core of the coordination among private, individual and collective interests in the PPP regulatory space. While both market-analogue and state-analogue models acknowledge the importance of discretion, they distrust it and develop formal solutions in the hope that these will promote trust and confidence among PPP actors and users: the

---

26 See Chapter 4, pp 192–4.

law should develop techniques to prevent any abuse of discretion. Discretion involves risks and has to be controlled through legal procedures (such as the competitive dialogue),[27] highly detailed contractual term,[28] forms of political and judicial accountability or regulatory techniques.[29] Yet PPP parties and users need to trust that their interests and needs will be met while engaging in PPPs/PFIs and that their investments and reliance on the services, rewards or other benefits generated by PPPs/PFIs will not be abruptly quashed. Indeed, they have all organised their strategies, either in terms of investments in firm development, provision for the public good or planning, with the aim of achieving personal development according to the services provided by PPPs/PFIs over a number of years. Therefore, different levels of trust need to be incrementally developed within the PPP regulatory space: namely personal, interpersonal and systemic trust. The values and practices of an ethic of care would both contribute to and be fostered by these different layers of trust in the PPP regulatory space.

Across the range of narratives and communities discussed earlier, trust is a recurring feature which allows for this displacement beyond one's legal position. Partnering signifies a willingness to find solutions without first insisting on legal entitlements. Parties trust each other to have a constructive mindset and to be committed to the project, to sharing information, and to devoting trained staff and suitable resources to doing so. Linkages and PSED convey the idea that public authorities lead by moral example. They also rely on the belief that public authorities use their discretion to carry out policies fostering the common good and not to favour some particular interests over others.[30] The common project narrative emphasises that parties trust each other to develop shared commitments to the success of the PPPs/PFIs, mindful of each other's expectations and commitments. In turn, these narratives strengthen trust as they provide occasions for trust to be expressed, experienced and incrementally integrated in parties' frames of reference regarding each other's behaviour. Trust needs, indeed, institutions or legal techniques as starting or strengthening points. However, if it has no occasion to be tested and expanded, it will not develop. Here narratives are helpful because they provide a map of what may be expected and trusted from which relationships, reducing (but not eliminating) the risks incurred by a

27 See Chapter 3, pp 108–11.
28 See Chapter 3, pp 124–40.
29 See Chapter 4, pp 160–68 and pp 168–82.
30 See Chapter 5, pp 230–32.

trusting attitude. Communities are also supportive as they offer a framework for testing and nurturing this trust.

However, trust in communities themselves may be needed, more especially trust in their legitimacy and accountability. Communities may indeed exercise powers alongside public authorities, for instance when they oppose public projects, such as in waste PFIs or in the Lewisham Hospital. This study has shown that techniques in this regard do not seem to have been developed. Fragmentation of communities may be one practical solution. Yet institutions and the law may not support communities and their contributions sufficiently. Further attention to their legal framing is needed. For this reason, an ethic of care may provide one alternative to a more comprehensive legal rethinking. It may provide a standard for calling communities to account but a standard which is not completely alien to them. An ethic of care emphasises, indeed, trusting that one entity will not seek to further just its own interests but also the ones of the individuals whose interests are entrusted to them.

A narrative of care would emphasise the need to find ways to implement theoretical or ideal conceptions of the common good in concrete and particularised situations that meet individuals' needs. An ethic of care values the differentiation in parties' positions within a relationship. Parties play nearly necessarily different functions depending on their relationships. An ethic of care does not offer a pre-defined set of priorities for how to achieve them. It brings a fresh perspective to the *VfM* that hybrid public–private solutions developed in the market-analogue model seek to achieve or to the control that the formalisation promoted in the state-analogue model seeks to develop. Indeed, if an ethic of care was to be pursued to explain PPP/PFI relationships, it might foster trust in a different way from how market-analogue or state-analogue models do. It would contribute to developing ways to maintain relationships in the long term and internalise competing interests within PPPs, therefore helping PPP actors to practice trust within the specific circumstances of particular PPPs and the issues arising in them.

BEYOND ENGLISH PPPs

This monograph focused on the coordination of private, individual and collective interests in English PPPs/PFIs and suggested that developing an ethic of care would be a fruitful approach to encapsulating three key dimensions of this coordination within the English PPP regulatory space:

communities, flexibility and trust. This approach to public–private relationships would benefit from further development in at least three different directions.

A first possible extension for this research would be the broadening of the research to kinds of public–private relationships used to provide public services with taxpayers' money other than PPPs/PFIs. This will be even more relevant as the government experiments with the provision of public services thanks to charities and non-profit organisations, new forms of PPPs/PFIs (such as PF2) and economic planning. Lessons drawn from the tensions and dynamics of coordination so far observed in PPPs/PFIs lead to highlighting the importance of acknowledging the protection of collective interests. Similar acknowledgment may be crucial for other public–private relationships to avoid repeating mistakes that have led to financial distress in PPPs/PFIs such as the London Underground PPPs or PFI hospitals. In this respect, developing an ethic of care such as the one that this monograph suggests may provide an alternative to a constitutional or legal framework for developing standards for the use of discretion in these public–private relationships and help to bring a balance between autonomy, solidarity and trust within them.

A second step forward in this research would be to explore further how the communities involved in PPPs/PFIs and similar public–private relationships could support the development of this ethic of care. This would require empirical research and sociological methods but would provide further insights into the interplay between legal techniques, narratives and ethical standards in shaping how public discretion coordinates private, individual and collective interests in the PPP regulatory space.

The third area for further research relates to the distinctiveness of English PPPs and English regulatory space, where public discretion features predominantly and where there is significant scope for an ethic of care because legal techniques shape discretion only to a limited extent. In other countries, the law plays a different role in coordinating public, private and collective interests, thus leaving open the question of how an ethic of care may be a useful resource for assessing how public discretion is used. France, for instance, has an administrative system in which the law conveys formal concepts such as 'public service' which generate legal consequences and have been historically developed to convey social cohesion. The USA is known for its pluralism, which organises the coordination of interests and the identification of the common good. Both systems have transplanted PPPs. Comparing the dynamics encountered there with the English ones may also highlight how English coordination of private, individual and collective interests might develop in the future and the possible challenges and disturbances that borrowing techniques from French or American approaches to public services could cause in the English regulatory space. It may also refine our understanding of ethical standards in the use of discretion in England and elsewhere.

These three further research directions would all contribute to greater mapping of an ethic of care which could be further developed, both in PPPs/PFIs and across other public services in England and abroad. If English PPPs/PFIs were once deemed to be 'a cultural change' in the delivery of public services, it may not only have been for their innovative financial instruments but also for their aptitude to guide our reflections about the ethical standards required from bodies in positions of trust when they take decisions involving users in a vulnerable position.[31]

[31] P Braun, 'The Practical Application of EC Public Procurement to the UK's Private Finance Initiative' (2003) EurLJ 575; echoing Treasury, 1993, Foreword (where PFIs were presented as 'a radical and far-reaching change in capital investment in public services') and Treasury, 1995, Foreword (where PFIs were presented as a 'profound change to the culture of government–procurement').

Select bibliography

BOOKS AND ARTICLES

Allen, G, *The Private Finance Initiative (PFI)*, (research paper 03/79 HC 2003)

Arrowsmith, S and Craven, R, 'Competitive Dialogue in the United Kingdom' in S Arrowsmith and S Treumer (eds), *Competitive Dialogue in EU Procurement* (CUP 2012) 181

Arrowsmith, S and Treumer, S, 'Competitive Dialogue in EU Law: A Critical Review' in S Arrowsmith and S Treumer (eds), *Competitive Dialogue in EU Procurement* (CUP 2012) 3

– and Kunzlik, P (eds), *Social and Environmental Policies in EC Procurement Law: New Directives and New Directions* (CUP 2009)

–, *The Law of Public and Utilities Procurement* (Sweet and Maxwell 2005)

–, 'Application of the U.K. Procurement Regulations to PFI Contracts: New Case Law' [2002] *Public Procurement Law Review* 84

–, 'Public Private Partnerships and the European Procurement Rules: EU Policies in Conflict?' (2000) 37 *Common Market Law Review* 709

Bachman, R, 'Conclusion: Trust – Conceptual Aspects of a Complex Phenomenon' in C Lane and R Bachman (eds), *Trust within and between the Organizations – Conceptual Issues and Empirical Applications* (OUP 2000) 298

Badcoe, P, 'Best Value – An Overview of the United Kingdom Government's Policy for the Provision and Procurement of Local Authority Services' [2001] *Public Procurement Law Review* 63

–, 'Public Private Partnerships in Local Government: the Legal, Financial and Policy Framework' [1999] *Public Procurement Law Review* 279

Baldwin, R and Hawkins, K, 'Discretionary Justice: Davis Reconsidered' [1984] *Public Law* 570

Beatson, J, 'Public Law Influences in Contract Law' in J Beatson and D Friedmann (eds), *Good Faith and Fault in Contract Law* (Clarendon Press 1995) 263

Bell, J, 'Public Interest: Policy or Principle?' in R Brownsword (ed), *Law and the Public Interest – Proceedings of the 1992 ALSP Conference* (Franz Steiner Verlag 1993) 27

–, 'Discretionary Decision-Making: A Jurisprudential View' in K Hawkins (ed), *The Uses of Discretion* (Clarendon Press 1992) 89
–, 'The Effect of Changes in Circumstances on Long-Term Contracts' in D Harris and D Tallon (eds), *Contract Law Today – Anglo-French Comparisons* (Clarendon Press 1991) 195
–, 'The Acceptability of Legal Arguments' in N MacCormick and P Birks (eds), *The Legal Mind: Essays for Tony Honoré* (Clarendon Press 1986) 45
Birkinshaw, P, Harden, I and Lewis, N, *Government by Moonlight: the Hybrid Parts of the State* (Unwin Hyman 1990)
Black J, 'Proceduralizing Regulation' (part I) (2000) 20 *Oxford Journal of Legal Studies* 597 and (part II) (2001) 21 *Oxford Journal of Legal Studies* 33
Braun, P, 'Strict Compliance versus Commercial Reality: The Practical Application of EC Public Procurement Law to the UK's Private Finance Initiative' (2003) 9 *European Law Journal* 575
Brookes, S, 'A Critical Evaluation of the Success of Project Partnering' (2008) 24 *Construction Law Journal* 314
Brown, A, 'The Impact of the New Procurement Directive on Large Infrastructure Projects: Competitive Dialogue or Better the Devil You Know' [2004] *Public Procurement Law Review* 160
Brownsword, R, 'From Co-operative Contracting to a Contract of Co-operation' in D Campbell and P Vincent-Jones (eds), *Contracts and Economic Organisation* (Dartmouth 1996) 14
Campbell, D, 'Relational Contracting and the Nature of Private Ordering: A Comment on Vincent-Jones' (2007) 14 *Indiana Journal of Global Legal Studies* 279
–, 'The Incompleteness of our Understanding of the Law and Economics of Relational Contract' (2004) *Wisconsin Law Review* 645
– and Harris, D, 'Flexibility in Long-Term Contractual Relationships: The Role of Co-Operation' (1993) 20 *Journal of Law and Society* 166
–, 'The Social Theory of Relational Contract: Macneil as the Modern Proudhon' (1990) 18 *International Journal of the Sociology of Law* 75
Cane, P, *Administrative Law* (5th edn, OUP 2011)
–, 'Public Law and Private Law: A Study of the Analysis and Use of a Legal Concept' in J Eekelaar and J Bell (eds), *Oxford Essays in Jurisprudence – 3rd Series* (Clarendon Press 1987) 57
Carolan, E, 'The Legitimacy of Public Service Reform: Democracy, Accountability and Experimentalism in the Big Society' [2013] *Public Law* 240
Cartlidge, D, *Public Private Partnerships in Construction* (Taylor and Francis 2006)
Collins, H, *Regulating Contracts* (OUP 1999)

Cotterrell, R, *Law, Culture and Society – Legal Ideas in the Mirror of Social Theory* (Ashgate 2006)
–, 'Trusting in Law: Legal and Moral Concepts of Trust' (1993) 46 *Current Legal Problems* 75
Cover, R, 'Foreword: Nomos and Narrative' (1983–84) 97 *Harvard Law Review* 4
Craig, P, *Administrative Law* (7th edn, Sweet and Maxwell 2012)
Daintith, T, 'Contractual Discretion and Administrative Discretion: A Unified Analysis' (2005) 68 *Modern Law Review* 554
–, 'Regulation by Contract: the New Prerogative' (1979) 32 *Current Legal Problems* 41
Davies, A, *The Public Law of Government Contracts* (OUP 2008)
–, *Accountability: A Public Law Analysis of Government by Contract* (OUP 2001)
Deakin, S and Michie, J, 'The Theory and Practice of Contracting' in S Deakin and J Michie (eds), *Contracts, Co-operation, and Competition – Studies in Economics, Management, and Law* (OUP 1997) 20
Deakin, S and Wilkinson, F, 'Contracts, Co-operation and Trust: the Role of the Institutional Framework' in D Campbell and P Vincent-Jones (eds), *Contract and Economic Organisation* (Dartmouth 1996) 95
– and Lane, C, '"Trust" or Law? Towards an Integrated Theory of Contractual Relations between Firms' (1994) 21 *Journal of Law and Society* 329
Elsenaar, M, 'Law, Accountability and the Private Finance Initiative in the National Health Service' [1999] *Public Law* 35
Entwistle, T and Martin, S, 'From Competition to Collaboration in Public Service Delivery: A New Agenda for Research' (2005) 83 *Public Administration* 233
Erridge, A and Greer, J, 'Partnerships and Public Procurement: Building Social Capital Through Supply Relations' (2002) 80 *Public Administration* 503
Freedland, M, 'Government by Contract Re-Examined – Some Functional Issues' in P Craig and R Rawlings (eds), *Law and Administration in Europe* (OUP 2003) 123
–, 'Public Law and Private Finance – Placing the Private Finance Initiative in a Public Frame' [1998] *Public Law* 288
–, 'Government by Contract and Public Law' [1994] *Public Law* 86
Fuller, L, 'The Forms and Limits of Adjudication' (1978–1979) 92 *Harvard Law Review* 353
Greve, C and Hodge, G, 'A Transformative Perspective on Public–Private-Partnerships' in T Christensen and P Laegreid (eds), *The Ashgate Research Companion to New Public Management* (Ashgate 2010) 265

Haley, G, 'PFI Contractors: Some Emerging Principles' (1999) 15 *Construction Law Journal* 220

Hancher, L and Moran, M, 'Organizing Regulatory Space' in L Hancher and M Moran (eds), *Capitalism, Culture and Economic Regulation* (Clarendon Press 1989) 271

Harden, I, *The Contracting State* (Open University Press 1992)

Harlow, C and Rawlings, R, *Law and Administration* (3rd edn, Law in Context, CUP 2009)

Hartley, K, 'Problems of Using Partnering and Similar Private Sector Practice in the Public Sector Environment: The Example of PPPs/PFIs', in S Arrowsmith and M Trybus (eds), *Public Procurement: The Continuing Revolution* (Kluwer 2003) 187

Held, V, 'Chapter 19: The Ethics of Care' in D Copp (ed), *The Oxford Handbook of Ethical Theory* (OUP 2006) 537

Hirst, M, 'Shared Risk and Reward – The Key to Partnering' (2009) *Construction Law* 20

Hodge, G, Greve, C and Boardman, A (eds), *International Handbook on Public–Private Partnerships* (Edward Elgar 2010)

Hodge, G and Greve, C (eds), *The Challenge of Public-Private Partnerships – Learning from International Experience* (Edward Elgar 2005)

Honey, R and Mort, J, 'Partnering Contracts for UK Building Projects: Practical Considerations' (2004) 20 *Construction Law Journal* 361

Hood, C and Margetts, H, *The Tools of Government in the Digital Age* (Palgrave 2007)

Kalbe, P, 'Public–Private Partnerships under the Constraints of EC Procurement Rules' [2005] *Public Procurement Law Review* na176

King, J, 'The Justiciability of Resource Allocation' (2007) 70 *Modern Law Review* 19

Lane, C, 'Introduction: Theories and Issues in the Study of Trust' in C Lane and R Bachman (eds), *Trust within and between the Organizations – Conceptual Issues and Empirical Applications* (OUP 2000) 1

Lindrup, G and Godfrey, E (eds), *Butterworths PFI Manual* (2 vol, Butterworths 1998–)

Luhmann, N, 'Trust' in N Luhmann, *Trust and Power – Two Works* (John Wiley & Sons 1979)

Macneil, I, 'Bureaucracy, Liberalism and Community-American Style' (1984–85) 79 *Northwestern University Law Review* 900

–, 'Values in Contract: Internal and External' (1983) 78 *Northwestern University Law Review* 340

–, 'The Many Futures of Contracts' (1974) 47 *Southern California Law Review* 691

Mason, J, 'The Views and Experiences of Specialist Contractors on Partnering in the United Kingdom' (2009) 25 *Construction Law Journal* 206

McCrudden, C, *Buying Social Justice – Equality, Government Procurement and Legal Change* (OUP 2007)

McEldowney, J, 'Public Expenditure and the Control of Public Finance' in J Jowell and D Oliver (eds), *The Changing Constitution* (OUP 2011) 334

Morgan, B and Yeung, K, *An Introduction to Law and Regulation – Text and Materials* (Law in Context, CUP 2007)

Morledge, R, Smith, A and Kashiwagi, D, *Building Procurement* (Blackwell/RICS Research 2006)

Morrison, N, 'Project Finance in the United Kingdom' (1996) 15 *International Banking and Financial Law* 25

Oliver, D, 'Review of (Non-Statutory) Discretions' in C Forsyth (ed), *Judicial Review and the Constitution* (Hart 2000) 307

–, *Common Values and the Public/Private Divide* (Butterworths 1999)

–, 'What is Happening to Relationships between the Individual and the State?' in J Jowell and D Oliver (eds), *The Changing Constitution* (3rd edn, Clarendon Press 1994) 441

O'Neill, O, *Bounds of Justice* (CUP 2000)

Osborne, S (ed), *Public–Private Partnerships – Theory and Practice in International Perspective* (Routledge 2000) 120

Page, A and Daintith, T, *The Executive in the Constitution: Structure, Autonomy and Internal Control* (OUP 1999)

Prosser, T, 'An Opportunity to Take a More Fundamental Look at the Role of Government in Society: the Spending Review as Regulation' [2011] *Public Law* 596

–, *The Regulatory Enterprise – Government, Regulation and Legitimacy* (OUP 2010)

–, 'Regulation and Social Solidarity' (2006) 33 *Journal of Law and Society* 364

–, 'Marketisation, Public Service and Universal Service' in D Nelken and J Feest (eds), *Adapting Legal Cultures* (Hart 2001) 223

–, 'Public Service Law: Privatization's Unexpected Offspring' (2000) 63 *Law and Contemporary Problems* 63

– and Moran, M, 'Privatization and Regulatory Change: The Case of Great Britain', in T Prosser and M Moran (eds), *Privatization and Regulatory Change in Europe* (Open University Press 1994) 35

–, *Nationalised Industries and Public Control – Legal, Constitutional and Political Issues* (Blackwell 1986)

Randall, H, 'The Private Finance Initiative' in H Randall (ed), *Local Government Contracts and Procurement* (Butterworth LexisNexis 2002) 279

Remington, K and Pollack, J, *Tools for Complex Projects* (Gower Publishing 2007)

Robinson, S, '*SoPC4* in the Spotlight' (2007) May *Local Authority Waste and Recycling* 23

Sah, M and Daintith, T, 'Privatisation and the Economic Neutrality of the Constitution' [1993] *Public Law* 465

Salamon, L, 'The New Governance and the Tools of Public Action: An Introduction' (2001) 28 *Fordham Urban Law Journal* 1611

Scott, C, 'Analysing Regulatory Space: Fragmented Resources and Institutional Design' [2001] *Public Law* 329

–, 'Accountability in the Regulatory State' (2000) 27 *Journal of Law and Society* 38

Selznick, P, *The Communitarian Persuasion* (Woodrow Wilson Center Press 2002)

–, *The Moral Commonwealth – Social Theory and the Promise of Community* (University of California Press 1992)

Skelcher, C, 'Chapter 15: Public-Private Partnerships and Hybridity' in E Ferlie, L Lynn and C Pollitt (eds), *The Oxford Handbook of Public Management* (OUP 2007) 347

Skilbeck, J, 'The Private Finance Initiative and Public Procurement' [1996] *Public Procurement Law Review* 148

Teubner, G, *Networks as Connected Contracts* (Hugh Collins (ed), Hart 2011)

–, 'Hybrid Laws: Constitutionalizing Private Governance Networks' in R Kagan, M Kryger and K Winston (eds), *Legality and Community – On the Intellectual Legacy of Philip Selznick* (Rowman & Littlefield Publishers 2002) 311

–, 'Juridification: Concepts, Aspects, Limits, Solutions' reprinted in R Baldwin, C Scott and C Hood (eds), *A Reader on Regulation* (OUP 1998) 389

Trepte, P, *Public Procurement in the EU – A Practitioner's Guide* (2nd edn, OUP 2007)

–, *Regulating Procurement – Understanding the Ends and Means of Public Procurement Regulation* (OUP 2004)

Tronto, J, *Moral Boundaries: A Political Argument for an Ethic of Care* (Routledge 1993)

Turpin, C, *Government Procurement and Contracts* (Longman 1989)

–, *Government Contracts* (Penguin 1972)

Vincent-Jones, P, *The New Public Contracting – Regulation, Responsiveness, Relationality* (OUP 2006)

–, 'Citizens Redress in Public Contracting for Human Services' (2005) 68 *Modern Law Review* 887
–, 'Review Article – Regulating Government by Contract: Towards a Public Law Framework' (2002) 65 *Modern Law Review* 611
–, 'Contractual Governance: Institutional and Organizational Analysis' (2000) 20 *Oxford Journal of Legal Studies* 317
Williamson, O, 'Transaction-Cost Economics: The Governance of Contractual Relations' (1979) 22 *Journal of Law and Economics* 233

PUBLICATIONS FROM PARLIAMENT

In alphabetic order and then in chronological order under the author

Business and Enterprise Committee, *Construction Matters* (127-I HC 2007–08)
CLGC, *Localism* (547 HC 2010–12)
EAC, *Measuring Well-being and Sustainable Development – Sustainable Development Indicators: Government Response to the Committee's Fifth Report of Session 2012–13* (139 HC 2013–14)
Health Committee, *The Role of the Private Sector in the NHS* (308-i HC 2001–02)
HC Deb, 28 February 2013, vol 559, col 611W
HC Deb, 31 January 2013, vol 557, col 1072
HC Deb, 23 June 2011, vol 530, cols 143–194
HC Deb, 12 November 1992, vol 213, cols 993–1016
HL Deb, 28 February 2013, vol 743, col 358WA
Liaison Committee, *Parliament and Government Finance – Recreating Financial Scrutiny* (426 HC 2007–08)
PAC, *Department of Health – The Franchising of Hinchingbrooke Health Care NHS Trust and Peterborough and Stamford Hospitals NHS Foundation Trust* (789 HC 2012–13)
–, *Department of Health – Securing the Future Financial Sustainability of the NHS* (389 HC 2012–13)
–, *Assurance for Major Projects* (384 HC 2012–13)
–, *Whole of Government Accounts 2009–10* (1696 HC 2010–12)
–, *PFI in Housing and Hospitals* (631 HC 2010–11)
–, *Department for Transport – The Failure of Metronet* (390 HC 2009–10)
–, *The Procurement of the National Roads Telecommunications Services* (578 HC 2007–08)
–, *The Cancellation of Bicester Accommodation Centre* (316 HC 2007–08)
–, *The Paddington Health Campus Scheme* (244 HC 2006–07)

–, *London Underground Public Private Partnerships* (446 HC 2004–05)
–, *The Operational Performance of PFI Prisons* (904 HC 2002–03)
–, *Delivering Better Value for Money from the Private Finance Initiative* (764 HC 2002–03)
PASC, *From Citizen's Charter to Public Service Guarantees – Entitlements to Public Services – Further Government Response to the Committee's Twelfth Report of Session 2007–08* (1147 HC 2007–08)
–, *From Citizen's Charter to Public Service Guarantees – Entitlements to Public Services* (411 HC 2007–08)
SCEA, *Private Finance Projects and Off-Balance Sheet Debt* (63 HL 2009–10)
Treasury Committee, *Private Finance Initiative* (1146 HC 2010–12)
–, *The Private Finance Initiative* (146 HC 1995–96)
Transport Committee, *Update on the London Underground and the Public–Private (PPP) Partnership Agreements* (100 HC 2009–10)
–, *The London Underground and the Public–Private Partnership Agreements* (45 HC 2007–08)

PUBLICATIONS FROM THE TREASURY AND RELATED BODIES

In alphabetic order and then in chronological order under the author

Ipsos/Mori, *Investigating the Performance of Operational PFI Contract – A Research Study Conducted for Partnerships UK on behalf of HM Treasury*, 2008 Survey of Operational PFI Projects, sd
Local Partnerships, *Corporate Briefing Paper*, 2009
OGC, *Policy through Procurement Action Plan*, 2010
–, *Annual Statement*, 2009
–, *Consultation Document 2nd Consultation on Implementing the New Remedies Directive (includes Draft Regulations)*, 2009
–, *Consultation Document – The Approach to Implementation of the EU Remedies Directive*, 2008
OGC Gateway™ Process, *Review 1 – Business Justification*, 2007
–, *Review 2 – Delivery Strategy*, 2007
OGC, *Risk Allocation Model for Project Strategy and Procurement*, 2006
–, Procurement Policy, *Practical Guidance on the Use of Competitive Dialogue*, Information Note 04/06 – 31 July 2006
OGC Kelly Report to the Financial Secretary to the Treasury, *Improving Competition and Capacity Planning in the Municipal Waste Market*, 2006
OGC, *Olympic Delivery Authority Delivery Partner Procurement Using Competitive Dialogue – A Lessons Learned Study*, 2006

–, *The Integrated Project Team – Teamworking and Partnering*, Achieving Excellence in Construction Procurement Guide, 2005
–, *Value for Money Evaluation in Complex Procurements,* 2002
–, *Green Public Private Partnerships*, 2002
–, *Best Practice: Risk Allocation in Long-Term Contracts*, 2002
–, *Best Practice, Forming Partnering Relationships with the Private Sector in an Uncertain World*, sd
–, *Working Together to Deliver Better Value,* sd
–, *The External Resources Framework Agreement (ERF*), OGC193, Contract Notice: TED 2007-220493EN
PRG, *Process and Code of Practice*, revised PRG code v 3.0, 2009
PUK, *Annual Report*, 2009
–, *Benchmarking and Market Testing – Help Pack*, 2007
Treasury, *Whole of Government Accounts – Year Ended 31 March 2011* (687 HC 2012)
–, *Major Project Authority – Integrated Assurance*, 2012
–, *A New Approach to Public Private Partnerships,* 2012
–, *Standardisation of PF2 Contracts, Draft*, 2012
–, *Standardisation of PFI Contracts: Version 4 Addendum (Amended Refinancing Provisions)*, 2012
–, *UK Private Finance Initiative Projects – Summary Data as at March 2012,* sd
–, *Making Savings in Operational PFI Contracts*, 2011
–, *Reform of the Private Finance Initiative,* 2011
–, *Treasury Minutes – Government Responses on the Fourteenth to the Eighteenth Reports from the Committee of Public Accounts Session 2010–11* (2011 Cm 8042)
–, *Whole of Government Accounts – Year Ended 31 March 2010* (1601 HC 2011)
–, *HM Treasury Review of Competitive Dialogue,* 2010
–, *Joint Ventures – A Guidance Note for Public Sector Bodies Forming Joint Ventures with the Private Sector*, 2010
–, *Public Private Partnerships – Technical Update*, 2010
–, *Spending Review* (2010 Cm 7942)
–, *Annual Report and Accounts 2008–09*, 2009
–, *Covering Note – SoPC4 Addendum April 2009: Amended Refinancing Provisions*, 2009
–, *Pre-Budget*, 2009
–, *Infrastructure Procurement: Delivering Long-Term Value*, 2008
–, *Implementation of Standardisation of PFI Contracts (SoPC) Version 4*, 2007
–, *Managing Public Money*, 2007

–, *Project Governance – A Guidance Note for Public Sector Project, Draft*, 2007
–, *Revision to Standardisation of PFI Contracts (SoPC),* 2007
–, *Standardisation of PFI Contracts (SoPC) Version 4*, 2007
–, *Standardisation of PFI Contracts – Version 4 – An Outline of Principal Changes*, 2007
–, *PFI: Strengthening Long-Term Partnerships*, 2006
–, *Value for Money Assessment Guidance*, 2006
–, *Standardisation of PFI Contracts (SoPC) Version 3*, 2004
–, *PFI: Meeting the Investment Challenge*, 2003
–, *Public Services – Meeting the Productivity Challenge*, 2003
–, *Public Private Partnerships – The Government Approach*, 2000
–, *Private Opportunity, Public Benefit – Progressing the Private Finance Initiative*, 1995
–, *The Private Finance Initiative – Breaking New Ground – Towards a New Partnership between the Public and the Private Sectors*, 1993
–, *The Green Book – Appraisal and Evaluation in Central Government*, sd
–, *Refinancing of Early PFI Transactions – Code of Conduct*, sd
Treasury and Cabinet Office, *Major Project Approval and Assurance Guidance,* 2011
Treasury and IUK, *Infrastructure Procurement Routemap – A Guide to Improving Delivery Capability*, 2013
–, *Infrastructure Procurement Routemap – Technical Note on Application,* 2013
–, *National Infrastructure Plan – Update 2012,* 2012
–, *Infrastructure Cost Review – Charter Commitments*, 2011
–, *Infrastructure Cost Review – Implementation Plan*, 2011
–, *National Infrastructure Plan 2011,* 2011
–, *Infrastructure Cost Review – Main Report,* 2010
–, *National Infrastructure Plan 2010*, 2010
–, *Strategy for National Infrastructure*, 2010
Treasury and OGC, *Competitive Dialogue in 2008*, 2008
–, *Managing Risks with Delivery Partners*, sd
Treasury (Operational Taskforce), *Note no 3 – Variations Protocol for Operational Projects* (*entered into prior to Standardisation of PFI Contracts version 4*), 2007
–, *Note no 2 – Project Transition Guidance*, 2007
–, *Note no 1 – Benchmarking and Market Testing Guidance*, 2006
Treasury Taskforce Private Finance, *Policy Statement no 5 – Provision of Information to Parliament*, 2000
–, *Technical Note no 6 – How to Manage the Delivery of Long Term PFI Contracts*, 2000

–, *Technical Note no 5 – How to Construct a Public Sector Comparator*, 1999
–, *Technical Note no 4 – How to Appoint and Work with a Preferred Bidder*, 1999
–, *Policy Statement no 2 – Public Sector Comparators and Value for Money*, 1998
–, *Technical Note no 2 – How to Follow EC Procurement Procedure and Advertise in the OJEC*, 1998
–, *Technical Note no 3 – How to Appoint and Manage Advisers to PFI Projects*, 1998
–, *Partnerships for Prosperity – The Private Finance Initiative*, 1997

PUBLICATIONS FROM THE NATIONAL AUDIT OFFICE

In chronological order

NAO, *Sustainable Procurement in Government – Briefing for the House of Commons Environmental Audit Select Committee*, 2013
–, *The Efficiency and Reform Group* (956 HC 2012–13)
–, *Ministry of Defence – The Major Projects Report 2012* (684-I HC 2012–13)
–, *HM Treasury – Planning for Economic Infrastructure* (595 HC 2012–13)
–, *Department of Health – Peterborough and Stamford Hospitals NHS Foundation Trust* (658 HC 2012–13)
–, *Department of Health – The Franchising of the Hinchingbrooke Health Care NHS Trust* (628 HC 2012–13)
–, *Department of Health – Securing the Future Financial Sustainability of the NHS* (191 HC 2012–13)
–, *Department of Transport – The Completion and Sale of High Speed 1* (1834 HC 2010–12)
–, *HM Treasury – Equity Investment in Privately Financed Projects* (1792 HC 2010–12)
–, *Lessons from PFI and Other Projects* (920 HC 2010–12)
–, *Cabinet Office – The Efficiency and Reform Group's Role in Improving Public Sector Value for Money* (887 HC 2010–11)
–, *Highways Agency – Procurement of the M25 Private Finance Contract* (566 HC 2010–11)
–, *HM Treasury – Financing PFI Projects in the Credit Crisis and the Treasury's Response* (287 HC 2010–11)
–, *PFI in Housing* (71 HC 2010–11)
–, *The Performance and Management of Hospital PFI Contracts* (68 HC 2010–11)

–, *Assurance for High Risk Projects*, 2010
–, *Regenerating the English Regions – Regional Development Agencies' Support to Physical Regeneration Projects* (214 HC 2009–10)
–, *Note on Optimism Bias – Lords Economic Affairs Committee Inquiry on Private Finance and Off-Balance Sheet Funding* (63-ii HL 2009–10)
–, *Private Finance Projects – A Paper for the Lords Economic Affairs Committee* (63-ii HL 2009–10)
–, *HM Revenue & Customs' Estate Private Finance Deal Eight Years On* (30 HC 2009–10)
–, *Annual Report*, 2009
–, *The Building Schools for the Future Programme – Renewing the Secondary School Estate* (135 HC 2008–09)
–, *Department for Environment, Food and Rural Affairs – Managing the Waste PFI Programme* (66 HC 2008–09)
–, *Department for Transport – The Failure of Metronet* (512 HC 2008–09)
–, *Allocation and Management of Risk in Ministry of Defence PFI Projects* (343 HC 2007–08)
–, *Making Changes in Operational PFI Projects* (205 HC 2007–08)
–, *Home Office – The Cancellation of Bicester Accommodation Centre* (19 HC 2007–08)
–, *Benchmarking and Market Testing the Ongoing Services Component of PFI Projects* (453 HC 2006–07)
–, *Improving the PFI Tendering Process* (149 HC 2006–07)
–, *A Framework for Evaluating the Implementation of Private Finance Initiative Projects*, 2 vol, 2006
–, *The Paddington Health Campus Scheme* (1045 HC 2005–06)
–, *The Termination of the PFI Contract for the National Physical Laboratory* (1044 HC 2005–06)
–, *Update on PFI Debt Refinancing and the PFI Equity Market* (1040 HC 2005–06)
–, *The Wider Markets Initiative* (799 HC 2005–06)
–, *The Refinancing of the Norfolk and Norwich PFI Hospital – How the Deal Can Be Viewed in the Light of Refinancing* (78 HC 2005–06)
–, *Progress on the Channel Tunnel Rail Link* (77 HC 2005–06)
–, *Department of Health – Innovation in the NHS: Local Improvement Finance Trusts* (28 HC 2005–06)
–, *Darent Valley Hospital – The PFI Contract in Action* (209 HC 2004–05)
–, *Accommodation Services for the Department for Work and Pensions – Transfer of Property to the Private Sector under the Expansion of the PRIME Contract* (181 HC 181 2004–05)

–, *London Underground PPP – Were They Good Deals?* (645 HC 2003–04)
–, *London Underground – Are the Public Private Partnerships Likely to Work Successfully?* (644 HC 2003–04)
–, *PFI – The STEPS Deal* (530 HC 2003-04) (NAO, *STEPS*, 2004)
–, *Refinancing the Public Private Partnership for National Air Traffic Services* (157 HC 2003–04)
–, *Government Communications Headquarters (GCHQ) – New Accommodation Programme* (955 HC 2002–03)
–, *PFI – The New Headquarters for the Home Office* (954 HC 2002–03)
–, *The Operational Performance of PFI Prisons* (700 HC 2002–03)
–, *PPP in Practice – National Savings and Investments' Deal with Siemens Business Services, Four Years On* (626 HC 2002–03)
–, *PFI – Construction Performance* (371 HC 2002–03)
–, *The PFI Contract for the Redevelopment of West Middlesex University Hospital* (49 HC 2002–03)
–, *PFI Refinancing Update* (1288 HC 2001–02)
–, *The Public Private Partnership for National Air Traffic Services Ltd* (1096 HC 2001–02)
–, *Ministry of Defence – Redevelopment of MOD Main Building* (748 HC 2001–02)
–, *Managing the Relationship to Secure a Successful Partnership in PFI Projects* (375 HC 2001–02)
–, *Innovation in PFI Financing – The Treasury Building Project* (328 HC 2001–02)
–, *The Financial Analysis for the London Underground Public Private Partnerships* (54 HC 2000–01)
–, *The Radiocommunications Agency's Joint Venture With CMG* (21 HC 2000–01)
–, *Department of the Environment, Transport and the Regions – The Channel Tunnel Rail Link* (302 HC 2000–01)
–, *The Department for Culture, Media and Sport – The Re-negotiation of the PFI-type Deal for the Royal Armouries Museum in Leeds* (103 HC 2000–01)
–, *Modernising Construction* (87 HC 2000–01)
–, *The Cancellation of the Benefits Payment Card Project* (857 HC 1999–2000)
–, *The New British Embassy in Berlin* (585 HC 1999–2000)
–, *The Refinancing of the Fazakerley PFI Prison Contract* (584 HC 584 1999–2000)
–, *National Savings – Public-Private Partnership with Siemens Business Services* (493 HC 1999–2000)

–, *The Private Finance Initiative – The Contract for the Defence Fixed Telecommunications System* (328 HC 1999–2000)
–, *The Contributions Agency – The Newcastle Estate Development Project* (16 HC 1999–2000)
–, *United Kingdom Passport Agency – The Passport Delays of Summer* 1999 (812 HC 1998–99)
–, *Examining the Value for Money of Deals under the Private Finance Initiative* (739 HC 1998–99)
–, *The PFI Contract for the New Dartford & Gravesham Hospital* (423 HC 1998–99)
–, *Department of Social Security – The PRIME Project – The Transfer of the Department of Social Security Estate to the Private Sector* (370 HC 1998–99)
–, *The Private Finance Initiative – The First Four Design, Build, Finance and Operate Roads Contracts* (476 HC 1997–98)
–, *The PFI Contracts for Bridgend and Fazakerley Prisons* (253 HC 1997–98)
NAO and HM Treasury, *From Private Finance Units to Commercial Champions – Managing Complex Capital Investment Programmes Utilising Private Finance,* 2010

OTHER OFFICIAL PUBLICATIONS

In alphabetic order and then in chronological order under the author

4Ps, *A Guide to Contract Management for PFI and PPP Projects*, 2007
–, *A Map of the PFI Process Using Competitive Dialogue,* 2006
AC, *Public Interest Report – South London Healthcare NHS Trust – Audit 2011/12*, 2012
–, *Well Disposed – Responding to the Waste Challenge*, 2008
–, *For Better, for Worse – Value for Money in Strategic Service-Delivery Partnerships*, National Report, 2008
–, *For Better, for Worse – Value for Money in Strategic Service-Delivery Partnerships*, Framework, 2008
–, *Governing Partnerships – Bridging the Accountability Gap*, 2005
–, *PFI in Schools*, 2003
Cabinet Office, *Accelerating Government Procurement – Management Summary of the Findings of a 'LEAN' Study to Investigate Waste and Inefficiencies in Government's Procurement Process,* 2011
Chartered Institute of Building, *The Impact of the Global Crisis on the Construction Industry*, 2009
CEPA, *Report to the London Underground PPP Arbiter: Approaches to Benchmarking Infraco Efficiency and Performance*, 2003

Construction Industry Council, *A Guide to Partnering Workshops*, 2005
–, *A Guide to Project Team Partnering*, 2nd edn, 2002
CLG, *Localism Bill – General Power of Competence for Local Authorities – Impact Assessment,* 2011
–, *Local Government PFI Project Support Guide (2009–10)*
–, *Reform of Council Housing Finance Consultation*, 2009
–, *Local Government PFI Project Support Guide (2008–09)*
–, *The National Procurement Strategy for Local Government – Final Report: Towards Public Service Transformation*, 2008
–, *Strong and Prosperous Communities – The Local Government White Paper* (2006 Cm 6939-I)
–, *Tenant Involvement in Housing Management – Supplementary Guidance*, sd
CHP/SHINE, *Invitation to go Green and Beyond – The Exemplar Sustainable Healthcare Buildings Programme*, sd
CHP, *LIFT – Enabling Integrated Services, Co-location and Partnership Working*, sd
Commission for Local Administration in England, *Special Report – Local Partnerships and Citizens Redress – Advice and Guidance*, 2007
DCSF, *Evaluation of Building Schools for the Future – 2nd Annual Report – Final Report*, 2008
–, *The Management of Building Schools for the Future – Wave 7 to 15*, 2008
Defra, *Forecasting 2020 Waste Arisings and Treatment Capacity,* 2013
–, *Spending Review 2010 – Changes to Waste PFI Programme – Supporting Analysis,* 2010
–, *Waste Infrastructure Delivery Programme Residual Waste Procurement Pack Module 4 – Part I: Payment Mechanism Principle*s, 2008
–, *Waste Infrastructure Delivery Programme Residual Waste Procurement Pack Module 4 – Part II: Payment Mechanism Drafting*, 2008
–, *Waste Strategy for England*, 2007
–, *Standardisation of Waste Management PFI Contracts – Guidance on SoPC Derogations*, 2006
DH, *NHS Trust and NHS Foundation Trust Special Administration – A Guide for Unsecured Creditors*, 2013
–, *Statutory Guidance for Trust Special Administrators Appointed to NHS Trusts*, 2012
–, *Transforming Community Services – Enabling New Patterns of Provision*, 2009
–, *The Private Finance Initiative – How to Conduct a Competitive Dialogue Procedure – Consultation*, 2006
DH PFU & PPP Forum, *Benchmarking and Market Testing in NHS PFI Projects – Code of Best Practice*, 2006

EFA, *Priority School Building Programme, Hertfordshire, Luton & Reading (HLR) Private Finance (PF) Batch – Bidders' Day*, 2013

Egan (Sir John), *Rethinking Construction – The Report of the Construction Task Force to the Deputy Prime Minister, John Prescott*, on the Scope for Improving the Quality and Efficiency of UK Construction, 1998

European Commission, *TEN – T-Trans-European Transport Network Implementation of the Priority Projects Progress Report*, 2008

–, *Interpretative Communication on the Application of Community Law on Public Procurement and Concessions to Institutionalised Public-Private Partnerships (IPPP)*, 5 February 2008, C(2007)6661.

–, *Explanatory Note – Competitive Dialogue – Classic Directive*, CC/2005/04, rev 1, 2005

–, *Green Paper on Public-Private Partnerships and Community Law on Public Contracts and Concessions*, 30 April 2004, COM(2004) 327 final

–, *Decision no 264/2002, London Underground Public Private Partnership*, 2 October 2002, *JO*, C, 12 December 2002

FoE, *Briefing – Private Finance Initiative (PFI) Funding for Waste Infrastructure*, 2008

Gershon, P, *Review of Civil Procurement in Central Government*, 1999

Health and Safety Executive, *Safety by Design in the Construction of Public Healthcare Estate*, SIM 07/2005/12, 2006

HM Government, *The Civil Service Reform Plan*, 2012

–, *Open Public Services – White Paper* (2011 Cm 8145)

–, *Creating Strong, Safe and Prosperous Communities Statutory Guidance*, 2008

–, *Code of Practice on Consultation*, version 3, 2008

James, S, *Review of Education Capital*, 2011

Latham (Sir Michael), *Constructing the Team – Final Report* (HMSO 1994)

Law Commission, *Administrative Redress: Public Bodies and the Citizen* (2010 HC 6, LC no 322)

Lord Fulton, *The Civil Service,* vol 1 (1968 Cmnd 3638)

Ministry of Justice, *Reform of Judicial Review: The Government Response*, 2013

Monitor, *Statutory Guidance for Trust Special Administrators Appointed to NHS Foundation Trusts*, 2013.

–, *Draft Risk Assessment Framework: Consultation Document*, 2013

–, *Guidance for Commissioners on Ensuring the Continuity of Health Care Services – Designating Commissioner Requested Services and Location Specific Services*, 2013

–, *Monitor's Response to the Consultation on Guidance for Commissioners on Ensuring the Continuity of Health Care Services*, 2013
ODPM, *Strategic Partnering Taskforce – Final Report*, 2004
–, *National Procurement Strategy for Local Government*, 2003
Office of the TSA, *Securing Sustainable NHS Services: the Trust Special Administrator's Report on South London Healthcare NHS Trust and the NHS in South East London*, 2013
ONS, *Measuring National Well-being: Life in the UK*, 2012
PPP Arbiter, *Reference for Direction and Guidance from London Underground Ltd in Respect of the Periodic Review of Tube Lines' PPP Agreement – Direction on Financing Impossibility*, 27 April 2010
–, *International Benchmarking of the Costs and Performance of Maintaining and Renewing Metro Systems*, 16 March 2010
–, *Analytical Approach to Calculating ISC – Consultation Draft*, 17 December 2009
–, *Reference for Directions and Guidance from London Underground Ltd in Respect of the Periodic Review of Tube Lines' PPP Agreement – Draft Direction on Costs and Related Matters and Initial Thoughts on ISC Setting and Financing*, 17 December 2009
–, *Updates Timetable for Periodic Review Reference*, 16 December 2009
–, *Procedural Approach to Periodic Review*, 2 March 2009
–, *Reference for Guidance from London Underground Ltd*, 9 December 2008
–, *References for Guidance from (i) Metronet BCV Rail Ltd and London Underground Ltd and (ii) Metronet SSL Rail Ltd and London Underground Ltd – Treatment of Investment at an Extraordinary Review*, 13 March 2007
–, *Proposed Changes to Procedural Framework and Approach Documents – A Consultation Paper*, 7 February 2007
–, *Treatment of Investment at an Extraordinary Review: Initial Guidance*, 1 December 2006
–, *Annual Metronet Report 2006 – References for Guidance from BCVB Rail Ltd and London Underground Ltd and Metronet SSL Rail Ltd and London Underground Ltd*, 16 November 2006
Transport Committee, *Too Close for Comfort: Passengers' Experiences of the London Underground* (LA 2009)
–, *Delays Possible: Maintaining and Upgrading the London Underground* (LA 2009)
PwC, *The Value of PFI Hanging in the Balance (sheet)?*, sd
PfS, BsF, *Standard Form BSF, Strategic Partnering Agreement*, 2008
–, *PFI Agreement – Payment Mechanism*, 2008
–, *OBC Appendix 3: VfM Guidance Note and Input Assumptions*, 2006

–, *Strategy for Change, Guidance for Local Authorities in BSF Wave 7-9*, Version 10

SoS, *South London Healthcare NHS Trust: Notice*, 2013

TfL, *Business Plan 2009/10 – 2017/18*

TUC, *Reform of the Private Initiative Response Template*, 2012

Unison, *Not so Great – Voices from the Front-Line at the Great Western PFI Hospital in Swindon*, 2003

–, *Reform of the Private Initiative Response Template*, 2012

Index

Introductory Note: Please note that PPPs stands for Public–Private Partnerships, while PFIs represents Private Finance Initiatives.